Clean Air Handbook

Fifth Edition

Hunton Andrews Kurth LLP

Bernan Press

Lanham • Boulder • New York • London

Published by Bernan Press
An imprint of The Rowman & Littlefield Publishing Group, Inc.
4501 Forbes Boulevard, Suite 200, Lanham, Maryland 20706
www.rowman.com

86-90 Paul Street, London EC2A 4NE

British Library Cataloguing in Publication Information available

Library of Congress Cataloging-in-Publication Data Available

Names: Brownell, F. William, author. | Hunton Andrews Kurth LLP (Richmond, Virginia), author.
Title: Clean air handbook / Hunton Andrews Kurth LLP ; prinicple author and contributor, F. William Brownell ; contributing authors, Shannon S. Broome [and others].
Description: Fifth edition. | Lanham : Bernan Press, 2023. | Includes bibliographical references and index.
Identifiers: LCCN 2023032875 (print) | LCCN 2023032876 (ebook) | ISBN 9781641434256 (paperback) | ISBN 9781641434263 (epub)
Subjects: LCSH: Air—Pollution—Law and legislation—United States.
Classification: LCC KF3812 .B769 2023 (print) | LCC KF3812 (ebook) | DDC 344.7304/6342—dc23
LC record available at https://lccn.loc.gov/2023032875
LC ebook record available at https://lccn.loc.gov/2023032876

SUMMARY CONTENTS

CONTENTS

PREFACE

The Clean Air Act (Act) is perhaps the most complex environmental legislation ever enacted. From modest beginnings in 1967, the Act has grown in length to hundreds of pages and is implemented through thousands of pages of regulations.

The Clean Air Act has led to the expenditure of billions of dollars annually on pollution control programs. It governs what industrial growth may take place in communities that have been unable to attain clean air goals. It dictates basic changes in lifestyle where necessary to achieve air quality standards. It allocates marketable rights to emit pollution among regions of the country. And it defines the levels of public health risks that are acceptable as a result of exposure to air pollution. For these reasons, the Clean Air Act has generated intense political debate over the past four decades.

This fifth edition of the *Clean Air Handbook* provides a starting point for understanding how this complex legislation has developed and been implemented over the years. Beyond offering an introduction to the history and structure of the Act, the handbook discusses the efforts of the U.S. Environmental Protection Agency (EPA or Agency) to implement the Act. The handbook discusses EPA initiatives to impose more stringent emission reduction requirements through more stringent air quality standards promulgated in the new millennium; it addresses EPA rules and guidance implementing the Title I nonattainment program and ongoing federal efforts to address interstate pollution; it summarizes EPA's rules for state-administered Title V operating permit programs and discusses issues applicable to Title V permit applications; it reports on EPA's implementation of the air toxics program under Title III of the 1990 amendments to the Act; and it reviews the key rules promulgated by EPA to implement the Title IV acid rain program. This edition of the *Clean Air Handbook* also addresses developments under the stratospheric ozone protection program (Title VI of the 1990 amendments), EPA's actions to resolve controversies concerning the applicability of new source review requirements, and EPA's implementation of key Title II programs regarding motor vehicles, fuels, and fuel additives. The handbook reviews recent developments in civil and criminal enforcement under the Act, including EPA's enforcement effort under the new source review program. Finally, this edition of the *Clean Air Handbook* addresses EPA's recent efforts to regulate visibility and greenhouse gas emissions.

The Clean Air Act is constantly evolving. Because of continuing gridlock in Congress, more than thirty years have passed since the Act last underwent a major amendment. This has caused EPA to seek to accomplish new regulatory objectives under an old framework that, in many cases, is poorly suited to its objectives. This, in turn, has resulted in several EPA programs being overturned by the courts and in consequent uncertainty for the regulated community. The challenge for industry over the next several years will be not only to determine how to comply with these numerous regulatory requirements but also to determine how best to participate in future proceedings to ensure the development of sound rules.

Besides developing new rules, EPA continues to supplement its existing rules with guidance documents and policy statements. These materials are often critical to evaluating one's compliance obligations. As a result, it is important to consult various EPA websites for agency guidance as well as the materials referenced in this handbook, responsible regulatory personnel, and environmental counsel when confronted with specific regulatory compliance issues. With this caveat in mind, we hope that this handbook provides a useful starting point for understanding the Clean Air Act.

F. WILLIAM BROWNELL
Washington, D.C.
April 2023

Chapter 1

FEDERAL-STATE PARTNERSHIP: AN OVERVIEW OF THE CLEAN AIR ACT

The Clean Air Act (CAA or Act) has been with us for over fifty years. During that time, the Act has evolved from a set of principles to guide states in controlling sources of air pollution (the Air Quality Act of 1967) to an extensive series of programs designed initially by the federal government and administered in coordination with the states.

The evolution of air quality regulation has tracked advances in our understanding of the environment. As our knowledge of the environment has improved, new concerns have emerged and shortcomings have been identified in methods provided by the Act for regulating air pollution. A brief review of the experience with the Clean Air Act beginning in the 1960s is helpful context for understanding the multiple layers of regulatory requirements that exist today.

I. The Air Quality Act of 1967

In response to concerns about deteriorating urban air quality, Congress in 1967 enacted the Air Quality Act.[1] The purposes of the 1967 Act were:

- To protect and enhance the quality of the Nation's air resources so as to promote the public health and welfare and the productive capacity of its population;
- To initiate and accelerate a national research and development program to achieve the prevention and control of air pollution;
- To provide technical and financial assistance to State and local governments in connection with the development and execution of their air pollution prevention and control programs; and
- To encourage and assist the development and operation of regional air pollution control programs.[2]

The 1967 Act focused on regulation of ambient air quality to protect public health and welfare. The centerpiece of this regulatory program was the development of air quality "criteria" by the Department of Health, Education, and Welfare's (HEW) Air Quality Advisory Board for widespread and pervasive pollution.[3] The "criteria" documents were to "accurately reflect the latest scientific knowledge" on the health and welfare effects of individual pollutants, such as sulfur dioxide (SO_2), nitrogen oxides (NOx), and particulate matter (PM).[4] Although Congress gave the federal government, through HEW, the responsibility for developing air quality criteria, air quality problems were viewed principally as state and local concerns. Congress therefore left to the states the responsibility for developing, administering, and enforcing specific standards based on the federal criteria.[5]

By contrast, Congress in 1967 viewed mobile source regulation as a federal concern. The Act therefore directed the Secretary of HEW to establish nationally applicable emissions standards and a fuel and fuel additive registration program.[6] The Act required that these standards take into account economic and technological feasibility.[7]

These first efforts at air quality control were hampered by scientific uncertainties and technical difficulties that continued to challenge regulatory agencies over the subsequent decades. The criteria document development process proved long and cumbersome. States had difficulty translating the information made available by HEW into source-specific standards. Techniques for relating source-specific emissions to air quality impacts (e.g., atmospheric dispersion models) were not well developed. And the focus on improving ambient air quality through state and local action proved unduly narrow. Because air quality is influenced by regional as well as local factors, more broadly based regulatory programs and control methods were needed.

II. The 1970 Clean Air Act

This early experience with air quality regulation provided a starting point for comprehensive amendments to the Clean Air Act in 1970.[8] The 1970 amendments remain the centerpiece of the current Act.

To overcome the inertia experienced in implementing the 1967 Air Quality Act, Congress in 1970 gave the federal government a more prominent role in regulating air quality. Now, not only was the federal government required to develop criteria describing levels of air quality associated with specific public health and welfare concerns, but the federal government, through the newly created U.S. Environmental Protection Agency (EPA or Agency), was required to establish national ambient air quality standards (NAAQS) that define specific levels of air quality that must be achieved to protect against those public health and welfare concerns.[9] The NAAQS, in turn, would serve as the basis for individual source emission limitations to be established by the states in state implementation plans (SIPs).[10]

Congress also directed EPA to develop regulatory guidance to be used by states in implementing the NAAQS for individual sources through their SIPs and for EPA to use in reviewing the adequacy of these SIPs. Congress gave EPA a continuing oversight role to ensure that states continued to implement and enforce the requirements of the SIP.[11] If a state did not develop an adequate SIP, did not act in a timely fashion to adopt a SIP, or did not respond promptly to a notice from EPA that its SIP failed to meet the requirements of the Act, EPA would step in to implement the Act for the state through a federal implementation plan (FIP).[12] This basic federal-state partnership—referred to as "cooperative federalism"—remains a hallmark of Clean Air Act regulation today.

In an attempt to make this system of air quality regulation work in a more timely fashion, Congress set regulatory deadlines to spur administrative decision making. In response to delays experienced in criteria document development and implementation of associated air pollution control measures, for example, Congress set deadlines for developing criteria documents, for developing NAAQS based on those documents, and for state development and EPA review of SIPs.[13]

Besides creating a more detailed regime for the protection of public health and welfare through ambient air quality regulation, Congress in 1970 adopted stringent control technology requirements for new sources, called the new source performance standards (NSPS) program of section 111 of the Act. Congress added a preconstruction review program to ensure that emissions from new facilities that had not yet been reviewed under the SIP program were reviewed for compliance with the NAAQS prior to construction.[14] Congress made clear in the Act's general purposes clause that a key objective guiding implementation of the Act was not only improving poor air quality, but the prevention of significant deterioration (PSD) of air quality in clean air areas.[15]

In 1970, Congress recognized and began to address pollution problems other than those associated with the "criteria" pollutants regulated under the NAAQS. For example, Congress in the same year enacted the first program to regulate hazardous air pollutants (HAPs), or air toxics, under section 112 of the Act.

Finally, Congress continued to refine regulation of mobile sources in Title II of the Act. Recognizing the political and technical difficulties associated with control of vehicle tailpipe emissions, Congress balanced environmental and economic concerns and set specific, technology-forcing emissions standards and deadlines for their attainment.[16]

III. The 1977 Clean Air Act Amendments

In the early 1970s, EPA and the states began to implement the basic regulatory programs of the 1970 amendments, including the NAAQS, the NSPS, PSD preconstruction review, and the HAPs program. These activities produced controversies that gave rise to the first wave of regulatory litigation under the Clean Air Act and ultimately led to comprehensive amendments to the Act in 1977.

The 1977 Clean Air Act amendments[17] refined the basic programs of the 1970 Act. For example, Congress adjusted the dates for attainment of the NAAQS[18] and provided additional guidance for development by the states of programs for areas that remained out of compliance with the NAAQS (i.e., the "nonattainment" SIP requirements) in Title I, Part D.[19] With respect to the hazardous air pollutants program, Congress directed EPA to consider regulation of several specific substances (radioactive pollutants, cadmium, arsenic, and polycyclic organic matter) and required EPA to make regulatory decisions regarding these and other pollutants according to specific deadlines.[20]

Congress in the 1977 amendments codified the PSD program,[21] and adopted requirements aimed at improving visibility in national parks.[22] In an early attempt to deal with regional transport of pollution, Congress adopted limitations on the degree to which a source could rely on atmospheric dispersion of its emissions (e.g., through "tall stacks") to achieve the NAAQS.[23] These concerns about air pollution's effects on aesthetics and regional air quality foreshadowed a lengthy debate that continues today regarding the need for more prescriptive programs for regional transport of criteria pollutants, visibility, and greenhouse gases.

Finally, as the scope of the Act expanded, Congress became more sensitive to the impact of the Act on significant sectors of the national economy. For the NSPS program, for example, Congress acted to protect the jobs of high sulfur coal miners by requiring that large, new fossil fuel-fired boilers install "flue gas desulfurization" systems, or SO_2 scrubbers.[24] Congress also enacted measures that could be used to prevent economic disruption or unemployment associated with standards that disrupted the use of locally or regionally available coal.[25]

IV. Efforts to Implement the Programs of the 1977 Clean Air Act Amendments

The 1977 Clean Air Act amendments can be summarized in terms of three categories of programs. The first addresses air quality regulation. In this category fall the NAAQS and SIP programs,[26] which are designed to regulate widespread and pervasive air pollution problems. The substances addressed by the NAAQS are referred to as "criteria pollutants" and include SO_2, NOx, PM, carbon monoxide (CO), lead, and ozone. All sources of air pollution are subject to the NAAQS and are regulated as necessary through emission limitations set by states in SIPs (although the states are limited in their regulation of mobile sources). A stationary source must either take steps necessary to meet the NAAQS or shut down.[27] In this sense, the NAAQS program is the most important technology-forcing program of the Act.

The SIPs are the principal Clean Air Act tool for control of emissions from existing stationary sources of air pollution. In areas with clean air, emission limitations in SIPs must be set at a level that ensures maintenance of the NAAQS. In areas that do *not* attain the NAAQS (i.e., "nonattainment areas"), sources are subject to more stringent controls designed to bring those areas into attainment with the NAAQS. States with nonattainment areas must develop requirements that ensure "reasonable further progress" toward attainment, and large existing stationary sources of nonattainment pollutants must install "reasonably available control technology" (RACT).[28]

The second type of program contained in the 1977 amendments involves regulation of new and modified stationary sources of air pollution.[29] Categories of stationary sources that cause or contribute significantly to air pollution may be listed for regulation under the section 111 NSPS program. Emission limitations are then set for sources in that source category to reflect best adequately demonstrated control technology. New sources in areas that attain the NAAQS are also subject to the PSD preconstruction review program, which requires compliance with (1) "air quality increments" that represent levels of ambient air quality more stringent than the NAAQS,[30] and (2) control technology requirements that must be at least as stringent as NSPS (i.e., that must reflect "best available control technology," or "BACT," for that individual source).[31] New and modified sources in areas that do not attain the NAAQS are subject to a different preconstruction permitting program, called nonattainment new source review (NNSR). This program requires that major stationary sources (1) offset projected emission increases of nonattainment pollutants with emission reductions of those pollutants at existing facilities and (2) install control technology to achieve the "lowest achievable emission rate" (LAER) for that pollutant for that source category.[32]

The third category of programs under the 1977 amendments concerned special pollution problems that Congress felt needed attention beyond the air quality and control technology programs discussed above. The most important of these address national emission standards for hazardous air pollutants (NESHAPs),[33] and the protection of visibility in national parks.[34]

A. The NAAQS/SIP Program

EPA originally promulgated the NAAQS for criteria pollutants in the early 1970s in response to the 1970 amendments. As amended in 1977, the Act called on EPA to review these standards at five-year intervals to determine whether different or stricter standards are necessary to protect public health and welfare.

Pursuant to this mandate, EPA has periodically reviewed both the "primary" (i.e., health-based) and "secondary" (i.e., welfare-based) NAAQS for each criteria pollutant since 1977. Over the following decades, this review produced new standards for small particles, minor adjustments to the CO standards, and a host of administrative proceedings and litigation regarding the need to revise the NAAQS for other criteria pollutants. The history of this periodic review program in the 1980s and beyond illustrates the impact of congressional deadlines and the evolution of science.

In 1987, for example, EPA revised the PM NAAQS, changing the basis for the standard from total particulate matter (which included large particles) to "PM_{10}," or particles with an aerodynamic diameter of ten micrometers or less.[35] In 1997, EPA once again revised the PM NAAQS, adding standards for "$PM_{2.5}$," or particles with an aerodynamic diameter of two and a half micrometers or less.[36] EPA revised and tightened the $PM_{2.5}$ standard again in 2006[37] and 2012.[38]

EPA considered during the 1980s whether to adopt a stringent, short-term average (i.e., five-minute to one-hour) NAAQS for SO_2 to address "peak" emission episodes to protect asthmatics. This effort lagged, however, and in 1989, EPA was ordered by a federal court to complete its review of the primary SO_2 NAAQS.[39] EPA ultimately decided not to revise the NAAQS,[40] but then, in 2007, began another review of the SO_2 NAAQS in response to a court order.[41] This further review produced a revised, more stringent SO_2 NAAQS in 2010.[42]

With respect to the NAAQS for ozone, EPA originally established a NAAQS in 1971, relaxed it after a review proceeding in 1979,[43] and concluded in 1993 that the existing data did not support further revision of that NAAQS.[44] Nevertheless, EPA began yet another of the required statutory reviews after issuance of the 1993 notice, and in 1997 it tightened that standard significantly.[45] In 2008, EPA revised that standard yet again to make it even more stringent,[46] and tightened it again in 2015.[47]

Since many areas of the country were unable to meet even the then-existing NAAQS for ozone by the 1987 attainment date set by the 1977 amendments, EPA in 1987 proposed a policy for bringing such areas into attainment with the NAAQS.[48] Under EPA's policy, sanctions for failure to meet the Act's attainment deadlines (e.g., a moratorium on new construction) would not apply as long as the SIP for the area was revised to provide for reasonable further progress toward attainment with a demonstration of attainment within a set period of time. This policy prompted litigation that cast doubt on EPA's authority to provide flexibility for states to meet attainment deadlines,[49] and ultimately led Congress to amend the Act in 1990 to adopt new deadlines for attainment and more prescriptive nonattainment programs.

B. New Source Control Programs

The control technology programs for new and modified sources of air pollution (i.e., the NSPS and PSD/NNSR program) have proven to be among the more successful Clean Air Act programs. By the end of the 1980s, EPA had developed NSPS for over 60 source categories. Given the difficulty that EPA experienced with hazardous air pollution regulation during the 1980s, EPA began in the late 1980s to explore how the NSPS program might be used to regulate HAPs.

Rulemaking proceedings to establish and revise NSPS, however, proved increasingly costly and time-consuming. Starting in the late 1980s, this led to an increased focus on the use of policy statements and guidance to refine, and even to revise, the new source programs. Two issues exemplify EPA's efforts since the 1980s to find a means other than legislative rulemaking to implement these programs.

First, EPA undertook, through guidance and enforcement actions, to expand the reach of the new source programs. Under the so-called WEPCo policy,[50] EPA stated that work undertaken to repair deteriorated equipment to allow a facility to operate up to its prior capacity could result in application of more stringent new source standards and preconstruction review under the PSD program. The Seventh Circuit rejected EPA's decision[51] and, in response, EPA issued guidance and rule changes in 1992 addressing when existing sources that undertake repair or replacement projects would become subject to new source controls under the NSPS, PSD, and NNSR programs.[52] These administrative determinations and guidance continue to be controversial in EPA enforcement and regulatory actions today.

Second, EPA attempted to limit state discretion to determine BACT for new or modified sources in the PSD preconstruction review permitting process. Under the so-called "top-down" BACT policy announced in 1987, EPA said that new sources would have to apply the most stringent control technology available unless use of that technology could be shown to be infeasible at a given source. Litigation regarding the guidance memoranda that embodied the top-down

BACT policy resulted in a settlement, pursuant to which EPA made clear that states could elect to use, or not to use, that policy.[53]

Both the WEPCo guidance and the top-down BACT policy reflect an effort to find less burdensome means of implementing the Act by avoiding lengthy and contentious notice-and-comment rulemaking proceedings. As discussed below, the search for new approaches to implement the Act intensified in the wake of the 1990 amendments and has influenced Clean Air Act litigation ever since.

C. Specific Pollution Concerns

In addition to the NAAQS and new source control programs, Congress addressed several specific pollution concerns in the 1977 Act. EPA's efforts to implement these programs were no less controversial than its efforts to implement the NAAQS and new source programs, and those controversies helped shape the 1990 amendments to the Act.

1. Hazardous Air Pollutants

In 1970, the section 112 HAPs program targeted a limited number of especially hazardous substances.[54] Under the 1977 amendments, by contrast, section 112 directed EPA to list and regulate as a hazardous air pollutant any substance that can cause serious health problems when emitted into the ambient air. Once listed, EPA was required to regulate the substance at a level that would protect public health with an ample margin of safety.

By 1977, EPA had implemented this program for only a few substances. In the 1977 amendments, Congress therefore directed EPA to determine whether to regulate four other specific pollutants under section 112.[55]

Virtually every aspect of this 1977 statutory directive resulted in litigation. Environmental advocacy organizations argued that EPA had an obligation to list for regulation under this provision every known or probable carcinogen. They argued that, once listed, EPA was obligated to regulate every source category of the substance, regardless of the magnitude of risk associated with emissions from the source category. According to these groups, EPA in setting emission standards was, required to eliminate all risks of adverse health effects.[56] In response to these controversies, Congress stepped in to revamp the hazardous air pollutant program in 1990 to provide a new and more broadly applicable control technology-based program for hazardous air pollutants.

2. *Visibility Protection*

In response to the 1977 Act, EPA in 1980 adopted the so-called "Phase I" visibility program, addressing visible emission plumes from defined emission points such as smokestacks that impact the viewsheds of national parks and wilderness areas.[57] EPA did not promulgate rules to address the more widespread problem of "regional haze"—visibility impairment that is not clearly attributable to a single, identifiable source of pollution or a discrete group of sources. Rather, given the lack of techniques for attributing regional haze to individual sources, EPA left this concern for a future "Phase II" visibility program. The limited scope of the initial visibility program gave rise during the 1980s to litigation, including an attempt to force EPA to set a secondary, visibility-based NAAQS for fine particles.[58]

While resisting development of a Phase II regulatory program in light of scientific uncertainties, EPA did take a step in that direction in the late 1980s in the case of one individual source. Based on the alleged contribution of the Salt River Project's Navajo Generating Station to regional haze in Grand Canyon National Park,[59] EPA imposed on this source a "best available retrofit technology" (BART) requirement under the Phase I visibility program, which resulted in control expenditures in excess of $1 billion for the facility.[60] This decision foreshadowed lengthy rulemaking and litigation following the 1990 amendments regarding requirements for sources that allegedly contribute to haze in national parks.[61]

3. *Regional and International Air Pollution*

During the 1980s, EPA was also the target of persistent litigation to force it to regulate acid rain and other forms of acidic deposition under section 115 of the 1977 Act, which addresses international air pollution concerns. Ultimately, the courts refused to grant relief to environmental advocacy organizations and Northeastern states (which claimed that pollution from Midwestern sources was causing acid deposition in the Northeast United States as well as in Canada), leaving the litigants to seek relief by filing administrative petitions with the Agency under section 115. At the same time, the executive branch undertook an effort to negotiate an agreement with Canada addressing transboundary pollution. Most activity in this area was, once again, overtaken by the 1990 amendments to the Act, in which Congress enacted a comprehensive program targeting utility emissions that contribute to acid rain.

The 1980s also saw the first attempts by states to force pollution reduction in other states through a petition process created in section 126 of the Act. These interstate petitions were ultimately unsuccessful but laid the groundwork for more aggressive efforts to address interstate pollution transport beginning in the 1990s.

V. The 1990 Clean Air Act Amendments

Substantial agency resources were devoted to the implementation of the Clean Air Act through the 1970s and 1980s. Based on this experience, Congress in 1990 acted to guide and expedite the regulation of air pollution through yet another set of major amendments to the Act.[62] The 1990 amendments were more lengthy and complex than any previous environmental legislation. They were also far different in form and content than the changes sought by either industry or environmental advocacy organizations in the early 1980s. Reflecting the complexity of the task, Congress has not undertaken substantial amendments to the Act since 1990.

The 1990 amendments confirmed much of the structure that Congress had created in 1970 and 1977 but also added to that structure. For example, while the 1990 amendments retained the SIP program, Congress enacted a comprehensive operating permit program to group together all source-specific requirements in one document for each major emitting facility in the country. While Congress created a comprehensive regulatory program addressing acid rain, it retained provisions that had been used in earlier attempts to regulate acid deposition, including the 1977 amendments' international pollution provisions and dispersion technique prohibition. And Congress set even more deadlines for agency action to implement the new programs of the 1990 amendments.

In short, the 1990 amendments created substantial new regulatory responsibilities while leaving in place most of the preexisting system of air pollution control. Briefly, Congress made the following major changes to the Clean Air Act in 1990:

First, Congress addressed in 1990 the continuing difficulty experienced in many areas of the country in attaining the ozone and other NAAQS by establishing new attainment deadlines and more prescriptive regulatory requirements keyed to the seriousness of the nonattainment problem. These requirements are discussed in detail in chapter 2.

Second, to increase transparency of environmental requirements and facilitate enforcement, Congress enacted an operating permit program as a new Title V to the Act. The purpose of these permits is to assemble in one place all Clean Air Act requirements applicable to an individual source. The Title V permitting program is discussed further in chapter 4.

Third, Congress completely revamped the system for regulation of HAPs. Under the new regulatory approach, 189 substances were listed for regulation as HAPs,[63] with directions for EPA to list source categories and establish control technology-based standards by specific deadlines. EPA's regulation of HAPs is addressed in chapter 5.

Fourth, Congress substantially tightened mobile source emission standards in 1990, requiring significant reductions in tailpipe emissions from motor vehicles. Congress also established two new fuel-related programs designed to achieve emission reductions: the reformulated fuels program and the clean fuel vehicle program. Regulation of mobile sources is addressed in chapter 8.

Fifth, Congress debated extending new source control technology requirements to existing facilities, by requiring existing utility boilers either to retrofit new source control technologies or to shut down at age thirty. At the end of the day, Congress rejected expansion of these command-and-control new source programs. Instead, Congress adopted the Title IV acid rain program for utility boilers. This "cap-and-trade" program has become an important and highly successful example of how market-based principles can be used to control air pollution and is discussed further in chapter 9.

Finally, although ozone in the lower atmosphere can have adverse effects on public health, ozone in the upper atmosphere—or stratosphere—is desirable because it helps shield the earth's surface from harmful radiation. Congress added Title VI to the Act in 1990 to address stratospheric ozone protection, and this program is addressed in chapter 10.

VI. New Directions in Air Pollution Regulation

The extensive regulatory programs of the 1970, 1977, and 1990 Clean Air Act amendments have spawned complex rulemaking and litigation addressing both the Agency's substantive obligations and regulatory schedules. The experience with air pollution regulation in the decades since the 1990 amendments suggests a number of themes that will continue to shape air quality regulation in this century.

First, air pollution is not merely a local concern but must be addressed in a broader geographic context. This has led to efforts by EPA to redefine the federal-state relationship in ways that strengthen the federal partner. EPA's continuing challenge remains finding the proper balance of federal compulsion and state discretion to reconcile national, regional, and local interests.

Second, to ensure that the EPA acts, Congress increasingly has relied on statutory deadlines for regulatory action. Merely telling the Agency to act by a certain date does not guarantee timely action, however, and acting without sufficient deliberation does not produce sound regulation. EPA will continue to struggle with meeting deadlines that environmental advocacy organizations and states have found can readily be enforced by citizen suit.

Third, as deadlines have proliferated and statutory mandates have become more complex, EPA has looked for alternatives to rulemaking for implementing the Act. This trend was evident during the 1990s, as the Agency moved away from legislative rulemaking in several areas to explore strategies that required less public involvement, and therefore, supposedly, less controversy and delay. Policy statements, adjudications, and enforcement guidance have all played, and will continue to play, an important role in Clean Air Act implementation.

Fourth, Congress' attention to aesthetic and welfare-based concerns has resulted in an escalation in the costs of regulation, which in turn has provided a strong incentive for market-oriented solutions to air quality problems. Congress specifically adopted a market-based approach to regulation of acid rain in the 1990 amendments, and EPA has encouraged the states to employ market mechanisms in other areas of air quality regulation. The success of the Clean Air Act over the coming years will be influenced by the degree to which market-based alternatives can be used in place of the traditional command-and-control approach to regulation.

Fifth, with the maturation of many Clean Air Act programs, enforcement has assumed an increasingly important role. EPA's enforcement office is playing an active role in Clean Air Act implementation as well as enforcement, and that role includes shaping the interpretation of important Clean Air Act programs. Enforcement is discussed in more detail in chapter 11.

Finally, each decade has presented a key air quality issue for national debate—from criteria pollutants in the 1970s to air toxics in the 1980s, acid rain in the 1990s, and visibility protection in the 2000s. The issue for the next decade is climate change. Because Congress has been unsuccessful in legislating a regulatory program for greenhouse gas emissions, advocacy groups have promoted regulatory programs for climate change under the Clean Air Act. These efforts, which are discussed in chapter 7, will test the limits of the federal-state partnership in clean air regulation.

Each of these themes is reflected in ongoing controversies over the implementation and enforcement of the Clean Air Act, the most complex environmental legislation ever enacted by Congress. Each aspect of the current Clean Air Act is discussed in more detail in the following chapters.

Notes

1. *See* Air Quality Act of 1967, Pub. L. No. 90–148, 81 Stat. 485 (codified as amended at 42 U.S.C. §§ 1857–1857*l* (1967)) (AQA).

2. AQA § 101(b).
3. *Id.* §§ 107(b)(1), 110.
4. *Id.* § 107(b)(2).
5. *Id.* § 108.
6. *Id.* §§ 202, 210.
7. *Id.* § 202.
8. *See* Clean Air Amendments of 1970, Pub. L. No. 91–604, 84 Stat. 1676 (codified as amended at 42 U.S.C. §§ 1857, *et seq.* (1970)).
9. CAA §§ 108, 109, 42 U.S.C. §§ 1857c-3, 1857c-4 (1976).
10. *Id.* § 110, 42 U.S.C. § 1857c-5 (1976).
11. *Id.* § 110(a), 42 U.S.C. § 1857c-5(a) (1976).
12. *Id.* § 110(c), 42 U.S.C. § 1857c-5(c) (1976).
13. *Id.* §§ 108(a), 109(a)(1), 110(a), 42 U.S.C. §§ 1857c-3(a), 1857c-4(a)(1), 1857c-5(a) (1976).
14. *Id.* § 110(a)(2)(D), (a)(4), 42 U.S.C. § 1857c-5(a)(2)(D), (a)(4) (1976).
15. *See Sierra Club v. Ruckelshaus*, 344 F. Supp. 253 (D.D.C.), *aff'd per curiam*, 4 Env't. Rep. Cas. (BNA) 1815 (D.C. Cir. 1972), *aff'd by an equally divided Court sub nom. Fri v. Sierra Club*, 412 U.S. 541 (1973).
16. CAA § 202, 42 U.S.C. § 1857f-1 (1976).
17. Clean Air Act Amendments of 1977, Pub. L. No. 95–95, 91 Stat. 685 (1977).
18. CAA § 171(a), (b), 42 U.S.C. § 7501(a), (b) (1982).
19. Titles of the CAA correspond to subchapters in the U.S. Code.
20. CAA §§ 112, 122, 42 U.S.C. §§ 7412, 7422 (1982).
21. *Id.* §§ 160–169, 42 U.S.C. §§ 7470–7479 (1982); *see Ala. Power Co. v. Costle*, 636 F.2d 323 (D.C. Cir. 1980).
22. CAA § 169A, 42 U.S.C. § 7491 (1982).
23. *Id.* § 123(a), 42 U.S.C. § 7423 (1982); *see Nat. Res. Def. Council v. Thomas*, 838 F.2d 1224, 1232–33, 1237–38 (D.C. Cir. 1988); *Sierra Club v. EPA*, 719 F.2d 436, 439, 440–42 (D.C. Cir. 1983).
24. *See* Bruce A. Ackerman & W.T. Hassler, *Clean Coal/Dirty Air* 32-33, 98-99 (Yale University Press 1981).
25. CAA § 125, 42 U.S.C. § 7425 (1982).
26. *Id.* §§ 109, 110, 42 U.S.C. §§ 7409, 7410 (1982).
27. *Union Electric Co. v. EPA*, 427 U.S. 246, 266 (1976).
28. CAA § 172(b)(3), 42 U.S.C. § 7502(b)(3) (1982).
29. *See id.* §§ 111, 165, 173, 42 U.S.C. §§ 7411, 7475, 7503 (1982).
30. *Id.* § 163, 42 U.S.C. § 7473 (1982).
31. *Id.* § 165(a), 42 U.S.C. § 7475(a) (1982).
32. *Id.* § 173, 42 U.S.C. § 7503 (1982).
33. *Id.* § 112, 42 U.S.C. § 7412 (1982).
34. *Id.* § 169A, 42 U.S.C. § 7491 (1982).
35. Revisions to the National Ambient Air Quality Standards for Particulate Matter, 52 Fed. Reg. 24,634 (July 1, 1987).

36. National Ambient Air Quality Standards for Particulate Matter, 62 Fed. Reg. 38,652 (July 18, 1997).

37. National Ambient Air Quality Standards for Particulate Matter, 71 Fed. Reg. 61,144 (Oct. 17, 2006).

38. National Ambient Air Quality Standards for Particulate Matter, 78 Fed. Reg. 3086 (Jan. 15, 2013).

39. *See Env't Def. Fund v. Thomas*, 870 F.2d 892, 894 (2d Cir. 1989).

40. National Ambient Air Quality Standards for Sulfur Oxides (Sulfur Dioxide)—Final Decision, 61 Fed. Reg. 25,566 (May 22, 1996).

41. *See* Consent Decree, *Ctr. for Biological Diversity v. Johnson*, Civ. No. 1:05-cv-01814-LFO (D.D.C. Nov. 19, 2007), ECF No. 41; *see also* Stipulation to Amend Consent Decree, *Ctr. for Biological Diversity v. Johnson*, Civ. No. 1:05-cv-01814-LFO (D.D.C. Dec. 4, 2008), ECF No. 48.

42. Primary National Ambient Air Quality Standard for Sulfur Dioxide, 75 Fed. Reg. 35,520 (June 22, 2010).

43. Revisions to the National Ambient Air Quality Standards for Photochemical Oxidants, 44 Fed. Reg. 8202 (Feb. 8, 1979).

44. National Ambient Air Quality Standards for Ozone—Final Decision, 58 Fed. Reg. 13,008, 13,011–12, 13,013–16 (Mar. 9, 1993).

45. National Ambient Air Quality Standards for Ozone, 62 Fed. Reg. 38,856 (July 18, 1997).

46. National Ambient Air Quality Standards for Ozone, 73 Fed. Reg. 16,436 (Mar. 27, 2008).

47. National Ambient Air Quality Standards for Ozone, 80 Fed. Reg. 65,292 (Oct. 26, 2015).

48. State Implementation Plans; Approval of Post-1987 Ozone and Carbon Monoxide Plan Revisions for Areas Not Attaining the National Ambient Air Quality Standards, 52 Fed. Reg. 45,044 (proposed Nov. 24, 1987).

49. *See Abramowitz v. EPA*, 832 F.2d 1071, 1072–73, 1079 (9th Cir. 1987).

50. *See* Letter from Don R. Clay, Acting Assistant Adm'r for Air & Radiation, EPA, to John W. Boston, Vice President, Wisconsin Electric Power Co. (Feb. 15, 1989); Letter from Lee M. Thomas, Adm'r, EPA, to John W. Boston, Vice President, Wisconsin Electric Power Co. (Oct. 14, 1988); Memorandum from Don R. Clay, Acting Assistant Adm'r for Air & Radiation, EPA, to David A. Kee, Dir., Air & Radiation Div., EPA Region V, Applicability of Prevention of Significant Deterioration (PSD) and New Source Performance Standards (NSPS) Requirements to the Wisconsin Electric Power Company (WEPCO) Port Washington Life Extension Project (Sept. 9, 1988). These documents are maintained in an EPA database called the New Source Review Policy and Guidance Document Index.

51. *Wis. Elec. Power Co. v. Reilly*, 893 F.2d 901, 918 (7th Cir. 1990) ("*WEPCo*").

52. *See* Requirements for Preparation, Adoption and Submittal of Implementation Plans; Approval and Promulgation of Implementation Plans; Standards of Performance for New Stationary Sources, 57 Fed. Reg. 32,314 (July 21, 1992).

53. *See* Prevention of Significant Deterioration (PSD) and Nonattainment New Source Review (NSR), 61 Fed. Reg. 38,250, 38,282 (proposed July 23, 1996) (addressing EPA's obligation under then-pending settlement agreement); *see also Alaska Dep't of Env't Conservation v. EPA*, 540 U.S. 461, 476 n.7 (2004) ("Nothing in the Act or its implementing regulations mandates top-down analysis.").

54. *See* S. Rep. No. 91-1196 at 415, 490–91 (1970), *reprinted in* 1 COMM. ON PUBLIC WORKS, A LEGISLATIVE HISTORY OF THE CLEAN AIR AMENDMENTS OF 1970 (1974).

55. CAA § 122, 42 U.S.C. § 7422 (1982).

56. *See Nat. Res. Def. Council v. Thomas*, 885 F.2d 1067, 1072–75 (2d Cir. 1989); *Nat. Res. Def. Council v. EPA*, 824 F.2d 1146, 1147–48 (D.C. Cir. 1987).

57. Visibility Protection for Federal Class I Areas, 45 Fed. Reg. 80,084 (Dec. 2, 1980).

58. *See, e.g., Nat. Res. Def. Council v. Adm'r, U.S. EPA*, 902 F.2d 962, 965 (D.C. Cir. 1990).

59. Assessment of Visibility Impairment, 54 Fed. Reg. 36,948, 36,949 (proposed Sept. 5, 1989).

60. *See Cent. Ariz. Water Conservation Dist. v. EPA*, 990 F.2d 1531, 1533–34, 1537, 1542 (9th Cir. 1993).

61. *See, e.g., Am. Corn Growers Ass'n v. EPA*, 291 F.3d 1, 3–5 (D.C. Cir. 2002).

62. Clean Air Act Amendments of 1990, Pub. L. No. 101-549, 104 Stat. 2399 (1990).

63. CAA § 112(b), 42 U.S.C. § 7412(b) (1990).

Chapter 2

NATIONAL AMBIENT AIR QUALITY STANDARDS

The centerpiece of the Clean Air Act (CAA or Act) is a system for achieving healthful "ambient," or outdoor,[1] air through national air quality standards (NAAQS) promulgated by the U.S. Environmental Protection Agency (EPA or Agency) and implemented primarily by the states. The core provisions of the Act regarding NAAQS are sections 108, 109, and 110 of Title I.[2]

I. National Ambient Air Quality Standards

A. The Statutory Requirements

Section 108 of the Act requires EPA to list air pollutants that, in the judgment of the Administrator, "cause or contribute to air pollution which may reasonably be anticipated to endanger public health or welfare" and "the presence of which in the ambient air results from numerous or diverse mobile or stationary sources."[3] These listed pollutants are known as the "criteria" pollutants under the Act, so called because EPA must issue "air quality criteria" for each of them. These criteria must contain information that "accurately reflect[s] the latest scientific knowledge useful in indicating the kind and extent of all identifiable effects on public health or welfare which may be expected from the presence of such pollutant in the ambient air, in varying quantities."[4] The criteria pollutants are sulfur oxides (SOx), particulate matter (PM) (both coarse PM (PM_{10}) and fine PM ($PM_{2.5}$)),[5] carbon monoxide (CO), ozone, oxides of nitrogen ("NOx"), and lead.

Section 109 directs EPA to promulgate, through public notice-and-comment rulemaking, NAAQS for each of the criteria pollutants.[6] The NAAQS apply uniformly throughout the country.[7] For each pollutant, EPA must establish "primary" NAAQS at a level that, in the Administrator's judgment, is "requisite to protect the public health" with "an adequate margin of safety," and must establish "secondary" NAAQS at a level that the Administrator judges "requisite to protect the public welfare from any known or anticipated adverse effects associated with the presence of such air pollutant in the ambient air."[8] The Act defines "effects on [public] welfare" broadly to include effects on soils, water, crops, vegetation, man-made materials, animals, wildlife, weather, visibility, climate, property damage, transportation hazards, economic values, and personal comfort and well being.[9]

At least every five years, EPA must review the air quality criteria and the NAAQS, taking into account advice from EPA's Clean Air Scientific Advisory Committee (CASAC), a committee established by the Act.[10] After considering CASAC's recommendations, the Administrator may revise the criteria and NAAQS and promulgate new NAAQS if he or she determines such actions are "appropriate" in accordance with the statute.[11]

Once EPA sets or revises NAAQS, states have the primary responsibility for implementing them.[12] The first step in the implementation process is "designation" of areas for the new NAAQS according to their air quality. Under section 107 of the Act, within one year after promulgation of a NAAQS (or such earlier date that EPA may reasonably require, but not earlier than 120 days after promulgation of the NAAQS),[13] each state is to submit to EPA a list of all areas in the state, designating—for the new NAAQS—each area as (1) nonattainment, if it does not meet (or if it "contributes to ambient air quality in a nearby area that does not meet") the NAAQS; (2) attainment, if it meets the NAAQS (and is not included in a nonattainment area under the "nearby area" clause); or (3) unclassifiable, if it cannot be classified as attainment or nonattainment "on the basis of available information" (generally, information from ambient air quality monitoring devices).[14] EPA must review the states' lists and, within two years after NAAQS promulgation (a period that EPA may extend by up to one year if it has "insufficient information"), promulgate designations, modified from the states' lists as necessary in EPA's judgment.[15] Section 107 also contains provisions governing state- and EPA-initiated redesignations of areas, for example, from nonattainment to attainment, attainment to nonattainment, and unclassifiable to attainment or nonattainment.[16]

States also are responsible for a plan, known as a "state implementation plan" or "SIP," that ensures the NAAQS are attained and maintained. Within three years after the promulgation of a new or revised NAAQS (or a shorter period if the Administrator so specifies), states must submit a SIP to EPA that provides for implementation, maintenance, and enforcement of the NAAQS in each air quality control region within the state.[17] States in which nonattainment areas are located must also address additional statutory requirements in their SIPs after nonattainment designations are finalized. These requirements are intended to bring nonattainment areas into attainment as expeditiously as practicable.

Although states take the lead in NAAQS implementation, EPA has ongoing authority to review SIPs and to require states to revise their SIPs as necessary.[18] If a state does not promptly revise its SIP in response to a new or revised NAAQS, or to an EPA finding of SIP inadequacy, EPA has the authority to step in and to set emission limitations for sources within that state; when EPA takes that step, it promulgates these limitations in the form of a "federal implementation plan," or "FIP."[19]

The SIP program and the Act's nonattainment requirements are discussed in Section II.

B. The Current Standards

The following table summarizes the NAAQS promulgated as of April 2023:

Pollutant	Type of NAAQS	Level (Year Adopted)	Form	Citation
SO_x (measured as sulfur dioxide) (SO_2)	Primary	0.030 parts per million (ppm) (1971)	Annual arithmetic mean	40 C.F.R. § 50.4(a)
		0.14 ppm (1971)	24-hour average, not to be exceeded more than once per calendar year	40 C.F.R. § 50.4(b)
		75 parts per billion (ppb) (2010)	99th percentile of daily Maximum 1-hour values averaged over 3 years	40 C.F.R. § 50.17[20]
	Secondary	0.5 ppm (1971)	3-hour average, not to be exceeded more than once per calendar year	40 C.F.R. § 50.5
PM_{10}	Primary & Secondary	150 micrograms per cubic meter (μg/m³) (2006)	24-hour average, not expected to be exceeded more than once per calendar year	40 C.F.R. § 50.6
$PM_{2.5}$	Primary	15.0 μg/m³ (1997)	Annual arithmetic mean, based on 3 years of data	40 C.F.R. §§ 50.7,[21] 50.13

Pollutant	Type of NAAQS	Level (Year Adopted)	Form	Citation
		65 μg/m^3 (1997)	98th percentile 24-hour concentration, based on 3 years of data	40 C.F.R. § 50.7
		35 μg/m^3 (2006)	98th percentile 24-hour concentration, based on 3 years of data	40 C.F.R. §§ 50.13, 50.18
		12.0 μg/m^3 (2012)	Average annual arithmetic mean based on 3 years of data	40 C.F.R. § 50.18
	Secondary	15.0 μg/m^3 (1997)	Annual average, based on 3 years of data	40 C.F.R. §§ 50.7, 50.13
		65 μg/m^3 (1997)	98th percentile 24-hour concentration, based on 3 years of data	40 C.F.R. § 50.7
		35 μg/m^3 (2006)	98th percentile 24-hour concentration, based on 3 years of data	40 C.F.R. § 50.13
CO	Primary	9 ppm (1971)	8-hour average, not to be exceeded more than once per year	40 C.F.R. § 50.8
		35 ppm (1971)	1-hour average, not to be exceeded more than once per year	40 C.F.R. § 50.8
Ozone	Primary & Secondary	0.12 ppm 1979)	1-hour average, not expected to be exceeded more than once per calendar year	40 C.F.R. § 50.9[22]

Pollutant	Type of NAAQS	Level (Year Adopted)	Form	Citation
		0.08 ppm (1997)	Average annual fourth-highest daily maximum 8-hour average, based on 3 years of data	40 C.F.R. § 50.10[23]
		0.075 ppm (2008)	Average annual fourth highest daily maximum 8-hour average, based on 3 years of data	40 C.F.R. § 50.15
		0.070 ppm (2015)	Annual average fourth highest daily 8-hour average, based on 3 years of data	40 C.F.R. § 50.19
NOx (with nitrogen dioxide (NO_2) as the indicator)	Primary	53 ppb (1971)	Annual average	40 C.F.R. § 50.11(a)
		100 ppb (2010)	3-year average of the annual 98th percentile of daily maximum 1-hour values	40 C.F.R. § 50.11(b) & (f)
	Secondary	0.053 ppm (2010)	Annual arithmetic mean	40 C.F.R. § 50.11(c)
Lead	Primary & Secondary	1.5 μg/m^3 (1978)	Maximum arithmetic mean, averaged over a calendar quarter	40 C.F.R. § 50.12[24]
		0.15 μg/m^3 (2008)	Arithmetic mean concentration over a 3-month period	40 C.F.R. § 50.16

Reviews of the CO and lead standards were last completed in 2011[25] and 2016,[26] respectively. Reviews of the primary NOx and SO_2 standards were last completed in 2018[27] and 2019,[28] respectively. EPA completed reviews of the 2015 ozone standard and the existing PM standards in December 2020, deciding to retain the current standards.[29] Both of those actions are the subject of judicial challenges.[30] In 2021, Biden EPA announced it would reconsider the previous administration's decisions to retain the current $PM_{2.5}$ and ozone standards. The judicial challenges were held in abeyance pending completion of the reconsideration process. In January 2023, EPA proposed to strengthen the primary (health-based) annual $PM_{2.5}$ standard to a level between 9 and 10 micrograms per cubic meters.[31]

II. Overview of the General State Implementation Plan Program

As noted above, sections 107 and 110 of the Act give each state primary responsibility for protecting air quality within its borders. This is achieved through the development of SIP requirements specifying how the primary and secondary NAAQS will be achieved. To ensure that SIP requirements are adequate to attain and maintain the NAAQS, all SIPs submitted by the states to EPA must meet certain minimum requirements specified in section 110 of the Act. The following discussion reviews the substantive and procedural requirements of the Act pertaining to SIP development and approval.

A. Minimum Substantive Requirements for All SIPs

Section 110(a)(2) of the Act requires that all SIPs be adopted after reasonable notice and a public hearing. Section 110(a)(1) requires that a SIP to implement a NAAQS, which EPA refers to as an "infrastructure SIP,"[32] be submitted to EPA not later than three years after promulgation of that NAAQS, although EPA may establish a shorter submission deadline. Other provisions of the Act add further requirements for SIPs. (As described here, a later submission deadline applies to nonattainment SIP provisions.)

The general provisions that must be included in a SIP are:

Enforceable Emission Limitations. A SIP must include enforceable emission limitations and other control measures, including economic incentives and timetables, as well as schedules and compliance timetables.[33]

Air Quality Data. A SIP must include provisions for monitoring, compiling, and analyzing data on ambient air quality that must be made available to EPA.[34]

Enforcement and Permitting Authority. A SIP must establish an enforcement program and include provisions regulating modification and construction of stationary sources, including permit programs for prevention of significant deterioration (PSD) in attainment areas and for sources in nonattainment areas as required by Parts C and D of Title I of the Act.[35] The operation of existing stationary sources, however, is also subject to regulation and enforcement under the federal operating permit program established by Title V of the Act. The preconstruction and operating permit programs are discussed further in chapter 4.

Means To Address Interstate Air Pollution. A SIP must prohibit emissions activities within the state from (1) "contribut[ing] significantly to nonattainment in, or interfer[ing] with maintenance [of the NAAQS] by, any other State," or (2) interfering with measures required to be included in another state's SIP under the PSD or visibility protection provisions of Title I, Part C. A SIP also must include provisions ensuring compliance with applicable requirements in sections 126 and 115, which authorize certain actions by EPA to address interstate and international pollution, respectively.[36]

Adequate Personnel, Funding, and Authority. A SIP must provide assurances that the state (or state-designated local regulatory authority) has adequate resources and power to carry out the SIP under state or local laws. A SIP must also provide assurances that the state has retained ultimate responsibility for implementation despite any delegation of authority to local governments.[37]

Monitoring and Emission Data. A SIP must require monitoring and periodic reporting of emissions by stationary sources. It also must require that the state correlate those emission reports with relevant emission limitations and make the reports available for public inspection.[38]

Contingency Plans. A SIP must provide authority for certain emergency powers and adequate contingency plans to restrict emissions of pollutants that present an imminent and substantial danger.[39]

Revision Authority. A SIP must provide for its revision as necessary to take into account any revisions to the NAAQS, improved methods of attainment, or any finding by EPA that the SIP is "substantially inadequate" to attain the NAAQS or to meet other Clean Air Act requirements.[40]

Part D Requirements for Nonattainment Areas. For states that have a nonattainment area, a SIP must meet the requirements of Part D of Title I of the Act, which establishes more stringent provisions for those areas.[41] These requirements are discussed in more detail in Section II.B.

Air Quality Modeling. A SIP must provide for air quality modeling and submission of related data as prescribed by the Administrator. Air quality modeling is used to predict the effect of the emissions of any criteria pollutant on ambient air quality.[42] The Act requires EPA to "specify with reasonable particularity each air quality model or models to be used under specified sets of conditions" in performing ambient air quality analyses with respect to new sources under the PSD program.[43] EPA regulations require the use of models to demonstrate the source-specific SIP requirements will assure attainment and maintenance of the NAAQS.[44] EPA's Guideline on Air Quality Models identifies the models that EPA recommends be used for a wide variety of applications, discusses the data required for their use, and specifies the procedures that are to be followed if the Agency has not recommended a model for a particular situation or if approval is sought for the use of a model other than the one recommended by EPA.[45]

Permit Fees. A SIP must include provisions requiring the owner or operator of each major stationary source to pay, as a condition of any Clean Air Act-required permit, a fee sufficient to cover the reasonable costs of reviewing and acting on permit applications and implementing and enforcing permits (not including costs for court actions or other enforcement actions) until superseded by a fee program under the state's Title V operating permit program.[46] As states have received EPA approval of their Title V programs, including Title V permit fee provisions, section 110(a)(2)(L) has become largely moot. The Title V permitting program is discussed in chapter 4.

Local Consultation. A SIP must provide for consultation with and participation by local political subdivisions affected by the plan.[47]

Conformity Requirements. Section 176(c) prohibits the federal government from engaging in, supporting, licensing, or approving any activity that does not conform to an approved SIP, Transportation Improvement Plan, or FIP. EPA's rules address two types of conformity: transportation conformity and general conformity. EPA's transportation conformity rule, which was developed in coordination with the Department of Transportation, was last updated in 2012.[48] EPA's rule on general conformity was last significantly revised in 2010.[49]

Technical Assistance for Small Business Sources. Under section 507 of the Act, each state must establish a "small business stationary source technical and environmental compliance assistance program." These programs must meet certain minimum requirements, including mechanisms for the development and collection of information concerning compliance technologies, assistance with pollution prevention, designation of a state agency to serve as an ombudsman, assistance with permit applications and compliance auditing, and procedures for modifying compliance methods and milestones.[50]

EPA has provided guidance, outlining alternative control technologies and pollution prevention methods for small business stationary sources.[51] In addition, states and EPA must consider factors such as the financial resources and technical capabilities of small business stationary sources when imposing permit or other fees, when applying continuous emission monitoring requirements, and when issuing control technique guidelines (CTGs) under the Act.[52] EPA must develop a program assisting small business if a state fails to submit one.[53]

Other Requirements. A SIP must meet the requirements of Part C of Title I of the Act (relating to PSD and visibility protection[54]), section 121 (relating to consultation with local governments and federal land managers with authority over federal lands to which the SIP would apply), and section 127 (relating to public notification of instances in which NAAQS are exceeded).[55]

B. Additional Requirements for Nonattainment Area SIPs

In addition to the general requirements described above, SIPs for states that contain nonattainment areas also must provide a mechanism for attainment (and maintenance) of the relevant NAAQS, as specified in Subpart 1 of Title I, Part D (sections 171–179B). Specifically, the SIP must include provisions designed to achieve attainment by the "attainment date" specified by EPA. The general rule is that, for a particular nonattainment area, the attainment date is to be "the date by which attainment can be achieved as expeditiously as practicable."[56] For primary NAAQS, attainment is required "no later than 5 years from the date such area was designated nonattainment," except that EPA may extend that date to as long as 10 years from the date of designation "considering the severity of nonattainment and the availability and feasibility of pollution control measures."[57] EPA may classify nonattainment areas for purposes of applying an attainment date (and unspecified other purposes) according to the severity of nonattainment and the availability and feasibility of emission control measures for achieving attainment.[58] In addition, EPA may provide up to two additional one-year extensions of the attainment date under certain circumstances.[59]

These general provisions concerning nonattainment area SIPs are supplemented by the following additional subparts of Title I Part D: Subpart 2 addressing ozone (sections 181–185B), Subpart 3 addressing CO (sections 186–187); Subpart 4 addressing PM (sections 188–190); and Subpart 5 addressing SOx, NO_2, and lead (sections 191–192). As EPA began to implement these new subparts, it published a "general preamble" and several supplements explaining the

Agency's interpretations of these provisions of the 1990 amendments.[60] The requirements of Subparts 1–5 are described here.

1. General Requirements for Nonattainment Area SIPs

Subpart 1 of Title I Part D of the Act specifies additional requirements for nonattainment area SIPs, for the purpose of "provid[ing] for attainment of the national primary ambient air quality standards."[61] These requirements include:

Reasonably Available Control Technology. SIPs must require all reasonably available control measures (RACM) as expeditiously as practicable and must, at a minimum, require reasonably available control technology (RACT) for existing sources of nonattainment pollutants.[62] Only technology that will accelerate attainment is considered RACT.[63]

Reasonable Further Progress. SIPs must provide for such "annual incremental reductions" in emissions of relevant air pollutants as are "reasonably" required by EPA to ensure attainment of the NAAQS by the applicable attainment date.[64] In some cases, measures that are otherwise required in nonattainment area SIPs may satisfy the requirement for reasonable further progress ("RFP).[65]

Inventory of Current Emissions. SIPs must include "a comprehensive, accurate, current inventory of actual emissions from all sources of the relevant pollutant or pollutants in [the nonattainment] area." EPA may require periodic revisions to the inventory.[66]

Permits for New and Modified Major Stationary Sources. SIPs must require permits for the construction and operation of new or modified "major stationary sources" anywhere in the nonattainment area.[67] Plans must meet the requirements of the nonattainment-new source review (NNSR) program, which are discussed in chapters 3 and 4.

Quantify New Emissions To Be Allowed. SIPs must identify and quantify emissions that will be allowed from certain new or modified major stationary sources and demonstrate that those emissions will be consistent with the achievement of RFP toward attainment.[68]

Contingency Measures. SIPs must provide specific measures that will automatically be implemented if an area either fails to make RFP toward attainment or fails to attain the primary NAAQS by the applicable attainment date.[69]

Equivalent Techniques. EPA may allow, upon application by the state, the use of equivalent modeling, emission inventory, and planning techniques if they are, taken together, not less effective than the methods specified by EPA.[70]

Other Measures The Act also contains a catch-all requirement that the SIP include, in addition to the specific provisions discussed above, "enforceable emission limitations, and such other control measures, means or techniques (including economic incentives such as fees, marketable permits, and auctions of emission rights), as well as schedules and timetables for compliance, as may be necessary or appropriate to provide for attainment of such standard in such area by the applicable attainment date."[71]

2. SIP Requirements for Ozone Nonattainment Areas (Subpart 2 of Part D)

The 1990 amendments to the Act made major changes to the program for addressing areas that failed to attain the ozone NAAQS, which at that time was a 1-hour standard of 0.12 ppm, not to be exceeded more than once in a calendar year.[72] These changes, as summarized below, involved classification of ozone areas as a matter of law, specification of new requirements for SIPs based on those classifications, imposition of new federal measures, and provision for multi-state ozone transport regions.

Following the 1990 amendments, EPA replaced the 1-hour ozone NAAQS with a more stringent NAAQS with an 8-hour averaging time. After the Supreme Court determined that the requirements of Subpart 2 also largely apply to SIPs for areas designated as nonattainment for the 8-hour NAAQS,[73] EPA had to translate some of the requirements in Subpart 2 for application to those standards.

a. Classifications and Attainment Deadlines

Section 181(a)(1) of the Act classified areas that were nonattainment for the 1-hour ozone NAAQS based on the area's ozone "design value" (a measure of how far the area was out of compliance with the NAAQS) and established attainment deadlines for areas in each classification. Section 181(a)(5) authorized EPA to adjust the classifications for areas that were on the margin between classifications and to grant up to two one-year extensions of the attainment deadline under specified circumstances.[74] Newly designated ozone nonattainment areas were to be classified at the time of their nonattainment designation and provided with time to reach attainment equivalent to that allowed for areas that were classified upon enactment of the 1990 amendments.[75]

In certain cases, the Act required areas to be reclassified to a higher classification, or "bumped up." Such areas would receive a later attainment date but also face the additional requirements associated with the higher classification. If EPA finds that an area classified as *marginal, moderate, or serious* has failed to attain the NAAQS by its attainment date (including any extensions of that date), that area will be reclassified by operation of law to the higher of either (1) the next higher classification or (2) the classification associated with its design value when EPA found it had not attained, but not as high as *extreme* nonattainment.[76]

A state may also request a voluntary bump-up (including *extreme* nonattainment), which EPA must grant.[77]

Following its 1997 adoption of an 8-hour ozone NAAQS, EPA adjusted the categories and associated attainment deadlines that Congress had codified for the 1-hour standard in section 181(a)(1) of the Act as follows:[78]

Classification	Design Value (ppm)	Attainment Deadline (years)
Marginal	0.085 to 0.092	3
Moderate	0.092 to 0.107	6
Serious	0.107 to 0.120	9
Severe-15	0.120 to 0.127	15
Severe-17	0.127 to 0.187	17
Extreme	0.187 and above	20

Following adoption of the revised 8-hour ozone NAAQS in 2008, EPA determined that nonattainment area would again be classified under a modification of the classifications in section 181(a)(1) of the Act as follows:[79]

Classification	Design Value (ppm)	Attainment Deadline (years)
Marginal	0.076 to 0.086	3
Moderate	0.086 to 0.100	6
Serious	0.100 to 0.113	9
Severe-15	0.113 to 0.119	15
Severe-17	0.119 to 0.175	17
Extreme	0.175 and above	20

Thereafter, EPA used the same approach to establish the following classifications for the 8-hour ozone NAAQS that it promulgated in 2015:[80]

Classification	Design Value (ppm)	Attainment Deadline (years)
Marginal	0.071 to 0.081	3
Moderate	0.081 to 0.093	6
Serious	0.093 to 0.105	9
Severe-15	0.105 to 0.111	15
Severe-17	0.111 to 0.163	17
Extreme	0.163 and above	20

After adopting its first 8-hour ozone NAAQS in 1997, EPA determined that the 1-hour NAAQS would no longer apply to any area one year after the effective date of designations for the 8-hour standard as long as the area met specified anti-backsliding requirements.[81] Thus, the Agency reasoned, it would not make findings of failure to attain for the 1-hour NAAQS and would not "bump-up" areas to a higher nonattainment classification for the 1-hour NAAQS under Subpart 2 of the Act.[82] Furthermore, EPA concluded it had no mechanism to redesignate such 1-hour nonattainment areas to attainment, allowing them to terminate measures implementing the anti-backsliding requirements and establish a "redesignation substitute."[83] EPA applied these same approaches to transitioning from the 0.08 ppm 8-hour NAAQS set in 1997 to the 0.075 ppm 8-hour NAAQS promulgated in 2008.[84]

In 2018, however, the U.S. Court of Appeals for the District of Columbia Circuit (D.C. Circuit) held that the requirement to reclassify areas that had not been redesignated to attainment applied even for NAAQS that had been revoked.[85] The court also vacated the provision for a "redesignation substitute."[86] As a result, EPA has begun terminating anti-backsliding requirements for areas that it determines have met the criteria for redesignation to attainment for ozone NAAQS that no longer apply in an area.[87]

b. Required SIP Revisions

States with ozone nonattainment areas are required by Subpart 2 of Part D to make the following revisions to their SIPs. While some of these requirements apply regardless of classification, for others, the requirements become increasingly onerous for higher classifications.[88]

(1) State Planning and Demonstration Requirements

Emission Inventories. States must provide a "comprehensive, accurate, current inventory" of actual emissions of VOCs and NOx in all ozone nonattainment areas.[89] These inventories are used by states in air quality modeling and to assess compliance with emission reduction requirements. States must update their emission inventories every three years until attainment is achieved.[90]

Percent Reductions for RFP. Each state with an ozone nonattainment area classified as *moderate or above* for ozone must provide for annual reductions in VOC emissions in the area of at least 15 percent over an initial six-year period in order to show "reasonable further progress" toward attainment.[91] For any area other than an *extreme* area, however, a percentage of less than 15 percent for VOC reductions is permitted if specific additional requirements are imposed.[92]

To be creditable, emission reductions must be "real, permanent, and enforceable" and must be the result of emission reduction strategies implemented "in the designated nonattainment area."[93] Sources of creditable reductions include (1) RACT or motor vehicle inspection and maintenance (I/M) reductions not associated with required SIP corrections (i.e., reductions from lower emission rates or applicability thresholds); (2) application of regulations to areas not previously subject to them; (3) adoption of transportation control measures (TCMs) not previously included in the SIP; and (4) improvements in "rule effectiveness."[94]

Emission reductions may not be "double-counted" (e.g., counted for both a new source offset and for RFP).[95] In addition, emissions eliminated by regulations governing motor vehicle exhaust or evaporative emissions promulgated by January 1, 1990, Reid Vapor Pressure, RACT "fix-up," corrections to existing I/M programs, and pre-enactment banked emission reduction credits are not creditable toward the 15 percent reduction.[96] All other reductions from the implementation of control measures under the SIP, from EPA-adopted federal control measures, or from the state's operating permit program are creditable.[97]

Each state containing an ozone nonattainment area classified as *serious or above* for ozone also is required to provide for reductions in VOC emissions thereafter of at least 3 percent per year averaged over each subsequent three-year period (i.e., 9 percent over each three-year period) until attainment. A reduction of less than 3 percent may be allowed for any area other than an *extreme* area upon a demonstration that the plan includes all measures that can "feasibly" be implemented in light of "technological achievability."[98] In lieu of these reductions in VOC emissions, states may provide for a combination of NOx and VOC emission reductions if those reductions would result in a reduction in ozone concentrations equivalent to the reduction that would result from VOC emission reductions alone.[99]

Nonattainment areas first designated nonattainment for the 2008 ozone NAAQS had three years after that designation to submit their 15 percent RFP plan and four years to submit a plan providing for the additional 3 percent per year until attainment.[100] EPA maintained these timeframes for implementation of the 2015 NAAQS.[101]

Attainment Demonstrations. Each state with an ozone nonattainment area classified as *moderate* is required to provide for "such specific annual reductions" in emissions of VOCs and NOx in the area "as necessary to attain" the ozone NAAQS by the applicable deadline.[102] States are required to demonstrate through application of EPA-approved computer air quality modeling techniques described in EPA's "Guidelines on Air Quality Models," 40 C.F.R. part 51, Appendix W, that the specified reductions and other control strategy measures will be sufficient to achieve attainment. These demonstrations generally involve use of photochemical grid modeling. Such modeling or other analytical method determined by the Administrator" to be "at least as effective" is required for areas classified as *serious or above*.[103]

States had three years to submit required attainment demonstrations for the 1997 NAAQS.[104] States had three years to submit attainment demonstrations for *moderate* nonattainment areas for the 2008 NAAQS and four years to submit attainment demonstrations for nonattainment areas classified as *serious or above* for that NAAQS.[105] EPA maintained those timeframes for attainment demonstrations for the 2015 NAAQS.[106]

Milestone Demonstrations. States with ozone nonattainment areas classified as *serious or above* must demonstrate compliance with any required milestones (including the 15 percent and 3 percent reduction requirements under section 182(b)(1) and (c)(2)) every three years.[107]

For the 2008 ozone NAAQS, EPA established a baseline year of 2011,[108] meaning the first milestone compliance demonstration date was 2014. The Agency also offered states the alternative for a baseline year between 2008 and 2012, *id.*, but the D.C. Circuit vacated that option.[109] For the 2015 NAAQS, EPA established the year of the most recent triennial inventory as the baseline year, noting that for areas designated nonattainment in 2018 that would be 2017.[110] Using this baseline, the first milestone compliance demonstrations were due in 2020. EPA's implementation rule also offered the alternative of a baseline year that corresponds with the effective date of the nonattainment designation, and the D.C. Circuit upheld that option.[111]

Within 90 days after each milestone, the state must submit to EPA a demonstration that the reduction has been met. The Administrator has 90 days to determine whether the demonstration is adequate.[112]

In addition, for each ozone nonattainment area classified as *serious or above*, states must submit a demonstration every three years that certain relevant transportation parameters (including aggregate vehicle mileage, aggregate vehicle emissions, and congestion levels) are consistent with projections made in the area's attainment demonstration. If the parameters exceed those projected, the state has 18 months to submit a SIP revision with TCMs, including TCMs listed in section 108(f) of the Act, that are capable of bringing emissions within the projected levels. The revisions must be consistent with EPA guidelines.[113] TCMs listed in section 108(f) include requirements for employer-based transportation management plans and employer-sponsored flexible work schedules.

Contingency Measures. States with *moderate or above* ozone nonattainment areas must comply with a section 172(c)(9) requirement to provide for contingency measures that are to be undertaken if an area fails to make reasonable further progress or to achieve attainment by the deadline.[114] Measures must take effect "without further action" by EPA or the state.

Enhanced Ozone Monitoring Programs. EPA has promulgated rules for enhanced ambient monitoring of ozone, NOx, and VOCs and for enhanced emissions monitoring of NOx and VOCs under section 182(c)(1).[115] States with *serious and above* ozone nonattainment areas must adopt and implement a monitoring program based on those rules.

(2) Required Revisions Affecting Stationary Sources

SIPs must address the following requirements and control measures for stationary sources.

Annual Emission Statements for Stationary Sources. All states with ozone nonattainment areas must require stationary sources of NOx and VOCs to submit emission statements annually, showing actual emissions.[116] States may waive the requirement, however, for any class of sources emitting less than 25 tons per year of the relevant pollutant if the state includes those sources' emissions in its periodic inventories.[117]

Requirements for Permit Programs. All states with ozone nonattainment areas must address in their SIPs permits for the construction or modification of major new or modified stationary sources of NOx or VOCs in the nonattainment area.[118] The SIPs must apply the following definitions of "major stationary source" (based on potential to emit) and emission offset ratios (i.e., ratio of total emission reductions to total increased emissions):[119]

Classification	"Major Source"	Emissions Offset Ratio
Marginal	100 tons per year	1.1 to 1
Moderate	100 tons per year	1.15 to 1
Serious	50 tons per year	1.2 to 1
Severe	25 tons per year	1.3 to 1
Extreme	10 tons per year	1.5 to 1

For *severe* and *extreme* areas, a ratio of 1.2 to 1 may be used if all existing major sources use the "best available control technology."[120]

Special provisions apply in *serious*, *severe*, and *extreme* ozone nonattainment areas to evaluate proposed "modifications" to determine whether new source review will apply.[121]

RACT. States are required to impose RACT in areas classified as *moderate or above*. Specifically, SIPs for all *moderate or above* ozone nonattainment areas must require RACT at all existing stationary sources of VOCs for which EPA has issued a CTG specifying RACT for the source category. In addition, states must require RACT at all existing "major stationary sources" of VOCs in the area not covered by a CTG.[122]

Clean Fuel for Boilers. New, modified, and existing electric utility and industrial and commercial boilers emitting more than 25 tons per year of NOx that are located in an *extreme* ozone nonattainment area are required to either burn "clean fuel" (generally, natural gas, methanol, or ethanol) at least 90 percent of the time or use "advanced control technology" (e.g., catalytic control technology) for NOx emissions.[123] As the only state to contain an *extreme* ozone nonattainment area, California is the only state to which this provision currently applies.

(3) Required Revisions Related to Mobile Sources

States with ozone nonattainment areas are required to submit the following SIP revisions for the control of emissions from mobile sources.

Motor Vehicle I/M Programs. I/M programs are aimed at reducing hydrocarbons and NOx in ozone nonattainment areas. Areas classified as *marginal* or *moderate* are required to implement a basic I/M program.[124] Areas classified as *serious or above* must have an enhanced I/M program that meets the requirements set out in section 182(c) (including the use of computerized emission analyzers and on-road testing devices), as well as all published guidelines.[125] Requirements for I/M programs are codified in Subpart S of 40 C.F.R. Part 51.

Clean-Fuel Vehicle Programs in Some Areas. States with certain highly populated *serious or above* ozone nonattainment areas must require a specific percentage of clean-fuel vehicles in centrally fueled fleets for each area covered by the clean-fuel vehicle program of Title II.[126] A centrally fueled fleet is ten or more vehicles that are owned or operated by a single person and that are, or are capable of being, centrally fueled. Alternatively, states can adopt control measures resulting in reductions equal to those that would be achieved with a clean-fuel vehicle program. Requirements for the Clean-Fuel Fleet program are codified in 40 C.F.R. part 88.

Transportation Control Measures. For areas classified as *severe or above*, states must adopt specific, enforceable TCMs sufficient to offset any growth in emissions of VOCs from an increase in vehicle miles traveled (VMT) in the area and to help attain the required periodic emissions reductions for reasonable further progress.[127] EPA has issued guidance on TCMs.[128] States must consider implementing the TCMs listed in section 108(f), which include employer-based transportation management plans and employer-sponsored flexible work schedules. In addition, each state with a *serious or above* ozone nonattainment area must submit a demonstration every three years that aggregate vehicle mileage, aggregate vehicle emissions, and congestion levels (as well as other relevant parameters) in the area are consistent with projections made in the area's attainment demonstration. If the parameters exceed the projections, the state has 18 months to submit a SIP revision with TCMs for the area (including, but not limited to, those listed under section 108(f)) capable of bringing emissions within the projected levels.[129]

Although EPA took the position that TCMs were required only to offset growth in motor vehicle emissions in the aggregate, the U.S. Court of Appeals for the Ninth Circuit ruled that TCMs were mandatory if emissions increased due to increased VMT, even if there was no overall increase in motor vehicle emissions (i.e., emissions due to increased VMT were offset by emissions decreases for other reasons such as fleet turnover).[130] As a result, EPA issued guidance to facilitate state determination of situations in which additional TCMs would not be required.[131]

Reformulated Fuels. To reduce VOC emissions, the Act prohibits the sale of non-reformulated gasoline in certain ozone nonattainment areas.[132] The prohibition applies to nine highly polluted ozone nonattainment areas as specified under section 211(k)(10)(D). It may be applied to other ozone nonattainment areas at the request of the governor of the relevant state.[133] EPA's regulations on reformulated gasoline currently are found in 40 C.F.R. part 1090. The reformulated fuel program is discussed in greater depth in chapter 8.

Sale of Low Emission Vehicles (LEV). Section 209 of the Act preempts the states from establishing their own standards directly regulating emissions from motor vehicles. California is entitled, under the statute, to a waiver from this preemption. A state may adopt vehicle emission standards different from the federal standards, however, if those standards (1) are "identical to the California standards for which a waiver has been granted" and (2) are adopted at least two years before commencement of the model year of the vehicles to which they will apply. States cannot adopt standards so different from the federal or the California standards that they effectively call for a "'third vehicle.'"[134] Implementation of this program is discussed in chapter 8.

(4) Requirements for Ozone Transport Regions/Northeast Ozone Transport Region

Under the general SIP requirement of section 110(a)(2)(D), all SIPs must, consistent with the provisions of Title I of the Act, prohibit emissions that interfere with certain Clean Air Act requirements in other states. To help ensure that this requirement is met, the 1990 amendments established a new provision, section

176A,[135] to address interstate transport of air pollutants. Under section 176A, whenever the Administrator determines (on the Administrator's own motion or upon petition from a state) that interstate transport of pollutants from one or more states is contributing significantly to a violation of a NAAQS in another state or states, the Administrator may establish a "transport region" that includes those states (both the "contributing" and the "receiving" states).[136] After designating a transport region, EPA must establish a "transport commission," made up of representatives of the states and EPA.[137] The transport commission "shall assess the degree of interstate transport . . . throughout the transport region, assess strategies for mitigating the interstate pollution, and recommend to the Administrator such measures as the Commission determines to be necessary to ensure" that the relevant states' SIPs satisfy the requirements of section 110(a)(2)(D).[138]

Further, under section 176A(c), a transport commission may ask EPA to issue a SIP call pursuant to section 110(k)(5) of the Act,[139] finding that the SIP for one or more states in the transport region is "substantially inadequate" to meet those requirements and must be revised.[140] EPA must approve, disapprove, or partly approve and partly disapprove any such request within 18 months, and, to the extent EPA approves it, EPA must issue the SIP call to the relevant state or states at the time of the approval.[141]

While section 176A addresses transport generally, section 184 of the Act[142] addresses *ozone* transport specifically. Section 184(a) of the Act specifically created an ozone transport region (the only transport region established under Part D thus far) consisting of Connecticut, Delaware, Maine, Maryland, Massachusetts, New Hampshire, New Jersey, New York, Pennsylvania, Rhode Island, Vermont, and the Consolidated Metropolitan Statistical Area that includes the District of Columbia (an area that encompasses part of Virginia).[143] This region is called the "Northeast Ozone Transport Region." Under section 184(b), all states within an ozone transport region are required to revise their SIPs to include: (1) enhanced I/M for motor vehicles in all Metropolitan Statistical Areas with a population of 100,000 or more; (2) RACT for all "major stationary sources" of VOCs and for VOC sources for which EPA issues or had issued a CTG; and (3) new source review for "major stationary sources" of VOCs.[144] For ozone transport regions, the term "major stationary source" is defined as all sources with the potential to emit 50 tons or more per year of VOCs.[145] "Major stationary sources" of NOx in ozone transport regions could also be required to comply with RACT and new source review under section 182(f).[146] These requirements must be met in all areas in an ozone transport region, regardless of their attainment status.

Section 184(a) provides that section 176A(a)(1) and (2) apply to any ozone transport region, including the Northeast Ozone Transport Region. Those sections in turn provide that the Administrator, "on the Administrator's own motion or petition from the Governor of any State, or upon the recommendation of a transport commission," may: (1) add any state (or part of a state) to an existing transport region if EPA "has reason to believe that the interstate transport of air pollutants" from the state "significantly contributes" to a NAAQS violation in the transport region; or (2) remove any state (or part of a state) from a transport region if EPA "has reason to believe that the control of emissions" in that state (or the relevant part of the state) "will not significantly contribute" to NAAQS attainment "in any area in the [transport] region."[147] Section 176A(a) requires EPA to approve or disapprove such a petition or recommendation—after public notice and comment—within 18 months after receiving it.[148]

In 2013, several of the Northeast Ozone Transport Region states submitted a petition to EPA under section 176A(a) asking EPA to expand the transport region by adding nine upwind states: Illinois, Indiana, Kentucky, Michigan, North Carolina, Ohio, Tennessee, Virginia (i.e., the part of Virginia outside the Washington, D.C. metropolitan area), and West Virginia. The petitioning states argued that emissions from the upwind states significantly contribute to NAAQS violations in the transport region and that those states should be made subject to the emission control requirements applicable to the existing transport region states. In 2017, after receiving and considering public comments, EPA denied the petition.[149] EPA's action was challenged in the D.C. Circuit, which affirmed the denial.[150]

In 2022, EPA approved a petition from Maine to remove a large portion of the state based on continued attainment and technical analysis showing that additional controls of emissions would not significantly contribute to attainment of any standard in any portion of the Ozone Transport Region.[151]

As discussed above, section 176A includes provisions authorizing a transport commission to ask EPA to issue a SIP call requiring one or more states in the transport region to prepare and submit SIP revisions to address interstate pollution. Section 184(c)[152] contains similar—but, in some respects, more specific—provisions for ozone transport regions, including the Northeast Ozone Transport Region. An ozone transport commission by majority vote of the member states may, upon petition by a member state, adopt recommendations to EPA "for additional control measures to be applied within all or a part of [the ozone] transport region if the commission determines such measures are necessary to bring any area in [the transport] region into attainment" by the applicable attainment deadline.[153] EPA must publish a notice of any such recommendation in the *Federal Register*, provide an opportunity for a public hearing within 90 days, and—within nine months after receiving the recommendation—determine whether to approve, disapprove, or partly approve and partly disapprove the recommendation (and must publish its determination in the *Federal Register*).[154] Section 184(c)(4)[155] describes criteria that any EPA decision to disapprove or partly disapprove an ozone transport commission recommendation must meet. If EPA approves the recommendation in whole or in part, it must issue a SIP call to the affected state or states in the ozone transport region, requiring them to make the necessary SIP revisions within one year after EPA issues its determination.[156]

In 2019, Maryland proposed to its fellow Northeast Ozone Transport Region states that the transport commission recommend to EPA additional NOx emission control measures for certain electric generating facilities in Pennsylvania (which is also in the Northeastern Ozone Transport Region). In June 2020, the commission approved the proposed recommendation by a majority vote and transmitted it to EPA. EPA published notice of its receipt of the recommendation,[157] held a public hearing, and accepted comments on the recommendation and information,[158] but as of April 2023 had not taken other action.

(5) National Measures for Consumer or Commercial Products

EPA was required under section 183(e) to issue regulations for control of consumer and commercial products at the national level. EPA has adopted VOC emission standards for: (1) 24 categories of household consumer products ranging from bathroom and tile cleaners to hair mousse;[159] (2) automobile refinish coatings;[160] and (3) a variety of architectural coatings.[161] EPA was permitted to issue CTGs for consumer or commercial products in lieu of regulations if it determined they would be substantially as effective as regulations at reducing VOC emissions.[162] EPA has made this determination and issued CTGs for a variety of products.[163]

(6) Consequences of the Failure by a Serious, Severe, or Extreme Area To Meet a Milestone or an Attainment Deadline

While *marginal, moderate, and serious* areas that fail to attain the ozone NAAQS will, as discussed above, be "bumped up" to a higher classification, other remedies may be applied in *severe and extreme* ozone nonattainment areas. If they fail to attain it by their attainment date, these areas must implement a fee program under section 185.[164] Until the NAAQS is attained, each major stationary source of VOCs in the area must pay an annual fee of $5,000 (adjusted upward for inflation) for each ton of VOC emitted by the source during the year in excess of 80 percent of a "baseline" amount of the lower of actual or allowable VOC emissions.[165] The fee provisions also may apply to major stationary sources of NOx under section 182(f).[166]

These areas—as well as areas classified as *serious*—also face sanctions if they fail to meet a milestone, as discussed above. For *serious and severe* areas, the state may elect to have the area "bumped up," to implement contingency measures adequate to meet the next milestone, or to adopt an economic incentive program.[167]

An *extreme* ozone nonattainment area that fails to meet a milestone is required to adopt such a program.[168]

3. SIP Revisions for CO Nonattainment Areas (Subpart 3 of Part D)

Subpart 3 of Part D discusses classifications and attainment deadlines for areas designated nonattainment for the CO NAAQS, as well as the content of SIPs for such nonattainment areas. No CO nonattainment areas remain. Thus, the provisions of Subpart 3 have no current applicability.

4. SIP Revisions for PM Nonattainment Areas (Subpart 4 of Part D)

a. Classification and Attainment Deadlines

Certain areas were designated nonattainment for PM_{10} by operation of law under section 107(d)(4) of the Act. All of these areas were initially classified as *moderate*[169] and had an attainment deadline of December 31, 1994.[170] The Administrator was authorized to reclassify as *serious* any area that EPA determined "cannot practicably attain" the PM_{10} NAAQS by that date.[171] These areas were given an attainment deadline of December 31, 2001.[172] Areas subsequently designated as nonattainment were required to attain within six years if classified as *moderate* or within ten years if classified as *serious*.[173] Extensions of these attainment deadlines were available, provided certain conditions are met.[174] In addition, the Act permits the Administrator to waive a specific attainment date upon determining that non-manmade sources of PM_{10} "contribute significantly" to violations of the PM_{10} NAAQS in the area.[175]

After EPA promulgated NAAQS using $PM_{2.5}$ as the indicator, EPA initially took the position that Subpart 4 did not apply to nonattainment areas for the $PM_{2.5}$ NAAQS. In 2013, the D.C. Circuit held that the requirements of Subpart 4 apply to nonattainment areas for the NAAQS set using a $PM_{2.5}$ indicator.[176] In 2016, EPA promulgated regulations concerning implementation of these NAAQS under Subpart 4.[177]

The following discussion addresses Subpart 4 requirements for PM NAAQS, whether the indicator for the NAAQS is PM_{10} or $PM_{2.5}$.

b. Required SIP Revisions

States must submit a SIP for each initial *moderate* PM nonattainment area that provides for attainment by the applicable deadline,[178] or demonstrate that attainment by such a deadline is "impracticable," thereby qualifying them for reclassification as *serious*.[179] SIPs are required for later-designated *moderate* nonattainment areas within eighteen months of that designation.[180]

The SIP must also include a permitting program for new or modified major stationary sources of PM[181] and assure implementation of RACM. Finally, the SIP must contain quantitative milestones to be achieved every three years until the area is redesignated for attainment and provide for demonstrations that those milestones were met.[182] Control requirements applicable to major stationary sources of PM also must be applied to major stationary sources of precursor pollutants unless the Administrator determines that such sources do not contribute significantly to PM levels that exceed the NAAQS.[183]

Areas reclassified as *serious* following their failure to attain must submit revised SIPs addressing additional requirements applicable to serious nonattainment areas within eighteen months of that reclassification.[184] Other areas receiving the *serious* classification have four years after their nonattainment designation to submit SIPs addressing the requirements.[185] In either case, these SIPs have to assure implementation of the *best* available control measures (BACM), including best available control technology (BACT), within four years of the *serious* classification.[186] Furthermore, the SIP must define any stationary source or group of stationary sources located within a contiguous area as a "major source" or "major stationary source" if it had the potential to emit 70 tons per year of PM or a PM precursor.[187] The state must provide a modeled demonstration that the measures in the SIP will provide for attainment by the applicable attainment date or, if attaining by that date would be "impracticable," provide for attainment "by the most expeditious alternative date practicable."[188]

c. Consequences of Failure To Meet a Milestone or an Attainment Deadline

States are required to submit a demonstration that a milestone specified in the SIP has been met within ninety days of the date of the milestone.[189] The Administrator must determine the adequacy of that demonstration within ninety days of its submission and, if the milestone is not met, must require revision of the SIP within nine months to assure that the next milestone will be met or the NAAQS will be attained.[190]

Moderate nonattainment areas that fail to attain the standard by the relevant deadline are automatically reclassified as *serious*.[191] As noted above, they must submit a revised SIP addressing the requirements for serious nonattainment areas within eighteen months.[192]

A state in which a *serious* area fails to reach attainment by the applicable deadline must submit a revised SIP within twelve months of that failure.[193] This plan must provide for attainment of the PM NAAQS and for annual reductions in PM or PM precursor emissions within the area of not less than 5 percent until the NAAQS is attained.[194] An area that fails to demonstrate attainment of a milestone is required to submit a SIP revision that assures that the next milestone date of that attainment will be achieved if the attainment date is less than three years in the future.[195]

5. SIP Revisions for SO_2, NO_2, and Lead Nonattainment Areas (Subpart 5 of Part D)

Subpart 5, which concerns requirements for nonattainment areas for the SO_2, NO_2, and lead NAAQS, allows less time for the submission of SIPs for newly designated nonattainment areas than does Subpart 1 (which concerns nonattainment plans in general)—eighteen months compared to three years.[196] Moreover, whereas other subparts of Part D specifically provide for attainment date extensions, Subpart 5 does not. It requires attainment "as expeditiously as practicable but no later than 5 years from the date of the nonattainment designation."[197]

C. Procedural Requirements for SIPs

1. EPA Action on New or Revised SIPs

The 1990 amendments to the Clean Air Act added section 110(k), which sets out the requirements for EPA action on SIPs and revisions to SIPs that the states submit for approval. Section 110(k) required EPA to promulgate minimum criteria that a SIP or SIP revision submittal must meet to be deemed "complete."[198] Those criteria are codified at 40 C.F.R. part 51, Appendix V.

Within 60 days of receiving a SIP or SIP revision, EPA must determine whether the completeness criteria have been met. If, after six months, EPA has not determined whether the criteria have been met, the plan or revision is deemed complete.[199] If EPA determines during the six-month period that the plan or any part of the plan does not meet the completeness criteria, the state is treated as not having made the submission.[200]

Once a plan submission is deemed complete under the criteria, EPA must approve or disapprove the plan within 12 months.[201] A plan that meets all of the requirements of the Act will be approved in whole. If part of the plan does not meet the requirements, EPA may approve it in part or disapprove it in part. In addition, EPA may give conditional approval, contingent on the state adopting specific enforceable measures by a date certain no later than one year after the conditional approval.[202] If a state fails to make a required submission, makes a submission that EPA determines is incomplete, or if the Administrator disapproves a SIP submission in whole or in part, EPA must promulgate a FIP within two years. A FIP is not required if the state corrects the deficiency and obtains EPA approval of the SIP or SIP revision before EPA promulgates the FIP.[203]

Whenever EPA finds that a SIP is "substantially inadequate" to (1) attain or maintain a NAAQS, (2) mitigate interstate pollutant transport as described in the Act's interstate transport provisions (§§ 176A and 184), or (3) comply with any other requirement of the Act, EPA is to issue a SIP call. In a SIP call, EPA provides formal public notification to the state of the SIP deficiency and establishes a reasonable deadline for submission of SIP revisions. That deadline may not be later than 18 months after the notification to the state. EPA may adjust applicable deadlines as appropriate, except that attainment dates prescribed by the Act may not be adjusted unless the deadline has already passed.[204]

SIP revisions required for nonattainment areas in response to a finding by EPA of SIP inadequacy must correct the deficiency and satisfy all other applicable requirements of section 110 and Part D of Title I. To facilitate submittal of adequate and approvable plans, EPA is to issue, as appropriate, guidelines, interpretations, and information to the states and the public.[205]

EPA must approve a SIP revision unless the Agency determines that it would interfere with requirements for attainment, reasonable further progress toward attainment, or any other requirements of the Act.[206] EPA may make corrections to an approval, disapproval, or promulgation of a plan, or to an area designation or classification, without further submissions from the state. Corrections, along with their bases, must be provided to the state and announced to the public.[207]

If EPA revises a primary NAAQS in a way that makes the NAAQS less stringent, EPA must, within 12 months, promulgate emission control requirements for all areas that are nonattainment for that NAAQS. Notwithstanding the NAAQS relaxation, the new emission control requirements may not be less stringent than those in effect before the relaxation.[208]

2. Sanctions for Inadequate SIP Submittals or Implementation

If EPA finds that a state either has failed to submit an approvable SIP or SIP revision as required by the Act, or has failed to implement any requirement of an approved plan, EPA must impose certain sanctions on the state. Under section

179 of the Act, EPA may use two kinds of sanctions against states: (1) EPA may require the state to increase the emission offset ratio for new or modified major stationary sources to at least a 2-to-1 ratio;[209] and (2) EPA may cut off the state's federal highway funds (except for certain safety projects and certain other specific projects).[210] (EPA also may withhold federal grants for air pollution planning and control programs.[211]) EPA's rules on the timing and sequence of the sanctions are codified at 40 C.F.R. § 52.31. Under these rules, once 18 months have passed since the state's failure, the offset requirement is imposed. If the deficiency is not corrected after another 6 months, a highway-fund cut-off is imposed in addition to the offset provision. Sanctions are triggered in this sequence unless EPA decides in a case-specific rulemaking to alter it.[212] In addition, as discussed above, EPA must promulgate a FIP within two years of a state default pursuant to section 110(c)(1) of the Act. These sanctions may not be applied on a statewide basis if only one or more political subdivisions within the state are "principally responsible" for the deficiency.[213] Finally, if a state fails to comply with any requirement regarding new source review in a nonattainment area (including failure to submit an approvable program), EPA may ban construction or modification of any major stationary source in the area.[214]

3. Consequences of Failure to Meet Attainment Deadlines

EPA must determine whether an area has attained the NAAQS and publish the determination in the *Federal Register* as expeditiously as practicable, but not later than six months after the applicable attainment date. The determination is to be made based on the area's air quality as of the attainment date.[215] If the area has not achieved attainment, the state must submit a SIP revision within one year after EPA's publication of notice of its determination that includes all measures that EPA "may reasonably prescribe" and that "can be feasibly implemented in the [nonattainment] area in light of technological achievability, costs, and any nonair quality and other air quality-related health and environmental impacts."[216]

D. SIP Revision After Promulgation of a More Stringent NAAQS

When EPA promulgated rules in 2004 that addressed implementation of the 1997 8-hour ozone standard, the Agency adopted anti-backsliding provisions requiring the retention of control measures in areas designated as nonattainment for the less-stringent 1-hour NAAQS that was being revoked.[217] Although section 172(e) of the Act only requires retention of control requirements in nonattainment areas if a NAAQS is relaxed, EPA reasoned that Congress also would have intended to retain controls when a NAAQS is made more stringent.[218]

Accepting this EPA policy judgment, the D.C. Circuit has identified additional measures as "controls" that must be retained, including provisions governing new source review in nonattainment areas, penalties imposed on major stationary sources in certain areas that do not meet an applicable attainment deadline, contingency plans, and motor vehicle emissions budgets for conformity determinations for the revoked NAAQS.[219] That court subsequently added reclassification upon failure to attain by an applicable deadline, other conformity requirements, requirements to adopt outstanding applicable requirements for a revoked NAAQS, and requirements for maintenance plans to the list of measures that must be maintained.[220] Although these anti-backsliding requirements have been established in the context of the ozone NAAQS, to the extent that they are based on an interpretation of section 172(e) of the Act, they likely also will apply if other NAAQS are replaced by more stringent ones.

III. EPA Rules Addressing Interstate Transport

As discussed above, the Act addresses the interstate transport of air pollution through multiple provisions. Among those, the so-called "Good Neighbor Provision" of section 110 requires each state's SIP to include, among other things, "adequate provisions . . . prohibiting . . . emissions activity within the State from emitting any air pollutant in amounts which will . . . contribute significantly to nonattainment in, or interfere with maintenance by, any other State with respect to any" NAAQS.[221] Under section 110(a)(1) of the Act,[222] states must submit SIP provisions to address interstate transport with respect to any new or revised NAAQS within three years of promulgation of the new or revised NAAQS. The Act further requires EPA to promulgate a FIP if a state fails to submit, or EPA disapproves, a good neighbor SIP.

In addition, section 126 authorizes states to petition EPA for a finding that upwind sources emit pollution in violation of the good neighbor provision,[223] thus bypassing the SIP and FIP processes and obtaining direct federal regulatory action. The Act sets an outer deadline of eight months after receipt of a petition[224] for the Administrator either to "make such a finding"—thereby granting the petition—or "deny the petition." If EPA makes the requested finding, then "any major existing source" is prohibited from "operat[ing] more than three months after such finding has been made with respect to it" unless EPA decides to "permit the continued operation of [the] source . . . beyond the expiration of such three-month period if such source complies with such emission limitations and compliance schedules" as established by EPA "to bring about compliance with the requirements" of the Good Neighbor Provision.[225]

A. The NOx SIP Call and Related Rules

Since the mid-1990s, EPA has recognized that the interstate transport of pollutants is a significant factor in nonattainment in the Eastern United States. In 1998, EPA issued a SIP call to address the contribution of interstate transport of ozone and ozone precursors to ozone nonattainment (the "NOx SIP Call"). The NOx SIP Call found the SIPs of twenty-two states and the District of Columbia "substantially inadequate" with respect to interstate transport and required them to submit SIP revisions that would reduce emissions of NOx within their boundaries between May 1 and September 30 of each year (the "ozone season") to meet specific statewide NOx emissions budgets.[226] The NOx SIP Call permitted interstate trading as a way of meeting these budgets. The rule was largely upheld after a judicial challenge,[227] although the court subsequently extended the date for full implementation of control measures from May 1, 2003, to May 31, 2004.[228]

After adopting new NAAQS for ozone and $PM_{2.5}$ in 1997, EPA proposed to find that twenty-nine states and the District of Columbia contributed significantly to nonattainment of either the 1997 ozone NAAQS or the 1997 $PM_{2.5}$ NAAQS, or both, in other states in the Eastern United States. Based on this finding, EPA proposed to require that the twenty-nine states and the District of Columbia revise their SIPs to eliminate such significant contributions, under a regional cap-and-trade program.[229] In 2005, EPA adopted the Clean Air Interstate Rule (CAIR).[230]

CAIR, which EPA generally modeled on the NOx SIP Call, required reductions of SO_2 and NOx in twenty-eight states and the District of Columbia.[231] The required reductions were to take place in two phases, with the first phase requiring NOx emission reductions beginning in 2009 and SO_2 emission reductions beginning in 2010, and the second phase requiring additional reductions in both NOx and SO_2 beginning in 2015. Most of the emission reductions were expected to come from electric generating facilities. The rule included an interstate trading program using emission allowances and permitted banking of reductions that occurred before the applicable deadlines. According to EPA, implementation of CAIR was expected to bring several areas into attainment of the 1997 ozone and $PM_{2.5}$ NAAQS and make attaining those standards less expensive in the remaining nonattainment areas. Thus, EPA encouraged states to take credit for emission reductions related to CAIR in preparing their SIPs. When it adopted CAIR, EPA decided that the requirements of the NOx SIP Call would no longer apply after 2008.

CAIR was challenged by several parties, including the state of North Carolina. Although none of the petitioners advocated vacatur of the rule, in 2008, the D.C. Circuit issued an opinion finding many problems with CAIR and vacating it.[232] Recognizing the disruptive effect of vacatur on state efforts to implement the ozone and $PM_{2.5}$ NAAQS, EPA petitioned the D.C. Circuit for rehearing on the decision and, in particular, on the remedy. The court granted EPA's rehearing petition to the extent of remanding CAIR to EPA without vacating the rule: "[A]llowing CAIR to remain in effect until it is replaced by a rule consistent with our opinion would at least temporarily preserve the environmental values covered by CAIR."[233]

In 2011, EPA adopted the Cross-State Air Pollution Rule (CSAPR) as a replacement for CAIR.[234] As promulgated, CSAPR required emission reductions in twenty-eight states, beginning in 2012.[235] At the same time, EPA issued FIPs for the covered states that incorporated the emission reductions—in the form of statewide emission budgets—required by CSAPR. EPA indicated that CSAPR would provide a template for future interstate air pollution rules if needed to address requirements for future, more stringent NAAQS.

As had been the case with CAIR, numerous parties sought judicial review of CSAPR. On December 30, 2011 (the last business day before the CSAPR FIPs were to take effect), the D.C. Circuit took the unusual action of granting motions to stay the effectiveness of the rule, and it directed EPA to continue to implement CAIR while the court considered challenges to CSAPR on the merits.[236] In August 2012, the court vacated both CSAPR and the FIPs implementing it and remanded them to EPA.[237] The court directed EPA to continue to administer CAIR until EPA promulgated a valid rule to replace it. EPA sought review of the D.C. Circuit's decision by the U.S. Supreme Court, which granted review.

Reversing the D.C. Circuit's decision, the Supreme Court in a 2014 decision[238] broadly upheld EPA's analytical framework for addressing interstate transport in CSAPR, including EPA's use of cost-effectiveness of emission controls as a factor in determining whether, and to what extent, an upwind state's contribution to a downwind state's problems attaining, or maintaining attainment of, NAAQS is "significant"—and, thus, whether and to what extent the upwind state's emissions may be subject to additional emission control requirements. Although the Supreme Court rejected facial challenges to CSAPR as a whole, it said that any "as-applied" challenges to emission budgets for individual states—on grounds that those budgets were more stringent than necessary to address downwind states' nonattainment or maintenance problems—could be considered by the D.C. Circuit on remand, along with certain other issues that the Supreme Court declined to adjudicate (and that the D.C. Circuit had not resolved in its 2012 decision).

In its 2015 decision on remand,[239] the D.C. Circuit largely rejected challenges to CSAPR but held that EPA had failed to justify the stringency of certain statewide emission budgets. Despite finding those budgets invalid on grounds of "over-control," the D.C. Circuit remanded them to EPA without vacating them, noting that vacatur could be disruptive to the emission allowance markets.[240] Indeed, following the Supreme Court's decision, EPA had filed a motion with the D.C. Circuit to lift that court's 2011 stay of CSAPR, and the court granted that motion in October 2014.[241] The result was that CSAPR took effect beginning in 2015.

Some of the remanded CSAPR statewide emission budgets—those involving SO_2 emissions—were addressed subsequently through state-specific proceedings. The majority of the remanded budgets, however, concerned ozone-season NOx emissions. EPA addressed the remanded CSAPR ozone-season NOx budgets as an element of its 2015–2016 rulemaking on an "update" to CSAPR to address interstate transport with respect to the more stringent ozone NAAQS that EPA had promulgated in 2008 (which the original CSAPR had not addressed due to the uncertain legal status of that NAAQS when EPA originally issued CSAPR in 2011). EPA's final "CSAPR Update" rule[242] established generally more stringent ozone-season NOx emission budgets for twenty-two CSAPR states[243] to address significant interstate contributions to nonattainment and "maintenance" problems in downwind states with respect to the stricter 2008 ozone NAAQS. These updated budgets reflected additional NOx emission reductions that EPA concluded were achievable through cost-effective emission controls that could be implemented at electric generating units (EGUs) in time for the 2017 ozone season, when the revised budgets first took effect. EPA focused on the 2017 ozone season because that was the last full ozone season in which ambient air quality readings would be used for nonattainment areas classified as *moderate*—which had a July 2018 attainment deadline—to show attainment with the 2008 ozone NAAQS. In promulgating the CSAPR Update, EPA explained that, for all but one of the twenty-two covered states, further analysis would be needed to determine whether any additional cost-effective emission reductions at EGUs, or any cost-effective emission reductions at non-EGU facilities were warranted to address significant contribution for the 2008 ozone NAAQS.[244]

Several states, industry parties, and environmental advocacy organizations challenged various elements of the CSAPR Update in the D.C. Circuit. In a 2019 decision,[245] the court affirmed the rule in most respects but held it invalid insofar as it "does not call for upwind States to eliminate their substantial contributions to downwind nonattainment in concert with the attainment deadlines" applicable to downwind states' nonattainment areas.[246] As in the litigation on the original version of CSAPR, the court, to avoid disrupting the program's operation, did not vacate the rule pending EPA's remand rulemaking to correct the deficiency identified by the court.[247]

While the litigation on the CSAPR Update was pending, EPA conducted a follow-up rulemaking in which it determined that the CSAPR Update had in fact fully satisfied all of the covered upwind states' interstate transport obligations for the 2008 ozone NAAQS.[248] In adopting this rule—called the "CSAPR Close-Out Rule"—EPA relied on air quality modeling projections for 2023. Those modeling projections showed no remaining nonattainment or maintenance problems with the 2008 ozone NAAQS in the relevant downwind states in 2023, which EPA determined was the soonest that substantial additional emission controls could be implemented if such controls were to be found necessary. In a decision issued shortly after its remand of the CSAPR Update, the D.C. Circuit invalidated the CSAPR Close-Out Rule because EPA had not shown that significant contributions from the upwind states would be eliminated by the 2021 attainment deadline for downwind nonattainment areas classified as "serious" under the 2008 ozone NAAQS.[249]

In the wake of the D.C. Circuit's decisions on the CSAPR Update and the CSAPR Close-Out rules, northeastern states obtained a judicial order directing EPA to take final action addressing the EPA's outstanding statutory obligations by March 15, 2021.[250] In April 2021, EPA finalized a rule—referred to as the "Revised CSAPR Update" rule—adopting revised FIPs with more stringent emission budgets for EGUs in twelve of the upwind states that are subject to the CSAPR Update.[251] A group of affected sources challenged the rule as arbitrary and capricious, criticizing, among other things, EPA's choice of emissions modeling techniques.[252] The D.C. Circuit upheld the rule as "an appropriate exercise of EPA's statutory authority."[253] Noting that the court "has never required EPA to use a particular modeling method to generate its data or adhere to past practice," the court found EPA's "analytical techniques rationally connected to the Revised Rule" and "appropriately explained," especially in light of the limited amount of time EPA had to complete its rulemaking before the next attainment deadline.[254]

The CSAPR Update and Revised CSAPR Update rules addressed interstate transport obligations for the 2008 ozone NAAQS. In June 2023, after notice-and-comment rulemaking, EPA finalized FIPs to address twenty-three states' obligations with respect to the more stringent 2015 ozone NAAQS.[255] That rule established more stringent NOx emissions budgets for EGU facilities in twenty-two states[256] and NOx emissions standards for certain large industrial non-EGUs in twenty states.[257] However, the final rule also exempts some sources that EPA had proposed to regulate and includes provisions for case-by-case relief in the form of an alternative limit if a source owner can demonstrate that a unit is unable to comply due to "technical impossibility or extreme economic hardship."[258] EPA met the pre-requisite for application of the FIPs to those states when it finalized disapproval of the SIP submission, or a finding of failure to submit, for each of those states.[259] Multiple parties, including states, have challenged the disapprovals and are almost certain to challenge the FIPs.

B. EPA Action on State Petitions

Although the SIP process has been the principal mechanism under which the impact of interstate transport on the ozone NAAQS has been addressed, it is not the only one. In recent years, some states have tried to use section 126 to obtain more stringent, EPA-imposed emission limitations at electric generating and industrial facilities in upwind states that, according to the section 126 petitioners, contribute significantly to nonattainment or interfere with maintenance of either the 2008 or the 2015 ozone NAAQS (or both) in the petitioning states. In 2016, Connecticut filed with EPA a section 126 petition targeting a single facility in Pennsylvania. EPA denied the petition,[260] an action that was not challenged through litigation. Also in 2016, Delaware filed four petitions, each targeting a single source in Pennsylvania or West Virginia, and Maryland filed a petition listing 36 EGUs in five states (Indiana, Kentucky, Ohio, Pennsylvania, and West Virginia). EPA denied all five of these petitions,[261] an action that drew litigation challenges in the D.C. Circuit from Delaware, Maryland, and environmental advocacy organizations. The court largely affirmed EPA's denial of those petitions,[262] although it remanded to EPA for further consideration of its decision as to a small subset of the upwind EGUs targeted by Maryland's petition.[263] Central to the D.C. Circuit's opinion was its agreement with EPA and industry intervenors that "EPA reasonably interpreted section 126(b) to require [the section 126 petitioner] to bear the burden of proof" to show that an affirmative finding under section 126 should be made with respect to the emission sources listed by the petitioner.[264]

The burden-of-proof issue figured prominently in the next section 126 court decision as well, concerning a petition that New York filed in 2018—listing about 350 upwind sources, both EGU and non-EGU facilities, located in nine states[265]—and that EPA denied the next year.[266] In a 2020 decision, the D.C. Circuit held that the denial was arbitrary and capricious because, in its public notice-and-comment proceeding on this petition, EPA failed to articulate a coherent and workable standard that New York, as the section 126 petitioner, would have to meet to satisfy its burden of proof under section 126.[267] In addition, as in the *Maryland* case, the court held it was impermissible for EPA to base its petition denial on air quality projections for a future year that was later than the relevant NAAQS attainment deadline.[268] Although the court vacated and remanded EPA's denial, it declined New York's request to impose a sixty-day deadline for EPA to develop and promulgate a new decision on the petition.[269] In a concurring opinion, Judge Griffith endorsed industry intervenors' argument that New York's petition—by listing hundreds of disparate facilities, geographically dispersed across a nine-state region—exceeded the bounds of section 126 because the listed facilities did not constitute in any meaningful sense a "group of stationary sources," as section 126(b)'s text requires where a petition targets more than one source.[270] But because EPA had not relied on this point in denying New York's petition, Judge Griffith agreed it was appropriate for the court not to resolve the merits of the issue in that case.[271] He added, however, that "in a future case, EPA may decide to enforce the textual and structural restrictions on the scope of a section 126 petition" and that "[p]rospective petitioners should act accordingly."[272]

As of April 2023, EPA had yet to respond to the remands of the Maryland and New York petition denials, although proposed rulemakings for both regularly appear on EPA's regulatory agenda. EPA's fall 2022 regulatory agenda estimated a proposal in the first half of 2023.

Notes

1. EPA regulations define ambient air as "that portion of the atmosphere, external to buildings, to which the general public has access." 40 C.F.R. § 50.1(e). EPA also has issued guidance on exclusions from that definition. *See, e.g.,* Memorandum from Andrew R. Wheeler, Adm'r, EPA, to Reg'l Adm'rs, Revised Policy on Exclusions from "Ambient Air" (Dec. 2, 2019). The Act does not authorize regulation of indoor air quality.

2. Titles of the CAA correspond to subchapters in the U.S. Code.

3. CAA § 108(a)(1), 42 U.S.C. § 7408(a)(1).

4. *Id.* § 108(a)(2), 42 U.S.C. § 7408(a)(2). EPA used to call the document containing this information a "Criteria Document," but now calls it an Integrated Science Assessment (ISA).

5. "PM_{10}" and $PM_{2.5}$" refer to particles with aerodynamic diameters less than or equal to 10 and 2.5 micrometers, respectively.

6. CAA § 109(a), 42 U.S.C. § 7409(a).

7. *See Am. Petroleum Inst. v. Costle,* 665 F.2d 1176, 1185 (D.C. Cir. 1981) (explaining that NAAQS "need not [be] tailor[ed] national regulations to fit each region or locale").

8. CAA § 109(b), 42 U.S.C. § 7409(b). "'[R]equisite,'" in this context means "not lower or higher than is necessary," a judgment that the Administrator makes without considering implementation costs. *Whitman v. Am. Trucking Ass'ns*, 531 U.S. 457, 475-76, 486 (2001). NAAQS are not required to eliminate risk. *Murray Energy Corp. v. EPA*, 936 F.3d 597, 610 (D.C. Cir. 2019) (per curiam).

9. CAA § 302(h), 42 U.S.C. § 7602(h).

10. CAA § 109(d)(2)(A), 42 U.S.C. § 7409(d)(2)(A).

11. *Id.* § 109(d)(1), 42 U.S.C. § 7409(d)(1). Although the Administrator must exercise reasoned judgment in the face of scientific uncertainty when reviewing NAAQS, *Murray Energy Corp.*, 936 F.3d at 620, the scientific uncertainty is sometimes so profound that reasoned judgment is impossible and no NAAQS revision can be appropriate. *Ctr. for Biological Diversity v. EPA*, 749 F.3d 1079, 1091 (D.C. Cir. 2014).

12. CAA § 107(a), 42 U.S.C. § 7407(a) ("Each State shall have the primary responsibility for assuring air quality within the entire geographic area comprising such State by submitting an implementation plan for such State which will specify the manner in which national primary and secondary ambient air quality standards will be achieved and maintained within each air quality control region in such State."). *See Union Elec. Co. v. EPA*, 427 U.S. 246, 256 (1976) (The Act "place[s] the primary responsibility for formulating pollution control strategies on the States.").

13. EPA has taken the position that the date of public distribution combined with signature of a final rule—not the date on which it is published in the *Federal Register* or its effective date—is the date of promulgation for purposes of interpreting CAA deadlines tied to promulgation. Extension of Deadline for Promulgating Designations for the 2010 Primary Sulfur Dioxide National Ambient Air Quality Standard, 77 Fed. Reg. 46,295, 46,295 n.1 (Aug. 3, 2012).

14. CAA § 107(d)(1)(A), 42 U.S.C. § 7407(d)(1)(A). The Act and EPA's implementing regulations provide for the exclusion of monitoring data influenced by exceptional events when making designations and for other purposes. *Id.* § 319(b), 42 U.S.C. § 7619(b). *See* 40 C.F.R. §§ 50.14, 51.930.

15. CAA § 107(d)(1)(B), 42 U.S.C. § 7407(d)(1)(B). EPA sometimes designates areas as attainment/unclassifiable. *See, e.g.*, Additional Air Quality Designations for the 2015 Ozone National Ambient Air Quality Standards, 83 Fed. Reg. 25,776, 25,774 (June 4, 2018). This is treated as a designation as attainment. *See Clean Wisconsin v. EPA*, 964 F.3d 1145, 1157 (D.C. Cir. 2020).

16. CAA § 107(d)(3), 42 U.S.C. § 7407(d)(3).

17. *Id.* § 110(a)(1), 42 U.S.C. § 7410(a)(1).

18. *Id.* § 110(k)(5); 42 U.S.C. § 7410(k)(5).

19. *Id.* § 110(c)(1), 42 U.S.C. § 7410(c)(1) (requiring EPA to promulgate a FIP within two years after the state fails to submit a complete SIP or within two years after EPA disapproves a SIP submission, unless the state corrects the deficiency (and EPA approves a new SIP) before EPA promulgates the FIP).

20. The annual and 24-hour primary NAAQS for SOx cease to apply one year after the effective date of designation for this NAAQS except in areas that are nonattainment for them or that are not meeting the requirements of a "SIP call" with respect to those NAAQS.

Those areas must receive approval of a plan for attaining and maintaining the 1-hour NAAQS before the annual and 24-hour NAAQS will no longer apply. 40 C.F.R. § 50.4(e).

21. Under 40 C.F.R. § 50.13(d), the 15.0 ppm primary annual NAAQS codified at 40 C.F.R. § 50.7 ceased to apply on October 24, 2016 as a result of EPA's revocation of the 1997 standard Fine Particulate Matter National Ambient Air Quality Standards: State Implementation Plan Requirements, 81 Fed. Reg. 58,010 (Aug. 24, 2016). This NAAQS continues to apply in any area designated nonattainment until the area is redesignated attainment.

22. The 1-hour ozone NAAQS have not applied since June 15, 2005, a year after designations for these NAAQS became effective. Adequate anti-backsliding measures are required, however, in areas that were designated nonattainment for the 1-hour NAAQS at the time of its revocation. See S. Coast Air Quality Mgmt. Dist. v. EPA, 472 F.3d 882, 899 (D.C. Cir. 2006).

23. Pursuant to 40 C.F.R. § 50.10(c), and subject to anti-backsliding requirements applicable to areas designated nonattainment for it, the 0.08 ppm NAAQS ceased to apply on April 6, 2016, a year after the effective date of EPA's rule on Implementation of the 2008 National Ambient Air Quality Standards for Ozone: State Implementation Plan Requirements.

24. The 1.5 µg/m3 lead NAAQS no longer applies anywhere because the one area designated nonattainment for it—a part of Jefferson County, MO—has received approval of a plan for attaining and maintaining the 0.15 µg/m3 NAAQS.

25. Review of National Ambient Air Quality Standards for Carbon Monoxide, 76 Fed. Reg. 54,294 (Aug. 31, 2011).

26. Review of the National Ambient Air Quality Standards for Lead, 81 Fed. Reg. 71,906 (Oct. 18, 2016).

27. Review of the Primary National Ambient Air Quality Standards for Oxides of Nitrogen, 83 Fed. Reg. 17,226 (Apr. 18, 2018).

28. Review of the Primary National Ambient Air Quality Standards for Sulfur Oxides, 84 Fed. Reg. 9866 (Mar. 18, 2019).

29. Review of the Ozone National Ambient Air Quality Standards, 85 Fed. Reg. 87,256 (Dec. 31, 2020); Review of the National Ambient Air Quality Standards for Particulate Matter, 85 Fed. Reg. 82,684 (Dec. 18, 2020).

30. *New York v. EPA*, No. 21-1028 (D.C. Cir. filed Jan.19, 2021) (ozone); *California v. EPA*, No. 21-1014 (D.C. Cir. filed Jan. 13, 2021) (PM).

31. Reconsideration of the National Ambient Air Quality Standards for Particulate Matter, 88 Fed. Reg. 5558 (proposed Jan. 27, 2023).

32. *See, e.g.,* EPA, Guidance on Infrastructure State Implementation Plan (SIP) Elements Under Clean Air Act Sections 110(a)(1) and 110(a)(2) (Sept. 2013).

33. CAA § 110(a)(2)(A), 42 U.S.C. § 7410(a)(2)(A).

34. *Id.* § 110(a)(2)(B), 42 U.S.C. § 7410(a)(2)(B).

35. *Id.* § 110(a)(2)(C), 42 U.S.C. § 7410(a)(2)(C).

36. *Id.* § 110(a)(2)(D), 42 U.S.C. § 7410(a)(2)(D). Section 110(a)(2)(D) is one of the provisions on which EPA has relied for a series of regulatory programs addressing interstate transport of air pollutants. Those rules are discussed in Section III. Requirements for visibility protection are discussed in chapter 6.

37. *Id.* § 110(a)(2)(E), 42 U.S.C. § 7410(a)(2)(E).

38. *Id.* § 110(a)(2)(F), 42 U.S.C. § 7410(a)(2)(F).

39. *Id.* § 110(a)(2)(G), 42 U.S.C. § 7410(a)(2)(G); *see also id.* § 303, 42 U.S.C. § 7603 (federal emergency enforcement authority).

40. *Id.* § 110(a)(2)(H), 42 U.S.C. § 7410(a)(2)(H); *see also id.* § 110(k)(5), 42 U.S.C. § 7410(k)(5) (providing EPA's SIP call authority, i.e., EPA authority to call for, or require, revisions to SIPs that EPA determines are substantially inadequate).

41. *Id.* § 110(a)(2)(I), 42 U.S.C. § 7410(a)(2)(I).

42. *Id.* § 110(a)(2)(K), 42 U.S.C. § 7410(a)(2)(K).

43. *Id.* § 165(e)(3)(D), 42 U.S.C. § 7475(e)(3)(D).

44. 40 C.F.R. §§ 51.112(a), 51.166(l).

45. 40 C.F.R. pt. 51, App. W. In November 2018, EPA issued additional guidance on modeling for particular SIP development needs. EPA, EPA 454/R-18-009, Modeling Guidance for Demonstrating Air Quality Goals for Ozone, $PM_{2.5}$, and Regional Haze (Nov. 2018).

46. CAA § 110(a)(2)(L), 42 U.S.C. § 7410(a)(2)(L).

47. *Id.* § 110(a)(2)(M), 42 U.S.C. § 7410(a)(2)(M); *see also id.* § 121, 42 U.S.C. § 7421.

48. Transportation Conformity Rule Restructuring Amendments, 77 Fed. Reg. 14,979 (Mar. 14, 2012) (codified at 40 C.F.R. §§ 93.101 to 93.119).

49. Revisions to the General Conformity Regulations, 75 Fed. Reg. 17,254 (Apr. 5, 2010). These rules are codified at 40 C.F.R. pt. 51, subpt. W and pt. 93, subpt. B.

50. CAA § 507(a), 42 U.S.C. § 7661f(a).

51. EPA, Guidelines for Implementation of Section 507 of the 1990 Clean Air Act Amendments: Final Guidelines (Jan. 1992).

52. CAA § 507(f)–(h), 42 U.S.C. § 7661f(f)–(h).

53. *Id.* § 507(b), 42 U.S.C. § 7661f(b).

54. The PSD regulations are codified at 40 C.F.R. § 52.21. The PSD program is discussed in more detail in chapter 4. The principal visibility protection regulations under Part C are codified at 40 C.F.R. § 51.300 *et seq.* and 40 C.F.R. part 51, Appendix Y. Visibility protection is discussed in more detail in chapter 6.

55. CAA § 110(a)(2)(J), 42 U.S.C. § 7410(a)(2)(J).

56. *Id.* § 172(a)(2)(A), 42 U.S.C. § 7502(a)(2)(A).

57. *Id.*

58. *Id.* § 172(a)(1)(A), 42 U.S.C. § 7502(a)(1)(A).

59. *Id.* § 172(a)(2)(C), 42 U.S.C. § 7502(a)(2)(C).

60. State Implementation Plans; General Preamble for the Implementation of Title I of the Clean Air Act Amendments of 1990, 57 Fed. Reg. 13,498 (Apr. 16, 1992) ("General Preamble"); State Implementation Plans; General Preamble for the Implementation of Title I of the Clean Air Act Amendments of 1990; Supplemental, 57 Fed. Reg. 18,070 (Apr. 28, 1992); State Implementation Plans; Nitrogen Oxides Supplement to the General Preamble for the Implementation of Title I of the Clean Air Act Amendments of 1990, 57 Fed. Reg. 55,620 (Nov. 25, 1992); State Implementation Plans for Lead Nonattainment Areas; Addendum to the General Preamble for the Implementation of Title I of the Clean

Air Act Amendments of 1990, 58 Fed. Reg. 67,748 (Dec. 22, 1993); State Implementation Plans for Serious PM-10 Nonattainment Areas, and Attainment Date Waivers for PM-10 Nonattainment Areas Generally; Addendum to the General Preamble for the Implementation of Title I of the Clean Air Act Amendments of 1990, 59 Fed. Reg. 41,998 (Aug. 16, 1994).

61. CAA § 172(c), 42 U.S.C. § 7502(c).

62. *Id.* § 172(c)(1), 42 U.S.C. § 7502(c)(1). The RACT requirement can be satisfied through averaging emissions within a nonattainment area. *S. Coast Air Quality Mgmt. Dist. v. EPA,* 882 F.3d 1138, 1154 (D.C. Cir. 2018).

63. *See Nat. Res. Def. Council v. EPA*, 571 F.3d 1245, 1253 (D.C. Cir. 2009) (per curiam).

64. CAA § 171(1), 42 U.S.C. § 7501(1). EPA can suspend the requirement for annual emission reductions once an area has air quality that meets the relevant NAAQS, even if the area has not been redesignated to attainment. *Nat. Res. Def. Council*, 571 F.3d at 1260-61.

65. CAA § 172(c)(2), 42 U.S.C. § 7502(c)(2).

66. *Id.* § 172(c)(3), 42 U.S.C. § 7502(c)(3).

67. *Id.* §§ 172(c)(5), 173, 42 U.S.C. §§ 7502(c)(5), 7503.

68. *Id.* § 172(c)(4), 42 U.S.C. § 7502(c)(4).

69. *Id.* § 172(c)(9), 42 U.S.C. § 7502(c)(9).

70. *Id.* § 172(c)(8), 42 U.S.C. § 7502(c)(8).

71. *Id.* § 172(c)(6), 42 U.S.C. § 7502(c)(6).

72. *See* 40 C.F.R. § 50.9.

73. *See Whitman*, 531 U.S. at 476–86.

74. CAA § 181(a)(5), 42 U.S.C. § 7511(a)(5); *see also id.* § 181(a)(4), 42 U.S.C. § 7511(a)(4).

75. *Id.* § 181(b), 42 U.S.C. § 7511(b).

76. *Id.* § 181(b)(2), 42 U.S.C. § 7511(b)(2).

77. *Id.* § 181(b)(3), 42 U.S.C. § 7511(b)(3).

78. Final Rule to Implement the 1997 8-Hour Ozone National Ambient Air Quality Standard: Classification of Areas That Were Initially Classified Under Subpart 1; Revision of the Anti-Backsliding Provisions to Address 1-Hour Contingency Measure Requirements; Deletion of Obsolete 1-Hour Ozone Standard Provision, 77 Fed. Reg. 28,424, 28,426 (May 14, 2012).

79. Implementation of the 2008 National Ambient Air Quality Standards for Ozone: Nonattainment Area Classifications Approach, Attainment Deadlines and Revocation of the 1997 Ozone Standards for Transportation Conformity Purposes, 77 Fed. Reg. 30,160, 30,163 (May 21, 2012).

80. Additional Air Quality Designations for the 2015 Ozone National Ambient Air Quality Standards, 83 Fed. Reg. 25,776, 25,780 (June 4, 2018).

81. Final Rule to Implement the 8-Hour Ozone National Ambient Air Quality Standard—Phase 1, 69 Fed. Reg. 23,951, 23,953 (Apr. 30, 2004). Anti-backsliding requirements are discussed below.

82. *Id* at 23,951.

83. *See* Implementation of the 2008 National Ambient Air Quality Standards for Ozone: State Implementation Plan Requirements, 80 Fed. Reg. 12,264, 12,304–05 (Mar. 6, 2015).

84. *Id.* at 12,265.

85. *S. Coast Air Quality Mgmt. Dist.*, 882 F.3d at 1147–48.

86. *Id.* at 1152.

87. *See, e.g.,* Air Plan Approval; Texas; Houston-Galveston-Brazoria Area Redesignation and Maintenance Plan for Revoked Ozone National Ambient Air Quality Standards; Section 185 Fee Program, 85 Fed. Reg. 8411 (Feb. 14, 2020).

88. Certain ozone nonattainment areas may be treated as *marginal* areas despite a higher design value. If the Administrator determines that sources of volatile organic compounds (VOCs) and NOx emissions in an ozone nonattainment area do not contribute significantly to the area's failure to meet the ozone NAAQS, EPA may designate the zone a rural transport area (RTA) subject only to the SIP requirements applicable to *marginal* areas, regardless of air quality. *Id.* § 182(h), 42 U.S.C. § 7511a(h). According to EPA, an RTA that fails to meet the *marginal* area attainment deadline will be "bumped up" to the appropriate classification (with the extended deadline) but will still only be subject to the SIP requirements for *marginal* areas as long as it meets the requirements of an RTA. General Preamble, 57 Fed. Reg. at 13,506.

89. CAA § 182(a)(1), 42 U.S.C. § 7511a(a)(1). Air emissions reporting requirements, generally, are codified at 40 C.F.R. part 51, subpart A.

90. CAA § 182(a)(3)(A), 42 U.S.C. § 7511a(a)(3)(A).

91. *Id.* § 182(b)(1)(A), 42 U.S.C. § 7511a(b)(1)(A). Areas are only subject to the 15 percent RFP requirement one time. *Nat. Res. Def. Council*, 571 F.3d at 1262.

92. CAA § 182(b)(1)(A)(ii), 42 U.S.C. § 7511a(b)(1)(A)(ii).

93. General Preamble, 57 Fed. Reg. at 13,507, 13,509.

94. *Id.* at 13,502, 13,503–04.

95. *Id.* at 13,509.

96. *See* CAA § 182(b)(1)(B), (D), 42 U.S.C. § 7511a(b)(1)(B), (D).

97. *Id.* § 182(b)(1)(C), 42 U.S.C. § 7511a(b)(1)(C).

98. *Id.* § 182(c)(2)(B)(ii), 42 U.S.C. § 7511a(c)(2)(B)(ii).

99. *Id.* § 182(c)(2)(C), 42 U.S.C. § 7511a(c)(2)(C).

100. 80 Fed. Reg. at 12,266.

101. Implementation of the 2015 National Ambient Air Quality Standards for Ozone: Nonattainment Area State Implementation Plan Requirements, 83 Fed. Reg. 62,998, 63,000 (Dec. 6, 2018).

102. *Id.* § 182(b)(1)(A)(i), 42 U.S.C. § 7511a(b)(1)(A)(i).

103. CAA § 182(c)(2)(A), 42 U.S.C. § 7511a(c)(2)(A).

104. Final Rule to Implement the 8-Hour Ozone National Ambient Air Quality Standard—Phase 2; Final Rule to Implement Certain Aspects of the 1990 Amendments Relating to New Source Review and Prevention of Significant Deterioration as They Apply in Carbon Monoxide, Particulate Matter, and Ozone NAAQS; Final Rule for Reformulated Gasoline, 70 Fed. Reg. 71,612, 71,615 (Nov. 29, 2005).

105. 80 Fed. Reg. at 12,266.

106. 83 Fed. Reg. at 63,000.

107. CAA § 182(g)(1), 42 U.S.C. § 7511a(g)(1).

108. 80 Fed. Reg. at 12,272.

109. *S. Coast Air Quality Mgmt. Dist.,* 882 F.3d at 1153.

110. 83 Fed. Reg. at 63,005.

111. *Sierra Club v. EPA*, 985 F.3d 1055, 1066–67 (D.C. Cir. 2021).

112. CAA § 182(g)(2), 42 U.S.C. § 7511a(g)(2). This demonstration must be based on actual emissions data. *Sierra Club,* 985 F.3d at 1063–66 (vacating EPA's rule authorizing reliance on implementation of a percentage of measures from the relevant plan).

113. CAA § 182(c)(5), 42 U.S.C. § 7511a(c)(5).

114. *Id.* § 172(c)(9), 42 U.S.C. § 7502(c)(9). Measures that have already been implemented do not qualify as contingency measures. *Sierra Club*, 985 F.3d at 1067–1068.

115. Revisions to Ambient Monitoring Quality Assurance and Other Requirements, 81 Fed. Reg. 17,248 (Mar. 28, 2016); Revisions to Ambient Air Monitoring Regulations, 71 Fed. Reg. 61,236 (Oct. 17, 2006); Ambient Air Quality Surveillance, 58 Fed. Reg. 8452 (Feb. 12, 1993). EPA's regulations on ambient air quality surveillance are codified in 40 C.F.R. part 58.

116. CAA § 182(a)(3)(B)(i), 42 U.S.C. § 7511a(a)(3)(B)(i). For 1997, 2008, and 2015 8-hour ozone nonattainment areas, these emission statements were to be submitted within two years of the nonattainment designation. 70 Fed. Reg. at 71,702; 80 Fed. Reg. at 12,266; 83 Fed. Reg. at 63,000.

117. CAA § 182(a)(3)(B)(ii), 42 U.S.C. § 7511a(a)(3)(B)(ii).

118. *Id.* § 182(a)(2)(C), 42 U.S.C. § 7511a(a)(2)(C). Requirements under Subpart 2 of Part D for major stationary sources of VOCs are also generally applicable to major stationary sources of NOx. The Administrator, however, may under specified conditions determine that the requirement for control of NOx emissions should not apply to or should be limited in a given area. *Id.* § 182(f), 42 U.S.C. § 7511a(f).

119. *Id.* § 182, 42 U.S.C. § 7511a. Emission offset requirements for ozone apply separately for NOx and VOCs. *Sierra Club,* 985 F.3d at 1059–63 (vacating rules allowing for interprecursor trading to comply with offset ratios for new source permitting).

120. CAA § 182(d)(2), (e)(1), 42 U.S.C. § 7511a(d)(2), (e)(1).

121. *See id.* § 182(c)(6), (7), (8), (e)(2), 42 U.S.C. § 7511a(c)(6), (7), (8), (e)(2).

122. *Id.* § 182(b)(2), 42 U.S.C. § 7511a(b)(2).

123. *Id.* § 182(e)(3), 42 U.S.C. § 7511a(e)(3).

124. *Id.* § 182(a)(2)(B), (b)(4), 42 U.S.C. § 7511a(a)(2)(B), (b)(4).

125. *Id.* § 182(c)(3)(B)–(C), 42 U.S.C. § 7511a(c)(3)(B)–(C).

126. *Id.* §§ 182(c)(4)(A), 246(a)(2)(A) and (3), 42 U.S.C. §§ 7511a(c)(4)(A), 7586(a)(2)(A) and (3).

127. *Id.* § 182(d)(1)(A), 42 U.S.C. § 7511a(d)(1)(A).

128. EPA, 450/2-89-020, Transportation Control Measure: State Implementation Plan Guidance (Sept. 1990).

129. CAA § 182(c)(5), 42 U.S.C. § 7511a(c)(5).

130. *Ass'n of Irritated Residents v. EPA*, 686 F.3d 668, 679–81 (9th Cir. 2012).

131. EPA, EPA-420-B-12-053, Implementing Clean Air Act Section 182(d)(1)(A): Transportation Control Measures and Transportation Control Strategies to Offset Growth in Emissions Due to Growth in Vehicle Miles Travelled (Aug. 2012).

132. CAA § 211(k)(5), 42 U.S.C. § 7545(k)(5).

133. *Id.* § 211(k)(6), 42 U.S.C. § 7545(k)(6).

134. Final Rule on Ozone Transport Commission; Low Emission Vehicle Program for the Northeast Ozone Transport Region, 60 Fed. Reg. 4712, 4727, 4729 (Jan. 24, 1995).

135. CAA § 176A, 42 U.S.C. § 7506a.

136. *Id.* § 176A(a), 42 U.S.C. § 7506a(a).

137. *Id.* § 176A(b)(1), 42 U.S.C. § 7506a(b)(1).

138. *Id.* § 176A(b)(2), 42 U.S.C. § 7506a(b)(2).

139. *Id.* § 110(k)(5), 42 U.S.C. § 7410(k)(5).

140. *Id.* § 176A(c), 42 U.S.C. § 7506a(c).

141. *Id.*

142. *Id.* § 184, 42 U.S.C. § 7511c.

143. *Id.* § 184(a), 42 U.S.C. § 7511c(a).

144. *Id.* § 184(b), 42 U.S.C. § 7511c(b)

145. *Id.* § 184(b)(2), 42 U.S.C. § 7511c(b)(2).

146. *Id.* § 182(f), 42 U.S.C. § 7511a(f).

147. *Id.* § 176A(a)(1), (2), 42 U.S.C. § 7506a(a)(1), (2).

148. *Id.* § 176A(a), 42 U.S.C. § 7506a(a).

149. Response to December 9, 2013, Clean Air Act Section 176A Petition From Connecticut, Delaware, Maryland, Massachusetts, New Hampshire, New York, Pennsylvania, Rhode Island and Vermont; Notice of Final Action on Petition, 82 Fed. Reg. 51,238 (Nov. 3, 2017).

150. *New York v. EPA*, 921 F.3d 257 (D.C. Cir. 2019).

151. Response to Clean Air Act Section 176A Petition from Maine, 87 Fed. Reg. 7734 (Feb. 10, 2022).

152. CAA § 184(c), 42 U.S.C. § 7511c(c).

153. *Id.* § 184(c)(1), 42 U.S.C. § 7511c(c)(1).

154. *Id.* § 184(c)(2), 42 U.S.C. § 7511c(c)(2).

155. *Id.* § 184(c)(4), 42 U.S.C. § 7511c(c)(4).

156. *Id.* § 184(c)(5), 42 U.S.C. § 7511c(c)(5).

157. Ozone Transport Commission; Recommendation That EPA Require Daily Limits for Emissions of Nitrogen Oxides from Certain Sources in Pennsylvania; Notice of Availability and Public Hearing, 85 Fed. Reg. 41,972 (July 13, 2020).

158. Ozone Transport Commission Recommendation that EPA Require Daily Limits for Emissions of Nitrogen Oxides from Certain Sources in Pennsylvania; Notice of Public Hearing and Supplemental Information, 86 Fed. Reg. 4049 (Jan. 15, 2021).

159. National Volatile Organic Compound Emission Standards for Consumer Products, 63 Fed. Reg. 48,819 (Sept. 11, 1998) (codified at 40 C.F.R. pt. 59, subpt. C).

160. National Volatile Organic Compound Emission Standards for Automobile Refinish Coatings, 63 Fed. Reg. 48,806 (Sept. 11, 1998) (codified at 40 C.F.R. pt. 59, subpt. B).

161. National Volatile Organic Compound Emission Standards for Architectural Coatings, 63 Fed. Reg. 48,848 (Sept. 11, 1998) (codified at 40 C.F.R. pt. 59, subpt. D).

162. CAA § 183(e)(3)(C), 42 U.S.C. § 7511b(e)(3)(C).

163. EPA maintains a listing of Control Techniques Guidelines and Alternative Control Techniques Documents on its website.

164. CAA §§ 181(b)(4)(A), 185, 42 U.S.C. §§ 7511(b)(4)(A), 7511d.

165. *Id.* § 185(b), 42 U.S.C. § 7511d(b). The D.C. Circuit vacated guidance that EPA issued offering states the possibility of developing an alternative program that was at least as stringent as the fees in section 185(b). *Nat. Res. Def. Council v. EPA,* 643 F.3d 311 (D.C. Cir. 2011).

166. The Act provides an exemption for nonattainment areas with a population of less than 200,000 that demonstrate that attainment is prevented by transport of ozone or ozone precursors from other areas. CAA § 185(e), 42 U.S.C. § 7511d(e).

167. *Id.* § 182(g)(3), 42 U.S.C. § 7511a(g)(3). EPA's regulations concerning such Economic Incentive Programs are codified at 40 C.F.R. part 51, subpart U.

168. CAA § 182(g)(5), 42 U.S.C. § 7511a(g)(5).

169. *Id.* § 188(a), 42 U.S.C. § 7513(a).

170. *Id.* § 188(c)(1), 42 U.S.C. § 7513(c)(1).

171. *Id.* § 188(b), 42 U.S.C. § 7513(b).

172. *Id.* § 188(c)(2), 42 U.S.C. § 7513(c)(2).

173. *Id.* § 188(c), 42 U.S.C. § 7513(c).

174. *Id.* § 188(d), (e), 42 U.S.C. § 7513(d), (e).

175. *Id.* § 188(f), 42 U.S.C. § 7513(f).

176. *Nat. Res. Def. Council v. EPA*, 706 F.3d 428, 433–437 (D.C. Cir. 2013).

177. Fine Particulate Matter National Ambient Air Quality Standards: State Implementation Plan Requirements, 81 Fed. Reg. 58,010 (Aug. 24, 2016).

178. CAA § 189(a)(2)(A), 42 U.S.C. § 7513a(a)(2)(A). After the D.C. Circuit determined that Subpart 4 applied to $PM_{2.5}$ NAAQS, EPA classified all nonattainment areas for the 1997 and 2006 $PM_{2.5}$ NAAQS as *moderate*. Identification of Nonattainment Classification and Deadlines for Submission of State Implementation Plan (SIP) Provisions for the 1997 Fine Particle ($PM_{2.5}$) National Ambient Air Quality Standard (NAAQS) and 2006 $PM_{2.5}$ NAAQS, 79 Fed. Reg. 31,566 (June 2, 2014). EPA also initially classified all nonattainment areas for the 2012 annual $PM_{2.5}$ NAAQS as *moderate*. Air Quality Designations for the 2012 Primary Annual Fine Particle ($PM_{2.5}$) National Ambient Air Quality Standards (NAAQS), 80 Fed. Reg. 2206 (Jan. 15, 2015).

179. CAA §§ 188(b)(1), 189(a)(1)(B), 42 U.S.C. §§ 7513(b)(1), 7513a(a)(1)(B).

180. *Id.* § 189(a)(2), 42 U.S.C. § 7513a(a)(2). All SIP elements to address *moderate* $PM_{2.5}$ nonattainment must be submitted within eighteen months of the effective date of a nonattainment designation. 81 Fed. Reg. at 58,026.

181. CAA § 189(a)(1)(A), 42 U.S.C. § 7513a(a)(1)(A).

182. *Id.* § 189(c), 42 U.S.C. § 7513a(c).

183. *Id.* § 189(e), 42 U.S.C. § 7513a(e). EPA has issued guidance for state demonstrations to exempt sources of $PM_{2.5}$ precursors from these controls. EPA, EPA-454/R-19-004, PM 2.5 Precursor Demonstration Guidance (May 2019).

184. CAA § 189(b)(2), 42 U.S.C. § 7513a(b)(2).

185. *Id.* Such *serious* $PM_{2.5}$ nonattainment areas have until the earlier of four years after reclassification or the end of the eighth year after nonattainment designation to submit an attainment demonstration and most other required SIP elements. 81 Fed. Reg. at 58,077.

186. CAA § 189(b)(1)(B), 42 U.S.C. § 7513a(b)(1)(B). For *serious* $PM_{2.5}$ nonattainment areas that received that classification for reasons other than failing to attain by the applicable deadline, this BACT/BACM plan submission and an updated emissions inventory is required within eighteen months of reclassification. 81 Fed. Reg. at 58,076–77.

187. CAA § 189(b)(3); 42 U.S.C. § 7513a(b)(3).

188. *Id.* § 189(b)(1)(A), (3), 42 U.S.C. § 7513a(b)(1)(A), (3).

189. *Id.* § 189(c)(2), 42 U.S.C. § 7513a(c)(2).

190. *Id.* § 189(c)(2), (3), 42 U.S.C. § 7513a(c)(2), (3).

191. *Id.* § 188(b)(2), 42 U.S.C. § 7513(b)(2).

192. *Id.*

193. *Id.* § 189(d), 42 U.S.C. § 7513a(d).

194. *Id.*

195. *Id.* § 189(c)(3), 42 U.S.C. § 7513a(c)(3).

196. *Compare id.* § 191(a), 42 U.S.C. § 7514(a), *with id.* § 172(b), 42 U.S.C. § 7502(b).

197. *Compare id.* § 192(a), 42 U.S.C. § 7514a(a), *with id.* §§ 172(a)(2), 42 U.S.C. § 7502(a)(2) (allowing an extension for a period no greater than 10 years from the data of designation and for two possible extension years), 181(a)(5), 42 U.S.C. § 7511(a)(5) (providing for two possible one-year extensions).

198. *Id.* § 110(k)(1)(A), 42 U.S.C. § 7410(k)(1)(A).

199. *Id.* § 110(k)(1)(B), 42 U.S.C. § 7410(k)(1)(B).

200. *Id.* § 110(k)(1)(C), 42 U.S.C. § 7410(k)(1)(C).

201. *Id.* § 110(k)(2), 42 U.S.C. § 7410(k)(2).

202. *Id.* § 110(k)(3), (4), 42 U.S.C. § 7410(k)(3), (4).

203. *Id.* § 110(c)(1), 42 U.S.C. § 7410(c)(1).

204. *Id.* §§ 110(k)(5), 172(d), 42 U.S.C. §§ 7410(k)(5), 7502(d).

205. *Id.* § 172(d), 42 U.S.C. § 7502(d).

206. *Id.* § 110(*l*), 42 U.S.C. § 7410(*l*).

207. *Id.* § 110(k)(6), 42 U.S.C. § 7410(k)(6).

208. *Id.* § 172(e), 42 U.S.C. § 7502(e).

209. *Id.* § 179(b)(2), 42 U.S.C. § 7509(b)(2).

210. *Id.* § 179(b)(1), 42 U.S.C. § 7509(b)(1).

211. *Id.* § 179(a), 42 U.S.C. § 7509(a).

212. If EPA finds that the state has not acted in good faith, EPA is to apply both the offset and highway funding sanctions at the 18-month point. CAA § 179(a), 42 U.S.C. § 7509(a).

213. *Id.* § 110(m), 42 U.S.C. § 7410(m). *See* 40 C.F.R. § 52.30.

214. CAA § 113(a)(5), 42 U.S.C. § 7413(a)(5).

215. *Id.* § 179(c), 42 U.S.C. § 7509(c).

216. *Id.* § 179(d)(2), 42 U.S.C. § 7509(d)(2).
217. 69 Fed. Reg. at 23,951.
218. *Id.* at 23,972.
219. *S. Coast Air Quality Mgmt. Dist.*, 472 F.3d at 901–5.
220. *S. Coast Air Quality Mgmt. Dist.*, 882 F.3d at 1147–48, 1149, 1155, 1156.
221. CAA § 110(a)(2)(D)(i), 42 U.S.C. § 7410(a)(2)(D)(i).
222. 42 U.S.C. § 7410(a)(1).
223. *Id.* § 126(b), 42 U.S.C. § 7426(b). On its face, section 126(b) actually cross-references section 110(a)(2)(D)(ii), 42 U.S.C. § 7410(a)(2)(D)(ii)—rather than the Good Neighbor Provision (section 110(a)(2)(D)(i))—but courts have held that this was a "scrivener's error" and that Congress intended to cross-reference section 110(a)(2)(D)(i). *GenOn REMA, LLC v. EPA*, 722 F.3d 513, 517 n.3 (3d Cir. 2013); *Appalachian Power Co. v. EPA*, 249 F.3d 1032, 1040–44 (D.C. Cir. 2001) (per curiam).
224. Section 126(b) sets a 60-day deadline for an EPA decision to grant or deny a petition, but section 307(d)(10) of the Act, 42 U.S.C. § 7607(d)(10), authorizes EPA to extend that deadline in a given proceeding by up to six months. *See* CAA § 307(d)(1)(N), 42 U.S.C. § 7607(d)(1)(N) (applying the provisions of section 307(d) to section 126 actions).
225. CAA § 126(c), 42 U.S.C. § 7426(c).
226. Finding of Significant Contribution and Rulemaking for Certain States in the Ozone Transport Assessment Group Region for Purposes of Reducing Regional Transport of Ozone, 63 Fed. Reg. 57,356, 57,456 (Oct. 27, 1998). The jurisdictions for which NOx emissions budgets were established were Alabama, Connecticut, Delaware, the District of Columbia, Georgia, Illinois, Indiana, Kentucky, Massachusetts, Maryland, Michigan, Missouri, North Carolina, New Jersey, New York, Ohio, Pennsylvania, Rhode Island, South Carolina, Tennessee, Virginia, West Virginia, and Wisconsin.
227. *Michigan v. EPA*, 213 F.3d 663 (D.C. Cir. 2000) (per curiam). The court vacated and remanded the rule with respect to Wisconsin, Missouri, and Georgia. *Id.* at 695.
228. *Michigan v. EPA*, No. 98-1497, 2000 WL 1341477, at *1 (D.C. Cir. Aug. 30, 2000).
229. Rule To Reduce Interstate Transport of Fine Particulate Matter and Ozone (Interstate Air Quality Rule), 69 Fed. Reg. 4566 (proposed Jan. 30, 2004); Supplemental Proposal for the Rule to Reduce Interstate Transport of Fine Particulate Matter and Ozone (Clean Air Interstate Rule), 69 Fed. Reg. 32,684 (proposed June 10, 2004).
230. Rule To Reduce Interstate Transport of Fine Particulate Matter and Ozone (Clean Air Interstate Rule); Revisions to Acid Rain Program; Revisions to the NOx SIP Call, 70 Fed. Reg. 25,162 (May 12, 2005).
231. The twenty-eight states were Alabama, Arkansas, Connecticut, Delaware, Florida, Georgia, Illinois, Indiana, Iowa, Kentucky, Louisiana, Maryland, Massachusetts, Michigan, Minnesota, Mississippi, Missouri, New Jersey, New York, North Carolina, Ohio, Pennsylvania, South Carolina, Tennessee, Texas, Virginia, West Virginia, and Wisconsin. Some of the states were covered only for emissions of either SO_2 or NOx, rather than for both.
232. *North Carolina v. EPA*, 531 F.3d 896, 900, 929–30 (D.C. Cir.) (per curiam), *modified in part on reh'g*, 550 F.3d 1176 (D.C. Cir. 2008) (per curiam).

233. *North Carolina v. EPA*, 550 F.3d 1176, 1178 (D.C. Cir. 2008) (per curiam).

234. Federal Implementation Plans: Interstate Transport of Fine Particulate Matter and Ozone and Correction of SIP Approvals, 76 Fed. Reg. 48,208 (Aug. 8, 2011).

235. The states subject to CSAPR were Alabama, Arkansas, Florida, Georgia, Illinois, Indiana, Iowa, Kansas, Kentucky, Louisiana, Maryland, Michigan, Minnesota, Mississippi, Missouri, Nebraska, New Jersey, New York, North Carolina, Ohio, Oklahoma, Pennsylvania, South Carolina, Tennessee, Texas, Virginia, West Virginia, and Wisconsin. Some of the states were included for only their NOx emissions or only their SO_2 emissions, rather than for both.

236. Order, *EME Homer City Generation, L.P. v. EPA*, No. 11–1302 (D.C. Cir. Dec. 30, 2011) (per curiam), ECF No. 1350421 (order granting motions for stay).

237. *EME Homer City Generation, L.P. v. EPA*, 696 F.3d 7 (D.C. Cir. 2012), *cert. granted*, 570 U.S. 916 (2013), *rev'd*, 572 U.S. 489 (2014).

238. *EPA v. EME Homer City Generation, L.P.*, 572 U.S. 489 (2014).

239. *EME Homer City Generation, L.P. v. EPA*, 795 F.3d 118 (D.C. Cir. 2015).

240. *Id.* at 132.

241. EPA then issued an interim final rule to reflect the new compliance dates. Rulemaking To Amend Dates in Federal Implementation Plans Addressing Interstate Transport of Ozone and Fine Particulate Matter, 79 Fed. Reg. 71,663 (Dec. 3, 2014).

242. Cross-State Air Pollution Rule Update for the 2008 Ozone NAAQS, 81 Fed. Reg. 74,504 (Oct. 26, 2016).

243. The twenty-two states are Alabama, Arkansas, Illinois, Indiana, Iowa, Kansas, Kentucky, Louisiana, Maryland, Michigan, Mississippi, Missouri, New Jersey, New York, Ohio, Oklahoma, Pennsylvania, Tennessee, Texas, Virginia, West Virginia, and Wisconsin.

244. The exception was Tennessee. 81 Fed. Reg. at 74,508 n.19, 74,521 n.84, 74,540. In addition, Kentucky submitted a SIP to EPA that relied on the CSAPR Update to fully satisfy that state's interstate transport emission reduction obligation for the 2008 ozone NAAQS, and EPA approved that SIP. Air Plan Approval; Kentucky; 2008 Ozone NAAQS Interstate Transport SIP Requirements, 83 Fed. Reg. 33,730 (July 17, 2018). No litigation challenge was filed on EPA's approval of Kentucky's SIP.

245. *Wisconsin v. EPA*, 938 F.3d 303 (D.C. Cir. 2019) (per curiam).

246. *Id.* at 318.

247. *Id.* at 336.

248. Determination Regarding Good Neighbor Obligations for the 2008 Ozone National Ambient Air Quality Standard, 83 Fed. Reg. 65,878 (Dec. 21, 2018).

249. *New York v. EPA*, 781 F. App'x 4 (D.C. Cir. 2019) (per curiam).

250. *New Jersey v. Wheeler*, 475 F. Supp. 3d 308 (S.D.N.Y. 2020).

251. Revised Cross-State Air Pollution Rule Update for the 2008 Ozone NAAQS , 86 Fed. Reg. 23,054 (Apr. 30, 2021); Revised Cross-State Air Pollution Rule Update for the 2008 Ozone NAAQS; Correction, 86 Fed. Reg. 29,948 (June 4, 2021). The twelve states for which EPA adopted more stringent emission budgets are Illinois, Indiana, Kentucky, Louisiana, Maryland, Michigan, New Jersey, New York, Ohio, Pennsylvania, Virginia, and West Virginia.

252. *Midwest Ozone Grp. v. EPA*, 61 F.4th 187 (D.C. Cir. 2023).

253. *Id.* at 189.

254. *Id.* at 192–93.

255. Federal "Good Neighbor Plan" for the 2015 Ozone National Ambient Air Quality Standards, 88 Fed. Reg. 36,654 (June 5, 2023).

256. The states are Alabama, Arkansas, Illinois, Indiana, Kentucky, Louisiana, Maryland, Michigan, Minnesota, Mississippi, Missouri, Nevada, New Jersey, New York, Ohio, Oklahoma, Pennsylvania, Texas, Utah, Virginia, West Virginia, and Wisconsin.

257. The states are Arkansas, California, Illinois, Indiana, Kentucky, Louisiana, Maryland, Michigan, Mississippi, Missouri, Nevada, New Jersey, New York, Ohio, Oklahoma, Pennsylvania, Texas, Utah, Virginia, and West Virginia.

258. 88 Fed. Reg. at 36,734.

259. *See* Air Plan Disapprovals; Interstate Transport of Air Pollution for the 2015 8-Hour Ozone National Ambient Air Quality Standards, 88 Fed. Reg. 9336 (Feb. 13, 2023); Findings of Failure To Submit a Clean Air Act Section 110 State Implementation Plan for Interstate Transport for the 2015 Ozone National Ambient Air Quality Standards (NAAQS), 84 Fed. Reg. 66,612 (Dec. 5, 2019).

260. Response to June 1, 2016 Clean Air Act Section 126(b) Petition From Connecticut, 83 Fed. Reg. 16,064 (Apr. 13, 2018).

261. Response to Clean Air Act Section 126(b) Petitions From Delaware and Maryland, 83 Fed. Reg. 50,444 (Oct. 5, 2018).

262. *Maryland v. EPA*, 958 F.3d 1185 (D.C. Cir. 2020) (per curiam).

263. *Id.* at 1207–08, 1211.

264. *Id.* at 1197. The D.C. Circuit faulted EPA for considering air quality modeling projections for a future year that was later than the next upcoming NAAQS attainment deadline applicable to the section 126 petitioning state (which, with respect to this issue, was Delaware). *Id.* at 1205. But the court held that this EPA error was "harmless" because EPA had independently based its decision on Delaware's failure to carry its burden of proof to show that downwind air quality problems were projected to occur in the relevant future attainment-deadline year. *Id.*

265. The nine states are Illinois, Indiana, Kentucky, Maryland, Michigan, Ohio, Pennsylvania, Virginia, and West Virginia.

266. Response to Clean Air Act Section 126(b) Petition From New York, 84 Fed. Reg. 56,058 (Oct. 18, 2019).

267. *New York v. EPA*, 964 F.3d 1214, 1222–25 (D.C. Cir. 2020).

268. *Id.* at 1226.

269. *Id.*

270. *Id.* at 1227–29 (Griffith, J., concurring).

271. *Id.* at 1229 (Griffith, J., concurring).

272. *Id.* (Griffith, J., concurring).

Chapter 3

CONTROL TECHNOLOGY REGULATION

The Clean Air Act (CAA or Act) provides for ambient air quality-based emission standards designed to protect public health and welfare and for control technology-based emission standards designed to ensure the use of advanced emission controls.

As discussed in chapter 2, both existing and new sources of air pollution are subject to the ambient air quality-based program through the national ambient air quality standards (NAAQS) established by the U.S. Environmental Protection Agency (EPA or Agency) and the emission limitations established by states in state implementation plans (SIPs).

In addition, the Act contains a general control technology program for *new* sources of air pollution. The "new source performance standard" (NSPS) program under section 111 authorizes establishment of emission standards for categories of major "new," "modified," or "reconstructed" sources based upon the capabilities of control technology.

On top of the NSPS program, the Act requires development of source-specific control technology standards for large new and modified sources of air pollution through a preconstruction permit program. The new source permitting program imposes control technology requirements of varying stringency, depending upon whether the source is located in an area that attains or that does not attain the NAAQS (i.e., in an "attainment" or a "nonattainment" area). In attainment areas, this control technology requirement is referred to as "best available control technology" (BACT). In nonattainment areas, it is referred to as "lowest achievable emission rate" (LAER), or the lowest rate achieved by any source in the same or a similar source category.

Although the Act does not establish a national control technology program for existing sources, existing sources may nonetheless be subject to control technology requirements if they fall within a source category regulated under the NSPS program, or within one of several programs that address special pollution problems. Under section 111(d), EPA is authorized to establish guidelines for states to set performance standards for certain existing sources of air pollutants. In addition, in nonattainment areas, existing sources of a nonattainment pollutant must install "reasonably available control technology" (RACT) to ensure progress toward attainment of the NAAQS. In areas close to larger national parks and wilderness areas (referred to as "mandatory Class I areas"), existing sources that contribute to visibility impairment may be required to install a best available retrofit technology" (BART), which is described in chapter 6. Finally, the 1990 amendments established a control technology-based regulatory program for new and existing stationary sources of hazardous air pollutants (HAPs), which is described in chapter 5.

This chapter focuses first on the generally applicable new source control technology requirements of the Act—that is, the NSPS, BACT, and LAER requirements. It then discusses the circumstances under which existing sources of air pollution may become subject to these new source control technology requirements under the "reconstruction" and "modification" rules. Finally, this chapter summarizes other control technology requirements that may apply in specific cases to existing sources that contribute to specific pollution problems.

I. Control Technology Requirements for New Sources

A. New Source Performance Standards

In enacting the 1970 and 1977 amendments to the Act, Congress expressed concern that retrofitting existing sources with state-of-the-art control technologies could be prohibitively expensive. Congress concluded that it would be more cost-effective to require such technologies at new sources, which have more flexibility with respect to location and design than do existing sources.[1]

Under section 111 of the Act, Congress required the EPA Administrator to identify categories of new and modified sources that contribute significantly to air pollution that endangers public health or welfare (referred to as an "endangerment finding").[2] An endangerment finding applies to source categories as a whole. EPA also may identify subcategories of sources based on class, type, and size for purposes of creating standards.[3] To date, EPA has identified about 80 such source categories, including most major industrial processes. The 1990 amendments imposed new regulatory schedules for source categories that were listed but not regulated under section 111 prior to enactment of the 1990 amendments.[4] As a consequence, EPA published a priority list of source categories for

NSPS development.[5] The list of currently regulated source categories as shown on EPA's website appears in Appendix 2.

For these source categories, EPA sets emission standards that reflect the "degree of emission limitation achievable" through the best technology or system of emission reduction that the Agency determines has been "adequately demonstrated," taking into consideration "nonair quality health and environmental impact and energy requirements."[6] These standards appear at 40 C.F.R. part 60. Where numerical emission limitations are not feasible, NSPS may take the form of design, equipment, work practice, or operational standards.[7]

NSPS apply to facilities on which construction (or "reconstruction") is commenced after proposal of the emission standards or which are "modified" after the date of proposal. The terms "modification" and "reconstruction" are by no means simple to apply and are discussed at length in the second section of this chapter. Once set, NSPS serve as the *minimum* level of control that can be required through the control technology requirements of the new source preconstruction permitting program.

NSPS must be reviewed at least every eight years and, if appropriate, revised through notice-and-comment rulemaking.[8] Although EPA has often failed to revise the NSPS as frequently as mandated by the Act, it nevertheless has done so often enough that technology requirements tend to become more stringent as new technologies are developed and existing technologies are improved.

The 1990 amendments mandated several revisions to specific NSPS. For example, section 403 of the 1990 amendments repealed section 111(a)(1) of the Act, which included a percentage reduction requirement for sulfur dioxide (SO_2) emissions from large fossil fuel-fired boilers, and instead required EPA to set specific emission limits. In 1998, EPA finalized rules to revise the NSPS only for nitrogen oxide (NOx) emissions from those sources.[9] In 2006 and again in 2012, the Agency revised the NSPS for NOx, set an emission limit for SO_2, and revised the NSPS for particulate matter for this source category.[10]

B. New Source Permits and Control Technology Review

As noted above, the NSPS program sets a minimum level of control for new and modified sources of air pollution. More stringent control may be required under either the prevention of significant deterioration (PSD) or the nonattainment new source review (NNSR) preconstruction permitting programs. These source-specific control technology requirements are discussed below.[11]

1. The Best Available Control Technology Standard

Pursuant to the 1977 CAA amendments,[12] an applicant for a PSD permit must show that the proposed source will employ BACT for each regulated pollutant that it emits in significant amounts. According to the Act and EPA's regulations, BACT limits are to be determined on a case-by-case basis after taking into account energy, environmental, and economic impacts and other costs.[13] As Congress has explained, "[t]he weight assigned to such factors is to be determined by the State . . . . Flexibility and State judgment are the foundations . . ." of BACT determinations.[14] In making a BACT determination, therefore, the permitting authority should consider both environmental and economic factors, including "the size of the plant, the increment of air quality which will be absorbed by any particular major emitting facility, and such other considerations as anticipated and desired economic growth for the area."[15]

In a contemporaneous interpretation of the Act, EPA's 1978 Guidelines for Determining Best Available Control Technology state that the decision regarding how much weight should be assigned to energy, environmental, and economic factors should be made by the state. This will "allow[ ] some flexibility in emission control requirements depending on local energy, environmental and economic conditions and local preferences."[16]

In 1980, EPA issued a manual to improve consistency in the BACT review process.[17] The 1980 PSD Workshop Manual embraced a flexible balancing approach to making BACT determinations. The manual makes clear that where the environmental benefits of additional controls are negligible but the economic or energy costs of additional controls are significantly greater, BACT does not require application of the most stringent level of control.[18]

Starting in 1987, EPA sought to limit the discretion of state permitting agencies to balance the statutory criteria in making BACT determinations through its "top-down" approach to BACT. Under this policy, a source would have had to rank available controls starting with the most stringent and then adopt the most stringent control as BACT unless it could be shown to be technically infeasible.

In 1990, EPA's Office of Air Quality Planning and Standards sent to each of the EPA regional offices and states a draft Top-Down Best Available Control Technology Guidance Document (Guidance Document)[19] addressing virtually every aspect of BACT review. For example, the draft guidance: (1) addresses procedures for determining the range of technologies that a PSD permit applicant (and permit-issuing agency) must consider in a BACT demonstration; (2) defines a control technique to be "applicable" and worthy of BACT consideration if it has been used anywhere else, or even if someone has simply agreed to use it somewhere else; and (3) specifies how to calculate the cost of various control technologies (i.e., dollars per ton of pollutant removed).

Although the draft Guidance Document states that it is not binding, many states signed PSD delegation agreements with EPA[20] that require them to follow the top-down approach. EPA also incorporated the policy into a new draft of its NSR Workshop Manual in 1990.[21] The result has been relatively widespread adherence to the top-down policy.

In conducting a case-by-case BACT analysis, the permitting agency must consider site-specific and source-specific characteristics, such as the type of fuel that will be used (e.g., eastern bituminous coal versus Powder River Basin coal), the type of source (e.g., pulverized coal boiler versus natural gas-fired turbine), and geographic considerations (e.g., water availability). Consequently, case-by-case BACT analyses do not necessarily yield a single, independently correct BACT determination.[22] The permitting agency must exercise a high degree of technical judgment in any BACT analysis, particularly for facilities that can utilize a wide variety of fuels and raw material inputs.

EPA's Environmental Appeals Board (EAB) has found that BACT does not necessarily have to match the lowest limit reported, emphasizing the case-by-case nature of the determination and state discretion:

> [The] Petition [contains] a compilation of one-page printouts from the RBL Clearinghouse showing the CO [carbon monoxide] limits for 14 facilities with CO limits ranging from 7.4 ppmvd to 25 ppmvd. We first note that the [Illinois Environmental Protection Agency's ("IEPA's")] determination falls within this range, albeit at the top-end of the range. . . . Although this emission limit may be somewhat lower than the limit set by IEPA in the present case, it does not show clear error in IEPA's decision . . . . [Thus, the] Petition actually demonstrates that IEPA's CO limit in this case is consistent with other similar permitting decisions.[23]

In the final analysis, the permitting agency therefore determines what is achievable for a source, exercising its technical judgment on a case-by-case basis. "Achievable" means an emission limit that the source can meet on a continual basis over each averaging period for the lifetime of the facility. The penalties for noncompliance with a permitted BACT limit are severe. When establishing a BACT limit, the permitting agency should account for the permittee's obligation to meet the limit on a continual basis to avoid an enforcement action. BACT limits therefore do not reflect solely what a source can achieve on its best possible day. BACT limits should reflect what the source can achieve throughout its lifetime under all reasonably foreseeable conditions.

Reflecting this principle, the EAB has repeatedly supported the use of a safety factor to allow the permittee to be able to achieve compliance consistently:

> When [EPA] prescribes an emissions limitation representing BACT, the limitation does not necessarily reflect the highest possible control efficiency achievable by the technology on which the emissions limitation is based. Rather, [EPA] has discretion to base the emissions limitation on a control efficiency that is somewhat lower than the optimal level. . . . To account for these possibilities, a permitting authority must be allowed a certain degree of discretion to set the emissions limitation at a level that does not necessarily reflect the highest possible control efficiency, but will allow the permittee to achieve compliance consistently.[24]

For emissions from operating facilities to be demonstrated as achievable and thus applicable to a new facility, there must be sufficient data to gauge whether those emissions rates are achievable over the long term. Limited stack test data may be insufficient to evaluate what is achievable for new facilities and to establish BACT.[25]

A control technology must also be "available" to be considered in a BACT determination. Theoretical, experimental, or developing technologies are not "available" under BACT. A control technology is neither demonstrated nor available if government subsidies are required to fund evaluations of the technology. In many cases, a technology that is "available" at a smaller unit is not "available" at a larger unit. A control technology must also be "commercially available." This means that the technology must be offered for sale with commercial terms that allow the applicant to meet the limits in the permit.

The BACT analysis focuses on the determination of an emission limitation for the applicant's "proposed facility."[26] Consistent with this reading that BACT applies to the source as proposed, EPA has long observed that the BACT requirements are "not intended to redefine the source."[27] In 2005, EPA reconfirmed in the context of whether an applicant for a proposed pulverized coal facility needed to include an evaluation of an integrated gasification combined cycle (IGCC) unit that it "does not consider the BACT requirement as a means to redefine the basic scope of the source or change the fundamental scope of the project when considering available control alternatives."[28] Accordingly, BACT cannot be used to require a coal-fired facility to consider wind, gas, or hydroelectric processes to generate electricity.

Likewise, BACT does not require a source to change the type of raw material input proposed for the project.[29] In 2007, the U.S. Court of Appeals for the Seventh Circuit (Seventh Circuit) held that BACT at a proposed power plant in

Illinois that was located adjacent to a high sulfur coal mine did not require the consideration of burning low sulfur coal from a mine a thousand miles away.[30] While "clean fuels" constitute one of the control technologies that the Act requires EPA to consider, the Seventh Circuit rejected any requirement that the proposal evaluate the use of nuclear fuel, hydroelectric power, wind turbines, or low sulfur coal because such fuels would constitute a redesign of the project.[31]

When establishing BACT for individual pollutants, the permitting agency must also consider possible interactions among regulated pollutants.[32] As emission limits are driven lower, reducing emissions of one pollutant may increase emissions of another pollutant. The relationship between emissions of NOx and CO is an example of this type of interaction.

Similarly, some techniques to lower emissions of one pollutant may create interactions that produce deleterious effects on downstream equipment. For example, increasing the injection of ammonia to reduce NOx emissions can produce unacceptable levels of sulfur trioxide and ammonium bisulfates if the source uses a high sulfur fuel. These substances can cause serious maintenance and reliability problems in downstream equipment.

Decisions concerning technical feasibility are the responsibility of the permitting authority. A control technology that is "demonstrated" for a given type or class of sources is assumed to be technically feasible unless source-specific factors exist and are documented to justify technical infeasibility. Specifically, EPA's 1990 Draft NSR Workshop Manual states: "Technologies which have not yet been applied to (or permitted for) full-scale operations need not be considered available; an applicant should be able to purchase or construct a process or control device that has already been demonstrated in practice."[33]

2. The Lowest Achievable Emission Rate Requirement

To obtain a preconstruction permit in a nonattainment area, a new or modified major stationary source must demonstrate that it will install control technology that will comply with the LAER for that source category or similar source categories. The LAER requirement applies only for those pollutants for which an area is in nonattainment and which the source will emit in "major" amounts (defined generally as emissions of 100 tons per year (tpy) or more, except in the case of serious and worse nonattainment areas). Alternatively, nonattainment review and LAER apply when a major source proposes to undertake a modification that will result in a "significant" increase in emissions of the nonattainment pollutant for which the source is major.

LAER is defined as "the most stringent emission limitation . . . contained in the implementation plan of any State" or "the most stringent emission limitation

. . . achieved in practice [by the same or similar source category] . . . whichever is more stringent."[34] LAER must be at least as stringent as any NSPS that applies to the source category. The House Report accompanying the 1977 amendments emphasizes that cost is less of a factor in LAER determinations than it is in setting NSPS, but notes that "if the cost of any given . . . means of compliance is so great that new . . . sources could not build and operate, then emission reductions which necessitate [its] use . . . would not be considered achievable . . . ."[35]

As a practical matter, the LAER requirement has been applied to require the most sophisticated control technologies that are available with respect to the nonattainment pollutant.[36] The most stringent technologies for NOx, volatile organic compounds (VOCs), and CO, for example, were historically found in Southern California, where nonattainment problems for several pollutants (including NOx) are particularly severe. The full range of technologies to be considered can typically be identified based on EPA's BACT/LAER Clearinghouse but may also require consideration of foreign experience. Once the most stringent technologies have been identified, the owner or operator of the proposed facility has the burden of demonstrating that the particular control technology is so expensive that it should not be considered "feasible" or "achievable" as applied in the specific circumstances of the proposed facility.

The nonattainment provisions of the 1990 amendments contain a variety of special rules pertaining to LAER. For example, in serious and severe ozone nonattainment areas, source modifications with a potential to emit VOCs or NOx of less than 100 tpy may apply BACT as opposed to LAER.[37] Larger projects may avoid LAER if they obtain an "internal emission offset" in a ratio of at least 1.3 to 1.[38]

II. Control Technology Regulation of Existing Sources Through the "Reconstruction" and "Modification" Rules

A critical issue for existing sources concerns when the new source requirements discussed above apply. New source requirements can be triggered by either reconstruction of a source (in the case of the NSPS program) or modification of a source (in the case of the NSPS, PSD, or nonattainment programs). The 1990 amendments provided refinements to the reconstruction and modification principles in several specific contexts. Additionally, from 1992 through 2007, EPA promulgated and proposed a number of important revisions to the rules applicable to modifications. Finally, the scope of the modification program has been shaped by a series of enforcement actions filed by EPA starting in the late 1990s. These issues are discussed below.

A. The Reconstruction Rule

EPA promulgated the reconstruction rule in 1975 to address projects designed to extend the useful life of existing industrial facilities.[39] The rule defines when a project to rebuild an existing facility becomes so extensive that it is "substantially equivalent to totally replacing it at the end of its useful life with a newly constructed affected facility."[40]

Work to rebuild or replace parts of an existing facility requires notification to EPA under the reconstruction rule when the project involves expenditures that are more than 50 percent of what it would cost to construct a comparable entirely new facility.[41] Triggering the reconstruction rule does not automatically result in application of NSPS. Rather, recognizing that control technology standards developed for new facilities may not be applicable to existing facilities, if the notification requirement is triggered, the Administrator then determines whether reconstruction has occurred by balancing costs, remaining useful life, potential emission reductions, and other considerations.[42]

When EPA promulgated the reconstruction rule, it stated that it did not anticipate that many facilities would trigger reconstruction review and that it would address more specific concerns with life extension of existing facilities in rulemakings establishing NSPS for specific source categories.[43] It is important, therefore, to examine the NSPS rules applicable to an individual source category for further guidance on when capital projects trigger reconstruction review.

For example, the NSPS for emissions of VOCs from synthetic organic chemical manufacturing industry distillation operations specifically lumps together all components that are replaced over any two-year period for purposes of determining whether the 50 percent capital expenditure notice requirement has been triggered.[44] This provision ensures that no owner or operator could spread out the costs of a single project over two years as a means of avoiding review under the reconstruction rule.

An issue that commonly arises under the reconstruction rule concerns what parts of a facility must be taken into account in determining whether the 50 percent capital expenditure threshold will be triggered. The "affected facility" for purposes of the NSPS program is the piece of equipment that produces the regulated emissions (e.g., the boiler at a power plant). The capital expenditure computation is made based on repair and replacement costs that pertain to this "affected facility."[45]

It should be noted that, in contrast to the modification rule, the reconstruction rule applies regardless of whether the work in question causes an increase in the emissions of a regulated pollutant. In addition, all work that forms part of the project—including routine repair and replacement—is considered under the capital expenditure test.[46]

The reconstruction rule was developed under the NSPS program. After enactment of the 1977 amendments, EPA considered whether to apply the reconstruction concept to the PSD program as well. After notice-and-comment rulemaking, the Agency decided that "the general PSD objective of safeguarding existing air quality from significant degradation" would be adequately served by review of major new sources and major modifications without the reconstruction rule.[47] Similarly, EPA has declined to adopt the reconstruction rule for the nonattainment permit program.

B. The Modification Rule

Unlike the reconstruction rule, the modification rule applies to the PSD and nonattainment programs as well as the NSPS program.[48] The modification rule has the same basic elements for each of these programs. That is, a modification occurs when there is a physical change or change in the method of operation at a source that results in an increase in emissions of a regulated pollutant from the source. The modification rule also provides examples of specific activities (e.g., routine repair, replacement, and maintenance) that are not considered modifications. Together, these elements of the modification rule define the construction activities that trigger application of the new source programs at existing sources.[49]

The scope and meaning of each of these elements of the modification rule are further defined in EPA guidance and applicability determinations. Unfortunately, there is no single document that compiles all of the relevant reference materials and indeed, individual guidance memoranda may have taken contradictory positions. Understanding the modification rule is further complicated by court decisions issued in recent years.

Reflecting the confusion that has existed regarding when activity at an existing facility triggers modification review, different U.S. district courts have read the same statutory and regulatory language and arrived at diametrically opposed conclusions.[50] The U.S. courts of appeals also have expressed differing views as to the scope and applicability of the modification provision.[51] In 2007, the U.S.

Supreme Court addressed one aspect of this program in *Environmental Defense v. Duke Energy*.[52] Unfortunately, the Supreme Court's decision did little to resolve the nature of the activity that triggers the modification program.

To begin to understand the modification rule, it helps to review the Seventh Circuit's decision in *Wisconsin Electric Power Company v. Reilly*[53] (*WEPCo*), the EPA interpretations that gave rise to that decision,[54] subsequent applicability determinations, recent judicial decisions, and recent rule revisions. The following sections follow this trail to make observations about the current state of this program.

1. The Modification Rule Before 1976

In the 1970 Clean Air Act, the term "modification" appeared in only one place—in the section 111 NSPS provision of the Act[55]—but governed two new source programs. First, under the 1970 Act, modification of an existing facility triggered application of any NSPS that applied to the source category.[56] Second, under the 1970 Act, modification of an existing facility could trigger preconstruction review of the modified facility to ensure compliance with the NAAQS.[57]

EPA originally promulgated a modification rule for the NSPS program in 1971.[58] In language that parallels the statutory definition, the rule defines a "modified" facility as one at which a "physical or operational change" occurs that "results in an increase in the emission rate of any pollutant to which a standard applies."[59] In a later clarification of this rule, EPA provided that an emission rate increase would be determined using the facility's emission rate measured in kilograms per hour (kg/hr).[60] EPA explained that, under this test, increased hours of operation were irrelevant to whether a "modification" occurred.[61]

To address further the scope of this provision, the modification rule provided examples of activity that does not constitute a "modification." Such activities include: (1) "[routine] [m]aintenance, repair, and replacement"; (2) "[a]n increase in production rate . . . [or] hours of operation" that can be "accomplished without a capital expenditure"; and (3) fuel conversions where the facility was originally designed to accommodate the alternative fuel.[62] As EPA explained in the preamble to the rule, such activities do not trigger NSPS because they do not create "new" pollution.[63] In other words, this definition anticipated that an existing facility can use its existing capacity.

As noted above, the 1970 Act also required review of the location of new or modified sources to ensure that emissions from those facilities that were *not* reviewed by states in establishing SIP emission limits (i.e., "new" pollution) were reviewed for compliance with the NAAQS.[64] Under the 1970 Act, this preconstruction review program applied to modified facilities as defined in section 111 of the Act.

In 1974, EPA adopted regulations defining "modification" for the newly developed preconstruction review program, generally conforming the definition of "modification" for the PSD regulatory program to the definition of that term under the NSPS program.[65] As EPA explained when it promulgated the PSD modification rule, it intended this rule to be consistent with the NSPS modification rule.[66]

2. The "Major Modification" Rule

Prior to 1976, the only definition of "modification" for preconstruction review was the NSPS/PSD regulatory definition. In 1976, EPA issued an interpretive rule on preconstruction review of new and modified facilities located in areas not attaining an applicable NAAQS (i.e., "nonattainment" areas). In that interpretive rule, EPA coined a new regulatory term—"major modification."[67] Under this interpretive rule, a "modification" in a nonattainment area (as defined under the NSPS/PSD regulatory definition of that term) would become subject to the more stringent nonattainment new source review requirements only when that modification was "major"—that is, when the modification caused an increase in emissions above a specified tonnage level.[68]

In 1977, Congress amended the Act to adopt *statutory* preconstruction review programs for PSD and nonattainment areas. In these amendments, Congress chose as the trigger for these new source review (NSR) programs the term "modification" (*not* "major modification") and defined "modification" by reference to its meaning and use under the NSPS program.[69] Congress further restricted application of these preconstruction review programs to "major stationary sources"[70] but other than providing that the 1976 interpretive rule would remain in effect until states adopted nonattainment SIPs,[71] did not address the term "major modification" created by EPA in 1976 for the nonattainment program.

Following the 1977 amendments to the Act, EPA left in place the definition of "modification" that it had promulgated in 1974 for the 1970 preconstruction review program. Activity that constituted a "modification" consistent with the NSPS modification rule, therefore, had to be reviewed to ensure compliance with the NAAQS.[72]

Following the 1977 amendments, however, EPA also adopted rules making "major modification" the trigger for review under the new statutory PSD and nonattainment programs. Under these rules, "modification" of existing facilities that are "major" must meet the *additional* requirements of these new source programs (e.g., the BACT and LAER control technology requirements discussed above), in addition to being reviewed to ensure compliance with the NAAQS and NSPS.

The 1980 PSD and nonattainment rules define a "major modification" as a physical or operational change that results in a "significant emissions increase

. . . of a regulated NSR pollutant . . . and a significant net emissions increase of that pollutant from the major stationary source."[73] A "significant net emissions increase" in turn is defined in terms of annual emissions (i.e., tpy) and allows a source to avoid NSR by offsetting increased emissions at the unit undergoing the modification with contemporaneous and enforceable emission reductions at other emitting units at the same stationary source.

The 1980 PSD rules addressed how a "significant net emissions increase" was to be calculated.[74] First, to determine whether a project is a "major modification," one must determine the amount of emissions, in tpy, from the emitting unit that would undergo the "change." The 1980 rules provided that where the unit had not begun normal operations, its emissions would be determined based on its potential to emit following construction or modification.[75] Thus, where a new emissions unit is added to a source or an existing facility is replaced by a new one, the emissions that must be offset in the "significant net emissions increase" calculation are based on the new emitting unit's "potential to emit," assuming operation of the new emitting unit at full capacity throughout the year (unless an enforceable restriction is imposed on the facility's operations, which restriction is then used to define the facility's potential to emit).[76]

Having defined the amount of the emissions increase (in tpy) that must be offset, the major modification rules then explained how one is to calculate offsetting emission reductions at other emitting units at the stationary source. In contrast to EPA's 1978 "major modification" rules, which would have allowed calculation of emission offsets based on the "potential-to-emit" of the other emitting units at the stationary source,[77] the 1980 rules required emission offsets to be calculated based on a unit's historical "actual emissions" during a representative baseline period.[78] That baseline was defined as the average emissions (in tpy) for a two-year period preceding the project that were "representative" of normal source operation.[79]

Although the 1980 NSR rules defined how to calculate the emissions that must be offset for an emitting unit that has not begun normal operations, they did not define how one calculates the increased emissions that must be offset for existing units that are established operations (i.e., that have begun normal operations).[80] This gap in the 1980 rules has been at the heart of the NSR enforcement controversy over the past two decades, and is discussed further below.

3. The WEPCo Decision

In 1988, the Wisconsin Electric Power Company sought to replace deteriorated equipment at its five-unit Port Washington station to address safety concerns. The deteriorated equipment had led to operation of four units at reduced capacity for an extended period and the shutdown of the fifth unit. All of the repair work involved replacement of broken equipment with equipment of similar design.[81]

The changes planned at these units were extensive—in the range of $80 million in capital costs in 1988 dollars. These costs, however, were only about 20 percent of the cost of comparable new units. As a result, the project did not trigger the reconstruction rule. EPA nevertheless expressed concern that because the project would permit the plant to operate as it had under its original design, all five of the Port Washington units should be treated as new units under both the NSPS and NSR programs if the project went forward.[82]

In reaching this conclusion, EPA found first that this project involved a "physical change" to the facilities, even though it consisted only of "like-kind" replacement of equipment that would not change the size, design, or nature of the facility's operations. While the Wisconsin Electric Power Company argued that the work was not a "physical change" because it constituted "routine" repair, replacement, and maintenance, EPA reasoned that whether replacement of broken equipment is routine must be evaluated on a case-by-case basis, based on consideration of the nature, purpose, cost, and extent of the project. Applying these factors, EPA concluded that the projects were not routine because, among other things, it could find "no examples of steam drum replacement" (the key component replaced) "at aged electric generating facilities."[83] Furthermore, according to EPA, the power company's air heater replacement projects were "too dissimilar to [other industry projects] . . . to support [the company's] contention that the work in question [was] routine."[84] Because the projects at issue had been undertaken at units that "comprise only a small fraction of total operating utility units" in the industry, and because the work at issue "was rarely, if ever, performed" in the utility industry, EPA reasoned that it could not be "routine."[85]

Having concluded that the Port Washington project was a physical change that did not fall within any of the regulatory exclusions, EPA examined the "emissions increase" issue. EPA found that only two of the five Port Washington units would undergo an NSPS "modification" (i.e., would have an hourly emission rate increase caused by the project), but nevertheless found that all five of the units would undergo "major modifications" triggering NSR. EPA reached this conclusion by filling the gap in the 1980 rules noted above and adopting an approach for projection of post-project emissions that would *always* result in an emissions increase finding. That is, EPA reasoned that a "major modification" that triggers NSR occurs when an existing unit's future *potential to emit* (measured in tpy) is greater than its past actual emissions. In reaching this conclusion, EPA specifically rejected the company's argument that it should be allowed under the 1980 rules to project its future actual emissions, as opposed to using its future potential to emit. According to EPA, the "[1980] PSD regulations provide no support for this view" that "'projected' actual emissions after the renovations" should be used to calculate post-project emissions for an existing emissions unit.[86]

Because no facility ever operates at full capacity twenty-four hours a day, every day of the year, this "actual-to-potential" approach to calculating post-project emissions would, as a practical matter, *always* result in a finding of an emissions increase whenever nonroutine work is proposed at an existing facility. According to EPA, one could avoid this result only by accepting a federally enforceable permit condition restricting operations of the existing facility to the level experienced during the two-year period used to establish the facility's emissions baseline.[87]

In the *WEPCo* decision, the Seventh Circuit rejected EPA's "actual-to-potential" approach to calculating a "significant net emissions increase" for units that had begun normal operations.[88] The court remanded the WEPCo PSD applicability determination to EPA to determine "whether the renovated plant would cause a significant net emissions increase if it were operated under present hours and conditions."[89]

As of 1990, therefore, three ways of calculating post-project emissions under the 1980 "major modification" rules had been advanced for emitting units that had begun normal operations. First, in its WEPCo determination, EPA advanced an interpretation under which future emissions would be based on the existing unit's "potential to emit." The Seventh Circuit, however, rejected this interpretation.[90] Second, in that same proceeding, WEPCo advanced an interpretation under which one would project the future actual emissions of an existing unit. EPA, in its 1988 WEPCo determination, however, rejected this interpretation as having no basis in its 1980 rules.[91] Third, as the Seventh Circuit directed, on remand, a "significant net increase" could be calculated under "present [representative] hours and conditions" of operation[92]—a position consistent with earlier EPA applicability determinations.[93] Many read this direction to mean that, for a unit that had begun normal operations, an emissions increase at that unit would require an increase in the hourly emission rate as required under the NSPS modification rule because annual emissions had to be calculated based on the same "representative" hours and conditions of operation before and after a project.[94] In *Duke III*, however, the Supreme Court ruled that a "reading of the 1980 PSD regulations, intended to align them with NSPS, was inconsistent with their terms and [would] effectively invalidate[] them."[95] Against this background, it is not surprising that the 1980 NSR rules were, for decades, the source of controversy.

4. The WEPCo Rule

After the Seventh Circuit's *WEPCo* decision, EPA sought to address some of the confusion created by the WEPCo determination and litigation by conducting a rulemaking. This 1992 rule is often referred to as the "WEPCo rule." This section summarizes the following provisions of the 1992 WEPCo rule, which remain relevant today: (i) the Routine Maintenance, Repair, and Replacement (RMRR) preamble guidance; (ii) the NSPS emissions test; (iii) the NSR "significant net emissions increase" test; (iv) the pollution control project exclusion; and (v) the demand growth/causation preamble discussion.

RMRR. In the WEPCo rule preamble, EPA addressed the "routine maintenance, repair and replacement" provision by promising to issue more formal "guidance on this subject as part of a NSR regulatory update package."[96] In the interim, EPA "clarif[ied] that the determination of whether the repair or replacement of a particular item of equipment is 'routine' under the NSR regulations, while made on a case-by-case basis, must be based on the evaluation of whether that type of equipment has been repaired or replaced by sources *within the relevant industrial category.*"[97]

NSPS emission rate increase. In the 1992 rulemaking, EPA clarified the NSPS emissions increase test by adding a new paragraph (h) to 40 C.F.R. § 60.14, which states that:

> No physical change, or change in the method of operation, at an existing electric utility steam generating unit shall be treated as a modification for the purposes of this section provided that such change does not increase the maximum hourly emissions of any pollutant regulated under this section above the maximum hourly emissions achievable at that unit during the 5 years prior to the change.[98]

In the preamble, EPA explains that this provision "*retain[s] the key concept in the [original] regulations* that the baseline be determined *during a period that is roughly contemporaneous with the proposed change at the affected facility*," thereby "enabl[ing] units to establish a baseline that is *representative* of [their] physical and operational capacity *in recent years,* while still precluding the use of a baseline tied to original design capacity, which . . . may bear no relationship to the facility's capacity in recent years."[99] This provision ensures that the NSPS regulations will not "unduly burden utilities undertaking physical or operational changes in conjunction with the acid rain program," by confirming that a source can "demonstrate that an earlier, higher capacity was more representative of the unit's maximum hourly emissions rate."[100]

NSR "significant net emissions increase" test. The WEPCo rule adds to the "major modification" rule a "projected actual" test for calculating a "significant net emissions increase." As promulgated, this 1992 "projected actual" test applies *only* to electric utility generating units because, as EPA explained, it lacked the time and resources to develop such a test for other industrial sectors.[101] Under this rule, all utility units, other than new or replacement units, can compare past actual emissions to a projection of "future representative actual emissions," a defined regulatory term.[102] In this way, a utility that projects that it would utilize a modified unit *less* than during the baseline period could avoid NSR even if it undertook a project that caused an hourly emission rate increase. To take advantage of this method, though, the utility must provide annual emissions reports for five to ten years after the project in question to confirm that utilization has decreased.[103]

As EPA explained, under the 1980 major modification rules, the "linchpin" for deciding whether to use "potential to emit" in calculating a significant net emissions increase is "whether the unit has '*begun normal operations*.'"[104] According to EPA, however, the *Puerto Rican Cement* and *WEPCo* cases "occasion[ed] a reexamination" of EPA's interpretation of the phrase "begun normal operations" and of the "usefulness of the regulatory language itself."[105]

The WEPCo rule, EPA explained, eliminates the "began normal operations" concept for use of the new "future actual representative emissions" test. Rather, *any* utility unit can use this test whether it has begun normal operations or not, *except* those that are an "addition of a new unit or constitute a replacement of an existing unit."[106] EPA implemented this test by adding a new clause (v) to 40 C.F.R. § 52.21(b)(21), stating that:

> For an electric utility steam generating unit (other than a new unit or the replacement of an existing unit) actual emissions of the unit following the physical or operational change shall equal the representative actual annual emissions of the unit, *provided* the source owner or operator maintains and submits to the permitting authority on an annual basis for a period of 5 years from the date the unit resumes regular operation, information demonstrating that the physical or operational change did not result in an emissions increase. A longer period, not to exceed 10 years, may be required by the [permitting authority] if [it] determines such a period to be more representative of normal source post-change operations.[107]

EPA explained in the preamble that, under this "future actual representative emissions" approach for calculating a "significant net emissions increase," one begins as under the 1980 rules by calculating baseline emissions for the modified unit.[108] According to EPA, the source owner or operator may "presume that any 2 consecutive years within the 5 years *prior to* the proposed change is representative of normal source operations for a utility."[109] Source owners or operators "desiring to use other than a 2-year period or a baseline period prior to the last 5 years" may seek EPA's "specific determination that such period is more representative of normal operations."[110]

As for future emissions, EPA defined the term "representative actual annual emissions" in a new 40 C.F.R. § 52.21(b) as:

> [T]he average rate, in tons per year, at which the source is projected to emit a pollutant for the two-year period after a physical change or change in the method of operation of a unit, (or a different consecutive two-year period within 10 years after that change, where the Administrator determines that such period is more representative of normal source operations), considering the effect any such change will have on increasing or decreasing the hourly emissions rate and on projected capacity utilization.[111]

The "future actual projection," therefore, "is the product of":

- The hourly emissions rate, which is based on the unit's physical and operational capabilities and federally enforceable operational restrictions that would affect the hourly emissions rate following the change; and
- Projected capacity utilization, which is based on consideration of available information regarding the unit's likely post-change capacity utilization.[112]

As noted above, this "projected actual" approach for electric utilities may be employed *only* if the "source owner or operator maintains and submits to the [permitting authority] on an annual basis for a period of 5 years from the date the unit resumes regular operation, information demonstrating that the physical or operational change did not result in an emissions increase."[113] If a utility declines to submit such information for a particular unit, the preexisting 1980 NSR rules would continue to apply.[114]

The Pollution Control Project Exclusion. In the preamble to the final WEPCo rule, EPA explained that "Congress did not intend that pollution control projects be considered the type of activity that should trigger NSR," in other words, new source review under the PSD and nonattainment permitting programs.[115] According to the Agency, "when Congress enacted the NSR provisions of the CAA, it provided that the term 'modification' in NSR shall have the same meaning as the term 'modification' under NSPS."[116] EPA described the NSR pollution control project exclusion under the NSR rules as "reflect[ing] the existing regulatory exclusion for pollution control activities under NSPS regulations, and several recent case-specific nonapplicability determinations under the NSR programs."[117]

The final rule added a new subclause (h) to 40 C.F.R. § 52.21(b)(2)(iii), providing that a "physical change or change in the method of operation" does not include the "addition, replacement or use of a pollution control project at an existing electric utility steam generating unit," with two qualifications. First, NSR may apply where the "Administrator determines that such addition, replacement, or use renders the unit less environmentally beneficial." Second, NSR may apply:

- "When the Administrator has reason to believe that the pollution control project would result in a significant net increase in representative actual annual emissions of any criteria pollutant over levels used for that source in the most recent air quality impact analysis in the area conducted for the purpose of title I, if any," *and*
- Where "[t]he Administrator determines that the increase will cause or contribute to a violation of any national ambient air quality standard or PSD increment, or visibility limitation."[118]

Corresponding regulatory changes were made to 40 C.F.R. § 51.166, the equivalent provision in the Part 51 rules concerning the requirements for approvable NSR SIPs.

Under the WEPCo rule, a "pollution control project" was defined as "any activity or project undertaken at an existing electric utility steam generating unit for purposes of reducing emissions from such unit." Such activities or projects were limited to:

- The installation of conventional or innovative pollution control technology, including but not limited to advanced flue gas desulfurization, sorbent injection for sulfur dioxide and nitrogen oxides controls and electrostatic precipitators;
- An activity or project to accommodate switching to a fuel which is less polluting than the fuel in use prior to the activity or project, including, but not limited to natural gas or coal re-burning, or the co-firing of natural gas and other fuels for the purpose of controlling emissions.[119]

The "pollution control project" definition also included certain permanent clean coal technology (CCT) demonstrations funded under the Further Continuing Appropriations Act of 1985 or by EPA, as well as permanent CCT demonstrations that constitute a repowering project.[120]

Following promulgation of the WEPCo rule, EPA in 1994 issued a guidance memorandum discussing when pollution control projects at non-electric utility sources should be excluded from NSR. This memorandum provided interim guidance pending promulgation of a formal regulatory exclusion for such projects in a future rulemaking. This guidance confirmed that the major modification rule did not apply to pollution control projects undertaken by industrial facilities.[121]

EPA ultimately promulgated a pollution control project exclusion applicable to *all* industries in 2002,[122] but those exclusions of the 2002 NSR rule and the 1992 WEPCo rule were vacated by the U.S. Court of Appeals for the District of Columbia Circuit (D.C. Circuit) in 2005 in a challenge by environmental advocacy organizations.[123] That decision, however, did *not* address the NSPS pollution control exclusion, nor did it address the NSR pollution control project exclusions contained in many SIPs.[124]

The Causation Requirement/Demand Growth Exclusion. In the preamble to the WEPCo rule, EPA recognized that the "NSR regulatory provisions require that the physical or operational change 'result in' an increase in actual emissions in order to consider that change to be a modification."[125] EPA explained that the modification rules are "in no way intend[ed] to discourage physical or operational changes that increase efficiency or reliability or lower operating costs, or improve other operational characteristics of the unit."[126] Further, EPA "recognize[d] that improvements such as these are desirable for economic reasons and to assure a reliable supply of electricity."[127]

To address these issues, the 1992 WEPCo rule contained a specific provision clarifying the "result in" requirement of the "modification" definition:

> In projecting future emissions, the Administrator shall:
>
> (i) Consider all relevant information, including but not limited to historical operational data, the company's own representations, filings with the State or Federal regulatory authorities, and compliance plans under Title IV of the Clean Air Act; and
>
> (ii) Exclude, in calculating any increase in emissions that results from the particular physical change or change in the method of operation at an electric utility steam generating unit, that portion of the unit's emissions following the change *that could have been accommodated during the representative baseline period and is attributable to an increase in projected capacity utilization at the unit that is unrelated to the particular change, including any increased utilization due to the rate of electricity demand growth for the utility system as a whole.*[128]

Although EPA explained that the amended rules "*clarify* this provision in the context of modifications at electric utility steam generating units,"[129] EPA also made clear that this change "merely incorporates into the actual-to-future actual methodology a requirement of the *pre-existing* statutory and regulatory scheme."[130]

In the preamble to the WEPCo rule, EPA identifies "physical or operational change[s] that significantly alter[] the efficiency of [a] plant" as the types of projects that could lead to increased emissions under this rule. EPA explains, however, that it "declines to create a presumption that every emissions increase that follows a change in efficiency is inextricably linked to the efficiency change" and that it "in no way intends to discourage physical or operational changes that increase efficiency or reliability or lower operating costs, or improve other operational characteristics of the unit." The WEPCo rule accomplishes this, EPA says, by making clear that "operational levels that a unit could *not* have achieved during the representative baseline period *but for* the . . . change are considered to result from the change." By contrast, where increased post-project operational levels could have been accommodated during the baseline period and are due to growth in demand, those increased operations are not "caused" by the project. Only where "efficiency improvements are *the predominant cause* of the change in emissions and demand growth is not," EPA continues, does "the exclusion [for increased emissions due to demand growth] . . . not apply."[131]

The "causation" element of the modification rule was addressed by the D.C. Circuit in *New York I*. First, the court recognized that "causation" is a statutory requirement, i.e., that a project must "cause" the emissions increase for there to be a modification. Second, the court upheld the WEPCo rule causation provision as a reasonable implementation of the statute.[132]

C. Changes to the Reconstruction and Modification Rules Made by the 1990 Amendments

Even though Congress decided not to address the modification provision generally in 1990, but rather to leave any needed clarifications to EPA,[133] Congress did address the reconstruction and modification issues in the context of several specific regulatory programs added by the 1990 amendments. These provisions are summarized below.

1. The Clean Coal Technology Program

To encourage the demonstration of CCT and the repowering of sources with such technologies, Congress clarified the applicability of NSPS and new source review to sources that undertake clean coal repowering and demonstration projects.

With respect to repowering projects, the 1990 amendments provide that NSPS does not apply unless there is an increase in the actual hourly emission rate of a regulated pollutant.[134] Qualifying repowering projects would also be given expedited consideration for PSD and/or nonattainment permits.[135] Moreover, any emissions increase must actually *result* from the repowering project before PSD review is required.[136]

Installation or cessation of temporary CCT demonstration projects (defined as projects operated for a period of five years or less) that comply with applicable SIP requirements would not trigger NSPS, PSD, or nonattainment review.[137] Moreover, EPA was required to promulgate regulations or interpretive rulings to revise the NSPS, PSD, and nonattainment modification requirements to facilitate CCT demonstration projects.[138] EPA did so as part of the WEPCo rule discussed above.[139]

2. The Nonattainment Program

To encourage progress toward attainment of the NAAQS, Congress changed the modification rules for certain nonattainment areas that make it more likely that a proposal to modify a source will trigger nonattainment review. For example, in ozone nonattainment areas, Congress changed the definition of "significant" emissions increase as follows: for serious and severe nonattainment areas, the threshold is 25 tpy (net increase over five years);[140] for extreme nonattainment areas, it is any emissions increase.[141] When nonattainment review is triggered in serious and severe areas, however, major sources emitting less than 100 tpy need only implement BACT as opposed to LAER.[142]

3. The Air Toxics Program

With the expanded emphasis on air toxics in the 1990 amendments, Congress specifically addressed the regulatory consequences of "modification" and "reconstruction" activities for air toxics emissions from existing sources. Under the amendments, a "modification" is defined as a physical or operational change that results in a greater than de minimis increase in *actual* emissions of a HAP.[143] A modification finding can be avoided, however, if the increase is offset by an equal or greater reduction of another HAP that is deemed more hazardous. EPA issued rules implementing this definition in 1996,[144] as discussed in chapter 5.

Under the air toxics program, a modification that takes place after the effective date of a state permit program must meet "maximum achievable emission limitations" for existing sources.[145] Reconstructed sources must meet maximum achievable emission limitations applicable to new sources.[146]

4. *The Operating Permit Program*

In Title V, Congress required the development of comprehensive state operating permit programs and specified the minimum elements that must be addressed in those programs. Among other things, permit programs must allow changes that do *not* constitute a modification without requiring a permit revision, provided that written notification of the change is given a minimum of seven days in advance.[147] In 1992, the Agency issued rules addressing this and other issues pertaining to state operating permit programs. These rules and subsequent litigation and rule revisions are discussed in chapter 4.

D. The NSR Enforcement Initiative

In the late 1990s, EPA filed a series of enforcement actions against industry, alleging that companies had been violating the NSR "major modification" rule by repairing and replacing broken or deteriorating equipment. NSR enforcement actions were filed against refineries, paper companies, electric utilities, and others.[148]

The most controversial of these NSR enforcement efforts was directed against the electric utility industry. In 1999, EPA instituted enforcement proceedings against seven utilities and the Tennessee Valley Authority (TVA) alleging that these companies modified their facilities without necessary new source preconstruction permits. The most complete statement of the EPA Enforcement Office's approach to the NSR modification rule is contained in an order of the EAB finding that TVA modified nine of its generating units without obtaining new source permits.[149]

TVA and others challenged the EAB Order in the U.S. Court of Appeals for the Eleventh Circuit. In 2003, the Eleventh Circuit found that the Clean Air Act provision for administrative compliance orders relied upon by the EAB was unconstitutional under due process and separation of powers principles.[150] The court also found that EPA's procedures for development and review of the EAB Order were inadequate and "ignor[ed] the concept of the rule of law."[151] The court therefore declared the TVA order "legally inconsequential" and directed that TVA was free to ignore it.[152] The Supreme Court then denied the Solicitor

General's petition for *certiorari* to the Eleventh Circuit.[153] Because the Eleventh Circuit declared the EAB decision legally inconsequential, courts have since refused to rely on that decision as having precedential value.[154]

Following the *TVA* decision, district courts that have addressed the substance of EPA's NSR enforcement arguments have reached conflicting conclusions. In *Ohio Edison*, for example, the court deferred to EPA's enforcement position, finding (i) that whether activity is "routine maintenance, repair or replacement" must be determined based on the frequency with which an activity is undertaken at an individual unit and that whether a project is common in the industry is irrelevant; and (ii) that a "significant net emissions increase" that triggers NSR can occur when hours of operation increase after a nonroutine project.[155] The court noted that EPA had not previously enforced the law in this manner but attributed this to an "abysmal breakdown" in the implementation and enforcement of NSR.[156] Although the court said that it would take this "abysmal breakdown" into account in fashioning an appropriate remedy, in 2005, Ohio Edison announced that it had settled the case.

By contrast, in *Duke I*, the district court refused to defer to EPA's enforcement arguments, finding them inconsistent with the statute, the regulations, and previous EPA positions.[157] According to the court, the Clean Air Act and EPA's regulations require (i) that "routine" be evaluated in light of industry practice in addition to whether an activity is frequent at a unit; and (ii) that a "significant net emissions increase" can occur only where activity causes an increase in the facility's annual emissions, holding hours and conditions of operation constant at pre-project "representative" operating levels.[158] The U.S. Court of Appeals for the Fourth Circuit issued a decision in 2005 affirming the district court decision on the grounds that the Clean Air Act requires that the term "modification" be defined "congruently" for the NSPS and NSR programs.[159] In 2007, however, the Supreme Court vacated the Fourth Circuit's decision.[160] After a remand to the district court, the case ultimately settled.

A number of other district courts have addressed these same NSR issues. For example, in *United States v. Alabama Power Company*, the Northern District of Alabama decided to follow the *Duke I* decision.[161] The Eastern District of Kentucky decided to follow the *Duke I's* decision on RMRR.[162] By contrast, the Southern District of Indiana decided to follow the *Ohio Edison* decision in *United States v. Cinergy Corp.*[163] A number of other utilities entered into settlements with EPA in order to avoid litigation.[164] One utility made two trips to the Sixth Circuit over ten years of litigation, producing five different opinions with three different interpretations of the NSR regulations from the same three-judge panel.[165] And one case—*Environmental Defense v. Duke Energy Corp.* (*Duke III*)—made it all the way to the Supreme Court.

E. *Environmental Defense v. Duke Energy Corp.*

As noted above, the Fourth Circuit in *Duke II* upheld the decision of the U.S. District Court for the Middle District of North Carolina rejecting EPA's NSR enforcement action against Duke Energy, finding that the Clean Air Act required "modification" to be defined "congruently" for the NSPS and NSR programs, such that "modification" had to be defined in terms of an hourly rate increase (not annual emissions) for both programs.

The Supreme Court's 2007 rejection of the Fourth Circuit's statutory analysis in *Duke III* found that the common definition of "modification" for the NSPS and NSR programs does *not* mandate a common definition of the term for those programs. According to the Court, "three points are relatively clear about the [Clean Air Act 'modification'] regime": (i) "[t]he Act defines modification . . . as a physical [or operational] change . . . that increases [emissions]"; (ii) "EPA's NSPS regulations require . . . [an emissions increase] measured in kilograms per hour"; and (iii) "EPA's 1980 PSD regulations require a permit for a modification . . . only when it is a major one and only when it would increase the actual annual emission of a pollutant above the actual average for the two prior years."[166] Otherwise, the Court observed that the 1980 rules are "no seamless narrative" and that the regulatory definition of "major modification" specifies "no rate at all" for emissions calculations.[167] Nevertheless, because the definitions of "significant" and "net emissions increase" refer to "annual" emissions, the Court observed that what the 1980 PSD rules seem to be "getting at is a measure of actual operations averaged over time, and the regulatory language simply cannot be squared with a regime under which 'hourly rate of emissions' . . . is dispositive."[168] Finally, the Court noted that it had no occasion to address the "charges" of Duke Energy and others in enforcement proceedings "that the agency has taken inconsistent positions and is now 'retroactively targeting twenty years of accepted practice.'"[169] These issues would be left, the Court said, for future proceedings.

As noted above, the 1980 major modification rule does not address how one computes increased emissions for emitting units that have begun normal operations. Of the three possible readings of the 1980 NSR rules that have been offered over time, the Seventh Circuit and EPA have said that calculating future emissions for such units based on "potential to emit" is "impermissible."[170] The Supreme Court has said that an interpretation of the 1980 rules to conform them to the NSPS "hourly rate" test would "effectively invalidate[]" them.[171] But the Supreme Court also said that what the major modification rule appears to be "getting at is a measure of actual operations averaged over time"[172]—that is, a projection of post-project actual emissions.

What type of activity at an existing, operational unit then is a "major modification" under the 1980 PSD rules? This persistent question has given rise to additional rulemaking and litigation in the new millennium.

F. The 2002 NSR Reform Rule and Related Litigation

Following promulgation of the WEPCo rule in 1992, EPA formed a workgroup to discuss further changes to the modification rule. As a result of the discussions of that group, EPA first issued a proposal to revise and clarify the rules.[173] EPA followed that two years later with a supplemental notice proposing to repeal principal portions of the WEPCo rule and the interpretations announced in the preamble to that rule.[174]

The final NSR reform rule, issued in 2002, had four components.[175] First, the rule confirmed that "environmentally beneficial" pollution control projects do not trigger new source review.[176] Listed pollution control projects could proceed once notice is provided to the permitting authority, while other pollution control projects must undergo review to ensure that they will not have adverse collateral impacts. The rule provided, however, that emission reductions achieved by a project that takes advantage of the pollution control project exclusion cannot be used in the future for netting or emission reduction credits.[177] Industry was directed to calculate an "emissions increase" using a "projected actual" test.[178]

Second, the rule provided a "clean unit" exclusion from NSR.[179] Under this provision, a unit that meets a BACT-equivalent level of emission control for an NSR pollutant could avoid triggering NSR for ten years, provided that it did not undertake an activity that causes an increase in the facility's allowable emissions rate.

Third, the rule provided criteria and procedures for the development of "plantwide applicability limits" (PAL).[180] A PAL is essentially a source-wide bubble. Once a PAL is established for a source, emissions-increasing activities can be undertaken at an emitting unit at the source as long as the activity does not cause an exceedance of the PAL.

Fourth, in an attempt to provide clarity regarding the emissions increase criterion, industry was directed to calculate an "emissions increase" using a "projected actual" test. Under the rule, if a source owner concludes that there is no "reasonable possibility" of an emissions increase based on his projection, he can proceed with construction provided he complies with certain recordkeeping and reporting requirements. EPA made it clear that it was not imposing any requirement for applicability determinations or for enforceable permit conditions to limit emissions to projected levels. Rather, EPA explained that existing recordkeeping and reporting requirements and certain new reporting requirements imposed by this rule would ensure either that emissions would not increase or would allow the permitting authority to address any NSR consequences if they did.[181]

The 2002 NSR reform rule was challenged by environmental advocacy organizations and certain states in the D.C. Circuit. Other states and industry intervened in defense of the rules. In 2005, the D.C. Circuit upheld most of the 2002 NSR Reform rule in *New York I*.[182] In particular, the court rejected challenges to EPA's "projected actual" emissions increase methodology, the PAL program, and the demand growth/causation requirement. The court, however, vacated the clean unit and pollution control project exclusions as unlawful and remanded certain recordkeeping requirements. As a result, pollution control retrofits have been required to evaluate preconstruction review and permitting before those projects can take place.

In 2007, in response to the D.C. Circuit's *New York I* decision, EPA issued a final rule clarifying the "reasonable possibility" recordkeeping and reporting standards of the 2002 NSR reform rule.[183] The rule utilizes a "'percentage increase trigger' option" and requires sources to determine if the projected actual emissions increase from the change is equal to or greater than 50 percent of the applicable NSR significance level, which would trigger the requirement to fulfill pre-change and, in some cases, post-change recordkeeping and reporting requirements.[184] The State of New Jersey challenged the rule. After a lengthy period during which EPA contemplated a voluntary reconsideration of the rule, the case moved forward, and in 2021, the D.C. Circuit upheld the rule.[185]

G. Subsequent NSR Reform Efforts

In 2017, at the beginning of the Trump administration, EPA began taking significant regulatory reform actions relating to the NSR regulations. Upon taking office in January 2021, President Biden issued an executive order directing the review of all actions taken by EPA in the prior four years that conflicted with certain of his administration's objectives.[186] The following describes the Trump administration's significant actions on NSR and the action's status under the Biden EPA.

Guidance on Enforceability and Use of Actual-to-Projected Actual Applicability Test. The Trump EPA's first action addressed the NSR preconstruction permitting requirements relating to enforceability and use of the actual-to-projected-actual applicability test in determining the applicability of major modifications of an existing facility.[187] In guidance issued in 2017, the Administrator stated that pending further review, EPA would consider it permissible for a facility to factor into its emission projection its intent to actively manage future emissions to prevent the occurrence of a significant emissions increase or a significant net emissions increase.[188] The letter also stated that, consistent with the Sixth Circuit's opinions in the DTE litigation, it would not second-guess source emission projections that "follow[ed] the objective calculation requirements of the regulations."[189] In 2022, the Biden EPA rescinded the memorandum without further explanation, stating only that EPA could continue to implement NSR consistent with the Act and applicable regulations.[190]

Reclassification of Major Source to Area Source Under Section 112. Next, in early 2018, the Trump EPA issued guidance superseding its "once in, always in" policy by allowing major sources subject to maximum achievable control technology (MACT) standards under section 112 of the Act to become area sources at any time by "tak[ing] an enforceable limit on [their] potential to emit (PTE) hazardous air pollutants (HAP) below the major source thresholds."[191] The guidance stated that the policy articulated by the Agency in 1995 was contrary to the plain language of the statute by imposing a temporal limit on conversion of a major source to an area source by allowing it to take place only by the "'first date a source must comply with an emission limitation or other substantive regulatory requirement.'"[192] This guidance was codified in a final rule in 2020.[193] A number of environmental advocacy organizations and states petitioned for reconsideration and challenged the rule judicially.[194] That litigation was placed on hold to allow EPA to review the rule under Executive Order 13990. EPA's fall 2022 regulatory agenda projected publication of a rulemaking proposal in the first half of 2023.

NSR Project Emissions Accounting Rule. In 2018, EPA overruled prior guidance by clarifying that it will consider emissions decreases and increases at a source at the first step in the major modification emissions increase calculation.[195] EPA also stated that for the step one analysis, which entails determining if the proposed project itself is "projected to result in a significant emissions increase,"[196] the facility may, within reason, define the scope of the project.[197] The guidance also provided that even a "'new unit'" (i.e., "'any emissions unit that is (or will be) newly constructed and that has existed *for less than 2 years* from the date such emission unit first operated'") could avoid an increase in potential emissions by offsetting its potential to emit with enforceable reductions at the source before it begins operations.[198] EPA stated that it wished to provide more clarity relating to NSR analysis so that projects that could "result in reduced emissions, even while production is maintained or expanded" are not foreclosed.[199] This guidance also was codified in a final rule in 2020.[200] After the change in administration, several environmental advocacy organizations petitioned for administrative reconsideration of the rule. Although the Biden EPA officially denied the petition,[201] and the Agency has indicated that it intends to initiate a discretionary rulemaking to consider addressing some of the issues raised in the petition. Judicial challenges by multiple states and environmental advocacy organizations are pending.[202]

Denial of Reconsideration and Lifting Stay of the 2009 Project Aggregation Rule. Less than a month later, EPA again addressed the question of what constitutes a project for the purposes of step one of the PSD applicability analyses.[203] According to this guidance, two concurrent projects that are separate and distinct need not be aggregated as one project, if they are technically distinct and are economically viable on their own.[204] The guidance was followed by a 2018 final action lifting a stay of a 2009 final rule, which provides that whether nominally separated activities that are "substantially related" could be aggregated depends on technical or economic dependence and that a rebuttable presumption exists that a gap of three years or more between the activities implies that they should not be aggregated for NSR purposes.[205] As of the end of 2022, the Biden EPA had not taken any public steps to alter this guidance.

Guidance on Significant Impact Levels (SILs) for Ozone and Fine Particulate Matter ($PM_{2.5}$). Later in 2018, EPA issued guidance relating to SILs for ozone and $PM_{2.5}$ for purposes of NAAQS and PSD review.[206] The guidance recognized that EPA had to vacate and remand its 2010 rulemaking on this topic because it did not preserve the permitting authorities' discretion to require additional analysis in certain circumstances, and it provided nonbinding SILs that the permitting authorities *could* use.[207] The memorandum states that EPA will seek to "learn generally about permitting agencies' experiences in applying SILs in particular PSD permitting decisions . . . [and] will use this experience . . . to . . . codify SIL values . . . in a future, potentially binding rulemaking."[208] The guidance states that the permitting authorities could use the suggested SILs to "support a case-by-case permitting decision, [but they] must justify the values and their use in the administrative record for the permitting action."[209] EPA further states that permitting authorities could also use their own SILs by providing similar justifications.[210] A 2020 judicial challenge to the guidance was dismissed for lack of subject-matter jurisdiction.[211] As of the end of 2022, the Biden EPA had not taken any public steps to alter this guidance.

Guidance on Source Definition and Common Control and Adjacency. Also in 2018, EPA's Office of Air and Radiation, in response to a request from the Pennsylvania Department of Environmental Protection, addressed a question relating to "source determinations." EPA affirmed that for purposes of NSR preconstruction permitting programs, "entities may be considered part of the same 'stationary source' or 'major source' if they (1) belong to the same industrial grouping; (2) are located on one or more contiguous or adjacent properties; and (3) are under the control of the same person (or persons under common control)."[212] The Agency stated that "the assessment of 'control' for . . . NSR permitting purposes [should] focus[] on the power or authority of one entity to dictate decisions of the other that could affect the applicability of, or compliance with, relevant air pollution regulatory requirements."[213] Later in 2018, in a draft guidance document issued on a related matter, EPA stated that it interprets "adjacency" to mean physical proximity for industries other than the oil and gas industry and that the concept of "'functional interrelatedness' of operations is not a relevant consideration" in deciding upon adjacency in case-by-case source determinations.[214] EPA issued a final guidance to this effect in 2019.[215] As of the end of 2022, the Biden EPA had not taken any public steps to alter this guidance.

Proposed Hourly Emissions Increase Test for Major NSR. Later in 2018, EPA proposed an NSR rule as part of the Affordable Clean Energy (ACE) rule aimed at giving electric generating units (EGUs) "more latitude to make the efficiency improvements that are consistent with EPA's proposed" best system of emission reduction (BSER) in the ACE proposal, "without triggering onerous and costly NSR permit requirements.[216] ACE proposed that for EGUs, states could elect to use an hourly emissions increase test as a qualifying step for the major NSR permitting requirements, with major NSR review applying only to projects that increased an EGU's hourly emissions rate.[217] However, EPA chose not to finalize the NSR revisions along with the ACE rule, instead stating that it "intends to take final action on the proposed NSR reforms in a separate final action at a later date."[218] However, the action no longer appears on the Agency's regulatory agenda.

Revised Policy on Exclusions from "Ambient Air." In 2019, EPA published guidance addressing the definition of "ambient air." According to EPA, "the atmosphere over land owned or controlled by the stationary source may be excluded from ambient air where the source employs measures, which may include physical barriers, that are effective in precluding access to the land by the general public."[219] The revised policy is not enforceable, and the agencies will make case-by-case determinations relating to adequacy of measures precluding public access from the zones to be excluded from the definition of ambient air.[220] As of the end of 2022, the Biden EPA had not taken any public steps to alter this guidance.

Guidance on Plantwide Applicability Limit (PAL) Provisions. In 2020, EPA continued its NSR reform efforts by publishing guidance on the PAL under the NSR regulations.[221] The guidance states that "the PAL should not be frequently and arbitrarily revised."[222] EPA states that if a source decides not to renew a PAL, EPA expects the reviewing authorities to accept the source's proposed distribution of the PAL emissions as long as the source provides supporting rationale and compliance demonstration methods.[223] The document states that EPA expects that for most of the PALs with baseline actual emissions plus a significant emissions level equal to or greater than 80 percent of the PAL, the PALs will be renewed at the same level, and for cases that sum less than 80 percent of the PAL, it expects that PALs will be renewed at a rate above baseline actual emissions that would allow for an adequate margin of safety, with the significant emission rate as a reasonable measure of such margin.[224] The Agency recommends a case-by-case approach to address requests to terminate a PAL prior to expiration.[225] The document also addresses a number of monitoring requirements for PALs, including emission factor adjustment, validation testing, and missing monitoring date.[226] The guidance states that for the purposes of both initial and subsequent NSR analyses, where the replacement unit is an existing emissions unit, any emission increase calculation must use the actual-to-projected-actual applicability test with the baseline actual emissions from the replaced unit.[227] As of the end of 2022, the Biden EPA had not taken any public steps to alter this guidance.

Interpretation of "Begin Actual Construction." Finally, in 2020, EPA issued a draft guidance memorandum setting forth a proposed change in EPA's interpretation of the phrase "begin actual construction" as it is used in the NSR regulations.[228] The draft guidance stated that after deviating from it in recent years, the Agency would return to the regulatory definition of the phrase according to which "begin actual construction" means "'in general, initiation of physical on-site construction activities on an emission[] unit which are of a permanent nature.'"[229] The draft guidance stated that the proposed change would allow facilities to perform more preparatory tasks while awaiting an NSR permit, but they would be doing so at their own risk.[230] EPA solicited comments on the draft but never finalized it, and it no longer appears on EPA's website.

H. Conclusion

The Clean Air Act modification provision was premised on a simple concept: If an existing industrial facility engages in activity that creates new pollution, that new pollution must be reviewed and regulated. Over the past thirty years, there have been repeated efforts to transform this simple program into one that regulates most, if not all, existing sources of air pollution. At stake in this controversy is the balance that Congress struck in the Act regarding regulation of new and existing sources. This controversy will continue over the coming years as EPA proceeds with additional NSR rulemaking and as the courts of appeals continue to address EPA's regulatory decisions.

III. Control Technology Requirements for Existing Sources

As discussed above, existing stationary sources are exempt from stringent new source control technology requirements unless they undertake projects that constitute "modification" or "reconstruction" of the source. Existing sources can be subject to any one of several control technology requirements, however, that address special environmental problems. These existing source control technology requirements are discussed briefly below.

A. "Reasonably Available Control Technology" in Nonattainment Areas

Existing stationary sources located in nonattainment areas may be required to install RACT.[231] RACT is defined as "devices, systems, process modifications, or other apparatus or techniques that are reasonably available taking into account: (1) [t]he necessity of imposing such controls in order to attain and maintain [the NAAQS]; (2) [t]he social, environmental, and economic impact of such controls; and (3) [a]lternative means of providing for attainment and maintenance . . . ."[232] EPA established RACT guidelines for over 30 categories of major sources of nonattainment pollutants and has guidelines under development for other categories.[233] These "control technique guidelines" (CTGs) are implemented by the states through their SIPs. The nonattainment provisions of the 1990 amendments set new deadlines for issuance of additional CTGs and imposition of RACT requirements in the 1990s.

B. "Best Available Retrofit Technology" Near National Parks

Any stationary source that is found to cause or contribute to impairment of visibility in a mandatory Class I area (i.e., larger national parks and wilderness areas) is subject to the BART requirement.[234] BART is defined as "an emission limitation based on the degree of reduction achievable through the application of the best system of continuous emission reduction for each pollutant which is emitted by an existing stationary facility."[235] BART limits are determined on a case-by-case basis, taking into consideration costs of compliance, energy and non-air quality environmental aspects of compliance, existing pollution control technology, the remaining useful life of the source, and the degree of improvement that might be expected from the use of such technology.[236] The BART requirement is discussed further in chapter 6.

C. "Maximum Achievable Control Technology" for Air Toxics

Section 112(d) of the Act imposes maximum achievable control technology (MACT) requirements for both existing and new sources of listed HAPs.[237] MACT must be equal to *at least* the level of control achieved by the best-performing 12 percent of regulated sources within the same source category. Where a category has fewer than 30 sources, MACT is defined as at least the level of control activity achieved by the best five sources. New source standards may be more stringent than existing source standards, and existing sources are subject to statutory schedules for retrofitting necessary technology.

The 1990 Clean Air Act amendments designated 189 chemicals to be regulated under section 112.[238] The air toxics provisions of the Act are discussed in chapter 5.

D. Existing Source Performance Standards

Under the NSPS program, EPA is authorized: to develop guidelines (1) on control technology standards for existing sources of pollutants for which NSPS have been set but which are not subject to NAAQS and where the source category is not regulated under section 112; and (2) to establish guidelines regarding implementation and enforcement of such standards. States are then required to implement these guidelines through their SIPs. In implementing these standards, states may consider, among other things, the remaining useful life of the existing source to which the standard applies. The Administrator is authorized to implement these standards for the state if the state fails to act.[239]

Initially, this provision of the Act was used rarely to regulate existing sources—only five times over fifty years. The Obama administration, however, seized on it as a potential basis for extensive regulatory programs for carbon dioxide emissions from existing power plants. These climate change programs are discussed in chapter 7.

Notes

1. S. Rep. No. 91-1196,15–18 (1970), *reprinted in* 1 Comm. on Public Works, A Legislative History of the Clean Air Amendments of 1970, at 415–18 (1974).

2. CAA § 111(b)(1)(A), 42 U.S.C. § 7411(b)(1)(A). EPA has generally interpreted this provision as only requiring a finding as to the source category and not the specific pollutant being regulated. In 2020, in the context of a specific NSPS, EPA determined that a separate finding was required for greenhouse gases. Pollutant-Specific Significant Contribution Finding for Greenhouse Gas Emissions from New, Modified, and Reconstructed Stationary Sources: Electric Utility Generating Units and Process for Determining Significance of Other New Source Performance Standards Source Categories, 86 Fed. Reg. 2542 (Jan. 13, 2021). But, after a change in administrations, EPA sought and received a voluntary vacatur of the rule based on procedural deficiencies. The rule is discussed in chapter 7.

3. CAA § 111(b)(2), 42 U.S.C. § 7411(b)(2).

4. *Id.* § 111(f)(1), 42 U.S.C. § 7411(f)(1).

5. *See* 40 C.F.R. § 60.16.

6. CAA § 111(a)(1), 42 U.S.C. § 7411(a)(1).

7. *Id.* § 111(h)(1), 42 U.S.C. § 7411(h)(1).

8. *Id.* § 111(b)(1)(B), 42 U.S.C. § 7411(b)(1)(B).

9. Revision of Standards of Performance for Nitrogen Oxide Emissions From New Fossil-Fuel Fired Steam Generating Units; Revisions to Reporting Requirements for Standards of Performance for New Fossil-Fuel Fired Steam Generating Units, 63 Fed. Reg. 49,442 (Sept. 16, 1998).

10. Standards of Performance for Electric Utility Steam Generating Units for Which Construction Is Commenced After September 18, 1978; Standards of Performance for Industrial-Commercial-Institutional Steam Generating Units; and Standards of Performance for Small Industrial-Commercial-Institutional Steam Generating Units, 71 Fed. Reg. 9866 (Feb. 27, 2006); National Emission Standards for Hazardous Air Pollutants From Coal- and Oil-Fired Electric Utility Steam Generating Units and Standards of Performance for Fossil-Fuel-Fired Electric Utility, Industrial-Commercial-Institutional, and Small Industrial-Commercial-Institutional Steam Generating Units, 77 Fed. Reg. 9304 (Feb. 16, 2012).

11. EPA currently maintains a "New Source Review Policy and Guidance Document Index" on its website at http://epa.gov/nsr/new-source-review-policy-and-guidance-document-index. Many of the documents discussed below are available on that webpage.

12. The 1977 provisions still apply; Congress did not amend this part of the Act in 1990.

13. CAA § 169(3), 42 U.S.C. § 7479(3); 40 C.F.R. § 52.21(b)(12).

14. *See* S. Rep. No. 95–127, at 31 (1977), *reprinted in* 3 Comm. on Public Works, A Legislative History of the Clean Air Act Amendments of 1977, at 1405 (1978).

15. *Id.*

16. EPA, Guidelines for Determining Best Available Control Technology (BACT) at 4 (Dec. 1978).

17. *See, e.g.*, EPA, Prevention of Significant Deterioration, Workshop Manual, EPA-450/2-80-081 (Oct. 1980) ("1980 PSD Workshop Manual").

18. *Id.* at I-B-2.

19. EPA, "Top-Down" Best Available Control Technology: Guidance Document (Mar 15, 1990).

20. EPA delegation of PSD program authority to states is discussed in chapter 4.

21. EPA, New Source Review Workshop Manual, Prevention of Significant Deterioration and Nonattainment Area Permitting, Draft (Oct. 1990) ("1990 Draft NSR Workshop Manual").

22. *Alaska Dep't of Env't Conservation v. EPA*, 540 U.S. 461, 488–89 (2004).

23. *In re Kendall New Century Dev.*, 11 E.A.D. 40, 52-53 (EAB 2003) (upholding state CO BACT determination).

24. *In re Masonite Corp.*, 5 E.A.D. 551, 560-61 (EAB 1994); *accord In re Knauf Fiber Glass, GmbH*, 9 E.A.D. 1, 15 (EAB 2000); *In re Three Mountain Power, LLC*, 10 E.A.D. 39, 53 (EAB 2001).

25. *See, e.g.*, *In re Newmont Nevada Energy Investment, LLC*, 12 E.A.D. 429 (EAB 2005).

26. CAA § 165(a)(4), 42 U.S.C. § 7475(a)(4).

27. *In re Pennsauken Cty., NJ, Res. Recovery Facility*, PSD Appeal No. 88-8, 1988 WL 249035, at *4 (EAB Nov. 10, 1988); *In re Spokane Reg'l Waste-to-Energy Applicant*, 2 E.A.D. 809, 811 n.7 (EAB 1989).

28. Letter from Stephen D. Page, Dir., Office of Air Quality Planning & Standards, EPA, to Paul Plath, Senior Partner, E3 Consulting, LLC, regarding Best Available Control Technology Requirements for Proposed Coal-Fired Power Plant Projects (Dec. 13, 2005).

29. *Id.* (concluding IGCC should not be considered in the BACT analysis for a pulverized coal-fired boiler).

30. *Sierra Club v. EPA*, 499 F.3d 653, 657 (7th Cir. 2007).

31. *Id.* at 655.

32. *Id.* at 657–58.

33. 1990 Draft NSR Workshop Manual at B.12.

34. CAA § 171(3), 42 U.S.C. § 7501(3).

35. H.R. Rep. No. 95-294, at 215 (1977), *reprinted in* 1977 U.S.C.C.A.N. 1077, 1294.

36. *See generally* EPA, New Source Review Prevention of Significant Deterioration and Nonattainment Area Guidance Notebook (Jan. 1988).

37. CAA § 182(c)(7), 42 U.S.C. § 7511a(c)(7).

38. *Id.* § 182(c)(8), 42 U.S.C. § 7511a(c)(8).

39. Part 60—Standards of Performance for New Stationary Sources; Modification, Notification, and Reconstruction, 40 Fed. Reg. 58,416, 58,420 (Dec. 16, 1975); 40 C.F.R. § 60.15.

40. 40 Fed. Reg. at 58,417.

41. 40 C.F.R. § 60.15(b)(1).

42. *Id.* § 60.15(b)(2), (f).

43. Standards of Performance for New Stationary Sources; Modification Notification, and Reconstruction, 39 Fed. Reg. 36,946, 36,948 (proposed Oct. 15, 1974).

44. Standards of Performance for New Stationary Sources; Volatile Organic Compound (VOC) Emissions From the Synthetic Organic Chemical Manufacturing Industry (SOCMI) Air Oxidation Processes, 55 Fed. Reg. 26,912, 26,930 (June 29, 1990).

45. *See, e.g.*, Letter from Donald R. Clay, Acting Assistant Adm'r for Air & Radiation, EPA, to John W. Boston, Wisconsin Electric Power Co., at 1–5 (Feb. 15, 1989) ("1989 Clay Letter").

46. *Id.* at 2-3.

47. Requirements for Preparation, Adoption, and Submittal of Implementation Plans; Approval and Promulgation of Implementation Plans, 45 Fed. Reg. 52,676, 52,703 (Aug. 7, 1980).

48. *See* Requirements for Preparation, Adoption, and Submittal of Implementation Plans; Approval and Promulgation of Implementation Plans; Standards of Performance for New Stationary Sources, 57 Fed. Reg. 32,314, 32,316 (July 21, 1992).

49. 40 C.F.R. §§ 51.165, 52.21(b)(2), 60.14.

50. *Compare United States v. Ohio Edison Co.*, 276 F. Supp. 2d 829 (S.D. Ohio 2003), with *United States v. Duke Energy Corp.*, 278 F. Supp. 2d 619 (M.D.N.C. 2003) ("*Duke I*"), *aff'd*, 411 F.3d 539 (4th Cir. 2005) ("*Duke II*"), *rev'd and judgment vacated sub nom.*, *Env't Def. v. Duke Energy Corp.*, 549 U.S. 561 (2007) ("*Duke III*").

51. *Compare Duke II*, 411 F.3d 539, *rev'd and judgment vacated*, *Duke III*, 549 U.S. 561, with *United States v. Cinergy Corp.*, 458 F.3d 705 (7th Cir. 2006), *cert. denied*, 549 U.S. 1338 (2007).

52. *Duke III*, 549 U.S. 561.

53. *Wis. Elec. Power Co. v. Reilly*, 893 F.2d 901 (7th Cir. 1990).

54. *See, e.g.*, Letter from Lee M. Thomas, Adm'r, EPA, to John W. Boston, Vice President, Wisconsin Electric Power Co. (Oct. 14, 1988) ("Thomas Letter"); 1989 Clay Letter.

55. CAA § 111, 42 U.S.C. § 1857c-6 (1970).

56. *Id.* § 111(a)(4), 42 U.S.C. § 1857c-6(a)(4) (1970).

57. *Id.* § 110(a)(2)(D), (4), 42 U.S.C. § 1857c-5(a)(2)(D), (4) (1970).

58. Part 60—Standards of Performance for New Stationary Sources, 36 Fed. Reg. 24,876 (Dec. 23, 1971).

59. 40 C.F.R. § 60.2.

60. *Id.* § 60.14(b); Standards of Performance for New Stationary Sources; Modification, Notification, and Reconstruction, 39 Fed. Reg. 36,946 (proposed Oct. 15, 1974); Part 60—Standards of Performance for New Stationary Sources; Modification, Notification, and Reconstruction, 40 Fed. Reg. 58,416 (Dec. 16, 1975).

61. 39 Fed. Reg. at 36,947 (A kg/hr test is "sensitive to increased production capacity . . . . [and] automatically allow[s] increases in operating hours.").

62. 40 C.F.R. § 60.14(e).

63. 39 Fed. Reg. at 36,946 ("[T]he intent of section 111 [is] controlling facilities only when they constitute a new source of emission.").

64. *See* CAA § 110(a)(2)(D), (4) (1970), 42 U.S.C. § 7410(a)(2)(D), (4) (1970).

65. Part 52—Approval and Promulgation of Implementation Plans, Prevention of Significant Air Quality Deterioration, 39 Fed. Reg. 42,510 (Dec. 5, 1974); *compare* 40 C.F.R. § 60.14 *with* 40 C.F.R. § 52.01(d).

66. 39 Fed. Reg. at 42,513.

67. Part 51—Requirements for Preparation, Adaption, and Submittal of Implementation Plans, Air Quality Standards, Interpretative Ruling, 41 Fed. Reg. 55,524 (Dec. 21, 1976).

68. *See id.* at 55,528 ("[A] 'major modification' shall include a modification . . . which increases the allowable emission rate by the amounts set forth above.").

69. *See* CAA §§ 169(2)(c), 171(4), 42 U.S.C. §§ 7479(2)(c), 7501(4).

70. *Id.* §§ 165(a), 169(1), 42 U.S.C. §§ 7475(a), 7479(1).

71. Clean Air Act Amendments of 1977, Pub. L. No. 95-95, § 129(a)(1), 91 Stat. 685, 745 (1977).

72. 40 C.F.R. §§ 52.01(d), 52.10.

73. *Id.* § 52.21(b)(2).

74. *See id.* § 52.21(b)(3).

75. *Id.* § 52.21(b)(21)(iv).

76. *But see Puerto Rican Cement Co. v. EPA,* 889 F.2d 292 (1st Cir. 1989). In *Puerto Rican Cement*, the company proposed building a new cement kiln to replace two older kilns. Then-Judge Breyer observed that it might be unreasonable in certain circumstances to assume operation at full capacity, even absent an enforceable restriction on operations. *Id.* at 297–98; *see also WEPCo*, 893 F.2d at 917.

77. Part 52—Approval and Promulgation of State Implementation Plans; 1977 Clean Air Act Amendments to Prevent Significant Deterioration, 43 Fed. Reg. 26,388 (June 19, 1978).

78. 40 C.F.R. § 52.21(b)(21)(ii). This change in the "netting" rules in 1980 was in response to the concern that allowing offsets based on an emitting unit's "potential to emit" would allow what EPA called "paper credits" (i.e., offsets based on unutilized emitting capacity). *See* 45 Fed. Reg. at 52,717–719.

79. 40 C.F.R. § 52.21(b)(21)(ii).

80. As EPA explained in an early enforcement action, the plain language of the 1980 rules "obviously describes a method of quantifying *past* [i.e., pre-project] emissions," but does not "define[] post-change emissions." Response of Plaintiff United States to Duke Energy's Motion for Summary Judgment at 4 n.9, *United States v. Duke Energy Corp.*, No. 1:00-cv-001262-WO-JEP (M.D.N.C. Mar. 31, 2003), ECF No. 152.

81. *See* Memorandum from Don Clay, Acting Assistant Adm'r for Air & Radiation, EPA, to David A. Kee, Dir., Air & Radiation Div., EPA Region V, Applicability of Prevention of Significant Deterioration (PSD) and New Source Performance Standards (NSPS) Requirements to the Wisconsin Electric Power Company (WEPCO) Port Washington Life Extension Project at 4 (Sept. 9, 1988) ("1988 Clay Memo").

82. Thomas Letter at 1.
83. *Id.* at 4.
84. 1989 Clay Letter at 7.
85. 1988 Clay Memo at 5; 1989 Clay Letter at 7 n.6.
86. 1988 Clay Memo at 7 n.4.
87. *WEPCo*, 893 F.2d at 916.
88. *Id.*; *see also Puerto Rican Cement*, 889 F.2d at 297–98.
89. *WEPCo*, 893 F.2d at 918 n.14.
90. *Id.* at 917.
91. 1988 Clay Memo at 7 n.4.
92. *WEPCo*, 893 F.2d at 918 n.14. Of course, if a unit has begun normal operations, only one period of "representative" operations should be necessary to characterize its "representative" operations.
93. *See Duke I*, 278 F. Supp. 2d at 641–43.
94. *See id.* at 645-46. Indeed, if an existing emission unit had begun normal operations, only one "representative" period would be needed to characterize those "normal" operations. Otherwise, differences in emissions would be driven merely by variations in "representative" operations, not the project at issue.
95. *Duke III*, 549 U.S. at 566.
96. Requirements for Preparation, Adoption and Submittal of Implementation Plans; Approval and Promulgation of Implementation Plans; Standards of Performance for New Stationary Sources, 57 Fed. Reg. 32,314, 32,326 (July 21, 1992).
97. *Id.* at 32,326 (emphasis added).
98. 40 C.F.R. § 60.14(h).
99. 57 Fed. Reg. at 32,330 (emphases added).
100. *Id.* at 32,331.
101. *Id.* at 32,332–33.
102. 40 C.F.R. § 52.21(b)(33), 57 Fed. Reg. at 32,337.
103. *Id.* § 52.21(b)(21)(v), 57 Fed. Reg. at 32,336.
104. 57 Fed. Reg. at 32,317 (emphasis added).
105. *Id.*
106. *Id.*
107. 40 C.F.R. § 52.21(b)(21)(v), 57 Fed. Reg. at 32,336 (emphasis added).
108. 57 Fed. Reg. at 32,323.
109. *Id.* (emphasis added).
110. *Id.*
111. 40 C.F.R. § 52.21(b)(33), 57 Fed. Reg. at 32,337.
112. 57 Fed. Reg. at 32,323.
113. *See* 40 C.F.R. § 52.21(b)(21)(v), 57 Fed. Reg. at 32,336.
114. *See Duke I*, 278 F. Supp. 2d at 647 n.25.
115. 57 Fed. Reg. at 32,321.
116. *Id.* at 32,319.
117. *Id.*

118. 40 C.F.R. § 52.21(b)(2)(iii)(h), 57 Fed. Reg. at 32,336.
119. *Id.* § 52.21(b)(32), 57 Fed. Reg. at 32,337.
120. *Id.* § 52.21(b)(32)(iii), (iv), 57 Fed. Reg. at 32,337.
121. Memorandum from John S. Seitz, Dir., EPA Office of Air Quality Planning & Standards, to Regional Dirs., EPA Regions I–X, Pollution Control Projects and New Source Review (NSR) Applicability (July 1, 1994).
122. Prevention of Significant Deterioration (PSD) and Nonattainment New Source Review (NSR): Baseline Emissions Determination, Actual-to-Future-Actual Methodology, Plantwide Applicability Limitations, Clean Units, Pollution Control Projects, 67 Fed. Reg. 80,186, 80,232 (Dec. 31, 2002).
123. *New York v. EPA,* 413 F.3d 3, 40 (D.C. Cir. 2005) (per curiam) ("*New York I*").
124. The D.C. Circuit specifically declined to address this issue. *New York v. EPA*, 431 F.3d 801, 801 (D.C. Cir. 2005) ("Because no specific retroactive application . . . is before the court, it would be premature to rule on this request [for clarification].)."
125. 57 Fed. Reg. at 32,326.
126. *Id.* at 32,327.
127. *Id.* (emphasis added).
128. 40 C.F.R. § 52.21(b)(33), 57 Fed. Reg. at 32,337 (emphasis added).
129. 57 Fed. Reg. at 32,326 (emphasis added).
130. *Id.* at 32,327 (emphasis added).
131. *Id.* (emphases added).
132. *New York I*, 413 F.3d at 31–33.
133. *See, e.g.*, H.R. Rep. 101-952, at 344–45 (1990), *reprinted in* 1 COMM. ON PUBLIC WORKS, A LEGISLATIVE HISTORY OF THE CLEAN AIR ACT AMENDMENTS OF 1990, at 1794–95 (1993) (as addressed in Joint Explanatory Statement of Conference Committee).
134. CAA § 409(d), 42 U.S.C. § 7651h(d).
135. *Id.* § 409(e), 42 U.S.C. § 7651h(e).
136. *Id.* § 415(b)(3), 42 U.S.C. § 7651n(b)(3).
137. *Id.* § 415(b)(1), 42 U.S.C. § 7651n(b)(1).
138. *Id.* § 415(b)(3), 42 U.S.C. § 7651n(b)(3).
139. 57 Fed. Reg. at 32,329–30.
140. CAA § 182(c)(6), 42 U.S.C. § 7511a(c)(6).
141. *Id.* § 182(e)(2), 42 U.S.C. § 7511a(e)(2).
142. *Id.* § 182(c)(7), 42 U.S.C. § 7511a(c)(7).
143. *Id.* § 112(g)(1)(A), 42 U.S.C. § 7412(g)(1)(A).
144. Hazardous Air Pollutants: Regulations Governing Constructed or Reconstructed Major Sources, 61 Fed. Reg. 68,384 (Dec 27, 1996).
145. CAA § 112(g)(2)(A), 42 U.S.C. § 7412(g)(2)(A).
146. *Id.* § 112(g)(2)(B), 42 U.S.C. § 7412(g)(2)(B).
147. *Id.* § 502(b)(10), 42 U.S.C. § 7661a(b)(10).
148. EPA maintains a list of air enforcement actions and settlements on its website.
149. Final Order on Reconsideration, *In re Tenn. Valley Auth.*, CAA Docket No. 00-6, 9 E.A.D. 357, 418, 439, 481–98 (EAB Sept. 15, 2000).

150. *TVA v. Whitman*, 336 F.3d 1236, 1239–40, 1249, 1260 (11th Cir. 2003).
151. *Id.* at 1246.
152. *Id.* at 1239–40.
153. *Leavitt v. TVA*, 541 U.S. 1030 (2004).
154. *See, e.g.*, *Duke I*, 278 F. Supp. 2d at 630 n.8.
155. *Ohio Edison Co.*, 276 F. Supp. 2d at 855–56, 862–69.
156. *Id.* at 832–33.
157. *Duke I*, 278 F. Supp. 2d at 637, 647.
158. *Id.*
159. *Duke II*, 411 F.3d at 550.
160. *Duke III*, 549 U.S. at 582.
161. *United States v. Alabama Power Co.*, 372 F. Supp. 2d 1283, 1292–99, 1305–06 (N.D. Ala. 2005).
162. *United States v. East Kentucky Power Coop.*, 498 F. Supp. 2d 970, 972 (E.D. Ky. 2007).
163. *United States v. Cinergy Corp.*, 384 F. Supp. 2d 1272, 1278 (S.D. Ind. 2005), *aff'd*, 458 F.3d 705, 710–11 (7th Cir. 2006).
164. The key aspects of these settlements involve (i) EPA's confirmation of the traditional understanding of the NSR emissions increase test (as described in *Duke I*), in return for (ii) companies agreeing to install controls over the next 10 years that they were generally planning to install under other Clean Air Act programs. Makram B. Jaber, *Utility Settlements in New Source Review Lawsuits*, 18 NAT. RESOURCES & ENV'T 22, 25–26 (2004).
165. In the first decision by the three-judge panel, the majority rejected the Government's arguments for establishing an emissions increase, but stated that even if the construction has not resulted in an actual increase in emissions, the court should examine whether the source's emissions projection complied with the objective requirements of the regulations for projecting emissions. *See United States v. DTE Energy Co.*, 711 F.3d 643, 649–50, 652 (6th Cir. 2013). The dissenting judge opined that without any post-construction emissions increase, there is nothing to enforce. *See id.* at 652–53 (Batchelder, J., dissenting). The second time, after the district court found that the company's emission projections complied with the NSR rules, the three-judge bench provided three different opinions with the two judges who wrote the majority opinion for the first case disagreeing on the allowable extent of EPA's second guessing of the facility's future emissions projections. *United States v. DTE Energy Co.*, 845 F.3d 735 (6th Cir. 2017). The dissenting judge from the first case found that the majority opinion in the first case entitled EPA to pursue enforcement based on an improper projection, and would have remanded again for further proceedings consistent with the prior remand. *Id.* at 742 (Batchelder, J., concurring).
166. *Duke III*, 549 U.S. at 569.
167. *Id.* at 577.
168. *Id.* at 577–78 (internal citation omitted).
169. *Id.* at 581–82.

170. *WEPCo*, 893 F.2d at 917; 57 Fed. Reg. at 32,317 (For projects that "do[] not 'change or alter' the design or nature of the facility . . . 'normal operations' have begun and the actual-to-potential test is impermissible."); *see also Ohio Edison Co.*, 276 F. Supp. 2d at 863 (The plant "was operational at the time the activities were proposed. Thus, any use of the actual to potential to emit test is not legally supportable.").

171. *Duke III*, 549 U.S. at 566.

172. *Id.* at 578.

173. Prevention of Significant Deterioration (PSD) and Nonattainment New Source Review (NSR), 61 Fed. Reg. 38,250 (proposed July 23, 1996).

174. Notice of Availability; Alternatives for New Source Review (NSR) Applicability for Major Modifications; Solicitation of Comment, 63 Fed. Reg. 39,857 (July 24, 1998).

175. Prevention of Significant Deterioration (PSD) and Nonattainment New Source Review (NSR): Baseline Emissions Determination, Actual-to-Future-Actual Methodology, Plantwide Applicability Limitations, Clean Units, Pollution Control Projects, 67 Fed. Reg. 80,186 (Dec. 31, 2002).

176. *Id.* at 80,234–36.

177. *Id.* at 80,232–39 (discussing pollution control project exclusion).

178. *See, e.g., id.* at 80,189, 80,191–92

179. *Id.* at 80,249–51.

180. *Id.* at 80,255–58.

181. *Id.* at 80,259.

182. *New York I*, 413 F.3d at 3.

183. Prevention of Significant Deterioration and Nonattainment New Source Review: Reasonable Possibility in Recordkeeping, 72 Fed. Reg. 72,607 (Dec. 21, 2007).

184. *Id.* at 72,610.

185. *New Jersey v. EPA*, 989 F.3d 1038 (D.C. Cir. 2021).

186. Exec. Order 13990, Protecting Public Health and the Environment and Restoring Science To Tackle the Climate Crisis (Jan. 20, 2021), *reprinted in* 86 Fed. Reg. 7037 (Jan. 25, 2021) ("EO 13990"). President Biden's executive orders are discussed in more detail in chapter 12.

187. Memorandum from E. Scott Pruitt, Adm'r, EPA, to Reg'l Adm'rs, New Source Review Preconstruction Permitting Requirements: Enforceability and Use of the Actual-to-Projected-Actual Applicability Test in Determining Major Modification Applicability (Dec. 7, 2017).

188. *Id.* at 2.

189. *Id.* at 8.

190. Memorandum from Michael S. Regan, Adm'r, EPA, to Reg'l Adm'rs, New Source Review Preconstruction Permitting Requirements: Enforceability and Use of the Actual-to-Projected-Actual Applicability Test in Determining Major Modification Applicability: Rescission of 2017 Memorandum (Dec. 9, 2022).

191. Memorandum from William L. Wehrum, Assistant Adm'r, EPA Office of Air & Radiation, to Reg'l Air Div. Dirs., Reclassification of Major Sources as Area Sources Under Section 112 of the Clean Air Act at 1 (Jan. 25, 2018).

192. *Id.* (citation omitted).

193. Reclassification of Major Sources as Area Sources Under Section 112 of the Clean Air Act, 85 Fed. Reg. 73,854 (Nov. 19, 2020).

194. *California Communities Against Toxics et al. v. EPA*, No. 21-1024 (and consolidated cases) (D.C. Cir. filed Jan. 15, 2021).

195. Memorandum from E. Scott Pruitt, Adm'r, EPA, to Reg'l Adm'rs, Project Emissions Accounting Under the New Source Review Preconstruction Permitting Program at 1 (Mar. 13, 2018).

196. *Id.* at 2.

197. *Id.* at 2, 9.

198. *Id.* at 7 (citation omitted).

199. *Id.* at 2.

200. Prevention of Significant Deterioration (PSD) and Nonattainment New Source Review (NNSR): Project Emissions Accounting, 85 Fed. Reg. 74,890 (Nov. 24, 2020).

201. Denial of Petition for Reconsideration and Administrative Stay: ''Prevention of Significant Deterioration (PSD) and Nonattainment New Source Review (NNSR): Project Emissions Accounting," 86 Fed. Reg. 57,585 (Oct. 18, 2021).

202. *New Jersey et al. v. EPA,* No. 21-1033 (and consolidated cases) (D.C. Cir. filed Jan. 19, 2021).

203. Letter from William L. Wehrum, Assistant Adm'r, EPA Office of Air & Radiation, to LeAnn Johnson Koch, Perkins Coie at 4 (Apr. 5, 2018).

204. *Id.* at 4–5.

205. Prevention of Significant Deterioration (PSD) and Nonattainment New Source Review (NNSR): Aggregation; Reconsideration, 83 Fed. Reg. 57,324, 57,326–327 (Nov. 15, 2018).

206. Memorandum from Peter Tsirigotis, Dir., EPA Office of Air Quality Planning & Standards, to Reg'l Air Div. Dirs., Regions 1–10, Guidance on Significant Impact Levels for Ozone and Fine Particles in the Prevention of Significant Deterioration Permitting Program at 1 (Apr. 17, 2018).

207. *Id.* at 2.

208. *Id.*

209. *Id.* at 3.

210. *Id.*

211. *Sierra Club v. EPA*, 955 F.3d 56 (D.C. Cir. 2020) (holding that the guidance was not final agency action).

212. *See* Letter from William L. Wehrum, Assistant Adm'r, EPA Office of Air & Radiation, to Patrick McDonnell, Sec'y, Pennsylvania Dep't of Env't Prot. at 1 (Apr. 30, 2018) (footnote omitted) (referred to as the "Meadowbrook Letter").

213. *Id.* at 6 (emphasis omitted).

214. Memorandum from William L. Wehrum, Assistant Adm'r, EPA Office of Air & Radiation, to Reg'l Air Div. Dirs., Regions 1–10, Interpreting "Adjacent" for New Source Review and Title V Source Determinations in all Industries Other Than Oil and Gas, Draft at 6 (Sept. 4, 2018).

215. Memorandum from Anne L. Idsal, Acting Assistant Adm'r, EPA Office of Air & Radiation, to Reg'l Adm'rs, Regions 1–10, Interpreting "Adjacent" for New Source Review and Title V Source Determinations in All Industries Other Than Oil and Gas (Nov. 26, 2019).

216. Emission Guidelines for Greenhouse Gas Emissions From Existing Electric Utility Generating Units; Revisions to Emission Guideline Implementing Regulations; Revisions to New Source Review Program, 83 Fed. Reg. 44,746, 44,748 (proposed Aug. 31, 2018).

217. *Id.* at 44,780–81.

218. Repeal of the Clean Power Plan; Emission Guidelines for Greenhouse Gas Emissions From Existing Electric Utility Generating Units; Revisions to Emission Guidelines Implementing Regulations, 84 Fed. Reg. 32,520, 32,521 (July 8, 2019).

219. Memorandum from Andrew R. Wheeler, Adm'r, EPA, to Reg'l Adm'rs, Revised Policy on Exclusions from "Ambient Air" at 1 (Dec. 2, 2019) (emphasis omitted).

220. *Id.*

221. Memorandum from Anne L. Austin, Principal Deputy Assistant Adm'r, EPA Office of Air & Radiation, to Reg'l Air Div. Dirs. Regions 1–10, Guidance on Plantwide Applicability Limitation Provisions Under the New Source Review Regulations (Aug. 4, 2020).

222. *Id.* at 3 (citation omitted).

223. *Id.* at 4–5.

224. *Id.* at 6–7.

225. *Id.* at 9.

226. *Id.* at 9–13.

227. *Id.* at 14–15.

228. Memorandum from Anne L. Idsal, Principal Deputy Assistant Adm'r, EPA Office of Air and Radiation, to Reg'l Air Div. Dirs., Interpretation of "Begin Actual Construction" Under the New Source Review Preconstruction Permitting Regulations, Draft (Mar. 25, 2020).

229. *Id.* at 12–13.

230. *Id.* at 12.

231. CAA § 172(b)(1), 42 U.S.C. § 7502(b)(1).

232. 40 C.F.R. § 51.100(o).

233. EPA maintains a listing of Control Techniques Guidelines and Alternative Control Techniques Documents on its website.

234. CAA § 169A(b)(2)(A), 42 U.S.C. § 7491(b)(2)(A).

235. 40 C.F.R. § 51.301.

236. CAA § 169A(g)(2), 42 U.S.C. § 7491(g)(2).

237. *Id.* § 112(d), 42 U.S.C. § 7412(d).

238. Clean Air Act Amendments of 1990, Pub. L. No. 101-549, § 112, 104 Stat. 2399, 2531–74 (1990); 40 C.F.R. § 68.130.

239. CAA § 111(d), 42 U.S.C. § 7411(d).

Chapter 4

OPERATING AND PRECONSTRUCTION PERMITTING PROGRAMS

Before enactment of the 1990 amendments, the Clean Air Act (CAA or Act) was implemented principally through state implementation plans (SIPs), which specify the emission limitations applicable to individual sources of air pollution. With respect to permits, the Act provided only for a *preconstruction* permitting program for major new sources of air pollution and for major modifications of those sources.[1]

Although many states during the 1970s and 1980s established their own permit programs under state law to govern the operation of air pollution sources, the U.S. Environmental Protection Agency (EPA or Agency) maintained that it had no authority to require or enforce these state operating permits until the late 1980s. In 1989, the Agency issued guidance addressing when permits issued pursuant to a state operating permit program authorized by a federally approved SIP could be considered to embody "federally enforceable" emission limits and operating restrictions.[2] As a practical matter, however, from the standpoint of federal law, existing sources were regulated almost exclusively through the application of SIP provisions and the terms of preconstruction permits.

The 1990 amendments changed this by establishing a new *federal* operating permit program, contained in Title V of the Act, that requires a comprehensive, source-specific permit for major sources. Additional aspects of the new operating permit program are addressed in Title IV of the Act (the acid rain program) and in Title III of the 1990 amendments (the air toxics program). This federal operating permit program does not replace, but rather supplements, the preconstruction permitting requirements of the Act and existing state permit programs.

This chapter discusses the key elements of both the operating and preconstruction permit programs. It begins with an overview of the operating permit program, including the basic program elements, the content of permit applications and the permits themselves (including the treatment of current state operating permit requirements), the protections afforded by a permit, the consequences of failure to obtain or to comply with a permit, and the roles of EPA, the public, and contiguous states in the issuance and enforcement of operating permits. This chapter then reviews other aspects of the Title V operating permit program, including monitoring requirements required under the Compliance Assurance Monitoring (CAM) program, and the requirements of the acid rain and air toxic permit programs. Finally, this chapter addresses the preconstruction permit program for proposed new sources and modified sources of air pollutants regulated under the Act.

I. The Operating Permit Program

Title V of the Clean Air Act requires each state to develop and implement a comprehensive operating permit program for most sources of air pollution. The purpose of this new permit program is to consolidate in a single document all the federally enforceable regulations applicable to a source to facilitate source compliance and enforcement. With few exceptions, Title V does not authorize the creation of new substantive federal requirements. Permit programs are administered by the states; however, EPA retains authority to review and approve not only the overall permit program, but also each individual permit issued by the state. Additionally, after a permit is issued, EPA may terminate, modify, or revoke the permit upon determining that cause exists to do so.

This permitting program covers all major stationary sources, and certain nonmajor, stationary sources. Each covered source must apply for and operate in compliance with the terms of an operating permit that contains (1) enforceable emission limitations and operating conditions; (2) a schedule for complying with any statutory requirements not yet being met; (3) inspection, monitoring, and reporting requirements; and (4) other conditions and measures as necessary to "assure compliance" with Clean Air Act requirements.

In July 1992, the EPA issued final regulations addressing the minimum requirements for state operating permit programs.[3] These regulations are codified at 40 C.F.R. part 70 (Part 70). Based on these minimum requirements, most states developed Title V operating permit programs and had those Part 70 programs approved by EPA. If a state failed to develop an adequate program or fails to administer an EPA-approved program adequately, EPA may issue permits for sources in that jurisdiction pursuant to a federal program developed by EPA and codified at 40 C.F.R. part 71.[4]

Immediately after promulgation of the Part 70 regulations, several industry groups, environmental advocacy organizations, and states challenged the rules in federal court.[5] The parties jointly requested a stay in briefing for most issues in order to encourage settlement.[6] A number of the issues raised in the litigation were the focus of rulemaking proposals to amend several elements of the Part

70 regulations, including those pertaining to when sources must seek revisions to their operating permits and the procedures applicable to each type of revision.[7] The proposals sparked considerable debate concerning the scope of and procedures necessary for, the Title V program. EPA never finalized any of those proposed amendments.

The following discussion summarizes the general features of the current program.

A. Applicability

Pursuant to section 502(a) of the Act, the Title V regulations initially required state programs to provide for the permitting of at least the following sources:

- Any major source, defined in section 70.2 of the rules as any stationary source belonging to a single major industrial grouping and that is:
    - a major source under section 112 of the Act;
    - a major source of air pollutants that directly emits or has the potential to emit 100 tons per year (tpy) or more of any air pollutant (including any major source of fugitive emissions of any such pollutant); and
    - a major source as defined in Part D of Title I of the Act;
- Any source subject to a standard, limitation, or other requirement under section 111 of the Act;
- Any source subject to a standard or other requirement under section 112 of the Act (although a source is not required to obtain a permit solely because it is subject to regulation under section 112(r) dealing with accidental release prevention);
- Any affected source under Title IV of the Act; and
- Any source in a source category designated by EPA.[8]

In 2010, EPA revised the major source definition to limit the 100 tpy threshold to emissions of those air pollutants that are "subject to regulation," as newly defined in the rule. EPA adopted the revised definition to phase in over time the number of sources of greenhouse gases required to obtain Title V permits.[9] In 2011, EPA further limited applicability of the rule by excluding biogenic carbon dioxide emissions from that threshold for a period of three years,[10] but the U.S. Court of Appeals for the District of Columbia Circuit (D.C. Circuit) vacated the exemption.[11]

Section 502(a) of the Act provides EPA discretion to exempt one or more source categories upon finding that compliance is "impracticable, infeasible, or unnecessarily burdensome."[12] Under this authority, EPA has allowed states to defer regulation of nonmajor sources, excluding solid waste incinerators, until the Agency "determine[s] how the program should be structured for nonmajor sources."[13] For nonmajor sources subject to new source performance or air toxics standards after July 21, 1992, EPA has reviewed the source category and determined whether to grant an exemption at the time the new standard for such a source category is promulgated.[14] The rules also allow states to develop exemptions for insignificant activities based on size, emission levels, or production rate, as long as the exemptions would not interfere with the determination or imposition of any applicable requirement or the calculation of fees.[15]

Under Title V, a single permit may be issued for a facility with multiple emission units that constitute a "Part 70 source" (i.e., a source to which the Title V program applies).[16] The process of combining facilities for purposes of the permit application may not result in any reduction in permit fees, however.

Title V also provides that a permitting authority may issue a single permit for similar operations at multiple temporary locations. Such a permit must, however, include conditions that will assure compliance with all Clean Air Act requirements at all locations.[17]

Finally, states may establish general permits "by rule" covering "numerous similar sources."[18] Under this provision, individual sources in the identified categories would merely have to apply to the permitting authority for use of the general permit. EPA has indicated that examples of sources for which the general permit provision would be appropriate include dry cleaners, degreasers, gas stations, small boilers, and storage tanks.[19]

B. Development of State Permit Programs

Virtually all states (as well as local agencies with permitting authority) submitted, and received EPA approval for, operating permit programs. The states have some flexibility to tailor their programs to their objectives, while providing for the minimum elements of a Title V program as set out in Part 70. Whereas many programs received full approval, some programs initially were granted only interim approval because although those programs were found to "substantially meet" the requirements of Part 70, they were not fully approvable.[20] States initially were given two years to correct the deficiencies identified by EPA and to resubmit those elements of the program. To provide states with the opportunity to correct these deficiencies and simultaneously to modify their programs in response to the Agency's anticipated revisions to Part 70, EPA in 1997 delayed the date by which states with interim approval would have to amend their programs.[21] The last extensions of the interim approval deadline ended in 2001 when, as part of a litigation settlement with environmental advocacy organizations, EPA removed language from the Part 70 rules authorizing multiple extensions.[22]

EPA periodically audits each state's permit program to determine whether the program is being administered in accordance with EPA regulations and the conditions approved by EPA. If the Agency determines that the state is not administering and enforcing its permit program adequately, EPA must notify the state of the inadequacies. During the next 18-month period, EPA also *may* impose sanctions under section 179(a) of the Act (restriction of federal highway funds and the imposition of an emission offset reduction ratio of two-to-one for projects subject to preconstruction permitting in nonattainment areas). If the state fails to correct the program within 18 months, EPA *must* apply the sanctions. If the state has not corrected the deficiencies within six months thereafter, EPA must implement the federal operating permit program under Part 71.[23]

C. Permit Applications

Sources subject to the Title V program must submit to the state permitting authority a complete permit application, including a compliance plan describing how the source plans to comply with all applicable requirements where there is noncompliance. Initial applications were due within one year after the permit program became effective.[24] A permit program is effective upon approval by EPA, whether that approval is interim, partial, or full.

For new sources (or modified sources that previously were not subject to Title V), a Title V permit application must be filed within 12 months of commencing operation.[25] In cases where an existing Title V permit would prohibit construction or a certain operational change, however, the source would need to satisfy the permit revision requirements of section 70.7 of the Title V rules before commencing operation.[26]

After receipt of an application, the permitting authority must determine whether the application is complete within sixty days. Unless the permitting authority requests additional information or otherwise notifies the applicant of incompleteness within this period, the application is deemed complete by operation of law.[27]

In general, if a source submits a timely and complete permit application, failure to have a final permit is not considered a violation of the requirement contained in section 502(a) of the Act to operate with a permit, at least until the permitting authority takes final action on the application.[28] This protection is called the "application shield." The application shield may cease to exist, however, if, prior to the issuance of a final permit, the source fails to submit any additional information that the permitting authority has determined to be necessary to process the application.

A permit application must contain all information listed in section 70.5(c) of the rules, including: (1) emissions of pollutants for which the source is major and emissions of "regulated air pollutants"; (2) identification of all points of emissions; (3) emission rates in tons per year and in other terms necessary to establish compliance; (4) description of air pollution control equipment; (5) identification of all federal air pollution control requirements; (6) monitoring and measurement techniques used to demonstrate compliance with federal applicable requirements; and (7) a statement of current compliance status with respect to all federally applicable requirements, and a schedule for compliance in the event of noncompliance.

States have developed standard application forms for use in satisfying the Title V permit application requirement. A particularly critical step in preparing the Title V application is identifying those requirements that are federally enforceable, as distinct from those that are only enforceable by the state. The federally enforceable requirements are the true subject of Title V permits—and the requirements to which the enforcement mechanisms apply. States may independently require sources to identify—and include in their Title V permits—state-only requirements. To the extent such requirements are included, they should be identified as "state-only," or they become federally enforceable as well.[29]

A responsible corporate official must submit a certification of the compliance status of the source with respect to all applicable requirements of the Act. If necessary, this submission must also include a compliance schedule with respect to those applicable requirements with which the source will not be in compliance at the time of permit issuance.[30] The responsible official also must certify the truth, accuracy, and completeness of the application based on a standard of "reasonable inquiry."[31]

To streamline the application process and reduce permitting burdens associated with Title V, EPA issued two principal guidance documents, or "White Papers" in the early years of the program.[32] Many states have issued guidance or rules of their own to implement the principles contained in these EPA papers.

D. Permit Issuance

The permitting authority must take final action within 18 months after receiving a complete application.[33] Anticipating the administrative burden of establishing the new permitting program, however, Congress in section 503(c) of the Act provided for a phased schedule over three years for acting on initial Title V permit applications. The permitting authority was required to act on one-third of the permit applications received in the first year of the program in each year over a three-year period following program approval by EPA. EPA made clear in the preamble to the Title V rules that "act on" means final action rather than initial review.[34] As a practical matter, states had difficulty acting on permit applications within these deadlines.

The permitting authority must issue permits for a fixed term of no more than five years. Each permit must include: (1) applicable emission limitations and standards; (2) monitoring and related recordkeeping and reporting requirements; (3) a permit condition prohibiting emissions of sulfur dioxide (SO_2) exceeding any allowances held under Title IV of the Act (for affected sources); (4) a severability clause to ensure continued validity of remaining permit requirements if any provisions are challenged; (5) a statement that any permit noncompliance constitutes a violation of the Act, and that the permit may be modified, revoked, reopened, and reissued or terminated for cause; (6) a provision to ensure that a source pays fees consistent with an approved state permitting fee schedule; and (7) the terms and conditions for reasonably anticipated alternative operating scenarios.[35] The permit also must contain the compliance requirements listed in section 70.6(c) of the rules, including (1) compliance certification, testing, monitoring, reporting, and recordkeeping requirements to assure compliance with the permit; (2) inspection and entry requirements for permitting authority officials; and (3) a schedule of compliance and provisions for regular progress reports. Insignificant emission units must be covered by the permit to the extent they are subject to applicable requirements.[36] Monitoring required under the CAM rule, which was issued in late 1997, must also be included in Title V permits.[37]

From 1992 to 2004, EPA's interpretation of the requirement in section 70.6(c) of the rules that permits specify monitoring to assure compliance, as well as the requirement in section 70.6(a)(3)(i)(B) for periodic testing or monitoring representative of compliance, changed several times. Each change prompted some judicial challenge. The issue was resolved in 2008 when the D.C. Circuit vacated a 2006 rule revision that explicitly prohibited permitting authorities from supplementing monitoring requirements where existing rules already provided for "periodic monitoring." Specifically, the court found that because section 504(c) of the Act requires that Title V permits contain monitoring "to assure compliance," permitting authorities must have authority to supplement existing monitoring that is not adequate for that purpose.[38] The court did not decide, however, what would happen if EPA and a permitting authority could not agree on whether an existing monitoring requirement was adequate.

Another issue upon which EPA's view has changed over time is the appropriate level of review of prior permitting decisions. Among the applicable requirements that must be included in a Title V permit are the terms and conditions of any preconstruction permit.[39] As discussed in Section III, such permits are subject to their own procedures for participation by EPA, the public, and affected states, and appeal. When developing the initial Title V rules, EPA took the position that the terms of Title I preconstruction permits should be incorporated "without further permit revision and review."[40] Later on, however, EPA began using its Title V review authority to reexamine states' new source permitting determinations.[41] The issue came full circle in 2017 when EPA reinstated its prior view that substantive review (and second guessing) of underlying NSR permit terms as part of the Title V process is not appropriate.[42] To date, two U.S. courts of appeals have reviewed that position to different result.[43] EPA has in its recent actions responded to those cases by reverting to its pre-2017 standard of review, which it describes as similar to a "clearly erroneous" standard.[44] However, the Agency appears likely to pursue a regulatory solution, listing on its Fall 2022 regulatory agenda a long-term action (e.g., rulemaking in 2024) to clarify the definition of "applicable requirement" to address the extent to which other Clean Air Act requirements may be reviewed and/or modified through the Title V permitting process.

Finally, as discussed above, pursuant to section 70.6(b)(2) of the rules, the permit must "specifically designate as not being federally enforceable . . . any terms and conditions included in the permit that are not required under the Act or under any of its applicable requirements" (e.g., state-only requirements). Such terms and conditions are not subject to Title V requirements regarding permit issuance, permit modification, and EPA and affected state review. Any terms not otherwise designated that appear in the permit, however, *become federally enforceable* by either EPA or citizens under the citizen suit provisions of the Act.

E. EPA, Public and Affected State Participation in the Permit Process

1. EPA Review

Even after the state Title V program is in place, the Act gives EPA a significant role in overseeing the permitting process. Section 505(a)(1) requires the permitting authority to provide to EPA a copy of each permit application, draft permit, and final permit issued under Part 70.[45] EPA may comment on a permit application or draft permit. For example, once it receives a draft permit, EPA has 45 days to object in writing to the issuance of the permit (or permit modification/revision).[46] EPA must object to issuance of any proposed permit deemed not to be in compliance with the requirements of the Act. If EPA objects to a proposed final permit within 45 days of receipt, the permitting authority may not issue the permit. If the state does not revise and resubmit the permit in accordance with EPA's objections within 90 days, EPA must either issue or deny the permit pursuant to the federal program contained in 40 C.F.R. part 71.[47]

2. Public Involvement

Interested members of the public can be involved in virtually all phases of the Title V permitting process. Prior to permit issuance, the permitting authority must provide procedures for public notice, a comment period of at least 30 days, and the opportunity to request a public hearing on the draft permit.[48] The materials in the record must be made available for public review.

In addition to giving the public the right to review and comment on each draft permit, interested citizens may challenge the terms of any permit with which they disagree. Specifically, members of the public (including an affected state) may petition the Administrator to object to issuance of a permit based on objections that were raised "with reasonable specificity" during the comment period (unless the petitioner demonstrates that it was impracticable to raise such objections within that period, or unless the grounds for the objection arose after the comment period).[49] Such a petition must be filed within 60 days of the expiration of the 45-day period within which EPA may object to a permit (as discussed above). EPA must then grant or deny the citizen petition within 60 days.[50] If EPA denies the citizen petition, that denial is subject to judicial review.

Over the years, the process of reviewing and responding to petitions for objections to permits has consumed significant agency resources. In 2020, to improve the efficiency of the process and provide greater clarity for stakeholders, EPA revised the rules governing petitions to specify, among other things, the format, minimum content, and method of submission of such petitions.[51] In the preamble to that action, EPA also provided guidance in the form of "recommended practices" for ensuring a complete administrative record, and provided information on the Agency's interpretation of relevant statutory and regulatory provisions as reflected in previously issued orders responding to petitions. Although EPA is not required to publish petitions or objections, EPA also maintains an online searchable database of Title V petitions and EPA's responses, and publishes notice of its actions on petitions in the *Federal Register*.

After permit issuance, the public continues to have access to Title V materials, including compliance plans, emissions and compliance monitoring reports, and certifications. The public thus has access to information that could form the basis for enforcement actions brought under the Act.

3. Participation of Affected States

The permitting authority also must give notice of each draft permit to any affected state on or before the time public notice is provided.[52] An affected state is one whose air quality may be affected *and* that is contiguous to the state in which the source is located, or within fifty miles of the source. The affected state must be afforded the opportunity to submit written recommendations on the proposed permit. If the permitting state does not accept a recommendation from an affected state, it must provide both the affected state and EPA with its reasons for rejecting the recommendation.[53] Affected states may then avail themselves of the administrative petition process that is available to citizens, as described above.

F. Protections Afforded by an Operating Permit: The Permit Shield

Section 504(f) of the Act provides that compliance with the permit shall be deemed compliance with applicable provisions of the Act. This permit shield is optional with the states, however. Section 70.6(f) of EPA's Title V rules provides that the permitting authority may include in a permit an express statement that compliance with the conditions of the permit shall be deemed compliance with any applicable requirements *as of the date of issuance of the permit* if (1) the applicable requirements are specifically identified in the permit, or (2) the permitting authority determines in writing that other requirements specifically identified do not apply to the source and the permit includes that determination. If the permit does not expressly state that a permit shield applies, then no shield will be presumed. Consequently, a source must take care to identify not only applicable requirements, but also those Clean Air Act requirements that do *not* apply to the source. In addition, sources must continue to track newly promulgated requirements, because compliance with the terms of the Title V permit may not constitute full compliance with all requirements of the Act.

G. Renewal, Reopening, and Revision of the Title V Operating Permit

1. Renewal

Operating permits are to be issued for a specific period, not to exceed five years. Permit expiration terminates a source's right to operate unless a timely and complete renewal application has been filed.[54] To be timely, a renewal application must be filed no later than six months before the permit expires. The state, however, may require a source to file a renewal application up to 18 months before the permit expires.[55]

2. Reopening

An operating permit may also be "reopened" before it expires for a number of reasons, including changes in regulatory requirements and changes in source operations. A source must reopen its permit if additional requirements under the Act become applicable to the source and the remaining permit term is three or more years. Reopening for this reason must be undertaken within 18 months after the promulgation of the additional applicable requirement.[56] Reopening also is necessary if additional requirements become applicable to affected sources under Title IV.[57] Moreover, the permitting authority or EPA may seek to reopen the permit if they determine that the permit contains a material mistake, that inaccurate statements were made in establishing the permit terms, or that the permit must be revised to assure compliance with applicable requirements.[58] Proceedings to reopen a permit are subject to the same procedures applicable to initial permit issuance, but affect only those parts of the permit in question.[59] Procedures applicable to EPA when it seeks to reopen a permit are outlined in section 70.7(g) of the rules.

3. Revision

The Title V rules establish several categories of permit revisions (or "modifications"). These requirements were the subject of intense debate throughout the rulemaking and the ensuing litigation, with industry and state agencies generally arguing for limited review of permit revisions during the five-year permit term and environmental advocacy organizations arguing in favor of more extensive review. At the heart of this debate was the issue of how much flexibility a source should have to change its operations without having to undertake a full permit proceeding to accomplish that change.

As a result of the judicial challenges to the final rule, EPA proposed several revisions to the flexibility provisions of Part 70. First, in 1994, EPA proposed to provide for four revision tracks, rather than the three contained in the 1992 rules.[60] The complexity of this proposal, however, raised questions as to whether this four-track approach actually would further limit flexibility to change operations in response to competition and other market conditions. Numerous parties, including states and regulated industries, criticized the proposal as too complex for both sources and permitting authorities.

In response to this criticism, EPA proposed a fundamental restructuring of the permit revision portions of the Title V rules the next year.[61] Under that proposal, during the five-year permit term, a source would have been able to undertake many changes in operations that require a permit revision simply by notifying the permitting authority at the time of the change and submitting a statement describing the revised permit term or new applicable requirements. This statement would have been attached to the permit itself. For "environmentally significant" changes, this streamlined "notice-and-go" procedure would have been available for those changes for which (1) a public review process was afforded in conjunction with the development or implementation of the applicable requirement, and (2) that review process was equivalent to the Title V permit procedures. States would have had more discretion to establish the requisite procedures for less environmentally significant changes. Formal review under the Title V program would have occurred during the next permit renewal.

This second reproposal prompted continued debate about the scope and procedures of the permit revision provisions. EPA proposed additional revisions to the permit modification rules in 1997[62] but, in the end, did not finalize any of its proposed revisions.

Below is a summary of the permit revision system as set out in the current Title V rules, which effectively is the same as the original rule issued in 1992.

Scope. Under the current Title V rules, a source must seek a permit revision *only* if the contemplated change could not be operated without violating a term of the existing permit, or if the change would trigger an applicable requirement to which the source had not previously been subject.

Administrative permit amendments.[63] An administrative permit amendment is generally a simple revision that corrects typographical errors, identifies a change in name or similar information, requires more frequent monitoring, or incorporates requirements into the operating permit from a preconstruction review permit (if the state review for preconstruction permits also satisfies the procedural participation requirements of Title V). In light of the ministerial nature of the changes in this category, no public notice is required for administrative amendments. Administrative amendments may typically be implemented upon the filing of an application.

Minor permit revisions.[64] Minor permit revisions are subject to limited review requirements and streamlined procedures. The Title V rules do not require public review of such revisions, but do require that EPA and affected states be notified of the proposed change. To qualify for the minor permit revision procedure: (1) the source may not be in violation of the permit term it seeks to change; (2) the revision may not violate any requirement applicable to the source; (3) the revision may not involve significant changes to existing monitoring, reporting, or recordkeeping requirements; (4) the revision may not require or change a case-by-case determination of an emission limitation or other standard; and (5) the revision may not seek to change or establish a permit term or condition for which there is no corresponding underlying applicable requirement. The source may make the proposed change immediately but, once it makes the change, the source may be liable for violating its permit if the revision is ultimately denied (e.g., in response to EPA or affected state comments, or a citizen suit challenging the state's failure to object to the proposed change).

Significant permit revisions.[65] Significant permit revisions are those that would not qualify as administrative or minor revisions. They are subject to the procedural requirements applicable to permit issuance and renewal, including the requirements for public participation and review by affected states and EPA.

H. Achieving Operational Flexibility

Considering the constraints that a source may face if it wishes to revise its permit during the permit term, ensuring maximum flexibility when drafting the final permit is of critical importance. The Clean Air Act mandates that the permit program offer operational flexibility. For example, pursuant to section 502(b)(10), as interpreted by EPA, states must allow sources to engage in trading under a federally enforceable cap established in the permit.[66]

By far the best way to ensure operational flexibility, however, is to write a permit that specifies operation under all the reasonably anticipated operating scenarios of the facility ("alternative operating scenarios").[67] A source owner or operator is then obligated simply to record in a contemporaneous log which operating scenario is in effect. This approach becomes less effective to the extent that it is difficult or impossible for an industry to predict new products or new market demands over a five-year period.

In 2007, EPA proposed additional revisions to Part 70 as part of its Flexible Air Permitting Rule.[68] EPA's goal was to clarify how additional operational flexibility can be achieved through advance approvals under the Act's NSR provisions and the use of alternative operating scenarios (AOS). EPA also proposed to add major NSR requirements for something it termed "Green Groups," which would allow future changes to occur within a group of emissions activities, provided that they were ducted to a common air pollution control device determined to meet "best available control technology" (BACT) or "lowest achievable emission rate" (LAER) as applicable, and provided they complied with all relevant ambient air quality requirements. As finalized in 2009, the revisions added definitions for AOS and something called an "approved replicable methodology," and codified some clarifications to existing provisions.[69] EPA withdrew its Green Groups proposal, however, and instead encouraged states and sources to take advantage of flexibilities already provided under the major NSR regulations.

I. Permit Fees

States must establish a fee schedule that results in collection of revenue sufficient to cover permit program costs.[70] The costs to be covered by the fee schedule are listed in section 70.9(b)(1). A state fee schedule may include "emissions fees, application fees, service-based fees or other types of fees."[71] EPA will assume that the fees are adequate to cover the costs of the state program if the fees are equal to $25 per year multiplied by the total tons of the *actual* emissions of each regulated pollutant emitted.[72] States are free to propose a different fee schedule so long as they demonstrate that the fees generated thereunder are adequate. The fee schedule ultimately adopted by the state must be increased annually by the percentage increase in the Consumer Price Index to ensure adequate funding of the state program.[73] Many states initially adopted fees in the $25 to $30 per-ton range and established caps on the maximum fee that can be collected from a source.

J. The Title V Performance Task Force

In 2004, to address some of the outstanding disagreements over Title V implementation without litigation and to determine if further rulemaking is warranted, EPA formed a task force under the Agency's Clean Air Act Advisory Committee (CAAAC). The mission of the "Title V Performance Task Force" was to seek input from stakeholders on the performance of the Title V program, including what is working well (or poorly) and what improvements might be made. The Task Force's Final Report identified and discussed issues, summarized testimony of stakeholders, and provided recommendations for further action (although few were unanimous).[74]

In 2006, the CAAAC forwarded the Task Force's Final Report to EPA and directed the Agency to report back with a response and a plan for implementing the recommendations. EPA responded with a list of the recommendations it deemed to be of the highest priority along with a timeframe for Agency action. EPA estimated most of the recommendations would take between one and three years to implement. A number of the EPA actions described above, including rule revisions addressing "periodic monitoring," public notice, the petition process, and flexible air permitting were responsive to the Task Force's recommendations.

EPA also issued guidance addressing the Task Force's recommendations related to annual compliance certifications and the statement of basis for the permit.[75] However, some of EPA's priority recommendations have not been implemented.

II. Other Operating Permit Requirements

While Title V of the 1990 amendments contains the basic federal operating permit program, other provisions of the 1990 amendments address special operating permit requirements that apply under other Titles of the Act.

A. Compliance Assurance Monitoring

Under section 114(a)(3) of the Act, EPA was required to promulgate regulations that require "enhanced monitoring" and submission of compliance certifications for all major stationary sources.[76] EPA satisfied those requirements through promulgation of the Title V operating permit rules and the 1997 CAM rule. The CAM rule applies to significant emission units that use control devices to achieve compliance with emission limits and that are not already required to perform continuous compliance monitoring in the units of the applicable emission standard.[77]

Sources covered by the CAM rule must develop and implement "CAM plans" that document continued proper operation of control devices by monitoring control device parameters and keeping those parameters within a specified range of performance that provides a reasonable assurance of compliance with applicable emission limits.[78] To the extent that a source monitors excursions from the specified range, it must investigate and take corrective action as necessary to bring the control device parameters back to within the specified range.[79] If a source fails to adequately correct the performance of the control device, the source must develop and implement a quality improvement plan, which consists of additional investigation and corrective action phases.[80]

The CAM rule is implemented on a source-by-source basis through the Title V permitting program. To ensure enforceability, certain elements of required CAM plans must be reflected in a source's Title V permit.[81] In the regulatory impact analysis accompanying the CAM rule, EPA estimated that the rule would affect approximately 27,000 emission units. To stagger implementation, the CAM rule delayed implementation for all but the largest emission units until the source renewed its initial Title V permit.[82]

Like most of EPA's Title V rules related to emissions monitoring, the CAM rule was challenged judicially as insufficient to satisfy the compliance assurance requirements of the Act. In 1999, the rule was upheld by the D.C. Circuit as sufficient to satisfy the Agency's obligation to require "enhanced monitoring," but was remanded to require that responsible officials signing compliance certifications specify whether compliance was "continuous" or "intermittent," as required under section 114(a)(3) of the Act.[83] EPA revised the compliance certification rules in 2003 to implement that requirement.[84]

B. Permit Requirements of the Acid Rain Program

Recognizing that many Title V permits would not be issued by 1995, Congress took steps to ensure that sources covered by the Title IV acid rain program would be issued operating permits in time to comply with the requirements of that program. The Title IV acid rain permitting program is described in chapter 9.

C. Permit Requirements of the Air Toxics Program

1. Source-Specific Emission Standards

The Title V operating permit program must also address existing section 112 standards for sources of hazardous air pollutants (HAPs) as well as future control technology standards.[85] Under section 112(j), if the Administrator fails to promulgate a section 112 standard for a category or subcategory of major sources within 18 months of the applicable date set forth by EPA pursuant to section 112, the owner or operator of a source in that source category will be required to file a permit application that contains emission limitations that are "equivalent" to the limitations that would have applied if the source category standard had been promulgated.[86] These "equivalent" emission limitations must be determined on a case-by-case basis to require the maximum degree of reduction in emissions of HAPs (including a prohibition of such emissions, where achievable), taking into account cost, energy requirements, and non-air quality health and environmental impacts.[87]

The requirements of section 112(j) are discussed further in chapter 5.

2. Early Reductions

Under section 112(i)(5) of the Act, EPA, or a state acting under a Title V permit program, may allow an existing source to meet an alternative emission limitation if the source demonstrates that it has achieved reductions of 90 percent or more in emissions of non-particulate HAPs, or reductions of 95 percent or more in hazardous pollutants emitted as particulates.[88] Sources that make these reductions before a standard is proposed receive a six-year extension from the compliance date for meeting the otherwise applicable maximum achievable control technology (MACT) standard.[89] Extensions and alternative emission limitations are to be reflected in Title V permits. The provisions of the section 112(i)(5)(B) early reductions program are discussed further in chapter 5.

3. State Programs and Delegation of EPA Authority

Under section 112(*l*), states may develop and submit to EPA for approval programs to implement and enforce the air toxics standards.[90] Such state programs may provide for either full or partial delegation of EPA authority. The section 112(*l*) provisions are discussed further in chapter 5.

D. State Operating Permit Programs

Even though not required prior to 1990, many states developed their own operating permit programs. Operating permits issued pursuant to these programs may have included limits and standards that are also contained in the SIP, but may include additional requirements that are based on state law. Existing state operating permit programs were generally folded into the Title V program.

The 1990 amendments, however, provided that "[n]othing in [Title V] shall prevent a State, or interstate permitting authority, from establishing additional permitting requirements not inconsistent with this [Act]."[91] Elaborating on this provision, the House and Senate Conferees explained that "[c]onsistent with the general provisions of section 116 of the Clean Air Act, the conferees understand that a State may establish additional, more stringent permitting requirements, but a State may not establish permit requirements that are inconsistent with the national permitting requirements of this Act, including this title."[92]

While more stringent substantive requirements of existing operating permit programs may generally be continued in new state programs, section 70.6(b) of the Part 70 rules explains that "[a]ll terms and conditions in a Part 70 permit" are federally enforceable by the Administrator and citizen groups (through the citizen suit provision of the Act), unless the state specifically designates a provision as a state, rather than a federal, requirement.[93] As a result, individual sources should ensure that the states delineate carefully whether specific substantive requirements are based in federal or state law. If a state does not specifically identify more stringent state-law requirements, those requirements could become the subject of an enforcement action by private citizens under the Clean Air Act citizen suit provision.

III. New Source Review (NSR) Preconstruction Permits

Under the PSD and nonattainment NSR (NNSR) programs, major new sources of air pollution (and, under certain conditions, major modifications to large existing sources) are subject to preconstruction review and permitting. In other words, under these programs, a source owner cannot begin construction of a major new facility, or a major modification of a major existing facility, without first obtaining a permit.[94] The same may also be true for minor sources of air pollution as most, if not all, states require preconstruction permits for minor sources that exceed state-specific thresholds as part of their SIPs.[95]

These programs are not supplanted by the Title V operating permit program.[96] Nevertheless, because sources subject to the PSD and NNSR permitting programs, as well as some sources subject to minor source permitting programs, are also subject to the Title V operating permit program, they must pay attention to how those programs are coordinated. The following discussion provides an overview of the preconstruction permit program, including certain changes made by the 1990 amendments, and then discusses several issues related to coordination of the Title V and preconstruction permit programs.

A. The PSD Program

Under the Act, before constructing a "major" new source or undertaking a "major modification" to an existing major source in an area that attains the NAAQS, one must obtain a permit under the PSD program.[97] In order to receive a PSD permit, the owner or operator of a proposed facility must demonstrate that the proposed source will (1) comply with the NAAQS and the PSD "increments"; (2) employ "best available control technology" (BACT) for regulated pollutants emitted in significant amounts; and (3) have no adverse impact on other air quality-related values (AQRVs). The following discussion summarizes these requirements.

1. The Applicability Determination

a. Major Source

The PSD permit requirement applies to construction or major modification of a major source of a regulated air pollutant for which an area is classified as "attainment" (or is not classifiable). A "major source" for purposes of the PSD program is defined as either (1) a source that belongs to one of 28 listed source categories that has a "potential to emit" 100 tpy or more of a regulated pollutant;[98] or (2) any other source that has a "potential to emit" 250 tpy or more of a pollutant.[99]

The term source is defined broadly in EPA's PSD regulations to include all emission units at "contiguous or adjacent sites," that are subject to "common control," and that belong to the same Standard Industrial Classification (SIC) code.[100] All of these terms have been the subject of EPA guidance and policy statements or litigation. For example, EPA in the past has indicated that facilities separated by some distance may be considered "contiguous" or "adjacent" facilities, where they otherwise have some practical relationship.[101] However, the U.S. Court of Appeals for the Sixth Circuit rejected EPA's use of "relationship" in determining adjacency, finding it to be contrary to the plain meaning of the term.[102] Consistent with the opinion, EPA issued new guidance interpreting "adjacency" to entail physical proximity for all activities other than onshore oil and gas extraction activities.[103] For onshore oil and gas extraction activities, EPA promulgated regulations defining "adjacent" to mean activities located on the same site or sites located within one quarter mile of each other (measured from the center of the equipment not the site boundary) that share equipment.[104]

With respect to "common control," EPA historically interpreted that broadly to mean the power to direct environmental decisions for a facility.[105] In 2018, EPA refined that "multi-factor" position to make clear that it requires more than the ability to merely influence the decision, and that the focus should be "on control (power or authority) over operations . . . that could affect the applicability of, or compliance with, permitting requirements."[106] Later that year, EPA further clarified the relationship between "control" over a certain activity and whether multiple entities should be considered "persons under common control."[107]

Finally, facilities that do not belong to the same SIC code have been found to be part of the same facility where they are auxiliary or supporting facilities.[108]

The term "potential to emit" refers to the "maximum capacity" of a facility to emit pollution.[109] A source's potential to emit can be restricted, however, by enforceable restrictions placed on facility operations. EPA guidance currently addresses how operating restrictions must be written in order to be considered "enforceable" as a practical matter.[110] Historically, only "federally" enforceable restrictions could be taken into account, but this requirement was vacated by the D.C. Circuit in 1995.[111] EPA subsequently issued "interim" guidance addressing the issue[112] and in 2020, as part of a rulemaking on reclassification of major sources (discussed in chapters 3 and 5), EPA addressed the decision by removing the word "federally" from the definition of "potential to emit" in what the final rule called an "interim ministerial revision."[113]

b. Major Modification

Once a major source has been built, a "major modification" of that source must be preceded by issuance of a PSD permit. A "major modification" is defined in EPA's PSD rules as a "physical or operational change" that results in (1) a "significant emissions increase" and (2) a "significant net emissions increase" of a PSD pollutant.[114] What constitutes a "physical or operational change," and how one computes an "emissions increase," have been the subject of much debate over the past years. These topics are addressed at length in chapter 3 under the "modification" heading. EPA's rules establish "significance" levels for many of the regulated pollutants. For example, the significance level is 40 tpy for SO_2, 15 tpy for particulate matter (PM_{10}), and 40 tpy for nitrogen oxides (NOx).[115]

The "significant emissions increase" prong of EPA's rules is related to the project or activity itself that is determined to be a "change." That is, this first step of the emissions increase analysis requires an evaluation of whether the change itself would result in a significant emissions increase, taking into consideration increases and decreases resulting directly from the change (project emissions accounting).[116] This includes emissions changes from emissions units that themselves are not being modified but are nonetheless affected by the modification (i.e., debottlenecked emission units or changes in utilization of emissions units as a result of the project).[117] The rules provide two types of tests for making this evaluation (the so-called "actual-to-projected-actual" and "actual-to-potential" tests), and elaborate procedures for applying these tests, depending on the type of emissions unit involved and the source's election.[118]

EPA's rules specify that "[i]f the project causes a significant emissions increase, then the project is a major modification only if it also results in a significant net emissions increase."[119] In this second step of the emissions increase analysis, one must balance out contemporaneous emissions increases and decreases at the source.[120] EPA's rules provide criteria that govern when emissions decreases at existing units at a source can be used to offset emissions increases that result, for example, from the increase in potential emissions associated with the construction of a new emissions unit. This concept is referred to as "emissions netting."

Generally, "contemporaneous" emissions increases and decreases must be aggregated to determine if a significant net emissions increase has taken place. Emissions increases and decreases are "contemporaneous" if they take place within a period starting five years before construction of the proposed facility begins and the time the proposed facility commences operation.[121] Moreover, in order to use emissions decreases to "net out" of PSD review, those decreases (1) must be computed based on emission reductions from the lower of past actual or allowable emissions; (2) must have approximately the same qualitative significance for public health and welfare as that attributed to the increase from the particular change; and (3) must be made enforceable, for example, through a permit condition or SIP revision.[122]

In addition to netting out of NSR the owner or operator of a source may avoid review under EPA's Plantwide Applicability Limitation (PAL) program. Under the PAL program, plant changes do not trigger NSR as long as sourcewide emissions remain below a certain level specified in the source's PAL permit. The PAL program is summarized below in subsection 6.

c. Examples of Applicability Determinations

The PSD applicability rules can give rise to numerous difficult questions regarding whether emissions exceed either the "major source" definition or the "significance" thresholds. These questions often involve how one aggregates emission changes over time among the individual emission units that comprise a source.

For example, assume that a source is subject to the 100 tpy "major source" applicability threshold, but has a potential to emit only 90 tpy of SO_2. If an emissions unit that has a potential to emit 90 tpy of SO_2 is added to that source, would it be subject to PSD review?

Under EPA's rules, PSD review would *not* apply, because the new unit is not a "major source," and there is no existing major source for purposes of the "major modification" rule.[123] The addition of the 90 tpy unit, however, would result in an existing source that is "major" for purposes of any future additions (i.e., the potential to emit of the existing source after the addition would be 180 tpy). As a result, the next addition of an emissions unit with the potential to emit 40 tpy or more of SO_2 would trigger PSD review for the new emissions unit (but not the already constructed units).[124]

Determination of what is a significant "net" emissions increase may raise similar questions. For example, expanding on the case described above, assume that the 90 tpy source (1) adds an emissions unit in year one with a potential to emit 30 tpy of SO_2; (2) shuts down a 10 tpy SO_2 emissions unit in year four; (3) adds a 20 tpy SO_2 emission unit in year five; and (4) adds a 40 tpy SO_2 emission unit in year six. When would PSD review be triggered, and which of these facilities would be subject to review?

The source in this example would become "major" in year one, assuming the 100 tpy threshold applies (90 + 30 = 120). The addition in year five is not a "major modification" (i.e., emissions from the new unit are below the 40 tpy significance level), so no PSD permit would be required to construct this unit. The addition of a 40 tpy emissions unit in year six represents a "significant emissions increase," and thus requires an evaluation of "net" emissions to determine whether it constitutes a "major modification." The changes in years four, five and, six are "contemporaneous" and would equal 50 tpy (-10 + 20 + 40 = 50), thus exceeding the 40 tpy significance level. Therefore, PSD review would be triggered in year six. Only the additional unit in year six, however, would be subject to PSD review, *unless* the projects in years five and six had been intentionally split apart to avoid review.[125]

2. Best Available Control Technology

To receive a PSD permit, an applicant must show that it will employ BACT for each pollutant regulated under the Act that it emits in significant amounts. BACT is defined as the "maximum degree of [emission] reduction . . . achievable," taking into account economic, energy, and environmental factors. BACT must be at least as stringent as any new source performance standard (NSPS) or national emission standards for hazardous air pollutants (NESHAP) applicable to the source category.

The BACT determination is a matter of judgment for the state permitting authority, based on a balancing of the economic, energy, and environmental impact of alternative control technologies.[126] In December 1987, however, EPA issued guidance (referred to as the "top-down" BACT guidance) that can restrict state discretion in making BACT determinations. The history of the controversy over top-down BACT is discussed in the chapter 3 review of Clean Air Act control technology requirements.

In 2004, the Supreme Court confirmed in *Alaska Department of Environmental Conservation v. EPA*, that "[n]othing in the Act or its implementing regulations mandates top-down analysis,"[127] yet upheld an EPA order based on EPA's determination that the state, which sought to apply the top-down methodology, did not provide a reasoned analysis for rejecting the "top" technology choice under that methodology.[128] Therefore, while a state may not be required to follow a top-down methodology for determining BACT, the state must nonetheless properly apply that methodology once it has decided to use it in the permitting process.

3. Air Quality Issues

Although the BACT determination is perhaps the most important and controversial aspect of PSD permitting, a variety of other issues must also be resolved to receive a permit to construct a new or modified source. For example, the applicant must show that the proposed source will not cause or contribute to exceedances of either any applicable NAAQS or PSD increments (stringent air quality requirements designed to prevent significant deterioration of air quality in clean air areas). The applicant must also show that the proposed source will not adversely impact other air quality-related values. And the applicant may be required to consider the implications of its control technology proposals for unregulated emissions of air toxics. These issues are discussed below.

a. NAAQS and PSD Increment Compliance

A permit applicant must demonstrate that the proposed facility will not cause or contribute to an exceedance of any applicable NAAQS or PSD increment. PSD increments have been set for SO_2, PM_{10}, and NOx at a fraction of the NAAQS to preserve air quality in clean air areas.[129]

The Act provides three levels of PSD increments. The most stringent (Class I increments) apply in "mandatory Class I areas" (larger wilderness areas and national parks).[130] The rest of the country is subject to Class II PSD increments. States can opt into a less-stringent set of increments (Class III increments), as set out in section 164(a) of the Act, but none has elected to do so since enactment of the 1977 amendments.

Compliance with NAAQS and PSD increments is determined through application of atmospheric dispersion models. EPA continues to refine these models and the related guidance for application of the models. Accordingly, the latest version of EPA's Air Quality Modeling Guidelines[131] and EPA's Support Center for Regulatory Atmospheric Modeling (SCRAM)[132] should be consulted. Moreover, since disputes over how modeling should be conducted can delay receipt of a permit, one should consult the state and EPA Regional permitting staffs before filing a permit application in order to develop a protocol that resolves modeling issues. Questions that need to be addressed in this regard include the need for on-site meteorological data, the appropriate years for such data, how background pollution concentration should be defined including the need for preconstruction ambient air monitoring, the amount of interactive source modeling that must be performed, and the location and density of receptor grids for air quality modeling.

A common issue that arises with respect to air quality modeling concerns whether a PSD permit may be issued for a source where a NAAQS exceedance is predicted in the vicinity of the source based on emissions from nearby, existing sources. Such modeled exceedances may be discovered for the first time in the course of air quality modeling conducted in support of the new source permit.

Moreover, such modeled exceedances may be wholly artificial constructs of the modeling process, resulting from application of EPA's rules on "good engineering practice" stack height (which curtail the amount of dispersion credit one may use as input in air quality modeling).[133]

EPA's rules and guidance allow a source to receive a permit under the PSD program in this situation if it can be shown either that the proposed source will not have a "significant" ambient impact (as defined by EPA's nonattainment rules) for the pollutant,[134] or if it can be shown that the predicted ambient impact of the proposed new source will be insignificant at the point of the predicted exceedance.[135] If one of these showings cannot be made, the exceedance will have to be corrected (either through refined modeling or installation of additional controls) before a permit can be issued,[136] or the area in which the source proposes to locate may need to be redesignated as a nonattainment area so that permitting can proceed under the nonattainment program. Each approach can be time-consuming and burdensome.

b. Air Quality-Related Values and the Federal Land Manager

The PSD program was designed to prevent pollution concentrations in clean air areas from deteriorating to the level of the NAAQS. At the same time, this program was intended to be compatible with reasonable economic growth.[137]

Congress therefore designed the PSD increments to allow a greater margin of growth in urban and industrial areas. By contrast, in the case of certain national parks and wilderness areas (referred to as "mandatory Class I" areas), Congress provided for additional air quality protection, including more stringent PSD increments. Congress also authorized the Federal Land Manager (FLM) for mandatory Class I areas to participate in the preconstruction permitting process when the area "may be affected by emissions" from the construction or operation of a new source.[138] If the FLM demonstrates to the satisfaction of the state that the "proposed major emitting facility will have an adverse impact" on the AQRVs of the Class I areas,[139] the facility may not receive a permit, even if the allowable increments would not be exceeded.[140] On the other hand, if the FLM is satisfied that there will not be an adverse impact on AQRVs, the permit may be issued even if the allowable increments would be exceeded.[141]

In 2000, the Federal Land Managers' Air Quality Related Values Work Group (FLAG) (formed by the FLMs for the stated purpose of developing a more consistent approach for reviewing PSD permit applications) published recommendations for evaluating AQRVs and guidelines for completing and evaluating PSD permit applications.[142] The recommendations were revised in 2010.[143] According to the FLAG Report 2010, prior to submitting a permit application, the applicant should "consult" with the FLM to confirm preferred procedures for evaluating PSD Class I area impact, and the FLM "may ask . . . an applicant [to] address any or all of the areas of concern [to the FLM]. The primary areas of concern to the FLMs with respect to air pollution emissions are visibility impairment, ozone effects on vegetation, and effects of pollutant disposition on soils and surface waters."[144]

Since the 1990 Clean Air Act amendments, the FLMs have become increasingly involved in the PSD permitting process. Based on a relatively rigid application of the FLAG Report, particularly for visibility, FLMs have requested that sources mitigate the impact of their emissions.[145] If sources refuse to mitigate impacts to the satisfaction of the FLM, the FLM may issue an adverse impact finding, in which case the permitting authority will not issue the permit unless it disagrees with the FLM's determination.[146]

Because the FLMs have become more aggressive in the PSD permitting process, one should carefully consider the proximity of Class I areas in making decisions regarding the siting of proposed new facilities.

c. Consideration of Air Toxics

Air toxics have been considered in two ways in the PSD permitting process. First, prior to the 1990 amendments, the PSD rules required BACT review for *regulated* HAPs emitted in significant amounts. Because EPA never set "significance" levels for several HAPs (e.g., arsenic, benzene, and radionuclides), some took the position that *any* emissions of these pollutants should lead to BACT review.

Second, EPA's decision in the *North County* permitting case explained that permitting authorities must consider the effects of a control technology on *unregulated* HAPs in making BACT determinations for regulated pollutants.[147] Under this doctrine, a technology that controls emissions of an unregulated trace metal or organic compound would be preferable to one that did not, all else being equal. Similarly, a technology producing emissions of a hazardous substance would be less desirable than one that did not, all else being equal.

The 1990 amendments to the Act changed the law in this area, at least with respect to the first issue noted above. The amendments to section 112 specifically state that substances listed under the new air toxics program are *not* subject to the PSD program.[148] According to EPA, this exemption applies to federal PSD permits issued on or after November 15, 1990.[149] States with an approved PSD program, however, may continue to regulate air toxics if their PSD regulations provide an independent basis for such regulation.[150]

The air toxics list is extensive (188 substances and compounds are currently listed),[151] and this provision in section 112 obviates the need for BACT review for

HAPs for EPA's purposes. Because most states implement their own PSD permitting programs, the impact of the federal amendments on BACT considerations for HAPs will vary by state with some states requiring BACT for one or more HAPs. The 1990 amendments, however, did *not* affect the policy enunciated in the *North County* remand decision regarding consideration of HAPs in BACT determinations for regulated PSD pollutants.

4. Permissible Preconstruction Activities

Under the PSD rules, one cannot "begin actual on-site construction" of a new source, or of a major modification to an existing source, without obtaining a PSD permit. Over the years, EPA has addressed in guidance the types of "preconstruction" activities that can be undertaken before receiving a PSD permit. Such preconstruction activities include site preparation, grading, and other work preliminary to laying the foundation of the facility.[152] Concluding contractual arrangements also fall outside the scope of the "actual on-site construction" concept, at least as long as the contracts do not anticipate either on-site construction or off-site construction of unique, site-specific equipment or facilities, before receipt of a permit. In short, under its current interpretation, EPA considers almost every physical on-site construction activity that is of a permanent nature to constitute the beginning of "actual construction."

In the spring of 2020, EPA solicited comment on a new draft guidance entitled Interpretation of "Begin Actual Construction" Under the New Source Review Preconstruction Permitting Regulations (Mar. 25, 2020). Although EPA never finalized the guidance, and it no longer appears on EPA's website, the draft provides a useful compilation of EPA's historic determinations regarding permissible activities prior to permit issuance in a number of contexts.

To the extent that construction is begun without a permit, EPA may issue an administrative order to halt construction.[153] Such an order is enforceable in federal district court. In addition, EPA has authority to seek civil penalties for violation of such an order.[154] EPA's enforcement authority is discussed in chapter 11. Of course, states also have enforcement authority and could take steps to stop construction and seek penalties.

B. The NNSR Program

In areas that have not attained the NAAQS for a given pollutant (i.e., "nonattainment" areas), new or modified major stationary sources must receive an NNSR permit before construction of the proposed source or modification may begin.

States are responsible for implementing the nonattainment permit program. The state permit program must require, at a minimum, that major new sources or major modifications of existing sources install control technology that will achieve a standard defined as the "Lowest Achievable Emission Rate" (LAER). The nonattainment permit must also require that emissions of the nonattainment pollutant from the new or modified source be offset by emission reductions that have a similar air quality impact, that the source owner or operator certify that its other sources are in compliance (or on a schedule to comply) with all applicable air quality requirements, and that the benefits of the proposed source outweigh its costs.

1. The Applicability Determination

The Act defines a "nonattainment area" as one which "does not meet (or that contributes to ambient air quality in a nearby area that does not meet)" any NAAQS.[155] The designation is made separately for each pollutant, and an area is typically "nonattainment" for some pollutants and "attainment" for others.

SIPs for nonattainment areas must "require permits for the construction and operation of new or modified major stationary sources."[156] A major stationary source is one that has the potential to emit 100 tpy or more of a nonattainment pollutant.[157] In contrast to the PSD program, there is no separate category of 250 tpy sources.

The 1990 amendments imposed a more stringent definition of major source for certain ozone nonattainment areas, depending on the seriousness of the nonattainment areas. For "moderate" ozone nonattainment areas, the applicability threshold remains at 100 tpy for NOx and volatile organic compounds (VOCs).[158] For "serious" nonattainment areas, for NOx and VOCs the threshold is 50 tpy; for "severe" areas, it is 25 tpy; and for "extreme" areas, it is 10 tpy.[159] These more stringent major source thresholds may not apply to NOx emissions in ozone nonattainment areas if the state has found that reductions in NOx emissions in the area will not contribute to attainment of the ozone standard.[160]

In serious carbon monoxide (CO) nonattainment areas where the Administrator determines that stationary sources contribute significantly to CO concentrations, the 1990 amendments revised the major source threshold from 100 tpy to 50 tpy.[161] In serious PM_{10} and $PM_{2.5}$ nonattainment areas, the major source threshold is 70 tpy for PM_{10}, $PM_{2.5}$, and the $PM_{2.5}$ precursors.[162]

Like the PSD rules, the NNSR rules apply to physical or operational changes that result in a "significant" emissions increase. Significance levels are defined in EPA's rules.[163] The 1990 amendments made certain changes to these significance levels, however. For example, in serious and severe ozone nonattainment areas, an increase in 25 tpy of VOCs over a five-year period is defined as significant. In an extreme ozone nonattainment area, *any* increase in VOCs is defined as significant.[164] These significance thresholds also apply to NOx emissions unless EPA has granted a waiver.[165]

The definition of "major modification" under the NNSR program differs somewhat from the PSD program in other respects. Under the nonattainment rules, states have discretion as to whether to allow emissions "netting" in making applicability determinations—i.e., whether to allow a source to avoid review by making contemporaneous emissions decreases at existing emission units to avoid an emission increase from the source as a whole.[166] States generally have two options under the nonattainment program. Under the first option, referred to as the "dual source" definition, emissions from separate emission units at a common site are aggregated to determine whether the major source threshold is met. All proposed new facilities at a site are then aggregated to determine whether the "significant" increase threshold is met, but emissions decreases elsewhere at the source cannot be applied to "net out" of NNSR review.

A state may reject the "dual source" definition and adopt an emissions netting approach that is similar to that of the PSD applicability rules, subject to certain special requirements of the 1990 amendments. For example, the 1990 amendments specifically addressed the issue of emissions netting in serious and severe ozone nonattainment areas. For serious and severe areas, sources that have a potential to emit VOCs of less than 100 tpy can avoid triggering the modification rule if emission increases from the proposed facility are offset by emission decreases internal to the source at a ratio of 1.3 to 1 or more.[167] If such an offset is not obtained, the modification rule applies, but BACT can be substituted for the more stringent LAER. Sources in such areas with a potential to emit 100 tpy or more of VOCs can avoid LAER if they obtain 1.3-to-1 internal offsets.[168]

Finally, the NNSR program is a *state*-implemented program. As a result, there may be important state-to-state variations in nonattainment requirements, including applicability requirements. Some states, for example, have defined "significant" emissions increase in terms that are more stringent than the federal minimum. States also may adopt different approaches to the control of NOx emissions in ozone nonattainment areas under the 1990 amendments. Therefore, close examination of a state's NNSR program is important in developing a new source permitting strategy.

2. The "Lowest Achievable Emission Rate" Requirement

Like the PSD program, the nonattainment permit program requires the owner or operator of a proposed facility to install stringent control technology. Specifically, the source owner or operator must demonstrate that the proposed facility will use control technology for nonattainment pollutants emitted in significant amounts that complies with the "LAER" standard.

LAER is defined as "the most stringent emission limitation" contained in any SIP, or that is "achieved in practice" by the same or a similar source category, whichever is most stringent. If the owner or operator of the proposed source can demonstrate the most stringent technology is not feasible for its proposed facility, a less stringent technology can be established as LAER.

The LAER requirement is discussed further in chapter 3 of this regarding new source control technology requirements.

3. *Air Quality Issues*

Besides the LAER determination, several air quality issues must be addressed in a permit for construction of a major source or a major modification in a nonattainment area. These issues are summarized below and discussed in more detail in chapter 2 regarding the nonattainment program.

a. Emission Offsets

To ensure progress toward attainment of the NAAQS, a proposed new facility must offset its potential to emit nonattainment pollutants by securing emission reductions from nearby facilities at a greater than 1-to-1 ratio. Under the 1990 amendments, varying offset ratios and more inclusive definitions of "major source" apply to permit programs in ozone, CO, and PM_{10} nonattainment areas. Offset ratio requirements in ozone nonattainment areas vary between 1.1 and 1.5 to 1 according to the area's classification, with offset requirements for other nonattainment areas and pollutants being at least 1 to 1.[169]

The Administrator is given authority to set rules for determining the "baseline" against which emission offsets are to be credited.[170] Generally, a new or modified major stationary source may comply with offset requirements only by obtaining enforceable emission reductions from the same source or other sources in the same nonattainment region. States may allow a source to obtain the reductions in another nonattainment area, however, if the second area has a nonattainment classification of greater or equal seriousness and emissions from that area contribute to nonattainment in the first area.

Offsetting emission reductions must be in effect and enforceable by the time the new source commences operation, and offsets must be adequate to assure that the total tonnage of increased emissions are offset by reductions in actual emissions that are not otherwise required by law.[171]

b. Compliance Certification

To receive a nonattainment permit, the owner or operator of the proposed facility must certify that all other facilities it owns or operates in the same jurisdiction are in compliance with all air quality control requirements, or subject to an enforceable schedule to come into compliance. Emissions testing to verify compliance may be required in some jurisdictions.

c. Benefits of the Project and Mitigation Strategies

The Act requires that the owner or operator of the proposed facility undertake "an analysis of alternative sites, sizes, production processes, and environmental control techniques" for the proposed facility.[172] In order to receive a permit, that analysis must demonstrate that the "benefits of the proposed source significantly outweigh the environmental and social costs imposed as a result of its location, construction, or modification."[173] The extent of this provision is broad and varies from state to state.

C. EPA, Public, and Affected State Participation With Respect to State-Issued Preconstruction Permits

1. EPA Oversight

Reflecting EPA efforts to impose more uniformity on state BACT and LAER decisions through policy guidance, EPA Regions actively review state permit decisions to ensure state conformity with national guidance. The type of review authority exercised by the EPA Regions depends upon whether a state has developed its own permitting program as part of its SIP, or whether the state has been delegated authority by EPA to implement the federal program.[174]

a. SIP-Approved NSR Programs

When a state has developed its own program and EPA has approved that program as part of the SIP, EPA's authority to review state decisions is limited. EPA has authority to revoke its approval of the state's program, based on a showing by EPA that the state program is "substantially inadequate" to carry out the purposes of the NSR program.[175] The burden is on EPA, however, to show substantial inadequacy. Given that Congress intended states to have substantial discretion to implement the NSR program, this burden is a heavy one. By contrast, EPA has used its enforcement authority under sections 167 and 113(a)(5) of the Act to enforce SIP-approved NSR programs.

Section 167 authorizes EPA to issue orders, enforceable in district court, halting construction of projects that do not have valid PSD permits.[176] Section 113(a)(5), which was added by the 1990 amendments to the Act, authorizes the Administrator to issue enforcement orders upon finding that "a State is not acting in compliance with any requirement or prohibition of the [Act] relating to the construction of new sources or the modification of existing sources."[177] Violation of such orders can give rise to the assessment of administrative or civil penalties. Although such orders are clearly appropriate in the cases of clear-cut violations of the NSR program (for example, where construction has begun on a major modification without a PSD permit, or where the state issues a PSD permit that is deficient on its face, such as a permit that contains no BACT determination), EPA has also used these provisions in cases where it merely disagrees with the state's exercise of discretion with respect to specific NSR issues (for example, the choice among alternative control technologies as BACT). Although lower federal courts were initially reluctant to accept this latter assertion of authority,[178] the Supreme Court in 2004 held that "EPA has supervisory authority over the reasonableness of state permitting authorities' BACT determinations and may issue a stop construction order, under §§ 113(a)(5) and 167, if a BACT selection is not reasonable."[179] Because the touchstone of the Supreme Court's holding focused on whether the state's *BACT decision* is "reasonable," it remains to be seen how far EPA can go to "second guess" other types of state permit decisions in states that have SIP-approved PSD programs.

b. Delegated NSR Authority

Where a state has been delegated authority by EPA to implement the federal NSR rules, EPA has greater authority to control state decisions. For example, EPA may preserve in the delegation agreement the right to review state decisions. As a result, when seeking an NSR permit in such states, sources should consult the delegation agreement to ascertain precisely what role EPA may play regarding the NSR permit decision.

Regardless of the terms of the delegation agreement, EPA retains authority under the consolidated permit regulations to review NSR decisions by states that have been delegated permitting authority, based on a petition from a private party to EPA's Environmental Appeals Board (EAB) filed within 30 days of the state permit decision.[180] The filing of a timely petition stays the effectiveness of the permit.[181] The EAB also can review permits on its own initiative.[182]

EPA Regions and private citizen groups have actively sought administrative review of delegated state permit decisions. This has caused delays in obtaining NSR permits in states with delegated authority. In formulating a permitting strategy, therefore, knowledge of the status of the state's NSR permitting authority and establishment of a comprehensive record for the state's permit decision are both critical to reduce the risks associated with administrative appeals.

2. Public Participation

As with the Title V program, prior to permit issuance, the permitting authority must provide procedures for public notice, a comment period of at least 30 days, and the opportunity to request a public hearing on the draft permit.[183] The materials in the record must be made available for public review.[184] Members of the public that commented on the draft permit may challenge its issuance either in state proceedings for SIP-approved programs or in EPA administrative proceedings for delegated programs.

Although not required by the Act, many SIP-approved states as well as EPA delegated states consider environmental justice concerns when issuing permits. Generally, permitting authorities seek to ensure environmental justice communities have a meaningful voice in the permitting process and are not disproportionately impacted by emissions from the source or modification.

3. Participation of Affected States

As with the Title V program, the permitting authority must also give notice of each draft permit to any affected state on or before the time public notice is provided.[185] An affected state is one whose air quality may be affected by emissions from the source or modification. The affected state must be afforded the opportunity to submit written comments on the proposed permit.

D. The Plantwide Applicability Limitation Program

As mentioned above, the owner or operator of an existing source may avoid NSR review under EPA's PAL program.[186] Under the PAL regulations, as under the NSR netting regulations, so long as source-wide emissions do not increase (i.e., so long as any emissions resulting from a change at one emissions unit at the source are offset by decreases at another emissions unit at the same source), NSR does not apply. The PAL program may have an advantage over netting because a PAL is established once every ten years and covers all changes that occur during its term, while netting must be applied separately for every change. According to EPA, "[t]he added flexibility of a PAL allows sources to respond rapidly to market changes consistent with the goals of the NSR program."[187] However, concerns that certain elements of the regulation are unduly onerous or may create risk apparently has hindered widespread use of the program. As a result, in August 2020, EPA issued guidance to improve the understanding of PALS and address the concerns raised by stakeholders.[188]

1. What is a PAL?

A PAL is an emission limitation for a major stationary source expressed in tons per year and set on a pollutant-by-pollutant basis. It must be enforceable as a practical matter and established source-wide in accordance with EPA's PAL regulations.[189] In other words, a PAL is specific to a particular pollutant, and multiple permits can be established so that emissions of several regulated pollutants are limited. As long as a source is able to comply with its PALs, changes, including alterations to existing emissions units and the addition of new emissions units, may occur at the source without triggering NSR.[190]

2. Determining the PAL Level

In general, for each covered pollutant, the PAL is determined by summing the baseline actual emissions for all emissions units at the source and adding an amount equal to the applicable significance level for that pollutant. The applicant must determine the baseline actual emissions using the same 24-month period for all units but may use allowable emissions for any emissions unit added to the facility after the selected 24-month period (emissions from permanently shut-down units must be subtracted).

A reviewing authority must provide an opportunity for public participation on the application for a PAL, including a comment period and the opportunity for a public hearing.[191] The application for a PAL must contain a proposed monitoring system, and a facility with a PAL must perform monitoring of all applicable units to demonstrate that the PAL is not exceeded.[192] A facility must determine its actual emissions on a monthly basis and compare them to its PAL on a rolling 12-month total basis.[193] Emission calculations and deviation reports must be submitted to the regulatory agency at least semi-annually.[194]

3. Term of the PAL

The permitting authority may reduce a PAL during its term but only if a reduction is required due to the promulgation of a new regulatory standard (e.g., a new NSPS or MACT) or if the authority determines that the PAL may cause an exceedance of a NAAQS or have an adverse impact to a Federal Class I area.[195] Limits eliminated by a PAL (for example, limits in accordance with 40 C.F.R. § 52.21(r)) do not return upon the expiration of a PAL. Once a PAL is determined and approved, it remains valid for 10 years and is renewable every 10 years.[196]

At the conclusion of the term of a PAL, the permitting authority may renew the PAL at the original PAL level without considering other factors if the sum of the baseline actual emissions for the emissions units at the source (plus significance levels) is equal to or greater than 80 percent of the original PAL level.[197] If the recalculated baseline plus significance level is less than 80 percent of the original PAL level, the permitting authority may set the PAL at a level that it believes is appropriate, taking into account air quality needs, advances in control technology, anticipated economic growth in the area, and other factors identified by the authority.[198] The new PAL level cannot be higher than the potential to emit of the source or the existing PAL (unless PAL increase provisions are met).[199]

E. Resource Materials for Permit Applicants

As can be seen from the foregoing discussion, permitting authorities are called upon to make numerous, complex decisions under both the PSD and NNSR permit programs. These decisions will depend on the facts and circumstances of each case and will be influenced by EPA's latest NSR and air quality guidance.

In planning for permitting a new facility, therefore, it is important to consult the most recent versions of EPA's guidance documents as well as recent EPA and state permit decisions. Materials that should be consulted in preparing a PSD and/or NNSR permit application include the following:

- The PSD and NNSR regulations
- EPA's 1980 PSD Workshop Manual
- EPA's 1990 Draft NSR Workshop Manual
- The latest versions of the Air Quality Modeling Guidelines and EPA's Annual Model Clearinghouse Reports
- EPA's RACT/BACT/LAER Clearinghouse
- EPA's New Source Review Policy and Guidance Index
- EPA's Control Technique Guidelines and Alternative Control Techniques Documents

F. Combined Title V/Preconstruction Permit Programs

Some states have sought to combine the Title V permitting program with their existing PSD and NNSR permitting programs. The objective is to harmonize the procedural requirements of the two programs so that a source need not engage in two separate permitting processes, for example, when undertaking a modification that triggers NSR and requires a revision of an existing Part 70 permit. In some cases, however, this effort has raised questions about the scope of EPA's permit review authority and its use of Title V veto authority, which may be appropriate for certain Part 70 permit terms but not as directly for state PSD determinations.

Notes

1. Preconstruction permitting—also called new source review (NSR)—is addressed in the Act under the prevention of significant deterioration (PSD) program of Title I Part C and the nonattainment new source review (NNSR) program of Title I Part D. Additional state-specific preconstruction permitting requirements (minor source permitting) may also be part of an approved SIP under Title I Part A. Titles of the CAA correspond to subchapters in the U.S. Code.

2. Requirements for the Preparation, Adoption, and Submittal of Implementation Plans; Approval and Promulgation of Implementation Plans, 54 Fed. Reg. 27,274 (June 28, 1989).

3. Operating Permit Program, 57 Fed. Reg. 32,250 (July 21, 1992).

4. Federal Operating Permits Program, 61 Fed. Reg. 34,202 (July 1, 1996). The federal operating permit program would be administered either by EPA or by the state under a delegation of authority from EPA.

5. *Clean Air Implementation Project v. EPA*, No. 92-1303 (and consolidated cases) (D.C. Cir. filed July 21, 1992).

6. Although the case has been administratively terminated for lack of activity, any party could seek to resume the case at any time.

7. These proposals are discussed in Section I.G.3.

8. 40 C.F.R. § 70.3(a).

9. Prevention of Significant Deterioration and Title V Greenhouse Gas Tailoring Rule, 75 Fed. Reg. 31,514 (June 3, 2010). Certain portions of that rule were later vacated by the D.C. Circuit and removed. Prevention of Significant Deterioration and Title V Permitting for Greenhouse Gases: Removal of Certain Vacated Elements, 80 Fed. Reg. 50,199 (Aug. 19, 2015).

10. Deferral for CO_2 [Carbon Dioxide] Emissions From Bioenergy and Other Biogenic Sources Under the Prevention of Significant Deterioration (PSD) and Title V Programs, 76 Fed. Reg. 43,490 (July 20, 2011).

11. *Ctr. for Biological Diversity v. EPA*, 722 F.3d 401 (D.C. Cir. 2013).

12. 42 U.S.C. § 7661a(a).

13. 40 C.F.R. § 70.3(b)(1). The rules also authorize states to permanently exempt two source categories from Title V: wood stoves and asbestos renovation and demolition projects. *Id.* § 70.3(b)(4).

14. *Id.* § 70.3(b)(2); *see, e.g.*, National Emission Standards for Hazardous Air Pollutants for Source Categories: Gasoline Distribution Bulk Terminals, Bulk Plants, and Pipeline Facilities; and Gasoline Dispensing Facilities, 73 Fed. Reg. 1916 (Jan. 10, 2008);

National Emission Standards for Hazardous Air Pollutants for Area Sources: Polyvinyl Chloride and Copolymers Production, Primary Copper Smelting, Secondary Copper Smelting, and Primary Nonferrous Metals: Zinc, Cadmium, and Beryllium, 72 Fed. Reg. 2930 (Jan. 23, 2007); Standards of Performance for New Stationary Sources and Emission Guidelines for Existing Sources: Large Municipal Waste Combustors, 70 Fed. Reg. 75,348 (proposed Dec. 19, 2005).

15. 40 C.F.R. § 70.5(c).

16. CAA § 502(c), 42 U.S.C. § 7661a(c); *see* 40 C.F.R. §§ 70.2, 70.3(a).

17. CAA § 504(e), 42 U.S.C. § 7661c(e); 40 C.F.R. § 70.6(e).

18. CAA § 504(d), 42 U.S.C. § 7661c(d); 40 C.F.R. § 70.6(d).

19. *See, e.g.*, 57 Fed. Reg. at 32,279.

20. 40 C.F.R. § 70.4(d).

21. Extension of Operating Permits Program Interim Approvals, 62 Fed. Reg. 45,732 (Aug. 29, 1997).

22. *See* Revision to Interim Approval Requirements, 66 Fed. Reg. 27,008 (May 15, 2001).

23. *See generally* 40 C.F.R. § 70.10.

24. CAA § 503(c), 42 U.S.C. § 7661b(c); 40 C.F.R. § 70.5(a)(1)(i). Section 70.5(a)(1)(i) also stipulates, however, that the permitting authority may establish an earlier date for submission of a permit application.

25. 40 C.F.R. § 70.5(a)(1)(ii).

26. *Id.*

27. *Id.* § 70.7(a)(4).

28. CAA § 503(d), 42 U.S.C. § 7661b(d); 40 C.F.R. § 70.7(b).

29. *See* 40 C.F.R. § 70.6(b)(2).

30. *Id.* § 70.5(c)(8)-(9).

31. *Id.* § 70.5(d).

32. Memorandum from Lydia N. Wegman, Deputy Dir., Office of Air Quality Planning & Standards, EPA, to Dir., Office of Ecosystem Prot., Region I, et al., White Paper Number 2 for Improved Implementation of the Part 70 Operating Permits Program (Mar. 5, 1996); Memorandum from Lydia N. Wegman, Deputy Dir., Office of Air Quality Planning & Standards, EPA, to Dir., Air, Pesticides & Toxics Mgmt. Div., Regions I & IV, et al., White Paper for Streamlined Development of Part 70 Permit Applications (July 10, 1995).

33. 40 C.F.R. § 70.7(a)(2).

34. 57 Fed. Reg. at 32,266.

35. 40 C.F.R. § 70.6(a).

36. *See, e.g.*, Clean Air Act Final Interim Approval of Operating Permit Programs; State of Tennessee and Memphis-Shelby County, Tennessee, 61 Fed. Reg. 39,335, 39,337 (July 29, 1996).

37. The CAM rule is discussed in Section II.

38. *Sierra Club v. EPA*, 536 F.3d 673 (D.C. Cir. 2008).

39. 40 C.F.R. § 70.2.

40. 57 Fed. Reg. at 32,259.

41. *See, e.g.*, *In re Am. Elec. Power Serv. Corp., Sw. Elec. Power Co., John W. Turk Plant, Fulton, Ark.*, Petition No. VI-2008-01, 2009 WL 7698416 (EPA Dec. 15, 2009).

42. *See, e.g.*, *In re PacifiCorp Energy Hunter Power Plant, Emery Cty., Utah*, Petition No. VIII-2016-4, 2017 WL 10717295 (EPA Oct. 16, 2017).

43. *Compare Sierra Club v. EPA*, 964 F.3d 882 (10th Cir. 2020) (finding EPA's position in the PacifiCorp order inconsistent with the regulations) and *Env't Integrity Project v. EPA*, 969 F.3d 529 (5th Cir. 2020) (finding EPA's interpretation of Title V persuasive and therefore entitled to deference).

44. *See, e.g.*, *In re PacifiCorp Energy, Hunter Power Plant, Emery Ct., Utah*, Petition No. VIII-2022-2 at 17 n.30 (EPA Sept. 22, 2022).

45. *See also* 40 C.F.R. § 70.8(a).

46. CAA § 505(b)(1), 42 U.S.C. § 7661d(b)(1); 40 C.F.R. § 70.8(c)(1).

47. CAA § 505(c), 42 U.S.C. § 7661d(c); 40 C.F.R. § 70.8(c)(4). Courts interpreting EPA's obligation to issue or deny permits have held that, because the Act provides no explicit deadline for EPA's action, the timing is discretionary, and EPA's inaction does not authorize a suit to compel performance of a nondiscretionary duty. *See, e.g.*, *Zen-Noh Grain Corp. v. Jackson*, No. 12- 2535, 2013 WL 1856084 (E.D. La. Apr. 30, 2013); *WildEarth Guardians v. Jackson*, 885 F. Supp. 2d 1112 (D.N.M. 2012).

48. 40 C.F.R. § 70.7(h). In 2016, EPA revised the rules governing Title V and NSR permitting to authorize posting of notice of draft permits on a public website, rather than requiring notice in a newspaper. Revisions to Public Notice Provisions in Clean Air Act Permitting Programs, 81 Fed. Reg. 71,613 (Oct. 18, 2016).

49. 40 C.F.R. § 70.8(d).

50. CAA § 505(b)(2), 42 U.S.C. § 7661d(b)(2). Several U.S. courts of appeal have upheld EPA's discretion to determine whether a petitioner has demonstrated that a permit does not comply with the Act and found reasonable EPA's finding that the petitioners had not met that burden. *See, e.g.*, *Sierra Club v. EPA*, 557 F.3d 401 (6th Cir. 2009); *Sierra Club v. Johnson*, 541 F.3d 1257 (11th Cir. 2008); *Citizens Against Ruining the Env't v. EPA*, 535 F.3d 670 (7th Cir. 2008).

51. Revisions to the Petition Provisions of the Title V Permitting Program, 85 Fed. Reg. 6431 (Feb. 5, 2020).

52. CAA § 505(a)(2), 42 U.S.C. § 7661d(a)(2); 40 C.F.R. § 70.8(b)(1).

53. 40 C.F.R. § 70.8(b)(2).

54. *Id.* § 70.7(c).

55. *Id.* § 70.5(a)(1)(iii).

56. *Id.* § 70.7(f)(1)(i).

57. *Id.* § 70.7(f)(1)(ii).

58. *Id.* § 70.7(f)(1)(iii)-(iv).

59. *Id.* § 70.7(f)(2).

60. Operating Permits Program Rule Revisions, 59 Fed. Reg. 44,460 (proposed Aug. 29, 1994).

61. Operating Permits Program and Federal Operating Permits Program, 60 Fed. Reg. 45,530 (proposed Aug. 31, 1995).

62. *See* Operating Permits Program; Notice of Availability of Draft Rules and Accompanying Information, 62 Fed. Reg. 30,289 (proposed June 3, 1997).

63. 40 C.F.R. § 70.7(d).

64. *Id.* § 70.7(e)(2).

65. *Id.* § 70.7(e)(4).

66. How EPA provides for operational flexibility under the Title V rules has been a subject of intense controversy. Section 502(b)(10) of the Act provides that states shall "allow changes within a permitted facility . . . *without requiring a permit revision*, if the changes are not modifications under any provision of [Title] I and the changes do not exceed the emissions allowable under the permit." 42 U.S.C. § 7661a(b)(10) (emphasis added). The Act further contemplates that sources will provide EPA and the permitting authority notice seven days in advance of implementing the change. *Id.* The 1992 Title V rules contain provisions that require state programs to provide for these types of changes. 40 C.F.R. § 70.4(b)(12). The 1994 and 1995 proposals would have limited the scope of "Section 502(b)(10) changes" substantially.

67. 40 C.F.R. § 70.6(a)(9).

68. Operating Permit Programs and Prevention of Significant Deterioration (PSD) and Nonattainment New Source Review (NSR); Flexible Air Permitting Rule, 72 Fed. Reg. 52,206 (proposed Sept. 12, 2007).

69. Operating Permit Programs; Flexible Air Permitting Rule, 74 Fed. Reg. 51,418 (Oct. 6, 2009).

70. 40 C.F.R. § 70.9(b).

71. *Id.* § 70.9(b)(3).

72. *Id.* § 70.9(b)(2).

73. *Id.*

74. The Title V Task Force, Final Report to the Clean Air Act Advisory Committee on the Title V Implementation Experience (Apr. 2006).

75. Memorandum from Stephen D. Page, Dir., Office of Air Quality Planning & Standards, EPA, to Reg'l Air Div. Dirs., Regions 1–10, Implementation Guidance on Annual Compliance Certification Reporting and Statement of Basis Requirements for Title V Operating Permits (Apr. 30, 2014).

76. CAA § 114(a)(3), 42 U.S.C. § 7414(a)(3).

77. 40 C.F.R. § 64.2. Some emission limitations and standards, including those proposed by the Administrator after November 15, 1990, pursuant to section 111 or 112 of the Act, are exempt from the rule.

78. *Id.* § 64.3.

79. *Id.* § 64.7(d).

80. *Id.* § 64.8.

81. *Id.* § 64.6(c).

82. *Id.* § 64.5.

83. *Nat. Res. Def. Council, Inc. v. EPA*, 194 F.3d 130 (D.C. Cir. 1999).

84. State and Federal Operating Permits Program: Amendments to Compliance Certification Requirements, 68 Fed. Reg. 38,518 (June 27, 2003); *see also* Amendments to Compliance Certification Content Requirements for State and Federal Operating Permits Programs, 79 Fed. Reg. 43,661 (July 28, 2014) (correcting a subsequent inadvertent revision to those provisions).

85. *See generally* 57 Fed. Reg. at 32,259–60.

86. CAA § 112(j)(5), 42 U.S.C. § 7412(j)(5).

87. *Id.* § 112(d)(2), 42 U.S.C. § 7412(d)(2).

88. *Id.* § 112(i)(5), 42 U.S.C. § 7412(i)(5).

89. *Id.* § 112(i)(5)(B), 42 U.S.C. § 7412(i)(5)(B).

90. *Id.* § 112(*l*), 42 U.S.C. § 7412(*l*).

91. *Id.* § 506(a), 42 U.S.C. § 7661e(a).

92. H.R. Rep. No. 101-952, Conference Report on S. 1630 at 345 (1990), *reprinted in* 1 Env't and Natural Res. Policy Div., Library of Congress, A Legislative History of the Clean Air Act Amendments of 1990 at 1795 (1998).

93. 40 C.F.R. § 70.6(b)(1).

94. The PSD Program is contained in Title I Part C of the Act, and the NNSR program is contained in Title I Part D of the Act.

95. Minor source permitting programs are part of a state's SIP under Title I Part A of the Act to ensure compliance with the national ambient air quality standards (NAAQS). The requirements for obtaining a minor source preconstruction permit are varied and state-specific, with some being essentially the same as the PSD permit requirements. EPA's Fall 2022 regulatory agenda includes plans for a rulemaking to revise the minimum criteria for such programs in 40 C.F.R. §§ 51.160–164 to improve accountability in the minor NSR program.

96. CAA § 502(a), 42 U.S.C. § 7661a(a), provides that "[n]othing in this subsection shall be construed to alter the applicable requirements of this [Act] that a permit be obtained before construction or modification."

97. *See generally* 40 C.F.R. § 52.21. If an area attains the NAAQS for certain pollutants and not for others, a proposed source may be required to obtain both a PSD and a NNSR permit. The NNSR program is discussed below, following the PSD discussion.

98. This list of source categories is contained in Appendix 2.

99. CAA § 169, 42 U.S.C. § 7479; 40 C.F.R. § 52.21(b)(1)(i). Although PSD permitting requirements such as BACT may apply to greenhouse gas emissions (carbon dioxide, nitrous oxide, methane, hydrofluorocarbons, perfluorocarbons, and sulfur hexafluoride) of 75,000 tpy carbon dioxide equivalent (CO_2e) or more, they are not a "regulated pollutant" and are not considered in determining if a source is major. 40 C.F.R. § 52.21(b)(49).

100. *See id.* § 52.21(b)(5), (6); *see also* Requirements for Preparation, Adoption, and Submittal of Implementation Plans; Approval and Promulgation of Implementation Plans, 45 Fed. Reg. 52,676, 52,693-96 (Aug. 7, 1980) (preamble to EPA's 1980 PSD rules).

101. *See, e.g.*, Memorandum from Robert G. Kellam, Acting Dir., Info. Transfer & Program Integration Div., Office of Air Quality Planning & Standards, EPA, to Richard R. Long, Dir., Air Program, EPA Region 8, Analysis of the Applicability of Prevention

of Significant Deterioration (PSD) to the Anheuser-Busch, Incorporated Brewery and Nutri-Turf, Incorporated Landfarm at Fort Collins, Colorado (Aug. 27, 1996); Letter from Richard R. Long, Dir., Air Program, EPA Region 8, to Lynn R. Menlove, Manager, NSR Sec., Utah Dep't of Env't Quality (Aug. 8, 1997); Letter from Richard R. Long, Dir., Air & Radiation Program, EPA Region 8, to Dennis Myers, Construction Permit Unit Leader, Colorado Dep't of Pub. Health & Env't (Apr. 20, 1999).

102. *Summit Petroleum Corp. v. EPA,* 690 F.3d 733 (6th Cir. 2012).

103. Memorandum from Anne L. Idsal, Acting Assistant Adm'r, Office of Air & Radiation, EPA, to Reg'l Adm'rs, Regions 1–10, Interpreting "Adjacent" for New Source Review and Title V Source Determinations in All Industries Other Than Oil and Gas (Nov. 26, 2019).

104. 40 C.F.R. § 52.21(b)(6)(ii).

105. *See, e.g.*, Letter from William A. Spratlin, Dir., Air, RCRA, & Toxics Div., EPA Region VII, to Peter R. Hamlin, Chief, Air Quality Bureau, Iowa Dep't of Nat. Res. (Sept. 18, 1995).

106. *See* Letter from William L. Wehrum, Assistant Adm'r, Office of Air & Radiation, EPA, to Patrick McDonnell, Sec'y, Pennsylvania Dep't of Env't Prot. at Attachment pp. 7–8 (Apr. 30, 2018).

107. Letter from Anna Marie Wood, Dir. Air Quality Policy Div., Office of Air Quality Planning & Standards, EPA, to Gail Good, Dir. Bureau of Air Mgmt., Wisconsin Dep't of Nat. Res. (Oct. 16, 2018).

108. *See, e.g.*, Letter from Judith Katz, Air Prot. Div., EPA Region 3, to James Salvaggio, Dir. of Air Quality, Pennsylvania Dep't of Env't Prot. (undated, post 2000).

109. 40 C.F.R. § 52.21(b)(4).

110. *See* EPA, Air Enforcement Div., Office of Enforcement & Compliance Monitoring, Guidance on Limiting Potential to Emit in New Source Permitting (June 13, 1989); *see also* Memorandum from Kathie A. Stein, Dir., Air Enforcement Div., Office of Enforcement & Compliance Assurance, EPA, to Dir., Air & Pesticides & Toxics Mgmt. Div., Regions I & IV et al., Guidance an[d] Enforceability Requirements for Limiting Potential to Emit through SIP and § 112 Rules and General Permits (Jan. 25, 1995).

111. *Chem. Mfrs. Ass'n v. EPA*, 70 F.3d 637 (D.C. Cir. 1995) (per curiam) (vacating the requirement in light of *National Mining Ass'n v. EPA*, 59 F.3d 1351 (D.C. Cir. 1995) (per curiam)).

112. *See, e.g.,* Memorandum from John S. Seitz, Dir., Office of Air Quality Planning & Standards, Office of Air & Radiation, EPA, & Robert I. Van Heuvelen, Dir., Office of Regulatory Enforcement, Office of Enforcement & Compliance Assurance, EPA, to Reg'l Office Addresses, Release of Interim Policy an [*sic*] Federal Enforceability of Limitations on Potential to Emit (Jan. 22, 1996). EPA also subsequently issued guidance for the potential to emit from specific categories of sources. *See, e.g.*, Memorandum from John S. Seitz, Dir., Office of Air Quality Planning & Standards, Office of Air & Radiation, EPA, & Eric Schaeffer, Dir., Office of Regulatory Enforcement, Office of Enforcement & Compliance Assurance, EPA, to Dir., Office of Ecosystem Prot., Region I et al., Potential to Emit (PTE) Guidance for Specific Source Categories (Apr. 14, 1998).

113. Reclassification of Major Sources as Area Sources Under Section 112 of the Clean Air Act, 85 Fed. Reg. 73,854, 73,876 (Nov 19, 2020).

114. 40 C.F.R. § 52.21(a)(2)(iv)(*a*), (b)(2).

115. Significance levels for these and other regulated pollutants can be found at 40 C.F.R. § 52.21(b)(23)(i), and are contained in Appendix 3. States that have developed their own PSD programs may set more stringent significance levels.

116. Memorandum from E. Scott Pruitt, Adm'r, EPA, to Reg'l Adm'rs, Project Emissions Accounting Under the New Source Review Preconstruction Permitting Program (Mar. 13, 2018) (the source is responsible for defining the scope of the project); Prevention of Significant Deterioration (PSD) and Nonattainment New Source Review (NNSR): Aggregation; Reconsideration, 83 Fed. Reg. 57,324, 57,326 (Nov. 15, 2018) ("'Project aggregation,' therefore, ensures that nominally-separate projects occurring at a source are treated as a single project for NSR applicability purposes where it is unreasonable not to consider them a single project."). In 2020, EPA revised the applicable NSR regulations consistent with the 2018 Pruitt memorandum. Prevention of Significant Deterioration (PSD) and Nonattainment New Source Review (NNSR): Project Emissions Accounting, 85 Fed. Reg. 74,890 (Nov. 24, 2020). As discussed in chapter 3, EPA has indicated it plans to initiate a rulemaking to revise portions of the 2020 rule.

117. *See, e.g.,* Letter from Kate Kelly, Dir., Office of Air, Waste & Toxics, EPA Region 10, to Alan Prouty, Dir., Env't & Regulatory Affairs, J.R. Simplot Co., J.R. Simplot Company's Don Siding Plant and Issues related to Aggregation, Debottlenecking, and Projected Actual Emissions (Aug. 29, 2013).

118. 40 C.F.R. § 52.21(a)(2)(iv)(*b*)–(*c*).

119. *Id.* § 52.21(a)(2)(iv)(*a*).

120. *Id.* § 52.21(b)(3).

121. *Id.* § 52.21(b)(3)(i)(*b*).

122. *Id.* § 52.21(b)(3)(vi).

123. *See* 45 Fed. Reg. at 52,702.

124. *See id.*

125. *See* EPA Air Enforcement Division, Office of Enforcement and Compliance Monitoring Guidance on Limiting Potential to Emit in New Source Permitting at 10-13 (June 13, 1989). More detailed discussion of emissions netting, and examples of how the applicability rules apply in specific cases, are presented in EPA's Prevention of Significant Deterioration Workshop Manual, EPA-450/2-80-081, at I-A-25 to I-A-39, II-A-10 to II-A-11 (Oct. 1980) ("1980 PSD Workshop Manual"), and the 1990 draft update of that manual, *see* EPA, New Source Review Workshop Manual, Prevention of Significant Deterioration and Nonattainment Area Permitting, Draft, at A-28 to A-33 (Oct. 1990) ("1990 Draft NSR Workshop Manual").

126. *See, e.g.*, 1980 PSD Workshop Manual at I-B-2.

127. 540 U.S. 461, 476 n.7 (2004).

128. *See id.* at 497–99.

129. *See* 40 C.F.R. § 52.21(c). In addition, up to one year of air quality monitoring data may be required for pollutants for which the proposed facility will cause significant ambient concentrations, as defined in EPA's rules. *See id.* § 52.21(m).

130. *Id.* § 52.21(e)(1).

131. *Id.* pt. 51, App. W, Guideline on Air Quality Models.

132. EPA's SCRAM website provides access to air quality models and tools, modeling guidance and support, and meteorological data and processors.

133. *See* CAA § 123, 42 U.S.C. § 7423; 40 C.F.R. § 52.21(h).

134. *See* 40 C.F.R. pt. 51, App. S, § III.A.

135. *See, e.g.*, EPA, Model Clearinghouse: FY88 Summary Report 57 (Oct. 1988).

136. Theoretically, a permit to construct could be issued if a commitment were made: (1) to solve the exceedance problem; and (2) not to commence operation of the new facility until the problem had been resolved. *See* 40 C.F.R. pt. 51, App. S, § III.C.

137. *See, e.g.*, CAA § 160(3), 42 U.S.C. § 7470(3). As numerous legislators indicate through the entire legislative history of the PSD provisions, the PSD program is to be flexible and allow for controlled growth, even in or near Class I areas. *See* ENVIRONMENTAL POLICY DIVISION OF THE CONGRESSIONAL RESEARCH SERVICE OF THE LIBRARY OF CONGRESS, A LEGISLATIVE HISTORY OF THE CLEAN AIR ACT AMENDMENTS OF 1977, at 318, 367, 369, 726, 1033 (1978). There is to be a "balancing" of the need for clean air against the need for economic growth even in those pristine areas. *See, e.g.*, *id.* at 366, 726, 770, 774, 818, 899, 914, 923, 938, 1041.

138. CAA § 165(d)(2)(A), 42 U.S.C. § 7475(d)(2)(A); 40 C.F.R. § 52.21(p)(1).

139. CAA § 165(d)(2)(B), 42 U.S.C. § 7475(d)(2)(B); 40 C.F.R. § 52.21(p)(2). According to the legislative history of the Act, the term "air quality related values" means the "fundamental purposes for which such lands have been established and preserved by the Congress and the responsible Federal Agency." S. Rep. No. 95-127 at 36 (1977).

140. CAA § 165(d)(2)(C)(ii), 42 U.S.C. § 7475(d)(2)(C)(ii).

141. *Id.* § 165(d)(2)(C)(iii), 42 U.S.C. § 7475(d)(2)(C)(iii).

142. *See* U.S. Forest Service—Air Quality Program et al., Federal Land Managers' Air Quality Related Values Workgroup (FLAG) Phase I Report at iii (Dec. 2000) ("FLAG Report 2000").

143. National Park Service et al., Federal Land Managers' Air Quality Related Values Work Group (FLAG) *Phase I Report—Revised (2010)*, Natural Resource Report NPS/NRPC/NRR—2010/232 (Oct. 2010) ("FLAG Report 2010").

144. *Id.* at xii-xiii.

145. For example, the FLMs for the Dolly Sod and Otter Creek Wilderness Areas, both of which are part of the Monongahela National Forest, requested that a West Virginia source agree to a mitigation plan that included providing for offsets of SO_2 emissions to reduce impacts on visibility and acid deposition in those Class I areas. *See* West Virginia Dep't of Env't Prot., Final Determination/Fact Sheet for a Major New Source Construction at Longview Power LLC (Mar. 2, 2004).

146. For example, the FLM for the Mingo Wilderness Area issued an adverse impact finding for a new facility in Illinois, but the Illinois Env't Prot. Agency, after reviewing

all of the information, disagreed with the FLM and issued the permit. *See* Illinois Env't Protection Agency, Responsiveness Summary for the Prairie State Generating Station (Apr. 2005).

147. *See* Memorandum from Gerald A. Emison, Dir., Office of Air Quality Planning & Standards, EPA, to Reg'l Dirs., et al., EPA, Implementation of North County Resource Recovery PSD Remand (Sept. 22, 1987).

148. CAA § 112(b)(6), 42 U.S.C. § 7412(b)(6).

149. State Implementation Plans; General Preamble for the Implementation of Title I of the Clean Air Act Amendments of 1990; Supplemental, 57 Fed. Reg. 18,070, 18,075 (Apr. 28, 1992).

150. *Id.*

151. Information on the air toxics list and revisions to the list can be found on EPA's website.

152. *See* Flambeau Paper Corp., Park Falls, Wisconsin, Final Determination, 46 Fed. Reg. 37,777, 37,778 (July 22, 1981); Memorandum from Edward E. Reich, Dir., Stationary Source Compliance, Office of Air Quality Planning & Standards, EPA, to Robert R. DeSpain, Chief, Air Programs, EPA Region VIII, Construction Activities Prior to Issuance of a PSD Permit with Respect to "Begin Actual Construction" (Mar. 28, 1986); Memorandum from Roger Strelow, Assistant Adm'r for Air & Waste Mgmt., EPA, to Reg'l Adm'rs, PSD Regulations—Interpretation of Commencement of Construction (Dec. 18, 1975).

153. CAA §§ 113(a)(5), 167, 42 U.S.C. §§ 7413(a)(5), 7477.

154. *Id.* § 113(b)(3), 42 U.S.C. § 7413(b)(3).

155. *Id.* §§ 107(d)(1)(A)(i), 171(2), 42 U.S.C. §§ 7407(d)(1)(A)(i), 7501(2).

156. *Id.* § 172(c)(5), 42 U.S.C. § 7502(c)(5).

157. *Id.* § 302(j), 42 U.S.C. § 7602(j).

158. *Id.* § 182(b), 42 U.S.C. § 7511a(b).

159. *Id.* § 182(c)-(e), 42 U.S.C. § 7511a(c)-(e).

160. *Id.* § 182(f), 42 U.S.C. § 7511a(f).

161. *Id.* § 187(c)(1), 42 U.S.C. § 7512a(c)(1).

162. *Id.* § 189(b)(3), 42 U.S.C. § 7513a(b)(3); 40 C.F.R. § 51.165(a)(1)(iv)(A)(1)(vii)-(viii).

163. 40 C.F.R. § 51.165(a)(1)(x). These significance levels are listed in Appendix 3.

164. CAA § 182(c)(6), (e)(2), 42 U.S.C. § 7511a(c)(6), (e)(2).

165. *Id.* § 182(f), 42 U.S.C. § 7511a(f).

166. *See Chevron, U.S.A., Inc. v. Nat. Res. Def. Council, Inc.*, 467 U.S. 837 (1984).

167. CAA § 182(c)(7), 42 U.S.C. § 7511a(c)(7).

168. *Id.* § 182(c)(8), 42 U.S.C. § 7511a(c)(8).

169. 40 C.F.R. § 51.165(a)(9).

170. *Id.* § 173(a)(1)(A), 42 U.S.C. § 7503(a)(1)(A).

171. *Id.* § 173(c), 42 U.S.C. § 7503(c). A source with a complete permit application in place prior to the date the state's nonattainment SIP submittal for new source permitting was due (i.e., for VOCs, by November 15, 1992) was not subject to the new offset requirement. *See* Memorandum from John Seitz, Dir., Office of Air Quality Planning &

Standards, EPA, to Reg'l Dirs., New Source Review (NSR) Program Supplemental Transitional Guidance on Applicability of New Part D NSR Permit Requirements (Sept. 3, 1992).

172. CAA § 173(a)(5), 42 U.S.C. § 7503(a)(5).

173. *Id.*

174. A state may receive "full" delegation to implement EPA's NSR rules or more limited delegation to conduct certain technical aspects of review. Most states, however, have developed NSR programs as part of their SIPs. Information regarding NSR program status can be found on EPA's website. The state agency or EPA regional office should be contacted to determine the current status of an individual state's authority.

175. CAA §§ 110(a)(2)(H) and (k)(5), 42 U.S.C. § 7410(a)(2)(H) and (k)(5).

176. 42 U.S.C. § 7477.

177. CAA § 113(a)(5), 42 U.S.C. § 7413(a)(5).

178. *See, e.g.*, *United States v. Solar Turbines, Inc.*, 732 F. Supp. 535 (M.D. Pa. 1989); *see also Allsteel, Inc. v. EPA*, 25 F.3d 312 (6th Cir. 1994); *United States v. AM Gen. Corp.*, 34 F.3d 472 (7th Cir. 1994).

179. *Alaska Dep't of Env't Conservation*, 540 U.S. at 502.

180. 40 C.F.R. § 124.19.

181. *Id.* § 124.15.

182. Although this authority was removed for a period by the Trump EPA, *see* Streamlining Procedures for Permit Appeals, 85 Fed. Reg. 51,650 (Aug. 21, 2020), the Biden EPA later reversed many of those revisions. Revisions to the Permit Appeals Process To Restore the Organization and Function of the Environmental Appeals Board, 86 Fed. Reg. 31,172 (June 11, 2021).

183. 40 C.F.R. §§ 51.165(i), 51.166(q)(2)(iii) and (v), and 124.10–11.

184. *Id.* §§ 51.161(b), 51.166(q)(2)(ii), and 124.18.

185. *Id.* §§ 51.161(d), 51.166(q)(2)(iv), and 124.10(c)(1)(vii).

186. *See generally id.* §§ 51.165(f), *et seq.*, (for NNSR) and 52.21(aa), *et seq.* (for PSD). The PAL regulations were promulgated by EPA as part of its comprehensive "NSR Reform" rulemaking at 67 Fed. Reg. 80,186 (Dec. 31, 2002) and upheld in *New York v. EPA,* 413 F.3d 3, 36–38 (D.C. Cir. 2005) (per curiam). The program took effect in March 2003 in "EPA delegated" states; SIP-approved states were required to submit revised rules to EPA in 2006 to implement the program.

187. Agenda of Regulatory and Deregulatory Actions, 69 Fed. Reg. 38,154, 38,197 (June 28, 2004).

188. *See* Memorandum from Anne L. Austin, Principal Deputy Assistant Adm'r, Office of Air & Radiation, EPA, to Reg'l Air Div. Dirs., Regions 1–10, Guidance on Plantwide Applicability Limitation Provisions Under the New Source Review Regulations (Aug. 4, 2020).

189. *See, e.g.,* 40 C.F.R. §§ 51.165(f)(2)(v) and 52.21(aa)(2)(v).

190. *See id.* §§ 51.165(f)(1)(ii) and 52.21(aa)(1)(ii).

191. *See id.* §§ 51.165(f)(5) and 52.21(aa)(5).

192. *See id.* §§ 51.165(f)(12) and 52.21(aa)(12).

193. *See id.* §§ 51.165(f)(14) and 52.21(aa)(14).
194. *See id.*
195. *See id.* §§ 51.165(f)(8)(ii)(B) and 52.21(aa)(8)(ii)(*b*).
196. *See id.* §§ 51.165(f)(4)(i)(F), (f)(10) and 52.21(aa)(4)(i)(*f*), (aa)(10).
197. *See id.* §§ 51.165(f)(10)(iv)(A) and 52.21(aa)(10)(iv)(*a*).
198. *See id.* §§ 51.165(f)(10)(iv)(B) and 52.21(aa)(10)(iv)(*b*).
199. *See id.* §§ 51.165(f)(10)(iv)(C) and 52.21(aa)(10)(iv)(*c*). The provisions applicable to increasing a PAL are set forth in 40 C.F.R. §§ 51.165(f)(11) and 52.21(aa)(11).

Chapter 5

HAZARDOUS AIR POLLUTANTS

The 1990 Clean Air Act (CAA or Act) amendments completely revamped the preexisting system of hazardous air pollution control. Congress enacted Title III of the 1990 amendments[1] to respond to perceived problems with the prior risk-based system of hazardous air pollutant regulation. The old regulatory scheme required the U.S. Environmental Protection Agency (EPA or Agency) to establish a list of hazardous air pollutants (HAPs) and impose health-based emission standards for each pollutant. The new scheme initially identified 190 HAPs, directed EPA to identify the sources of those pollutants, and established a timeframe within which EPA must promulgate technology-based standards for each source category. Although the 1990 amendments shifted the emphasis of the air toxics program to technology-based standards, Congress did not entirely abandon risk-based standards. The amendments require EPA to assess the risk to public health likely to remain after implementation of the technology-based standards and to promulgate residual risk-based standards where necessary.

This chapter presents an overview of the air toxics provisions under the 1990 amendments, including the pollutants and sources subject to regulation and how emission standards have been and continue to be developed and implemented.

I. Listed Air Toxics

The 1990 amendments established a list of 190 HAPs that were to be addressed by the new air toxics program under the Act.[2] Through subsequent congressional action[3] and EPA listing and de-listing actions,[4] there are now 188 regulated pollutants. The list includes organics, metals, and chemical compounds common to many industrial processes. The list does not include lead or precursors to criteria pollutants subject to regulation under section 108(a).[5] A copy of the HAP list appears in Appendix 3.

The amendments also provide that "[n]o substance, practice, process or activity regulated under [Title VI of this Act regarding stratospheric ozone] shall be subject to regulation under this section solely due to its adverse effects on the environment."[6] As noted in chapter 4, the 1990 amendments provided that air toxics will no longer be regulated under the Prevention of Significant Deterioration (PSD) program.[7] Therefore, the HAPs currently listed under section 112(b) are not considered "regulated pollutants" for purposes of Part C of Title I.

A. Additions/Deletions by EPA

The 1990 amendments require the Administrator to review the list of HAPs periodically and revise it by rule as necessary.[8] Based on this review, the Administrator may add a pollutant to the list if it "present[s], or may present, through inhalation or other routes of exposure, a threat of adverse human health effects."[9] These substances include those that are "carcinogenic, mutagenic, teratogenic, neurotoxic, which cause reproductive dysfunction, or which are acutely or chronically toxic."[10]

The Administrator may also add a substance to the list that presents, or may present, adverse environmental effects through ambient concentrations, bioaccumulation, deposition, or other means. The 1990 amendments define "adverse environmental effect" to mean "any significant and widespread adverse effect, which may reasonably be anticipated, to wildlife, aquatic life, or other natural resources, including adverse impacts on populations of endangered or threatened species or significant degradation of environmental quality over broad areas."[11]

The current standard for listing HAPs is different from the standard that existed under the Act prior to the passage of the 1990 amendments. The 1990 amendments include a broader category of effects, including "adverse environmental effects."[12] Under the current standard, more substances could qualify for regulation as HAPs.

B. Petitions to Modify

Any person may petition the Administrator to add a substance to or delete a substance from the list. The petitioner must show "that there is adequate data on the health or environmental defects of the pollutant or other evidence" to support the addition or deletion of the substance.[13]

EPA has noted, in denying a petition to delist, that "[a]s a general matter, when EPA determines that a petition submitted under CAA section 112(b)(3) is deficient or incomplete, . . . EPA will afford the petitioner an opportunity to remedy the deficiency or supply the missing information prior to formal action on the petition."[14] When EPA determines that a petition is complete, it publishes a notice and solicits comment on the petition,[15] after which the Administrator has

18 months to grant or deny it and publish the reasons for doing so.[16] The 1990 amendments do not address what happens if the Administrator fails to respond to the petition to list or delist. Presumably, a suit could be brought in federal district court to compel EPA action.

The Act specifies that the Administrator's decision to grant a petition to add or delete a pollutant must be based on the petitioner's showing "or on the Administrator's own determination."[17] In making this decision, the Administrator can use any authority available to acquire the information needed on the health or environmental effects of a substance.[18] The Administrator, however, is prohibited from "deny[ing] a petition solely on the basis of inadequate resources or time for review."[19]

In 2020, when EPA granted a petition under section 112(b)(3) for the first time, EPA deferred the listing of the pollutant to a separate regulatory action.[20] When EPA subsequently listed the pollutant, the Agency suggested the two-step process it used may not be necessary as long as EPA provides sufficient opportunity for public review and comment on the decision.[21] However, EPA also announced its intent to propose new regulations to address the impacts and implementation of new requirements triggered by the addition of a new HAP and the impacts on regulated entities.[22] EPA's Fall 2022 regulatory agenda projects issuance of a proposal early in 2023.

A decision by the Administrator to add a pollutant to the list is not a final agency action subject to judicial review. That action becomes reviewable under section 307 of the Act only after EPA issues emission standards regulating that pollutant,[23] an action EPA maintains is not subject to any specific timetable.[24]

II. Sources Covered

EPA's first task under the new HAP program was to identify categories and subcategories of major and area sources of HAP.[25] A source's size, expressed in terms of tons of HAP per year, determines whether it is a "major" source and therefore subject to the most stringent level achievable with current technology or an "area" source to which EPA may apply a less-stringent standard. EPA promulgated the initial list of sources in 1992.[26] In the preamble, EPA made clear that "[t]he Agency considers the listing of categories of sources under section 112(c)(1) to be an ongoing process."[27] The statute requires EPA to revise the list of source categories listed under that provision from time to time, if appropriate, but no less than every eight years.[28] After establishing the original list, the Administrator has added categories and subcategories to the list based on the same criteria used to designate the original list.[29] EPA last published the required list in 2002.[30] The current major source and area source categories as listed on EPA's website are set out in Appendix 2.

EPA's listing of a source category is not final agency action subject to judicial review. A listing decision becomes reviewable only after EPA issues emissions standards for that source category.[31] The Act required EPA to promulgate regulations for all listed categories and subcategories within ten years of enactment.[32] As detailed below, this deadline was not met, which prompted legal challenge. The availability of judicial review for a decision by EPA not to list a source category is not explicitly addressed by section 112(e)(4) of the Act.

The following discussion summarizes the statutory standards governing the definition of "major" and "area" sources of air toxics.[33]

A. Major Sources

In general, a "major source" is

> any stationary source or group of stationary sources located within a contiguous area and under common control that emits or has the potential to emit . . . 10 tons per year or more of any hazardous air pollutant or 25 tons per year or more of any combination of hazardous air pollutants.[34]

A "stationary source" in this section has the same meaning ascribed to it in section 111(a), which is "any building, structure, facility, or installation which emits or may emit any air pollutant."[35] The 1990 amendments did not indicate whether there was any restriction on grouping together different types of pollutant-emitting activities, for example, whether the facilities in question need to be within the same Standard Industrial Classification code. In *National Mining Association v. EPA*, however, the U.S. Court of Appeals for the District of Columbia Circuit (D.C. Circuit) upheld EPA's approach of aggregating all HAP emissions at a plant to determine if the facility (and all its components) were a "major source," even if the component sources fell into different industrial categories.[36]

The Administrator can establish a lesser quantity cutoff for defining a major source based on "the potency of the air pollutant, persistence, potential for bioaccumulation, other characteristics of the air pollutant, or other relevant factors."[37] The Administrator also may establish different criteria than "tons per year" for determining whether facilities that emit radionuclides are "major sources."[38]

B. Area Sources

An "area source" is any stationary source that is not a major source. Area sources do not have Title V obligations, and the modification, construction, and reconstruction provisions of section 112(g) (discussed below) also do not apply to them.[39]

The 1990 amendments require the Administrator to include on the source category list each category and subcategory of area sources "which the Administrator finds presents a threat of adverse effects to human health or the environment (by such sources individually or in the aggregate) warranting regulation under this section."[40] The amendments also require EPA to list "sufficient categories or subcategories of area sources to ensure that area sources representing 90 percent of the area source emissions of the 30 hazardous air pollutants that present the greatest threat to public health in the largest number of urban areas are subject to regulation under this section."[41] In determining appropriate urban area sources, EPA was to develop a "comprehensive strategy to control emissions of hazardous air pollutants from area sources in urban areas" and transmit that strategy to Congress by November 1995.[42]

EPA published the final Urban Air Toxics Strategy pursuant to sections 112(k) and 112(c)(3) in 1999.[43] In that strategy, which addressed area and mobile sources (regulated under Title II of the Act), EPA identified the 33 HAPs presenting the "greatest potential threat to public health," 30 of which are emitted by area sources. EPA also identified area source categories that "emit a substantial portion of these HAPs, and which [EPA was] consider[ing] for regulation under section 112(d),"[44] but explained that additional action was needed to meet EPA's section 112(c)(3) duties.[45] After a legal challenge to EPA's delay in meeting those obligations and subsequent court-imposed rulemaking deadlines, Administrator Jackson announced in 2011 that EPA had promulgated all of the required area source rules to meet its section 112(c)(3) obligations.[46]

C. Reclassification of Sources

As discussed in Section III, major sources generally are subject to more stringent standards under section 112 than area sources. After EPA began implementing the requirements in the 1990 amendments, the Agency received questions asking whether a major source could become an area source by taking an enforceable emission limitation. In 1995, EPA issued guidance interpreting the Act as allowing a source that qualifies as major to become an area source any time up to the "first compliance date" of the relevant standard, but stating that after that date the source would remain subject to the standard regardless of its actual or potential emissions.[47] This was referred to as the "once in, always in" policy. In 2007, EPA proposed to revise that policy through rulemaking but did not take final action.[48]

EPA again sought to revise the policy in 2018, issuing a new memorandum analyzing section 112 and concluding that the 1995 policy was contrary to the plain language of the Act.[49] Under the revised policy, a major source could reclassify as an area source at any time by limiting its "potential to emit" below the major source threshold. California and a group of environmental advocacy organizations challenged the memorandum as an unlawful legislative rule adopted in violation of notice-and-comment requirements, but the D.C. Circuit dismissed the suit.[50]

EPA responded by issuing a new rulemaking, this time adopting final revisions to the General Provisions (discussed below in Section IV), codifying the interpretation laid out in the 2018 memorandum.[51] Multiple states and environmental advocacy organizations challenged the rule and petitioned for administrative reconsideration.[52] Following the change in administration in 2021, the case was placed in abeyance to allow the new administration to review the rule under President Biden's directive.[53] According to EPA's fall 2022 regulatory agenda, the Agency estimates proposing a new rule in the first half of 2023.

D. Deleting Sources from the List of Source Categories

EPA may delete any source category from the list of source categories to be regulated upon petition or on the Administrator's own motion if: (1) in the case of a carcinogen, no source in the category emits pollutants that may cause a lifetime risk of cancer greater than one-in-one million to the most exposed individual; or (2) in the case of pollutants that may cause an adverse health effect (other than cancer) or may cause adverse environmental effects, public health will be protected with an ample margin of safety and no adverse environmental effects will occur as a result of emissions of the pollutant.[54] EPA has deleted source categories on its own motion,[55] but not upon receipt of a petition.[56] Although EPA in one instance deleted source categories without making a section 112(c)(9) finding,[57] the D.C. Circuit has since suggested that in light of the Act's "plain text," EPA cannot "correct[] its own listing 'errors' except through section 112(c)(9)'s delisting process or court-sanctioned vacatur."[58]

The Administrator cannot exempt or delist a *sub*category (i.e., part of a category) from section 112 requirements. The D.C. Circuit struck down EPA's risk-based exemption for a subcategory of plywood and composite wood products sources in 2007 because EPA had "failed to make the required statutory determination that *no source* in the *category*, rather than in the low-risk subcategory, emits HAPs 'in quantities which may cause a lifetime risk of cancer greater than one in one million to the individual in the population who is most exposed to emissions . . . .'"[59]

III. Standards for Regulation of Air Toxics

The 1990 amendments provide for different types of emissions standards under the air toxics program. These include: (1) the technology-based standards, referred to as maximum achievable control technology (MACT) standards and generally available control technologies (GACT) standards; (2) work practice or operational standards; and (3) residual risk-based standards. This section discusses the statutory criteria governing development of these standards. EPA's standard-setting methodology, especially for MACT, has evolved considerably.

A. Technology-Based Standards

1. MACT Standards

Under section 112(d), EPA engages in a two-step MACT standard-setting process for listed HAPs unless EPA determines that GACT or work practice standards are appropriate. Step 1 is to set the "MACT floors" for new and existing major sources pursuant to section 112(d)(3)—that is, the emissions levels actually achieved by the best-performing sources in a category or subcategory.[60] For a new source category or subcategory, the MACT floor is "the emission control that is achieved in practice by the best controlled similar source, as determined by the Administrator."[61] Calculation of an existing source MACT floor depends on the number of sources in the category or subcategory.[62] For an existing source category or subcategory with thirty or more major sources, the MACT floor is the average emission limitation achieved by the best-performing 12 percent of the existing sources in the same source category or subcategory.[63] If there are fewer than thirty existing sources in the source category or subcategory, the MACT floor must be at least as stringent as the average emission limitation achieved by the best-performing five sources in that category or subcategory.[64]

In Step 2 of the MACT standard-setting process, EPA conducts a "beyond-the-floor" analysis to determine whether to make the emissions standards even more stringent. Under section 112(d)(2), EPA evaluates "the cost of achieving such emission reduction, and any non-air quality health and environmental impacts and energy requirements" in assessing the need for a more stringent standard.[65]

EPA has sought to employ a variety of MACT standard-setting methodologies, with considerable pushback from the D.C. Circuit. Through these challenges, several clarifications of and, in some cases, constraints on EPA's MACT methodology have developed:

- EPA must determine a MACT limit for all listed HAPs that a category or subcategory emits, not just those HAPs "controlled with technology";[66]
- In setting MACT standards for each HAP, EPA may use a surrogate pollutant (for example, particulate matter),[67] *but only* if EPA demonstrates a correlation between surrogate emissions and regulated HAP emissions and indicates for which HAPs a surrogate is used;[68]
- In determining the emissions *achieved* by the best-performing sources under section 112(d)(3), it is not necessary that EPA determine that the MACT floor is *achievable* by all sources,[69] and indeed, EPA cannot design a MACT solely to ensure that all sources that use a given technology can achieve the floor;[70]
- Any existing source MACT pool (i.e., group of best-performing sources used to determine a MACT floor) is to be identified using available "emissions information." The D.C. Circuit has concluded that regulatory data, such as compliance testing data, can qualify as suitable "emissions information."[71] If actual emissions information about the best performing sources is not available, only a "reasonable estimate" of emission control *achieved* by the best performing sources may be used to determine the MACT floor;[72]
- Although the control technology employed by the best performing source(s) may determine those source(s)' emissions and therefore the MACT floor, if factors *other than* control technology affect the best performing source(s)' emissions (for example, access to cleaner raw material due to an owner's/operator's geographic location), EPA is obligated to consider those non-technology factors in setting the MACT floor, even if they are not deliberate on the part of the owner/operator;[73]
- In accounting for emissions variability of the best-performing unit(s), EPA must demonstrate that its analysis is "'a reasonable estimate of emissions achieved by the best-performing sources,'"[74] and cannot, for example, use emissions data from worst-performing units that use the same control technology as the best-performing units to account for the best performing units' variability unless EPA shows that those data "actually predict" the best performers' emissions;[75] but EPA can use the upper prediction limit (UPL) statistical procedure to account for expected emissions variability not reflected in limited stack-testing data;[76]

- In making any beyond-the-floor determination, EPA is required to consider *each* of those factors set forth in section 112(d)(2);[77]
- However, EPA is not required by the Act to consider potential control device malfunctions when setting standards because the "best-controlled similar source" is unlikely to be a malfunctioning source;[78] and
- Nothing in the Act prevents EPA from setting standards on a "pollutant-by-pollutant" basis—that is, identifying the best-controlled source for each pollutant rather than a single source that, on balance, best controls all HAPs in the aggregate.[79]

The D.C. Circuit has also looked to section 129 in evaluating MACT floors issued by EPA under section 112.[80] Section 129, which also was added to the Act in 1990, governs regulation of emissions from "solid waste incineration units" using a standard-setting approach that is extremely similar to MACT standard-setting under section 112(d)(2) and (d)(3), albeit for only nine pollutants.[81] As sections 112 and 129 are "mutually exclusive" in their applicability to sources,[82] the question of which sources are subject to regulation under which section has proved difficult.[83] And the determination of which section applies can have "practical consequences."[84] For example, section 112 requires controls on the broadly defined "major source," but allows for less-stringent GACT standards (discussed below) for area sources and work practice standards, whereas section 129 requires control only on individual combustion units, but does so regardless of size and without other flexibilities.[85] In 2011, EPA finalized rules that defined "commercial and industrial solid waste incineration units" (CISWI), as well as non-hazardous secondary materials that are solid waste, and thereby delineated which units are subject to regulation under section 129 and which are subject to regulation under section 112.[86] EPA revised the CISWI rule on reconsideration in 2013, among other decisions, declining to set standards for certain units for which it lacked sufficient data.[87] In consolidated judicial challenges to the two CISWI rules, the D.C. Circuit held that EPA had a nondiscretionary duty to establish standards for all solid waste combustion units and therefore an obligation to collect the data it needed to do so.[88]

Although the section 112 air toxics program relies principally on technology-based regulation, there is some room for consideration of public health effects. For "pollutants for which a health threshold has been established, the Administrator may consider such threshold level, with an ample margin of safety, when establishing emission standards under this subsection."[89] EPA has invoked section 112(d)(4) to promulgate such "health-based" standards in only a limited number of rulemakings.[90]

2. GACT Standards

For area sources, EPA can promulgate standards or requirements "which provide for the use of generally available control technologies or management practices by such sources to reduce emissions of hazardous air pollutants" in lieu of setting MACT standards.[91] This provision reflects the potential inapplicability of the MACT concept to area sources and the need for separate control requirements. GACT may take the form of numerical emission limits, use of certain pollution control equipment, or employment of other types of management practices.[92] Although the Act provides no specific criteria for setting such standards, EPA has identified cost and economic impacts as relevant criteria.[93]

3. Deadlines for Development of Standards

The 1990 amendments imposed general deadlines on EPA to establish technology-based standards for source categories.[94] The amendments also required EPA to establish a regulatory schedule for promulgating standards for each source category consistent with that statutory schedule.[95] Failure to promulgate a standard according to its regulatory schedule could (and did) result in citizen suits pursuant to section 304 to establish court-ordered schedules for development of standards.

In addition, under section 112(d)(6), EPA must review and revise "as necessary" all section 112 standards at least every 8 years, "taking into account developments in practices, processes, and control technologies."[96] In undertaking this review—often referred to as the "technology review," EPA does not need to recalculate the prior MACT determination.[97] However, consistent with its obligation to set standards for every listed HAP the source category is known to emit, EPA must set limits for all HAP, even those not previously regulated.[98] As discussed below in Section IV, EPA has combined the section 112(d)(6) review process with development of residual risk standards under section 112(f).

4. Interim Technology-Based Standards

To ensure that emission standards for major sources are implemented, Congress added a "hammer" provision to section 112.[99] If "the Administrator fails to promulgate a standard for a category or subcategory of majors sources" pursuant to section 112(e)(1) and (3) within 18 months after the statutory deadline, the statute requires states to establish MACT standards for the affected sources on a case-by-case basis.[100] In those circumstances, the owner or operator of a major source must submit "a timely and complete [permit] application" to the state, and the state will establish a source-specific MACT limit.[101] That application must demonstrate how an emission unit will obtain the degree of emission reduction that the Administrator or the State has determined is at least as stringent as the emission reduction that would have been obtained had the relevant emission standard been promulgated according to the source category schedule.[102]

If an applicable MACT standard is promulgated after a permit application has been filed but before it is approved, the new federal standard will apply instead of the source-specific limitation.[103] If the new standard is promulgated after the permit is approved, however, the new standard will be included in the next renewal of the permit, and the source will be provided reasonable time to comply with that limit (but no longer than eight years from promulgation of the standard or permit renewal, whichever is earlier).[104]

Issued initially in 1994 and amended in 2002, the implementing regulations for section 112(j) set forth a two-part process for applications.[105] Those amended regulations were challenged by Sierra Club, and under a settlement agreement, EPA further amended the regulations.[106] In 2010, EPA proposed revisions that clarified the applicability of section 112(j) to situations in which MACT standards are completely vacated because EPA interpreted complete vacatur as "failure to promulgate" a standard under section 112(j)(2).[107] In its proposal, EPA also reminded that section 112(j) only applied to "initial[ly] list[ed]" categories and subcategories (i.e., those initially listed in 1992[108]), and amended obsolete portions of the regulations. EPA never took final action on those revisions.

Under section 112(g), Congress created another interim program that requires MACT standards to be applied on a case-by-case basis to newly constructed, reconstructed, and modified major sources until general, category-wide MACT standards are promulgated under section 112(d). This interim program was included in the 1990 amendments because Congress recognized that the most cost-effective time for implementing MACT standards is during the construction, modification, or reconstruction of a facility, but that category-wide MACT standards could not quickly be developed for all source categories. Facilities that are subject to case-by-case MACT under section 112(g) may be given up to eight additional years to come into compliance with a category-wide MACT standard once that standard is promulgated pursuant to section 112(d).

EPA promulgated regulations implementing section 112(g) in 1996.[109] Those regulations narrowed the scope of the program to cover only the construction or reconstruction of a facility. Modifications to a facility do not trigger section 112(g) MACT standards. EPA explained that construction of a major source could trigger the applicability of section 112(g) in one of two ways. First, section 112(g) is triggered by the construction of a major emitting source on a greenfield site. Second, section 112(g) would become applicable to the construction of a new "'process or production unit' at an existing site where the process or production unit is itself major emitting."[110]

A reconstruction of a source takes place when there is:

> replacement of components at an existing process or production unit that in and of itself emits or has th[e] potential to emit 10 tons per year of any HAP or 25 tons per year of any combination of HAP, whenever:
>
> (1) The fixed capital cost of the new components exceeds 50 percent of the fixed capital cost that would be required to construct a comparable process or production unit; and
> (2) It is technically and economically feasible for the reconstructed major source to meet the applicable maximum achievable control technology emission limitation for new sources established under this subpart.[111]

B. Work Practice Standards

If the Administrator determines that it is "not feasible . . . to prescribe or enforce an emission standard" for a hazardous air pollutant, EPA may "in lieu thereof, promulgate a design, equipment, work practice, or operational standard, or combination thereof, which in the Administrator's judgment is consistent" with MACT/GACT reductions or, in the case of risk-based standards (discussed below), the ample margin of safety standard.[112] The standards must include requirements that "will assure the proper operation and maintenance of any such element of design or equipment."[113]

The infeasibility requirement is met if the Administrator determines either: (A) "a hazardous air pollutant or pollutants cannot be emitted through a conveyance designed and constructed to emit or capture such pollutant, or that any requirement for, or use of, such a conveyance would be inconsistent with any Federal, State or local law"; or (B) "the application of measurement methodology to a particular class of sources is not practicable due to technological and economic limitations."[114]

If an owner or operator can demonstrate that an alternative means of emission limitation will achieve an emission reduction equal to the reduction required under a work practice standard, the Administrator must permit the use of that alternative.[115]

C. Residual Risk Standards

One of the most significant section 112 activities in recent years is EPA's residual risk-rulemaking program. The 1990 amendments do not completely abandon the concept of risk-based emission standards that existed before 1990. By November 1996, the Administrator was required to investigate and report to Congress on the risks to public health remaining or likely to remain after the application of MACT standards.[116] The report was to identify: (1) the significance of these risks; (2) the technologically and commercially available methods and costs of reducing these risks; and (3) "the actual health effects with respect to persons living in the vicinity of sources, any available epidemiological or other health studies, risks presented by background concentrations of hazardous air pollutants, any uncertainties in risk assessment methodology or other health assessment technique[s], and any negative health or environmental consequences to the community of efforts to reduce such risks."[117] The Administrator also was required to make recommendations for legislation regarding those risks. EPA submitted its residual risk report to Congress in 1999 and did not set forth any legislative recommendations.[118]

Unless Congress took legislative action pursuant to EPA's recommendation (which it did not), the Act directs EPA to make a decision on risk-based standards within eight years after promulgation of MACT standards for a major source category (or within nine years if a MACT standard was required within two years of enactment of the 1990 amendments) to protect the public health with an "ample margin of safety" and to prevent adverse environmental effects.[119] If MACT standards applicable to sources "emitting a pollutant (or pollutants) classified as a known, probable or possible human carcinogen do not reduce lifetime excess cancer risks to the individual most exposed to emissions from a source in the category or subcategory to less than one in one million," the Administrator is to "promulgate standards under this subsection for such source category."[120]

But a health-based standard need not reduce risks to all exposed individuals to one-in-one million, as clarified by the D.C. Circuit.[121] In *Natural Resources Defense Council v. EPA*, environmental advocacy organizations argued that EPA's residual risk review rule for the synthetic organic chemicals category violated section 112(f) because it did not reduce lifetime cancer risks to less than one-in-one million. The court held that while the statute requires EPA to "'promulgate standards,'" "it says nothing about the substantive content of those standards."[122] Therefore, "[i]f EPA determines that the existing technology-based standards already provide 'an ample margin of safety,' then the agency is free to readopt those standards during a residual risk rulemaking."[123]

In that case, the court found that EPA reasonably interpreted "ample margin of safety" in the same way as it did before the 1990 amendments. As the court observed, that interpretation—set forth in the benzene rulemaking conducted under the 1970 version of section 112[124]—grew out of the D.C. Circuit's holding in an earlier case also called *Natural Resources Defense Council v. EPA*.[125] That 1987 decision set forth "a two-step process for EPA to follow in making [ample margin of safety] judgments: first, determine a 'safe' or 'acceptable risk' level, and then set standards at the level—which may be equal to or lower, but not higher than, the 'safe' or 'acceptable' level—that protects public health with an ample margin of safety."[126] In the first step, which evaluates only health effects, a one in ten thousand lifetime risk of cancer for the maximally exposed individual is, generally speaking, presumptively "acceptable," though EPA may determine an alternate "acceptable" level.[127] In the second step, EPA determines the "ample margin of safety" through consideration of "'other relevant factors *including costs and economic impacts*, technological feasibility, and other factors relevant to each particular decision.'"[128] This "ample margin" cannot be higher than the "acceptable" level (i.e., floor) determined at step 1. Under this standard-setting process, reduction to a one-in-one million lifetime risk of cancer is "an aspirational goal," not a requirement.[129]

Residual risk standards are generally effective upon promulgation.[130] These standards, however, do not apply to existing sources until 90 days after their effective date.[131] The Administrator is authorized to grant waivers for up to two years for existing sources to come into compliance with these standards if the Administrator finds that it is necessary to install controls and if steps are taken to protect the health of persons from imminent endangerment during the waiver period.[132]

D. Preexisting Standards

The 1990 amendments contain a savings clause that preserves the effectiveness of air toxics emission standards promulgated prior to the 1990 amendments.[133] The savings clause provides that the amendments to section 112 will not affect existing standards that were promulgated before enactment (whether in effect at that time or not), unless they are modified under the pre-1990 section 112 or the new section 112. The savings provision contains a special rule for radionuclide emissions. Under this rule, no standard will be established under the new air toxics program "for radionuclide emissions from (A) elemental phosphorous plants, (B) grate calcination elemental phosphorous plants, (C) phosphogypsum stacks, or (D) any subcategory of the foregoing."[134] Regulatory decisions under the old section 112 will remain in effect for emissions from these sources. The savings provision also addresses radionuclide emissions from certain source categories.[135]

E. Compliance Deadlines Under Standards

A new source must comply with any emissions standards (as well as limitations or other regulatory requirements) in proposed or final form at the time that the new source "commences construction or reconstruction."[136] A new source will be given three years after promulgation for compliance, however, if (1) the requirement is "more stringent" in final form than in the proposed form in which it was written at the time the new source commenced construction or reconstruction and (2) the source complies with the proposed version during the interim three-year period.[137] Once emission standards are promulgated, existing sources can have up to three years to comply.[138] EPA, however, may require compliance sooner.

An existing source may obtain a one-year compliance extension from EPA or the source's Title V permitting authority if needed for "installation of controls."[139] Sources can also defer compliance with otherwise applicable MACT standards by participating in the early reductions program.[140] If, prior to proposal of an applicable MACT standard, an existing source reduces its hazardous air emissions by 90 percent (95 percent for particulates), it may qualify for a six-year compliance extension. A source that qualifies for the extension will be subject to an alternative emission limitation that will be included in the source's Title V operating permit.[141]

The President can exempt *any* stationary source from any standard or limitation, including MACT, for up to two years if the President determines that the "technology to implement such standard is not available" and "it is in the national security interests of the United States to do so."[142] This exemption can be extended by the President for an additional two-year periods. To date, no President has invoked this option.

IV. Implementation of the Air Toxics Program

A. General Provisions

EPA first promulgated the General Provisions for HAP regulation in 1994.[143] These provisions are meant to create basic, common standards and requirements for stationary sources that emit (or have the potential to emit) one or more of the listed HAPs. As source-specific standards are promulgated, General Provisions are superseded where they conflict with source-specific standards. Where source-specific standards do not address a requirement contained in the General Provisions, the General Provisions remain in effect.

The General Provisions provide procedures and criteria for implementing all section 112 standards. These include administrative procedures related to: (1) applicability determinations, such as definitions of "major source" and "potential to emit"; (2) compliance extensions; and (3) requests to use alternative means of compliance. In addition, compliance-related provisions outline the responsibilities of owners and operators to comply with relevant emission standards, such as: (1) compliance dates; (2) operation and maintenance requirements; (3) methods for determining compliance with standards; (4) procedures for emission performance testing and monitoring; and (5) reporting and recordkeeping requirements. Some of the issues addressed in the General Provisions are discussed below.

1. Potential to Emit

In determining whether any stationary source or a group of stationary sources located within a contiguous area and under common control is a major source, EPA considers that site's "potential to emit" HAPs.[144] In the General Provisions, EPA defines "potential to emit" as "the maximum capacity of a stationary source to emit a pollutant under its physical and operational design."[145] Moreover, until recently, the rules provided that "[a]ny physical or operational limitation on the capacity of the stationary source to emit a pollutant, including air pollution control equipment and restrictions on hours of operation or on the type or amount of material combusted, stored, or processed, shall be treated as part of its design *if the limitation or the effect it would have on emissions is federally enforceable*."[146] In response to a judicial challenge of that italicized requirement, the D.C. Circuit mandated that EPA explain its decision to consider only *federally* enforceable limitations and not, for example, "effective" emission limitations imposed by state or local regulations.[147] In 1995, after suit was brought but before the D.C. Circuit issued its opinion, EPA issued guidance setting out a transition policy that provided means to sources for treatment as nonmajor sources if they did not have federally enforceable limits in effect.[148] In that memorandum, EPA indicated that it intended to conduct rulemaking on the issue. EPA has since issued a number of additional guidance documents, but has yet to conduct a targeted rulemaking on the issue.[149] Instead, in 2020, as part of its rulemaking on reclassification of major sources (discussed above in Section II) EPA addressed the decision by removing the word "federally" from the definition of "potential to emit" in what the final rule called an "interim ministerial revision."[150]

2. Monitoring and Testing Requirements

The General Provisions also detail "monitoring" and "performance testing requirements" for major and area sources.[151] When EPA issued the General Provisions in 1994, EPA noted that it would incorporate the concept of "enhanced monitoring" directly into all new rules promulgated in section 112 standards for specific source categories.[152] As a result, in the Compliance Assurance Monitoring rule,[153] EPA exempted those "emission limitations or standards . . . proposed by the Administrator after November 15, 1990 pursuant to section 111 or 112 of the Act."[154] Thus, "enhanced monitoring" requirements for emission standards under section 112 are determined in individual rulemakings under section 112.

With regard to the performance testing requirements, the General Provisions stipulate when these tests must be conducted, the operating conditions under which the tests must be conducted, the content of the site-specific test plan, how long the agency has to review the test plan, how many runs are needed, procedures for applying for the use of an alternative test method, and procedures for requesting a waiver of the performance test, among other things.[155] In 2010, EPA added to the General Provisions a requirement for analysis of audit samples as part of each performance test as long as such samples are "commercially available."[156] "Commercial availability" is defined to require that samples be available from at least two providers. Because that is not always the case, owners and operators must refer to EPA's website to determine whether the requirement is in effect at the time.

3. Operation and Maintenance Requirements[157]

Of note, the General Provisions mandated that sources develop a "startup, shutdown, and malfunction plan" containing procedures for operating and maintaining the source during periods of startup, shutdown, and malfunction (SSM)[158] and exempted sources from complying with section 112(d) standards during SSM. The D.C. Circuit vacated the exemption provisions, however, as contrary to the Clean Air Act, finding the Act requires that "some section 112 standard apply continuously" to sources regulated under the HAP program.[159] EPA published a letter in the wake of the court's decision that indicated how the vacatur would affect section 112 implementation.[160] In the years since the decision, EPA has been revising individual source category standards that use similar SSM exemption language. EPA revised the General Provisions to remove the vacated provision in early 2021.[161]

4. Recordkeeping and Reporting Requirements

The General Provisions also contain requirements for recordkeeping and reporting.[162] These provisions detail information regarding dates and timelines for various requirements arising under the statute. The provisions also specify how notifications are to be sent to the Administrator, rules regarding record retention, and procedures for filing quarterly reports regarding the status of emissions and monitoring systems.

B. Title V Permits

All sources subject to regulation under section 112, including area sources, must apply for and operate in compliance with a Title V operating permit.[163] Operating permits issued pursuant to Title V must contain all of the Clean Air Act requirements applicable to a given source, including air toxics standards and limitations. The Title V operating permit program is discussed in more detail in chapter 4.

C. State Air Toxics Programs Under Section 112(*l*)

EPA is responsible for implementing and enforcing the Act's air toxics program until a state seeks EPA approval of a program for implementing and enforcing emission standards and other requirements for HAPs, including requirements for the prevention and mitigation of accidental releases under section 112(r).[164] The Act provides for either partial or complete delegation of the Administrator's authority and responsibilities, and imposes no deadline for a state to apply for such a delegation of authority.[165]

The Administrator must disapprove a state program if EPA finds one of the following:

- "[T]he authorities contained in the program are not adequate to assure compliance by all sources . . .";
- Adequate authority or resources "do[] not exist . . . to implement the program";
- "[T]he schedule for implementing the program and assuring compliance . . . is not sufficiently expeditious; or"
- "[T]he program is otherwise not in compliance" with the Administrator's guidance or will not satisfy the objectives of the Act.[166]

If the Administrator disapproves a state program, EPA must notify the state of the reasons for disapproval, and the state can revise and resubmit the program.[167] Moreover, the Administrator can withdraw approval of a state program after public hearing and notice to the state if the state is not administering and enforcing the program in accordance with EPA's guidance.[168] The state has 90 days after notification to take action to assure "prompt compliance" before the approval will be withdrawn.[169] Finally, the Act makes clear that, even if a state has been delegated authority to implement and enforce the air toxics program, the Administrator retains independent enforcement authority.[170]

The Administrator may also approve programs developed and submitted by a local pollution control agency (after consultation with the state). The local agency can implement its approved program and take any action authorized to be taken by a state under this section.[171] As with state programs, the Administrator retains the authority to enforce any applicable emission standard or requirement.

The Administrator initially published rules to implement section 112(*l*) in 1993, with revisions in 2000 and 2003.[172] Those rules allow states to assume enforcement responsibility either for federal standards or, alternatively, to enforce state laws that are "no less stringent" than federal law. The option of allowing states to displace federal law under section 112(*l*) by making state laws federally enforceable has been controversial. EPA's regulations were challenged by environmental advocacy organizations and industry alike, contending that EPA exceeded its authority. Both argued that the requirement that state law be "no less stringent" was ambiguous and would be difficult to apply in practice. As a result, environmental advocacy organizations feared that state standards that were actually less stringent would be made federally enforceable, and industry feared that more stringent state standards would become federally enforceable even though EPA would be barred from adopting those standards on its own. The D.C. Circuit declined to resolve the issue because, at that time, no state had attempted to federalize a state law under section 112(*l*).[173] In its 2000 revisions to Subpart E, EPA clarified its view that it "always retain[s] the right to enforce and implement" under section 112(*l*)(7) "Federal rules, including the [state, local, and tribal] rules or programs that are substituted for [EPA's] Federal rules and become the Federal rules."[174]

D. Combined "Risk and Technology Review"

As discussed above in Section III, within eight years of promulgating MACT standards for a source category, EPA is required to perform a review of developments in technology under section 112(d)(6) and to evaluate residual risk under section 112(f). The technology review must be completed every eight years thereafter to account for improvements in air pollution controls and/or prevention. Although not required by the Act, EPA has chosen to fulfill its obligations under these provisions through combined rulemakings commonly referred to as Risk and Technology Review (RTR). EPA first described its RTR methodology in a 2009 draft report,[175] which was then reviewed by EPA's Science Advisory Board.[176]

The majority of EPA's RTR rulemakings have been conducted under deadlines established by district courts following citizen suits to compel action under section 304.[177] According to EPA's Office of Inspector General, as of November 2021, EPA had ninety-three overdue RTRs, or technology reviews, almost half of which were overdue by more than five years.[178] Of the reviews that have been completed, many have been challenged judicially on a variety of grounds, including EPA's failure to address all regulated HAPs as required in the 2020 *LEAN* decision.[179]

E. Statutory Provisions Addressing Specific Source Types

The 1990 amendments contain special provisions governing several types of sources, including electric utility boilers, oil and gas wells, and facilities subject to the Resource Conservation and Recovery Act (RCRA).

1. Electric Utility Steam Generating Units

Electric utility steam generating unit (EGU) is defined in the air toxics program to mean "any fossil fuel fired combustion unit of more than 25 megawatts that serves a generator that produces electricity for sale."[180] It also includes "[a] unit that cogenerates steam and electricity and supplies more than one-third of its potential electric output capacity and more than 25 megawatts electrical output to any utility power distribution system for sale."[181]

These electric utility boilers were exempt from regulation under the air toxics provisions unless EPA conducted a study of their air toxics emissions and associated health risks and, through that study, determined regulation of EGUs to be "appropriate and necessary."[182] Congress specified that the study should examine the hazards to public health reasonably anticipated to occur as a result of air toxic emissions from fossil fuel-fired power plants "after imposition of the requirements of this [Act]."[183] If EPA determined that regulation of power plants under the air toxics provisions was "appropriate and necessary," the report was required to describe "alternative control strategies" for those emissions that warrant regulation.[184]

EPA submitted its final Utility Study to Congress in 1998. Following the completion of the study, EPA initially deferred the determination of whether regulation of EGU HAP emissions was "appropriate and necessary." Then, in mid-December 2000, as one of her last actions, Administrator Browner made a determination under section 112(n)(1)(A) that regulation of mercury from coal-fired EGUs and nickel emissions from oil-fired units was "appropriate and necessary" and listed those units under section 112(c).[185]

A coalition of electric utilities challenged the December 2000 listing because it was made without notice and opportunity for public comment and did not otherwise comply with the rulemaking requirements of the Administrative Procedure Act. The D.C. Circuit dismissed the challenge as premature, citing CAA § 112(e)(4) and 42 U.S.C. § 7412(e)(4).[186]

In 2005, in its first of many changes in position, EPA promulgated a final rule in which it concluded "it is neither appropriate nor necessary to regulate coal- and oil-fired Utility Units under section 112 [of the Act]."[187] EPA therefore removed coal- and oil-fired EGUs from the section 112(c) list based on information developed and received since the December 2000 determination. In place of section 112 regulation, EPA promulgated the Clean Air Mercury Rule (CAMR) to regulate mercury EGU emissions under section 111 of the Act through a market-based cap-and-trade program.[188] In 2008, the D.C. Circuit vacated EPA's 2005 delisting rule because the court found that EPA had not made findings required by section 112(c)(9).[189] Because EGUs were subject to section 112 regulation after vacatur of the delisting determination and EPA interpreted section 112 regulation as precluding section 111(d) regulation, the court also vacated CAMR.[190]

Subsequently, a coalition of electric utilities filed a section 112(c)(9) petition for delisting. However, EPA denied that petition and, in early 2012, finalized section 112 emission standards for coal- and oil-fired EGUs.[191] The rule provided existing sources three years from the effective date (i.e., until April 16, 2015) to comply with the standards. EPA predicted the rule would cost $9.6 billion to implement.[192] EPA subsequently granted petitions for administrative reconsideration on a limited set of issues and revised the new source standards[193] and the work practice standards applicable during periods of startup and shutdown.[194] EPA ultimately denied reconsideration on the remaining issues raised in the petitions.[195] All of those actions resulted in judicial challenges.[196]

Multiple parties also challenged the 2012 rule, arguing, among other things, that EPA failed to properly consider cost in its finding under section 112(n)(1)(A) that regulation of EGUs was "appropriate and necessary." The D.C. Circuit rejected that challenge.[197] However, the Supreme Court reversed the decision on appeal, holding that because "the phrase 'appropriate and necessary' requires at least some attention to cost," EPA must "consider cost—including, most importantly, cost of compliance—before deciding whether regulation is appropriate and necessary."[198] Of course, by the time the decision was issued, the requirements in the rule already had been implemented. In 2016, on remand, EPA finalized a "Supplemental Finding" that promulgated two alternative approaches to incorporate cost into the decision-making process, again finding regulation "appropriate and necessary."[199] Various petitioners then challenged that revised finding.[200]

Over the next seven years, EPA reversed its position twice on reconsideration following a change in administration. First, in 2020, the Trump EPA issued a rule reconsidering and revoking the 2016 supplemental finding and concluding that the regulation was not "appropriate."[201] EPA rejected the revised cost analyses as inconsistent with the Act as interpreted in *Michigan*.[202] EPA also reasoned that revocation of the finding would not affect the legal underpinnings of the rule because EPA had not met the Act's requirement for delisting the source category under section 112(c)(9), as that provision had been interpreted by the D.C. Circuit in *New Jersey v. EPA*.[203] The 2020 rule also incorporated the required eight-year RTR, in which EPA concluded under sections 112(d)(6) and (f)(2) of the Act that the current standards required no revision. Challenges to that action were placed in abeyance.[204]

On taking office in 2021, President Biden directed EPA to review the 2020 action under Executive Order 13990, and in March 2023, EPA published a final rule reconsidering the 2020 revocation and reaffirming the 2016 "appropriate and necessary" finding.[205] In that action, EPA stated its intent to provide notice of the results of its review of the 2020 RTR in a separate future action.

2. Oil and Gas Wells

The 1990 amendments provided that "emissions from any oil or gas exploration or production well . . . [and] its associated equipment . . . and . . . from any pipeline compressor or pump station [cannot] be aggregated with emissions from other similar units" to determine if they are major sources.[206] When EPA promulgated standards for oil and natural gas production major sources in 1999, EPA defined "associated equipment" as "equipment associated with an oil or natural gas exploration or production well, . . . includ[ing] all equipment from the wellbore to the point of custody transfer, except glycol dehydration units and storage vessels *with the potential for flash emissions*."[207] In 2012, EPA finalized a rule that, among other things, narrowed the definition of "associated equipment" by deleting the italicized phrase.[208] Petitions for administrative reconsideration and judicial review were filed, and the case was placed in abeyance.[209] EPA subsequently issued a request for information on certain storage vessels[210] and based on its analyses of the information received, issued a letter granting reconsideration on two issues,[211] but the rulemaking was delayed. In early 2023, EPA published a proposed consent decree setting a December 2025 deadline for EPA's action on a number of issues related to the rule, including a technology review under section 112(d)(6) of the Act and action on the 2012 petition for reconsideration.[212]

The 1990 amendments also excluded oil and gas production and exploration wells (and their "associated equipment") from the list of *area* sources, unless the Administrator established "an area source category for oil and gas production wells located in any metropolitan . . . area . . . with a population in excess of 1 million" because HAP emissions from these wells are found to "present more than a negligible risk of adverse effects to public health."[213] Although EPA proposed to list oil and natural gas production as an area source category in 1998, it did not finalize that proposed listing.[214] Instead, EPA listed oil and natural gas production as an area source category pursuant to the Urban Air Toxics Strategy later that year.[215] EPA published final standards for oil and natural gas production area sources in 2007.[216]

The 1990 amendments to the Act also required the Administrator "to assess the [risks] to public health and the environment resulting from the emission of hydrogen sulfide associated with the extraction of oil and natural gas . . . [and to] report to the Congress."[217] EPA published its final report in 1993.[218] In its study, EPA found that while routine emissions of hydrogen sulfide from oil and gas wells created the potential for human and environmental exposure, insufficient evidence existed to suggest that these exposures presented any significant threat.[219] Thus, EPA did not recommend further legislation pertaining to routine hydrogen sulfide emissions or accidental releases from oil and gas wells.[220]

3. RCRA Facilities

In developing emission standards for categories or subcategories of sources whose air emissions are regulated under the hazardous waste provisions of Subtitle C of RCRA, the Administrator is to take the applicable RCRA requirements into account, to the maximum extent practicable, in order to ensure the consistency of requirements under RCRA and the Clean Air Act.[221] This provision anticipates application of concurrent and consistent requirements under both of these regulatory programs.[222] EPA has attempted to harmonize its responsibilities under the Clean Air Act and RCRA. For example, EPA promulgated so-called "Subpart CC" rules under RCRA that allow certain covered facilities to meet Clean Air Act regulations in lieu of complying with some provisions of the Subpart CC rules.[223]

V. Accidental Release Prevention

Section 112(r) of the 1990 amendments created a new set of provisions that address accidental air releases of hazardous substances that have significant off-site consequences to human health and the environment. The accidental release prevention program covers owners and operators of stationary sources producing, processing, handling, or storing listed hazardous substances. The scope and content of this program are discussed below. A state may be delegated section 112(r) authority pursuant to section 112(*l*)(1).[224]

A. Substances Covered

Within 24 months of enactment, EPA was required to promulgate a list of not less than 100 substances that "in the case of an accidental release, are known to cause or may reasonably be anticipated to cause death, injury, or serious adverse effects for human health or the environment."[225] In developing the list, EPA was to use as a starting point the list of extremely hazardous substances (EHS) developed under section 302 of the Emergency Planning and Community Right-To-Know Act of 1986 (EPCRA).[226] Section 112(r) also required EPA to include 16 specific substances in the initial list of regulated substances, including chlorine, ammonia, and sulfur trioxide.[227]

Section 112(r) lists factors that EPA must consider in establishing the list of regulated substances. Among other things, no substance for which a primary NAAQS has been established is to be included on the list.[228] EPA may revise the list and must review it at least every five years.[229]

When listing a substance, EPA must establish by rule a threshold quantity for the substance, "taking into account the toxicity, reactivity, volatility, dispersibility, combustibility, or flammability of the substance and the amount of the substance which, as a result of an accidental release, is known to cause or may reasonably be anticipated to cause death, injury or serious adverse effects to human health for which the substance was listed."[230] In contrast to the emergency release notification provisions of CERCLA, the statute establishes no default threshold quantity that would apply in the absence of action by EPA.[231]

In 1994, EPA promulgated a list of section 112(r)-regulated substances and threshold quantities.[232] Subsequent to that initial listing determination, EPA deleted Division 1.1 explosives listed in Department of Transportation regulations in 49 C.F.R. § 172.101 from the section 112(r) list.[233] EPA also amended the listing for hydrochloric acid to include only those solutions that contain at least a 37 percent concentration of hydrogen chloride.[234] The current list includes 77 toxic substances and 63 flammable substances.[235] Sources that have one or more of the listed substances on site in quantities *greater than the threshold* established by this rule will be subject to *specific regulations* under section 112(r)(7) for prevention, detection, and response to accidental releases.

B. The General Duty Clause

Section 112(r)(1) of the accidental release prevention program imposes on owners and operators a general duty "to prevent the accidental release and to minimize the consequences of any such release of any substance listed pursuant to [section 112(r)(3)] *or any other extremely hazardous substance*."[236] In doing this, *any* facility that has extremely hazardous substances is required to "identify hazards which may result from [accidental] releases using appropriate hazard assessment techniques, to design and maintain a safe facility taking such steps as are necessary to prevent releases, and to minimize the consequences of accidental releases which do occur."[237] This "general duty" is self-implementing. That is, it can be used as a basis for enforcement actions by EPA,[238] even in the absence of any implementing regulations defining what steps are needed to comply with this "general duty."[239] The general duty clause, however, cannot be used as the basis for citizen suits or for suits seeking to recover for personal injury or property damage.[240]

C. Accidental Release Regulations

1. Statutory Requirements for Regulations

Section 112(r)(7) provides EPA with the authority to promulgate two sets of regulations. Under section 112(r)(7)(A), the Administrator *may* promulgate release prevention, detection, and correction requirements that would include monitoring, recordkeeping, reporting, training, vapor recovery, secondary containment, and other design, equipment, work practice, and operational requirements. Under section 112(r)(7)(B), EPA was required to promulgate within three years of enactment "reasonable regulations and appropriate guidance" regarding the prevention and detection of accidental releases from stationary sources of the listed substances and for response to such releases by owners and operators.

The latter set of regulations must require owners and operators of sources at which a regulated substance is present in more than a threshold quantity to prepare and implement a risk management plan (RMP) to detect and prevent or minimize accidental releases and to provide a prompt emergency response to any such releases in order to protect human health and the environment.[241] The RMPs must include a hazard assessment that evaluates the off-site consequences of accidental releases of covered substances. They also must cover the use, operation, repair, replacement, and maintenance of equipment to monitor, detect, inspect, and control releases. Finally, RMPs must address training and provide procedures and measures for emergency response after an accidental release. The RMPs must be registered with EPA and submitted to the Chemical Safety and Hazard Investigation Board (CSB), the state in which the facility is located, and its local emergency planning and response agency.[242] The RMPs also must be made available to the public.[243]

In developing these regulations, EPA also was required to consider, as appropriate, "differences in size, operations, processes, class and categories of sources and the voluntary actions of such sources to prevent such releases and respond to such releases."[244]

2. EPA's Regulations—40 C.F.R. Part 68

EPA first promulgated regulations implementing the requirements of section 112(r)(7)(B) in 1996.[245] Part 68, which as of 2019 applied to approximately 12,000 facilities,[246] regulates any "stationary source" that has a regulated substance present in a "process" above threshold quantities.[247] A "stationary source" is defined as "any buildings, structures, equipment, installations, or substance emitting stationary activities which belong to the same industrial group, which are located on one or more contiguous properties, which are under the control of the same person (or persons under common control), and from which an accidental release may occur," with some limited exceptions.[248] The regulations also specify that properties are "not . . . considered contiguous solely because of a railroad or gas pipeline right-of-way."[249]

The term "process" means "any activity involving a regulated substance including any use, storage, manufacturing, handling or on-site movement of such substances, or combination of these activities," and includes "any group of vessels that are interconnected, or separate vessels that are located such that a regulated substance could be involved in a potential release."[250]

Each covered facility is required to develop an RMP by the later of June 21, 1999, or whenever a regulated substance is initially present above the threshold quantity in a process at the facility. RMPs are filed through a central system[251] and must be made available to the public.[252] Sources are required to update their RMPs at least once every five years, unless certain circumstances dictate an earlier update.[253] The RMPs are subject to periodic audits.[254]

The rule established three levels of compliance, depending on the relative risk a covered source poses for accidental releases of hazardous substances that have off-site consequences.[255] The three compliance levels are called "Program 1," "Program 2," and "Program 3." Program 1, which contains the fewest requirements, applies to facilities that are considered to pose a relatively low risk for accidental releases with off-site consequences.[256] Program 3, which requires the highest level of compliance, applies to facilities that are considered to pose the greatest risk of accidental releases.[257] Program 2 is a somewhat streamlined version of Program 3 and is the default level for all covered sources that do not fall under Program 1 or Program 3.[258]

RMPs generally include three basic elements: (1) hazard assessment; (2) accidental release prevention program information; and (3) accidental release emergency response plan. The hazard assessment requirement of the RMP requires each covered source to evaluate the risk of catastrophic accidental releases of regulated substances from its facility and to estimate the likely impacts such releases would have on off-site receptors of concern (human health and sensitive environments). A hazard assessment must include a five-year history of accidental releases that resulted in significant off-site consequences.[259] The hazard assessment must also include analyses of a "worst-case" release scenario, as well as other alternative release scenarios, for each regulated substance present in a process above the threshold quantity.[260] The worst-case release analysis evaluates the off-site impacts that are likely to result from the accidental release of the largest quantity of a regulated substance from a vessel or process, taking into account administrative controls and passive mitigation.[261] The alternative release scenarios cover those releases that the source determines are more likely to occur than a worst-case release.[262] All covered facilities must conduct a hazard assessment, regardless of whether they fall under Program 1, Program 2, or Program 3.[263] Program 1 facilities are required, however, to analyze only their worst-case release scenarios and are not required to analyze any alternative release scenarios.[264]

The accidental release prevention program requirement of the RMP requires covered sources to develop and implement procedures designed to prevent catastrophic accidental releases from occurring. The rule outlines specific prevention program requirements, which generally parallel the requirements in the OSHA PSM.[265] The primary difference between the section 112(r)(7) rule and the OSHA PSM rule is that OSHA PSM addresses the prevention of accidental releases that have on-site impacts, whereas the section 112(r)(7) rule addresses the prevention of accidental releases that have off-site impacts.

Facilities that qualify for Program 1 regulation are not subject to the prevention program requirements.[266] Facilities in Program 2 have the option of complying with the specifically outlined prevention program requirements or developing their own prevention program according to general guidelines set out in the rule.[267] Program 3 facilities must comply with the fully outlined requirements.[268] Any facility that already is complying with OSHA PSM, however, need not undertake additional measures to be in compliance with the prevention program requirements of the section 112(r)(7) rule.[269]

The emergency response plan requirement of the RMP requires covered sources to develop procedures to respond to catastrophic accidental releases if they occur and to mitigate off-site consequences of those releases. Specific emergency response plan requirements are outlined in the rule and are the same for Program 2 and Program 3.[270] Facilities in Program 1 are not required to comply with these requirements but need only certify that emergency response procedures have been coordinated with the appropriate local agency.[271] A covered facility in Program 2 or Program 3 is not required to undertake additional measures to comply with the emergency response requirements of the section 112(r) rule if it can demonstrate that it already has a plan that complies with another comparable federal contingency plan regulation or is otherwise consistent with the National Response Team's Integrated Contingency Plan Guidance.[272] The rule also exempts a covered facility from the emergency response plan requirements if the facility can demonstrate that (1) its employees will not respond to accidental releases, (2) the facility has coordinated with local emergency response agencies for accidental releases, and (3) measures are in place for notifying the local emergency response agencies.[273]

Although the primary elements of EPA's rule have remained relatively unchanged since their adoption in 1996, the last ten years have seen significant changes in the details of portions of those rules. In 2013, in response to several catastrophic chemical facility incidents, President Obama issued an executive order directing Federal agencies to develop options for improved chemical facility safety and security.[274] In response, in 2017, in the last days of the Obama administration, EPA promulgated revisions to the accident prevention program requirements of the rule.[275] The revisions required, among other things, (1) additional safer technology and alternatives analysis (STAA) as part of the hazard analysis for some Program 3 processes; (2) third-party audits and incident investigation root cause analysis for Program 2 and Program 3 processes; (3) enhancements to the emergency preparedness requirements; and (4) increased public availability of chemical hazard information. The revisions also included changes to certain regulatory definitions and data elements submitted in risk management plans.[276] Although the rule was to take effect in sixty days, it allowed sources several years (e.g., until 2021 or 2022) to comply with the more significant changes.[277]

Multiple industry groups and states challenged the 2017 revisions[278] and submitted petitions for administrative reconsideration. Following the change in administration in 2017, the Trump EPA granted reconsideration, issued a 90-day stay of the effective date under section 307(d)(7)(B) of the Act, and convened a new rulemaking.[279] Just prior to expiration of that stay, EPA attempted to further delay the effective date of the rule through notice-and-comment rulemaking,[280] but that rule was vacated allowing the rule to go into effect.[281] The final rule on reconsideration, issued in 2019, repealed the most controversial portions of the 2017 rule, and modified others.[282] A number of environmental advocacy organizations challenged that 2019 final rule[283] and submitted petitions for administrative reconsideration, which EPA denied.[284]

After another change in administration in 2021 and President Biden's issuance of an executive order directing review of the 2019 rule, the challenges to the 2019 rule were held in abeyance. In 2022, EPA issued a new proposal to revise the 2019 rule that largely mirrors the provisions of the 2017 rule that were rescinded in 2019, while also adding new provisions to emphasize the need to address "natural hazards," including those caused by climate change.[285] According to EPA's fall 2022 regulatory agenda, the Agency projects issuing a final rule in 2023.

VI. Imminent and Substantial Endangerment

Whenever the Administrator determines that there may be "an imminent and substantial endangerment to the human health or welfare or the environment" from a listed substance, "the Administrator may secure such relief as may be necessary to abate such danger or threat."[286]

The federal district court in the area of the endangerment will have jurisdiction "to grant such relief as the public interest and the equities of the case may require."[287] The Administrator may take other actions, including "issuing such orders as may be necessary to protect human health."[288]

A. Chemical Process Safety Management

Section 304(a) of the 1990 amendments required the Secretary of Labor, in coordination with the EPA Administrator, to promulgate a chemical process safety standard to protect employees from hazards associated with accidental releases of highly hazardous chemicals in the workplace. Section 304(b) of the amendments required the Secretary of Labor to develop a list of such hazardous chemicals and include that list in the standard.

In 1992, the Secretary of Labor published the PSM rule.[289] The rule applies to any process involving a listed highly hazardous chemical at or above specified threshold quantities. The elements of the rule are largely replicated in the accidental release prevention program requirements under section 112(r)(7) and include requirements to develop process information, process hazard analyses, standard operating procedures, training, pre-startup review procedures, mechanical integrity requirements, management of change requirements, accident investigation procedures, safety audits, and emergency response procedures.

B. Chemical Safety Hazard Investigation Board

The 1990 amendments established an independent safety council called the Chemical Safety and Hazard Investigation Board, or CSB, which has up to five members appointed by the President of the United States.[290] The CSB is a non-enforcement agency that is independent and non-regulatory, with its main office in Washington, D.C. The purposes of the CSB are to: (1) investigate or cause to be investigated "any accidental release resulting in a fatality, serious injury or substantial property damages"; (2) issue periodic reports recommending measures to reduce the likelihood of these accidents and proposing corrective steps; and (3) establish by regulation requirements directing persons to report such accidental releases.[291] The CSB is one of the entities that receives risk management plans developed and submitted by facilities covered by EPA's regulations under section 112(r)(7).[292]

The President did not begin the appointment process of the CSB until 1997, after EPA and OSHA had promulgated the accidental release/risk management regulations. Consequently, the CSB did not participate in the rulemaking process for those regulations as contemplated by the statute.[293] Since the CSB began operations in 1998, it has coordinated with other agencies, including EPA and OSHA. The CSB has screened thousands of incidents, deployed to more than 170 incidents, published more than 100 investigation reports after conducting investigations (which routinely last six months to one year), issued more than 900 recommendations, and produced numerous safety videos since its inception. The CSB is currently operating under its 2022–2026 strategic plan.[294]

Despite the statutory directive that the CSB promulgate regulations requiring reporting of accidental releases, the CSB initially failed to implement that requirement. In 2009, the CSB published an advance notice of proposed rulemaking soliciting comment on such a rule,[295] but took no further action until an environmental advocacy organization sued to compel it.[296] The CSB took final action in 2020, promulgating a rule requiring reporting of basic information regarding accidental releases within eight hours of the release.[297]

VII. Study Provisions

Section 112 of the Act contains a number of study provisions, several of which have already been mentioned (including the electric utility study and oil and gas study). The amendments also required EPA to study mercury emissions and their health and environmental effects, atmospheric deposition of air toxics to the Great Lakes and other water bodies, and the potential hazards of hydrofluoric acid to human health and the environment. The amendments also mandated a comprehensive study of risk assessment methodology, its uses, and policy implications. These studies are discussed below.

A. The Mercury Studies

Section 112(n) required EPA to study the rate of mercury emissions from electric utilities, municipal waste incinerators, and other sources, the health and environmental effects of those emissions, and technologies available to control them. This study focused on both direct and indirect human health effects and environmental effects from mercury emissions. EPA released its eight-volume study in 1997.[298]

Section 112(n) also mandated a companion study by the National Institute of Environmental Health Science "to determine the threshold level of mercury exposure below which adverse human health effects are not expected to occur."[299] This report was submitted to Congress in 1993 and did not establish a health threshold for mercury.

B. The Great Waters Study

Section 112(m) of the Act requires EPA to study atmospheric deposition of air toxics to the Great Lakes, Lake Champlain, the Chesapeake Bay, and coastal waters and to determine whether additional emissions standards or control measures are necessary to prevent serious adverse health and environmental effects. This provision contains an ongoing reporting requirement. EPA was to submit its first report to Congress by November 1993 and to update that report every two years. If EPA determined, based on the results of the study, that additional controls are necessary, it was to promulgate regulations by 1995.

EPA released its First Great Waters Study in 1994, but declined to make a determination as to whether it needed additional regulatory authority to protect the Great Waters because of deficiencies in the data available.[300] EPA released its Second Great Waters Study in 1997[301] and then issued proposed findings that section 112 authorities are adequately protecting the Great Waters and that no additional regulations were "necessary and appropriate" under section 112(m)(6).[302] EPA finalized those findings in 1998.[303] In 2000, EPA issued its Third Great Waters Study, in which it evaluated more recent data and also committed to development of a work plan regarding air deposition problems.[304] EPA's Office of Air and Radiation and Office of Water released an *Air-Water Interface Work Plan* in 2001, that provided for collaborative efforts under the Clean Air Act and Clean Water Act. In 2007, EPA then issued a "Survey of New Findings in Scientific Literature Related to Atmospheric Deposition to the Great Waters," which focused on deposition of polycyclic aromatic hydrocarbons[305] and polychlorinated biphenyls.[306]

C. Hydrofluoric Acid

Section 112(n)(6) required the Administrator to complete a study of the potential hazards of hydrofluoric acid and make recommendations to Congress for the reduction of such hazards if appropriate. In 1993, EPA published its final report.[307] EPA's report did not recommend that Congress take any action to reduce the hazards associated with hydrofluoric acid. EPA found that the primary risk of exposure stemmed from potential accidental releases and that government agencies' authority, as well as the accidental release provisions of the Clean Air Act amendments, presented an appropriate framework for addressing that risk. The report did recommend, however, that EPA continue its Chemical Safety Audit program, investigate any chemical accidents associated with hydrofluoric acid, and investigate whether additional regulations are needed.

D. Risk Assessment and Management Commission

Section 303 of the 1990 amendments[308] established an independent commission called the Risk Assessment and Management Commission, which was required to "make a full investigation of the policy implications and appropriate uses of risk assessment and risk management in regulatory programs under various Federal laws to prevent cancer and other chronic human health effects which may result from exposure to hazardous substances."

The Commission was required to consider the National Academy of Sciences' report on risk assessment methodologies required under section 112(*o*) of the Act and to evaluate the use and limitations of risk assessment in setting standards, the most appropriate methods for measuring and describing risks, methods for reflecting uncertainties, and various risk management policy issues. The Commission also was required to comment on the possibility or desirability of developing "a consistent risk assessment methodology, or a consistent standard of acceptable risk, among various Federal programs."[309] The Commission's two-volume report was made available in 1997.[310]

Notes

1. Titles of the CAA correspond to subchapters in the U.S. Code.
2. CAA § 112(b)(1), 42 U.S.C. § 7412(b)(1).
3. Hydrogen sulfide was inadvertently included as a HAP but removed through a joint resolution by the House and Senate in 1991. *See* Joint Resolution to make a Technical Correction in Public Law 101-549, Pub. L. No. 102-187, 105 Stat. 1285 (1991). Hydrogen sulfide is still regulated under section 112(r), discussed below.
4. *See* Hazardous Air Pollutant List; Modification, 61 Fed. Reg. 30,816 (June 18, 1996) (deleting caprolactam); Redefinition of the Glycol Ethers Category Under Section 112(b)(1) of the Clean Air Act and Section 101 of the Comprehensive Environmental Response, Compensation, and Liability Act, 65 Fed. Reg. 47,342 (Aug. 2, 2000) (removing surfactant alcohol ethoxylates and their derivatives from the glycol ethers category); List of Hazardous Air Pollutants, Petition Process, Lesser Quantity Designations, Source Category List; Petition To Delist of Ethylene Glycol Monobutyl Ether, 69 Fed. Reg. 69,320 (Nov. 29, 2004) (removing ethylene glycol monobutyl ether from the glycol ethers group); List of Hazardous Air Pollutants, Petition Process, Lesser Quantity Designations, Source Category List, 70 Fed. Reg. 75,047 (Dec. 19, 2005) (deleting methyl ethyl ketone); Clean Air Act Section 112 List of Hazardous Air Pollutant: Amendments to the List of Hazardous Air Pollutants (HAP), 87 Fed. Reg. 393 (Jan. 5, 2022) (adding 1-bromopropane (1-BP)).
5. *See* CAA § 108(a), 42 U.S.C. § 7408(a).
6. *Id.* § 112(b)(2), 42 U.S.C. § 7412(b)(2).
7. *Id.* § 112(b)(6), 42 U.S.C. § 7412(b)(6).
8. *Id.* § 112(b)(2), 42 U.S.C. § 7412(b)(2).
9. *Id.*
10. *Id.*
11. *Id.* § 112(a)(7), 42 U.S.C. § 7412(a)(7).
12. *See id.* § 112(b)(2), 42 U.S.C. § 7412(b)(2).
13. *Id.* § 112(b)(3)(A), 42 U.S.C. § 7412(b)(3)(A).

14. Hazardous Air Pollutants List; Notice of Denial, 58 Fed. Reg. 4164, 4165 (Jan. 13, 1993); *see also* Hazardous Air Pollutants List; Notice of denial of petition to delist methanol, 66 Fed. Reg. 21,929, 21,930 (May 2, 2001).
15. 66 Fed. Reg. at 21,930.
16. CAA § 112(b)(3)(A), 42 U.S.C. § 7412(b)(3)(A).
17. *Id.* § 112(b)(3)(B), (C), 42 U.S.C. § 7412(b)(3)(B), (C).
18. *Id.* § 112(b)(4), 42 U.S.C. § 7412(b)(4).
19. *Id.* § 112(b)(3)(A), 42 U.S.C. § 7412(b)(3)(A).
20. Granting Petition to Add 1-bromopropane (Also Known as 1-BP) to the List of Hazardous Air Pollutants, 85 Fed. Reg. 36,851 (June 18, 2020).
21. 87 Fed. Reg. at 394.
22. *Id.*
23. CAA § 112(e)(4), 42 U.S.C. § 7412(e)(4).
24. 87 Fed. Reg. at 395.
25. CAA § 112(c), 42 U.S.C. § 7412(c)
26. Initial List of Categories of Sources Under Section 112(c)(1) of the Clean Air Act Amendments of 1990, 57 Fed. Reg. 31,576, 31,591–92 (July 16, 1992).
27. *Id.* at 31,576.
28. CAA § 112(c)(1), 42 U.S.C. § 7412(c)(1).
29. *See id.* § 112(c)(5), 42 U.S.C. § 7412(c)(5).
30. National Emission Standards for Hazardous Air Pollutants: Revision of Source Category List Under Section 112 of the Clean Air Act, 67 Fed. Reg. 6521 (Feb. 12, 2002).
31. CAA § 112(e)(4), 42 U.S.C. § 7412(e)(4).
32. *Id.* § 112(e)(1)(E), 42 U.S.C. § 7412(e)(1)(E).
33. EPA maintains an applicability determinations index regarding source-specific determinations under section 112 on its website.
34. CAA § 112(a)(1), 42 U.S.C. § 7412(a)(1). EPA interpreted the pre-1990 Act to require regulation only of source categories that pose significant public health risks. Environmental advocacy organizations, by contrast, argued that standards should be set for all sources of a HAP, no matter how small. The 1990 amendments take a middle ground—defining a tonnage threshold as the trigger for categorization and regulation, regardless of health risk.

In 2000, EPA issued "Guidance on the Major Source Determination for Certain Hazardous Air Pollutants" (signed Aug. 14, 2000), which clarified the application of the tonnage thresholds to listed aggregate groups of HAPs, such as xylenes and dibenzofurans.

35. *See* CAA § 111(a)(3), 42 U.S.C. § 7412(a)(3).
36. *Nat'l Mining Ass'n v. EPA*, 59 F.3d 1351, 1354–55 (D.C. Cir. 1995) (per curiam).
37. CAA § 112(a)(1), 42 U.S.C. § 7412(a)(1).
38. *Id.*
39. *Nat'l Mining Ass'n*, 59 F.3d at 1354.
40. CAA § 112(c)(3), 42 U.S.C. § 7412(c)(3).
41. *Id.*
42. *Id.* § 112(k)(3)(A), 42 U.S.C. § 7412(k)(3)(A).

43. National Air Toxics Program: The Integrated Urban Strategy, 64 Fed. Reg. 38,706 (July 19, 1999).

44. *Id.* at 38,706.

45. *Id.* at 38,720.

46. Completion of the Requirement To Promulgate Emission Standards, 76 Fed. Reg. 15,308 (Mar. 21, 2011). A compiled list of area source rules is available on EPA's Air Toxics Website.

47. Memorandum from John S. Seitz, Dir., Office of Air Quality Planning & Standards, EPA, to Linda Murphy, EPA Region I et al., Potential to Emit for MACT Standards—Guidance on Timing Issues at 9–10 (May 16, 1995).

48. National Emission Standards for Hazardous Air Pollutants: General Provisions, 72 Fed. Reg. 69 (proposed Jan. 3, 2007).

49. Memorandum from William L. Wehrum, Assistant Adm'r, Office of Air & Radiation, EPA, to Reg'l Air Div. Dirs., EPA, Reclassification of Major Sources as Area Sources Under Section 112 of the Clean Air Act (Jan. 25, 2018).

50. *Cal. Cmtys. Against Toxics v. EPA*, 934 F.3d 627, 638 (D.C. Cir. 2019) (finding the memorandum was not final action because it had "no direct and appreciable legal consequences").

51. Reclassification of Major Sources as Area Sources Under Section 112 of the Clean Air Act, 85 Fed. Reg. 73,854 (Nov. 19, 2020).

52. *Cal. Cmtys. Against Toxics v. EPA*, No. 21-1024 (and consolidated cases) (D.C. Cir. filed Jan. 15, 2021).

53. Exec. Order No. 13990, Protecting Public Health and the Environment and Restoring Science To Tackle the Climate Crisis (Jan. 20, 2021), *reprinted in* 86 Fed. Reg. 7037, 7038 (Jan. 25, 2021) ("Executive Order 13990").

54. CAA § 112(c)(9)(B), 42 U.S.C. § 7412(c)(9)(B).

55. *See, for example,* National Emission Standards for Hazardous Air Pollutants: Revision of Source Category List Under Section 112 of the Clean Air Act, 67 Fed. Reg. 6521 (Feb. 12, 2002); National Emission Standards for Hazardous Air Pollutants: Revision of Source Category List and Schedule for Standards Under Section 112 of the Clean Air Act, 66 Fed. Reg. 8220 (Jan. 30, 2001); National Emission Standards for Hazardous Air Pollutants: Revision of Source Category List and Schedule for Standards Under Section 112 of the Clean Air Act, 64 Fed. Reg. 63,025 (Nov. 18, 1999); National Emission Standards for Hazardous Air Pollutants; Revision of List of Categories of Sources and Schedule for Standards Under Section 112 of the Clean Air Act, 63 Fed. Reg. 7155 (Feb. 12, 1998); Delisting of Source Category and Revision of Initial List of Categories of Sources and Schedule for Standards Under Section 112(c) of the Clean Air Act, 60 Fed. Reg. 61,550 (Nov. 30, 1995).

56. EPA issued guidance entitled "Information on EPA's Delisting Process" for use by potential petitioners. Memorandum from Sally L. Shaver, Dir., EPA, to Potential Petitioners Seeking Delisting of Hazardous Air Pollutants or Source Categories, Information on EPA's Delisting Process (undated).

57. *E.g.*, National Emission Standards for Hazardous Air Pollutants; Revision of Initial List of Categories of Sources and Schedule for Standards Under Sections 112(c) and (e) of the Clean Air Act Amendments of 1990, 61 Fed. Reg. 28,197, 28,200 (June 4, 1996) ("The Agency is not invoking the authority within Section 112(c)(9) for deleting source categories . . . . Instead, in today's notice, the Agency is simply contending that the data originally used for listing were erroneous, and that, based on newer data, the original listings are not warranted.").

58. *New Jersey v. EPA*, 517 F.3d 574, 583 (D.C. Cir. 2008). This case is discussed further in Section IV.

59. *Nat. Res. Def. Council v. EPA*, 489 F.3d 1364, 1372 (D.C. Cir. 2007) (quoting CAA § 112(c)(9)(B)(i), 42 U.S.C. § 7412(c)(9)(B)(i)) (emphases added).

60. CAA § 112(d)(3), 42 U.S.C. § 7412(d)(3).

61. *Id.*

62. *See id.* § 112(d)(3)(A), (B), 42 U.S.C. § 7412(d)(3)(A), (B).

63. *Id.* § 112(d)(3)(A), 42 U.S.C. § 7412(d)(3)(A).

64. *Id.* § 112(d)(3)(B), 42 U.S.C. § 7412(d)(3)(B).

65. *Id.* § 112(d)(2), 42 U.S.C. § 7412(d)(2).

66. *Nat'l Lime Ass'n v. EPA*, 233 F.3d 625, 633–34 (D.C. Cir. 2000) (rejecting EPA's "no control" floors for certain HAPs); *see also Sierra Club v. EPA*, 479 F.3d 875, 883 (D.C. Cir. 2007) (per curiam) (same).

67. *Nat'l Lime Ass'n*, 233 F.3d at 637.

68. *Mossville Env't Action Now v. EPA*, 370 F.3d 1232, 1242–43 (D.C. Cir. 2004).

69. *Sierra Club,* 479 F.3d at 880–81.

70. *See Cement Kiln Recycling Coal. v. EPA*, 255 F.3d 885, 861 (D.C. Cir. 2001) (per curiam) ("EPA may not deviate from section 7412(d)(3)'s requirement that floors reflect what the best performers actually achieve by claiming that floors must be achievable by all sources using MACT technology.").

71. *See id.* at 867 (citing *Sierra Club v. EPA*, 167 F.3d 658, 662, 665 (D.C. Cir. 1999)).

72. *Mossville*, 370 F.3d at 1240–42; *Cement Kiln*, 255 F.3d at 866.

73. *Sierra Club*, 479 F.3d at 882–83.

74. *Mossville*, 370 F.3d at 1241 (quoting *Cement Kiln*, 255 F.3d at 865).

75. *Sierra Club*, 479 F.3d at 882.

76. *U.S. Sugar Corp. v. EPA,* 830 F.3d 579, 636 (D.C. Cir. 2016) (per curiam).

77. *Nat'l Lime Ass'n,* 233 F.3d at 634.

78. *U.S. Sugar*, 830 F.3d at 608.

79. *Id.* at 611.

80. *See, e.g.*, *Nat'l Lime Ass'n*, 233 F.3d at 632.

81. CAA § 129(a)(2), 42 U.S.C. § 7429(a)(2); *Ne. Md. Waste Disposal Auth. v. EPA*, 358 F.3d 936, 944 (D.C. Cir. 2004) (per curiam) (summarizing MACT analysis under section 129).

82. *Nat. Res. Def. Council*, 489 F.3d at 1256 (quoting section 129(h)(2)) ("'no solid waste incineration unit subject to performance standards under [sections 129 and 111] . . . shall be subject to standards under section 7412(d)'").

83. *See, e.g., id.* at 1254 (vacating an EPA rule that defined "commercial or industrial waste" for purposes of section 129); *Portland Cement Ass'n v. EPA*, 665 F.3d 177 (D.C. Cir. 2011) (per curiam) (vacating section 112 standards promulgated for Portland cement facilities because of interdependence issues between sections 112 and section 129).

84. *U.S. Sugar*, 830 F.3d at 596.

85. *Id.*

86. Standards of Performance for New Stationary Sources and Emission Guidelines for Existing Sources: Commercial and Industrial Solid Waste Incineration Units, 76 Fed. Reg. 15,704 (Mar. 21, 2011); Identification of Non-Hazardous Secondary Materials That Are Solid Waste, 76 Fed. Reg. 15,456 (Mar. 21, 2011).

87. Commercial and Industrial Solid Waste Incineration Units: Reconsideration and Final Amendments; Non-Hazardous Secondary Materials That Are Solid Waste, 78 Fed. Reg. 9112, 9116–17 (Feb. 7, 2013) (discussing division between sections 112 and 129).

88. *U.S. Sugar*, 830 F.3d at 664.

89. CAA § 112(d)(4), 42 U.S.C. § 7412(d)(4).

90. *See, e.g., Sierra Club v. EPA*, 895 F.3d 1 (D.C. Cir. 2018) (finding EPA's use of health-based standards for acid gas emissions from brick and ceramics kilns unreasonable on several grounds); *U.S. Sugar*, 830 F.3d at 624–26 (upholding EPA's refusal to set such a standard for boilers due in part to concerns regarding potential cumulative health impacts of other nearby sources and the co-benefits of enforcing a MACT floor).

91. CAA § 112(d)(5), 42 U.S.C. § 7412(d)(5).

92. *See, e.g.,* National Emission Standards for Hazardous Air Pollutants for Area Sources: Electric Arc Furnace Steelmaking Facilities, 72 Fed. Reg. 74,088, 74,089–91 (Dec. 28, 2007) (summarizing GACT requirements for electric arc furnace steelmaking facilities that are area sources).

93. *U.S. Sugar*, 830 F.3d at 595.

94. CAA § 112(e)(1), 42 U.S.C. § 7412(e)(1).

95. *Id.* § 112(e)(3), 42 U.S.C. § 7412(e)(3).

96. 42 U.S.C. § 7412(d)(6).

97. *Nat'l Ass'n for Surface Finishing v. EPA*, 795 F.3d 1, 8–9 (D.C. Cir. 2015); *Ass'n of Battery Recyclers, Inc. v. EPA*, 716 F.3d 667, 672 (D.C. Cir. 2013) (per curiam).

98. *La. Envt'l Action Network v. EPA*, 955 F.3d 1088 (D.C. Cir. 2020) (*LEAN*) (rejecting EPA's interpretation of the CAA as providing the Agency the option of limiting its review to previously regulated HAP).

99. CAA § 112(j), 42 U.S.C. § 7412(j).

100. *Id.* § 112(j)(2), 42 U.S.C. § 7412(j)(2).

101. *Id.* § 112(j)(2), (3), 42 U.S.C. § 7412(j)(2), (3). The application must be reviewed and approved or disapproved according to the Title V operating permit procedures discussed in chapter 5. *Id.* § 112(j)(4), 42 U.S.C. § 7412(j)(4).

102. 40 C.F.R. § 63.53.

103. CAA § 112(j)(6), 42 U.S.C. § 7412(j)(6).

104. *Id.*

105. 40 C.F.R. §§ 63.50–63.56.

106. National Emission Standards for Hazardous Air Pollutants for Source Categories: General Provisions; and Requirements for Control Technology Determinations for Major Sources in Accordance With Clean Air Act Sections, Sections 112(g) and 112(j), 68 Fed. Reg. 32,586 (May 30, 2003).

107. Requirements for Control Technology Determinations for Major Sources in Accordance With Clean Air Act Sections, Sections 112(g) and 112(j), 75 Fed. Reg. 15,655, 15,657 (proposed Mar. 30, 2010).

108. 57 Fed. Reg. at 31,576.

109. 40 C.F.R. §§ 63.40–63.44; *see also* Hazardous Air Pollutants: Regulations Governing Constructed or Reconstructed Major Sources, 61 Fed. Reg. 68,384 (Dec. 27, 1996); Hazardous Air Pollutants: Regulations Governing Constructed or Reconstructed Major Sources, 64 Fed. Reg. 35,029 (June 30, 1999) (extending period of time for EPA to make case-by-case determination if permitting authority does not yet have section 112(g) procedures in place).

110. 61 Fed. Reg. at 68,388.

111. 40 C.F.R. § 63.41.

112. CAA § 112(h)(1), 42 U.S.C. § 7412(h)(1).

113. *Id.*

114. *Id.* § 112(h)(2), 42 U.S.C. § 7412(h)(2); *see, for example., Sierra Club v EPA*, 884 F.3d 1185 (D.C. Cir. 2018) (upholding use of work practice standards for boilers during periods of startup and shutdown due to the infeasibility of setting numeric limits); *see also Sierra Club*, 479 F.3d at 884 (holding that lack of emissions data alone is not a sufficient basis for invocation of the need for work practice standards).

115. CAA § 112(h)(3), 42 U.S.C. § 7412(h)(3).

116. *Id.* § 112(f)(1), 42 U.S.C. § 7412(f)(1).

117. *Id.*

118. EPA, EPA-453/R-99-001, Residual Risk Report to Congress (Mar. 1999).

119. CAA § 112(f)(2), 42 U.S.C. § 7412(f)(2). The Administrator is not required to conduct any review or promulgate any emission limitations based on residual risk for area source categories or subcategories for which GACT emission standards have been promulgated. *Id.* § 112(f)(5), 42 U.S.C. § 7412(f)(5). EPA has interpreted the Act to only require residual risk review in connection with its initial adoption of MACT standards and not after each subsequent technology review and at least one court has concurred. *See Citizens for Pennsylvania's Future v. Wheeler*, 469 F. Supp. 3d 920 (N.D. Cal. 2020).

120. *Id.* § 112(f)(2)(A), 42 U.S.C. § 7412(f)(2)(A). In residual risk rulemaking, EPA may use any reasonable data source, including industry-supplied data. *See Nat. Res. Def. Council v. EPA*, 529 F.3d 1077, 1086 (D.C. Cir. 2008).

121. *Nat. Res. Def. Council,* 529 F.3d at 1077.

122. *Id.* at 1081.

123. *Id.* at 1083.

124. National Emission Standards for Hazardous Air Pollutants; Benzene Emissions From Maleic Anhydride Plants, Ethylbenzene/Styrene Plants, Benzene Storage Vessels, Benzene Equipment Leaks, and Coke By-Product Recovery Plants, 54 Fed. Reg. 38,044 (Sept. 14, 1989).

125. *Nat. Res. Def. Council v. EPA*, 824 F.2d 1146 (D.C. Cir. 1987).

126. 54 Fed. Reg. at 38,048.

127. *Id.* at 38,045.

128. *Nat. Res. Def. Council,* 529 F.3d at 1083 (quoting 54 Fed. Reg. at 38,045) (emphasis in original).

129. *Id.* at 1082.

130. CAA § 112(f)(3), 42 U.S.C.§ 7412(f)(3).

131. *Id.* § 112(f)(4)(A), 42 U.S.C.§ 7412(f)(4)(A).

132. *Id.* § 112(f)(4)(B), 42 U.S.C.§ 7412(f)(4)(B).

133. *Id.* § 112(q)(1), 42 U.S.C. § 7412(q)(1).

134. *Id.* § 112(q)(2), 42 U.S.C. § 7412(q)(2).

135. *Id.* § 112(q)(3), 42 U.S.C. § 7412(q)(3).

136. *Id.* §112(i)(2), 42 U.S.C.§ 7412(i)(2).

137. *Id.* § 112(i)(2)(A), (B), 42 U.S.C. § 7412(i)(2)(A), (B).

138. *Id.* § 112(i)(3)(A), 42 U.S.C.§ 7412(i)(3)(A).

139. *Id.* § 112(i)(3)(A), (B), 42 U.S.C. § 7412(i)(3)(A), (B). The Part 63 General Provisions, discussed below in further detail, provide additional information regarding the application for and the approval of section 112(i)(3)(B) compliance extensions. *See* 40 C.F.R. § 63.6(i).

140. CAA § 112(i)(5), 42 U.S.C. § 7412(i)(5).

141. *See* 40 C.F.R. pt. 63, subpt. D.

142. CAA § 112(i)(4), 42 U.S.C. § 7412(i)(4).

143. *See* 40 C.F.R. pt. 63, subpt. A.

144. CAA § 112(a)(1), 42 U.S.C. § 7412(a)(1).

145. 40 C.F.R. § 63.2.

146. *Id.* (emphasis added).

147. *Nat'l Mining Ass'n*, 59 F.3d at 1363–1364 ("What EPA has not explained is how its refusal to consider limitations other than those that are 'federally enforceable' serves the statute's directive to 'consider[] controls' when it results in a refusal to credit controls imposed by a state or locality even if they are unquestionably effective.").

148. Memorandum from John S. Seitz, Dir., Office of Air Quality Planning & Standards, EPA, & Robert I. Van Heuvelen, Dir., Office of Regulatory Enforcement, EPA, to EPA Reg'l Dirs., Options for Limiting the Potential to Emit (PTE) of a Stationary Source Under Section 112 and Title V of the Clean Air Act (Act) (Jan. 25, 2005).

149. *See, e.g.,* Memorandum from John S. Seitz, Dir., Office of Air Quality Planning & Standards, EPA, & Eric V. Schaeffer, Dir., Office of Regulatory Enforcement, EPA, to EPA Reg'l Dirs., Third Extension of January 25, 1995 Potential to Emit Transition Policy (Dec. 20, 1999); Memorandum from John S. Seitz, Dir., Office of Air Quality Planning & Standards, EPA, & Eric Schaeffer, Dir., Office of Regulatory Enforcement, EPA, to EPA Reg'l Dirs., Potential to Emit (PTE) Guidance for Specific Source Categories (Apr. 14, 1998); *see also* Memorandum from Bruce Buckheit, Dir., Air Enforcement Div., Office of Enforcement & Compliance Assurance, EPA, & Lydia Wegman, Deputy Dir., Office of Air Quality Planning and Standards, EPA, to Clean Air Act Advisory Comm. Subcomm.

on Permits/NSR/Toxic Integration, Discussion Paper on Options for the Potential to Emit Rulemaking (Nov. 3, 1997).

150. 85 Fed. Reg. at 73,875–76.

151. 40 C.F.R. §§ 63.7, 63.8. With regard to monitoring issues, whether under the General Provisions or specific MACT standards, courts are generally deferential to EPA. *See, e.g.*, *Nat'l Lime Ass'n v. EPA*, 233 F.3d at 634.

152. National Emission Standards for Hazardous Air Pollutants for Source Categories: General Provisions, 59 Fed. Reg. 12,408, 12,418 (Mar. 16, 1994).

153. *See* Compliance Assurance Monitoring, 62 Fed. Reg. 54,900 (Oct. 22, 1997). This rule is discussed in more detail in chapter 4.

154. *See* 40 C.F.R. § 64.2(b)(1).

155. 59 Fed. Reg. at 12,419.

156. Restructuring of the Stationary Source Audit Program, 75 Fed. Reg. 55,636 (Sept. 13, 2010).

157. *See* 40 C.F.R. § 63.6.

158. *Id.* § 63.6(e)(3).

159. *Sierra Club v. EPA*, 551 F.3d 1019, 1028 (D.C. Cir. 2008).

160. Letter from Adam M. Kushner, Dir., Office of Civil Enforcement, EPA, to Charles H. Knauss, Bingham McCutchen LLP et al., Vacatur of Startup, Shutdown, and Malfunction (SSM) Exemption (40 C.F.R. §§ 63.6(f)(1) and 63.6(h)(1)) (July 22, 2009).

161. Court Vacatur of Exemption From Emission Standards During Periods of Startup, Shutdown, and Malfunction, 86 Fed. Reg. 13,819 (Mar. 11, 2021).

162. *See* 40 C.F.R. §§ 63.9, 63.10.

163. 40 C.F.R. § 70.3(a)(3); Operating Permit Program, 57 Fed. Reg. 32,250, 32,295, 32,297 (July 21, 1992). The Title V permit rules allow states to exempt area sources from the permitting requirement for five years. 40 C.F.R. § 70.3(b)(1); 57 Fed. Reg. at 32,261, 32,297.

164. CAA § 112(*l*)(1), 42 U.S.C. § 7412(*l*)(1). The accidental release provisions of section 112(r) are discussed in the following section of this chapter.

165. *See* 40 C.F.R. § 63.99 (listing states and their delegation status).

166. CAA § 112(*l*)(5), 42 U.S.C. § 7412(*l*)(5).

167. *Id.*

168. *Id.* § 112(*l*)(6), 42 U.S.C. § 7412(*l*)(6).

169. *Id.*

170. *Id.* § 112(*l*)(7), 42 U.S.C. § 7412(*l*)(7).

171. *Id.* § 112(*l*)(8), 42 U.S.C. § 7412(*l*)(8).

172. 40 C.F.R. pt. 63, subpt. E.

173. *La. Env't Action Network v. Browner*, 87 F.3d 1379 (D.C. Cir. 1996).

174. Hazardous Air Pollutants: Amendments to the Approval of State Programs and Delegation of Federal Authorities, 65 Fed. Reg. 55,810, 55,814 (Sept. 14, 2000).

175. EPA, EPA-452/R-09-006, Rish and Technology Review (RTR), Risk Assessment Methodologies: For Review by the EPA's Science Advisory Board, Case Studies—MACT I Petroleum Refining Sources, Portland Cement Manufacturing (June 2009).

176. Letter from Drs. Deborah L. Swackhamer & Jana Milford, Chairs, Science Advisory Board, EPA, to Lisa Jackson, Adm'r, EPA (May 7, 2010) (transmitting Science Advisory Board's review of draft RTR report).

177. *See, e.g.*, *Cal. Cmtys. Against Toxics v. Pruitt*, 241 F. Supp. 3d 199 (D.D.C. 2017) (twenty source categories); *Blue Ridge Env't Def. League v. Pruitt*, 261 F. Supp. 3d 53 (D.D.C. 2017) (thirteen source categories); *Community In-Power and Dev. Ass'n v. Pruitt*, 304 F. Supp. 3d 212 (D.D.C. 2018) (nine source categories).

178. Office of Inspector General, U.S. EPA, Report No. 22-E-0026, The EPA Needs to Develop a Strategy to Complete Overdue Residual Risk and Technology Reviews and to Meet the Statutory Deadlines for Upcoming Reviews (Mar. 30, 2022). EPA maintains a list of the status of its RTR actions relative to court-ordered deadlines on its website.

179. 955 F.3d 1088.

180. CAA § 112(a)(8), 42 U.S.C. § 7412(a)(8).

181. *Id.*

182. *Id.* § 112(n)(1), 42 U.S.C. § 7412(n)(1).

183. *Id.* § 112(n)(1)(A), 42 U.S.C. § 7412(n)(1)(A).

184. *Id.*

185. Regulatory Finding on the Emissions of Hazardous Air Pollutants From Electric Utility Steam Generating Units; Notice of Regulatory Finding, 65 Fed. Reg. 79,825, 79,826 (Dec. 20, 2000).

186. *See Util. Air Regulatory Grp. v. EPA*, No. 01-1074, 2001 WL 936363, at *1 (D.C. Cir. July 26, 2001).

187. Revision of December 2000 Regulatory Finding on the Emissions of Hazardous Air Pollutants From Electric Utility Steam Generating Units and the Removal of Coal- and Oil-Fired Electric Utility Steam Generating Units From the Section 112(c) List, 70 Fed. Reg. 15,994, 15,994 (Mar. 29, 2005).

188. Standards of Performance for New and Existing Stationary Sources: Electric Utility Steam Generating Units, 70 Fed. Reg. 28,606 (May 18, 2005).

189. *New Jersey v. EPA*, 517 F.3d at 583.

190. *Id.*

191. National Emission Standards for Hazardous Air Pollutants From Coal- and Oil-Fired Electric Utility Steam Generating Units and Standards of Performance for Fossil-Fuel-Fired Electric Utility, Industrial-Commercial-Institutional, and Small Industrial-Commercial-Institutional Steam Generating Units, 77 Fed. Reg. 9304, 9364 (Feb. 16, 2012).

192. *Id.* at 9306, 9413, 9425.

193. Reconsideration of Certain New Source Issues: National Emission Standards for Hazardous Air Pollutants From Coal- and Oil-Fired Electric Utility Steam Generating Units and Standards of Performance for Fossil-Fuel-Fired Electric Utility, Industrial-Commercial-Institutional, and Small Industrial-Commercial-Institutional Steam Generating Units, 78 Fed. Reg. 24,073 (Apr. 24, 2013).

194. Reconsideration of Certain Startup/Shutdown Issues: National Emission Standards for Hazardous Air Pollutants From Coal- and Oil-Fired Electric Utility Steam

Generating Units and Standards of Performance for Fossil-Fuel-Fired Electric Utility, Industrial-Commercial-Institutional, and Small Industrial-Commercial-Institutional Steam Generating Units, 79 Fed. Reg. 68,777 (Nov. 19, 2014).

195. Reconsideration on the Mercury and Air Toxics Standards (MATS) and the Utility New Source Performance Standards; Final Action, 80 Fed. Reg. 24,218 (Apr. 30, 2015).

196. *See Chesapeake Bay Found, Inc. v. EPA*, No. 13-1200 (and consolidated cases) (D.C. Cir. filed June 24, 2013) (challenge to new source standards revisions in abeyance pending EPA's action on a voluntary remand of certain standards); *Chesapeake Climate Action Network v. EPA*, No. 15-1192 (and consolidated cases) (D.C. Cir. filed June 29, 2015) (challenge to denial of reconsideration of particulate matter standards in abeyance pending EPA's review of rule); *Chesapeake Climate Action Network v. EPA*, 952 F.3d 310 (D.C. Cir. 2020) (finding EPA did not provide the petitioners opportunity to comment on the basis for use of work practice standards rather than numerical emission limitations).

197. *White Stallion Energy Ctr., LLC v. EPA*, 748 F.3d 1222, 1237, 1241 (D.C. Cir. 2014) (per curiam).

198. *Michigan v. EPA*, 576 U.S. 743, 752, 759 (2015).

199. Supplemental Finding That It Is Appropriate and Necessary To Regulate Hazardous Air Pollutants From Coal-and Oil-Fired Electric Utility Steam Generating Units," 81 Fed. Reg. 24,420 (Apr. 25, 2016).

200. *Murray Energy Corp. v. EPA*, No. 16–1127 (and consolidated cases) (D.C. Cir. filed Apr. 25, 2016). This challenge was placed in abeyance.

201. National Emission Standards for Hazardous Air Pollutants: Coal- and Oil-Fired Electric Utility Steam Generating Units—Reconsideration of Supplemental Finding and Residual Risk and Technology Review, 85 Fed. Reg. 31,286 (May 22, 2020).

202. *Id.* at 31,299, 31,301.

203. *Id.* at 31,312.

204. *American Academy of Pediatrics v. Regan*, No. 20-1221 (and consolidated cases) (D.C. Cir. filed June 19, 2020) (challenge to the revocation); *Air Alliance Houston v. EPA*, No. 20–1268 (D.C. Cir. filed July 21, 2020) (challenge to the RTR determination). The latter case was placed in abeyance pending EPA's review of a petition for administrative reconsideration. A third challenge to the action, by a coal company, also was held in abeyance pending resolution of the other cases. *Westmoreland Mining Holdings LLC v. EPA*, No. 20–1160 (D.C. Cir. filed May 22, 2020).

205. National Emission Standards for Hazardous Air Pollutants: Coal- and Oil-Fired Electric Utility Steam Generating Units—Revocation of the 2020 Reconsideration and Affirmation of the Appropriate and Necessary Supplemental Finding, 88 Fed. Reg. 13,956 (Mar. 6, 2023).

206. CAA § 112(n)(4)(A), 42 U.S.C. § 7412(n)(4)(A).

207. National Emission Standards for Hazardous Air Pollutants: Oil and Natural Gas Production and National Emission Standards for Hazardous Air Pollutants: Natural Gas Transmission and Storage, 64 Fed. Reg. 32,610, 32,629 (June 17, 1999) (emphasis added).

208. Oil and Natural Gas Sector: New Source Performance Standards and National Emission Standards for Hazardous Air Pollutants Reviews, 77 Fed. Reg. 49,490, 49,569 (Aug. 16, 2012).

209. *Am. Petroleum Inst. v. EPA*, No. 12–1405 (and consolidated cases) (D.C. Cir. filed Oct. 15, 2012).

210. Oil and Natural Gas Sector: National Emission Standards for Hazardous Air Pollutants, 80 Fed. Reg. 74,068 (Nov. 27, 2015).

211. Letter from E. Scott Pruitt, Adm'r, EPA, to Petitioners (Oct. 6, 2017).

212. Proposed Consent Decree, Clean Air Act Citizen Suit, 88 Fed. Reg. 4178 (Jan. 24, 2023).

213. CAA § 112(n)(4)(B), 42 U.S.C. § 7412(n)(4)(B).

214. 64 Fed. Reg. at 32,611.

215. *See* 64 Fed. Reg. at 38,706.

216. National Emission Standards for Hazardous Air Pollutants for Source Categories From Oil and Natural Gas Production Facilities, 72 Fed. Reg. 26 (Jan. 3, 2007).

217. CAA § 112(n)(5), 42 U.S.C. § 7412(n)(5).

218. EPA, EPA-453/R-93-045, Report to Congress on Hydrogen Sulfide Air Emissions Associated with the Extraction of Oil and Natural Gas (Oct. 1993).

219. *Id.* at iii.

220. *Id.*

221. CAA § 112(n)(7), 42 U.S.C. § 7412(n)(7).

222. *See* EPA Region IV, CAA and RCRA Overlap Provisions in Subparts AA, BB, and CC of 40 CFR Parts 264 and 265, at vii (Oct. 2000); *see also Cement Kiln*, 255 F.3d at 858 (discussing overlap between RCRA and CAA).

223. Hazardous Waste Treatment, Storage, and Disposal Facilities and Hazardous Waste Generators; Organic Air Emission Standards for Tanks, Surface Impoundments, and Containers, 61 Fed. Reg. 59,932, 59,938 (Nov. 25, 1996).

224. 40 C.F.R. § 63.95.

225. CAA § 112(r)(3), 42 U.S.C. § 7412(r)(3).

226. *See* 42 U.S.C. § 11002. The EHS list is published at 40 C.F.R. part 355.

227. CAA § 112(r)(3), 42 U.S.C. § 7412(r)(3).

228. *Id.*

229. *Id.*

230. *Id.* § 112(r)(5), 42 U.S.C. § 7412(r)(5).

231. *See* Comprehensive Environmental Response, Compensation and Liability Act (CERCLA) §§ 102, 103, 42 U.S.C. §§ 9602, 9603. Section 102(b) of CERCLA establishes a default reportable quantity value of one pound unless EPA specifies otherwise by rule.

232. List of Regulated Substances and Thresholds for Accidental Release Prevention; Requirements for Petitions Under Section 112(r) of the Clean Air Act as Amended, 59 Fed. Reg. 4478 (Jan. 31, 1994) (codified at 40 C.F.R. § 68.130). In the 1994 rule, EPA also promulgated the applicability provisions and definitions for the section 112(r)(7) regulations (discussed below), which EPA promulgated in full in 1996.

233. List of Regulated Substances and Thresholds for Accidental Release Prevention; Amendments, 63 Fed. Reg. 640 (Jan. 6, 1998).

234. List of Regulated Substances and Thresholds for Accidental Release Prevention, 62 Fed. Reg. 45,130 (Aug. 25, 1997).

235. A copy of the list appears in Appendix 3.

236. CAA § 112(r)(1), 42 U.S.C. § 7412(r)(1) (emphasis added). Thus, the general duty clause applies regardless of whether that substance is listed under section 112(r)(3).

237. *Id.* EPA has issued guidance regarding the "general duty" clause. *See, e.g.*, EPA, EPA 550-B00-002, Guidance for Implementation of the General Duty Clause, Clean Air Act Section 112(r)(1) (May 2000).

238. For an example of EPA enforcement action under the "general duty" clause, *see* EPA, Office of Regulatory Enforcement, EPA 300-N-98-006, Enforcement Alert: Owners, Operators of Stationary Sources Must Comply with Clean Air Act's General Duty Clause (Aug. 1998).

239. This result was suggested by the citation to the Department of Labor's Office of Health and Safety Administration's (OSHA) general duty clause (29 U.S.C. § 654) in the legislative language. The OSHA general duty clause was interpreted by the D.C. Circuit to be self-implementing. *Int'l Union v. Gen. Dynamics Land Sys. Div.*, 815 F.2d 1570 (D.C. Cir. 1987).

240. CAA § 112(r)(1), 42 U.S.C. § 7412(r)(1).

241. *Id.* § 112(r)(7)(B)(i), (ii), 42 U.S.C. § 7412(r)(7)(B)(i), (ii).

242. *Id.* § 112(r)(7)(B)(iii), 42 U.S.C. § 7412(r)(7)(B)(iii). The CSB is discussed in Section VI.B.

243. *Id.* § 112(r)(7)(B)(ii), 42 U.S.C. § 7412(r)(7)(B)(ii).

244. *Id.* § 112(r)(7)(B)(i), 42 U.S.C. § 7412(r)(7)(B)(i).

245. 40 C.F.R. pt. 68. EPA has issued a number of guidance documents regarding the Risk Management Program, as well as guidance for specific types of facilities, including ammonia refrigeration, propane storage facilities, waste water treatment plants, warehouses, and chemical distributors. Current versions are available on EPA's website.

246. EPA, Office of Land and Emergency Management, Fact Sheet, EPA 550-R-20-001, Clean Air Act Section 112(r): Accidental Release Prevention/Risk Management Plan Rule (Apr. 2020).

247. Certain exemptions apply in making the threshold determination. *See* 40 C.F.R. § 68.115.

248. *Id.* § 68.3.

249. *Id.*

250. *Id.*

251. *Id.* § 68.150. Sources may submit reports that do not contain confidential business information to EPA using an online reporting tool called "RMP*eSubmit."

252. *Id.* § 68.210.

253. *Id.* §§ 68.150, 68.190.

254. *Id.* § 68.220.

255. *Id.* § 68.10. EPA has issued off-site consequence analysis guidance. EPA, Office of Solid Waste and Emergency Response, EPA 550-B-99-009, Risk Management Program Guidance for Offsite Consequence Analysis (Mar. 2009). A program called RMP*Comp™ also allows an owner/operator to complete off-site consequence analysis for planning purposes.

256. To qualify for Program 1 regulation, a facility must demonstrate that: (1) a worst-case release from a covered process would not impact any public receptors of concern; (2) the facility has not had any accidental releases with significant off-site consequences within the previous five years; and (3) the facility has coordinated emergency response procedures with local emergency planners and responders. 40 C.F.R. § 68.10(g).

257. Facilities subject to Program 3 requirements include those that are not eligible for Program 1 and are either subject to the OSHA Process Safety Management (PSM) standard or fall within North American Industry Classification System (NAICS) code 32211, 32411, 32511, 325181, 325188, 325192, 325199, 325211, 325311, or 32532. *Id.* § 68.10(i). OSHA PSM is discussed further below.

258. *Id.* § 68.10(h).

259. *Id.* § 68.42.

260. *Id.* §§ 68.25, 68.28.

261. *Id.* § 68.25.

262. *Id.* § 68.28.

263. *Id.* § 68.12.

264. *Id.* § 68.12(b)(1).

265. *Id.* §§ 68.65–68.87. The OSHA PSM rule is codified at 29 C.F.R. § 1910.119.

266. 40 C.F.R. § 68.12.

267. *Id.* §§ 68.12, 68.48–68.60.

268. *Id.* §§ 68.12, 68.65–68.87.

269. Accidental Release Prevention Requirements: Risk Management Programs Under Clean Air Act Section 112(r)(7), 61 Fed. Reg. 31,668, 31,670, 31,672 (June 20, 1996). EPA and OSHA have entered into agreements to address potential conflicts in accident investigation and enforcement authority over the similar and overlapping requirements of section 112(r)(7) and OSHA PSM: (1) Strategy for Coordinated EPA/OSHA Implementation of the Chemical Accident Prevention Requirements of the Clean Air Act Amendments of 1990 (Aug. 8, 1996); and (2) Memorandum of Understanding Between EPA (Office of Solid Waste and Emergency Response; Office of Enforcement and Compliance Assurance) and U.S. Dep't of Labor, OSHA on Chemical Accident Investigation (Dec. 1, 1996).

270. 40 C.F.R. § 68.95.

271. *Id.* § 68.12.

272. *Id.* § 68.95(b). The Integrated Contingency Plan Guidance, also known as the "One Plan," was developed by a multi-agency group called the National Response Team. The One Plan was published at 61 Fed. Reg. 28,642 (June 5, 1996), with corrections published shortly thereafter at 61 Fed. Reg. 31,103 (June 19, 1996).

273. 40 C.F.R. § 68.90.

274. Exec. Order No. 13650, Improving Chemical Facility Safety and Security, (Aug. 1, 2013), *reprinted in* 78 Fed. Reg. 48,029 (Aug. 7, 2013).

275. Accidental Release Prevention Requirements: Risk Management Programs Under the Clean Air Act, 82 Fed. Reg. 4594 (Jan. 13, 2017).

276. *Id.*

277. *Id.* at 4678.

278. *Am. Chemistry Council v. EPA*, No. 17−1085 (and consolidated cases) (D.C. Cir. filed Mar. 13, 2017). The case was placed in abeyance after reconsideration was granted.

279. Accidental Release Prevention Requirements: Risk Management Programs Under the Clean Air Act; Further Delay of Effective Date, 82 Fed. Reg. 13,968 (Mar. 16, 2017).

280. Accidental Release Prevention Requirements: Risk Management Programs Under the Clean Air Act; Further Delay of Effective Date, 82 Fed. Reg. 27,133 (June 14, 2017).

281. *Air Alliance Houston v. EPA*, 906 F.3d 1049 (D.C. Cir. 2018) (per curiam) (holding that EPA cannot use general rulemaking authority to circumvent the 90-day limit on stays pending reconsideration under Clean Air Action section 307(d)(7)(B)).

282. Accidental Release Prevention Requirements: Risk Management Programs Under the Clean Air Act, 84 Fed. Reg. 69,834 (Dec. 19, 2019).

283. *Air Alliance Houston v. EPA*, No. 19-1260 (and consolidated cases) (D.C. Cir. filed Dec. 19, 2019).

284. Accidental Release Prevention Requirements: Risk Management Programs Under the Clean Air Act; Final Action on Petitions for Reconsideration, 85 Fed. Reg. 55,286 (Sept. 4, 2020). Challenges to the denial later were consolidated with the challenges to the 2019 rule revisions.

285. Accidental Release Prevention Requirements: Risk Management Programs Under the Clean Air Act; Safer Communities by Chemical Accident Prevention, 87 Fed. Reg. 53,556, 53,566–75 (proposed Aug. 31, 2022).

286. CAA § 112(r)(9)(A), 42 U.S.C. § 7412(r)(9)(A).

287. *Id.*

288. *Id.*

289. Process Safety Management of Highly Hazardous Chemicals; Explosives and Blasting Agents, 57 Fed. Reg. 6356 (Feb. 24, 1992) (codified at 29 C.F.R. § 1910.119).

290. CAA § 112(r)(6), 42 U.S.C. § 7412(r)(6).

291. *Id.* § 112(r)(6)(C), 42 U.S.C. § 7412(r)(6)(C).

292. *Id.* § 112(r)(7)(B)(iii), CAA § 7412(r)(7)(B)(iii).

293. *See, e.g.*, *id.* § 112(r)(6)(K), 42 U.S.C. § 7412(r)(6)(K).

294. CSB, FY 2022–2026 Strategic Plan.

295. Chemical Release Reporting; Advance Notice of Proposed Rulemaking, 74 Fed. Reg. 30,259 (June 25, 2009).

296. Accidental Release Reporting, 85 Fed. Reg. 10,074, 10,075 (Feb. 21, 2020).

297. *Id.* The requirements are codified in 40 C.F.R. § 1604.

298. EPA, EPA-452/R-97-003, Mercury Study Report to Congress (Dec. 1997).

299. National Institute of Environmental Health Sciences, Report to Congress on Methylmercury (1993).

300. EPA, EPA-453/R-93-055, Deposition of Air Pollutants to the Great Waters: First Report to Congress (May 1994).

301. EPA, EPA-453/R-97-011, Deposition of Air Pollutants to the Great Waters: Second Report to Congress (June 1997).

302. Draft Determination of Adequacy of Section 112 Authorities And Draft Determination of Need for Additional Standard, 62 Fed. Reg. 36,436 (July 7, 1997).

303. Determination of Adequacy of Section 112 Authorities and Determination of Need for Additional Standard, 63 Fed. Reg. 14,090 (Mar. 24, 1998).

304. EPA, EPA-453/R-00-005, Deposition of Air Pollutants to the Great Waters: Third Report to Congress (June 2000).

305. EPA, EPA-452/R-07-011, Survey of New Findings in Scientific Literature Related to Atmospheric Deposition to the Great Waters: Polycyclic Aromatic Hydrocarbons (PAH) (Dec. 2007).

306. EPA, EPA-452/R-07-012, Survey of New Findings in Scientific Literature Related to Atmospheric Deposition to the Great Waters: Polychlorinated Biphenyls (PCB) (Dec. 2007).

307. EPA, EPA-550-R-93-001, Hydrogen Fluoride Study—Report to Congress: Section 112(n)(6) Clean Air Act as Amended (1993).

308. Clean Air Act Amendments of 1990, Pub. L. No. 101-549, § 303, 104 Stat. 2399, 2574–76 (1990).

309. *Id.* at 2575.

310. The Presidential/Congressional Commission on Risk Assessment and Risk Management, Framework for Environmental Health Management (1997).

Chapter 6

VISIBILITY PROTECTION

I. Background

The 1977 Clean Air Act (CAA or Act) amendments declared as a national goal "the prevention of any future and the remedying of any existing, impairment of visibility in mandatory class I Federal areas which impairment results from manmade air pollution."[1] Pursuant to the Act, the U.S. Environmental Protection Agency (EPA or Agency) identified 156 mandatory Federal Class I areas, which include many large national parks and wilderness areas, in which EPA determined visibility is an important value.[2] To implement the 1977 amendments, EPA in 1980 adopted a "Phase I" visibility program addressing "plume blight" (i.e., visible plumes) that impacts Class I areas.[3] Citing uncertainties that existed at that time in monitoring and modeling techniques for evaluating the more complex phenomenon of regional visibility impairment, or "regional haze,"[4] EPA decided at that time to postpone development of a "Phase II" program addressing regional haze.

The Phase I visibility program was difficult for many states to implement and was only rarely used. The most notable example of its use was the regulation of the Navajo Generating Station (NGS) to reduce the visibility impacts of that source's plume in Grand Canyon National Park.[5]

In 1990, Congress enacted amendments to the Act in response to EPA's continued deferral of a regional haze regulatory program. New section § 169B required research on monitoring and modeling of regional haze, required establishment of a Grand Canyon Visibility Transport Commission, and set a deadline for EPA to adopt a regional haze regulatory program consistent with section169A.[6]

II. The Regional Haze Regulatory Program

In 1999, EPA adopted final rules to implement a regional haze regulatory program,[7] including the two main components of the program: the "reasonable progress" requirement and the "best available retrofit technology" (BART) requirement. The 1999 regional haze rules were challenged in the U.S. Court of Appeals for the District of Columbia Circuit (D.C. Circuit) by both industry and environmental advocacy organizations. The reasonable progress program survived judicial review, but the court vacated the BART rules and remanded them to EPA for further rulemaking, finding that they impermissibly constrained the states' "broad authority over BART determinations."[8]

EPA undertook a BART remand rulemaking and issued revised BART rules in 2005.[9] Those rules included the so-called "BART Guidelines," which are legally binding with respect to state BART determinations for fossil fuel-fired power plants with total electric generating capacity exceeding 750 megawatts (MW).[10] For other sources, the Guidelines provide only guidance to the states.[11] Even for sources for which the Guidelines are not mandatory, however, states generally followed that guidance. After 2005, with the final BART program in place, the regional haze program shifted to the implementation stage.

States must implement the regional haze rules pursuant to section 110(a)(2)(J) of the Act, which requires each state to develop a state implementation plan (SIP) to address the Act's visibility protection requirements.[12] States develop regional haze SIPs and submit them to EPA for approval. Regional haze SIPs for the regional haze program's first "implementation period" (sometimes called the "planning period"), which addressed regional haze requirements through 2018, were due to EPA by December 17, 2007,[13] although most states did not meet that deadline. Future regional haze SIPs are expected to cover every 10-year period beyond 2018, until at least 2064, which is the nonbinding target date for completion of the program and achievement of natural visibility conditions in Class I areas.[14] The following sections describe the principal elements of the regional haze program and its implementation.

A. The Regional Planning Organizations

The regional haze rules require an expensive and intensive implementation effort by states. The states must analyze air quality monitoring data collected by the so-called IMPROVE (Interagency Monitoring of Protected Visual Environments) monitoring network for the Class I areas within their borders,[15] determine "reasonable progress goals" for those areas through air quality modeling and consideration of other factors,[16] determine BART emission limitations for applicable sources,[17] and adopt emission control strategies, known as each state's "long-term strategy," that are designed to achieve the reasonable progress goals.[18]

The 1999 rules encouraged states to join together in doing much of the analysis and technical work needed for implementation of the rules, and the 2005 rules and BART Guidelines retained a recommendation that states work collaboratively. In the years following EPA's promulgation of the 1999 and 2005 rules, states formed and participated in five "regional planning organizations" (RPOs), each covering a different section of the country: (1) the Mid-Atlantic/Northeast Visibility Union (commonly known as MANE-VU), (2) the Visibility Improvement State and Tribal Association of the Southeast (known as VISTAS), (3) the Midwest Regional Planning Organization (MRPO), (4) the Central Regional Air Planning Association (CenRAP), and (5) the Western Regional Air Partnership (WRAP). Each of these RPOs undertook a multi-year research effort involving monitoring and modeling to assist its member states in developing their regional haze SIPs for the first implementation period, which ended in 2018. Subsequently, these organizations, or in some cases successor organizations,[19] assisted and coordinated with states in the development of regional haze SIPs for the second implementation period, which covers the period from 2018 to 2028.

B. BART

The BART program applied only in the first implementation period (although, due to delays in some states' development and EPA review of SIPs addressing BART requirements and due also in certain cases to litigation concerning BART determinations, BART-related regulatory activity for some states continued into the second implementation period).[20] To meet the BART requirements, states reviewed stationary sources in 26 source categories and determined which of those sources are both "BART-eligible"[21] and "subject to BART." BART-eligibility for specific sources that fall within these source categories is determined by the potential emissions of the source (potential emissions of a visibility-impairing pollutant must be at least 250 tons per year) and by the date that the source began operation (the source must have been in existence on August 7, 1977, but must have begun operation after August 7, 1962).[22] A BART-eligible source is "subject to BART" if it may reasonably be anticipated to cause or contribute to visibility impairment in a Class I area.[23] EPA's rules allow a state either to assume that all BART-eligible sources in that state are subject to BART or to perform (or have the source perform) source-specific air quality modeling to evaluate whether an individual source causes or contributes to visibility impairment in a Class I area.[24] EPA's BART Guidelines indicate that, for source-specific modeling assessments, any source whose emissions contribute 1.0 (or more) "deciview"[25] of visibility impairment in a Class I area normally would be deemed to cause visibility impairment, and any source whose emissions contribute 0.5 (or more) deciview of visibility impairment in a Class I area normally would be deemed to contribute to visibility impairment.[26]

If a source is both BART-eligible and subject to BART, then the state must make a BART determination for that source.[27] In making the BART determination, the state must consider—in addition to the emission control technology that is available—the five statutory BART factors: (1) the costs of compliance; (2) the energy and non-air-quality environmental impacts of compliance; (3) any existing pollution control technology in use at the source; (4) the source's remaining useful life; and (5) the degree of visibility improvement that may reasonably be anticipated to result from use of the proposed BART control technology.[28]

EPA's BART Guidelines also list "presumptive" BART emission limits for nitrogen oxide (NOx) and sulfur dioxide (SO_2) for a variety of fossil fuel-fired electric generating unit (EGU) types, which EPA premised on a generalized assessment of the BART factors for various categories of EGUs.[29] Although states could choose to deviate from the presumptive limits based on a source-specific evaluation of the BART factors, EPA characterized the presumptive limits as "highly cost-effective" and "extremely likely to be appropriate for all greater than 750 MW power plants subject to BART."[30]

After its evaluation of the BART factors and relevant information, a state (or, in some cases, EPA) must make a BART determination for each facility that is subject to BART. The BART determination for a source is expressed as an emission limitation for that source for each of the visibility-impairing pollutants that the source emits (above de minimis levels[31]). These emission limitations are included in the source's Title V operating permit.

C. Reasonable Progress

The regional haze program's other major component is the reasonable progress requirement, which applies in addition to (not in lieu of) the program's BART requirements. The regional haze rules reflect an objective of attaining the goal of no manmade visibility impairment (so-called "natural conditions") in Class I areas by the year 2064. To help achieve reasonable progress toward this goal, the regional haze rules require states to identify emission sources to be assessed for potential additional emission control measures and evaluate whether and what kinds of control measures for visibility-impairing pollutants are warranted for each such source in light of four statutory factors: "the costs of compliance, the time necessary for compliance, . . . the energy and nonair quality environmental impacts of compliance, and the remaining useful life" of the source.[32] The state must include in its SIP "a description of the criteria it used to determine which sources or groups of sources it evaluated and how the four factors were taken into consideration in selecting the measures for inclusion in its long-term strategy."[33]

States are to define interim reasonable progress goals for each 10-year interval between a baseline period (2000–2004) and 2064, with the first reasonable progress goal occurring in the year 2018, the second in 2028, and so on. In connection with determining how to set reasonable progress goals, states calculate, for each Class I area within their borders, the linear rate of progress in visibility improvement between the 2000–2004 baseline conditions (the average annual visibility impairment for the annual most-impaired 20 percent of days in that baseline period, based on IMPROVE monitoring data) and the estimated natural conditions level, assuming that that level will be reached in 2064.[34] EPA refers to this linear improvement in visibility conditions as the "uniform rate of progress" or the "glidepath."[35] Although the uniform rate of progress does not establish a mandatory or enforceable requirement, it must be considered by states in developing their SIPs.

In developing its SIP, a state with a Class I area must establish a "reasonable progress goal" for that area, expressed numerically in deciviews. These goals, while also not constituting enforceable requirements,[36] are to be calculated by modeling

> the visibility conditions that are projected to be achieved by the end of the applicable implementation period as a result of those enforceable emissions limitations, compliance schedules, and other measures required under [the SIP's long-term strategy] . . . that can be fully implemented by the end of the applicable implementation period, as well as the implementation of other requirements of the CAA."[37]

Although states have significant discretion in choosing which sources to control—and in what ways and to what degree—to achieve reasonable progress in a given implementation period, and although neither the uniform rate of progress nor the reasonable progress goals are themselves enforceable, the specific emission control measures included in the SIP must be enforceable. Moreover, the rules constrain a state's discretion in that its SIP's "long-term strategy and the reasonable progress goals must provide for an improvement in visibility for the [20 percent] most impaired days since the [2000–2004] baseline period and ensure no degradation in visibility for the [20 percent] clearest days since the baseline period."[38]

D. Rulemaking and Litigation Regarding Plans for the First Implementation Period

Beginning in 2009, EPA proposed and took final action on regional haze SIPs submitted by most of the states for the first implementation period. In addition, where states failed to submit regional haze SIPs,[39] and in other special circumstances in which EPA has jurisdiction to implement the regional haze program directly (e.g., on some Tribal lands),[40] EPA proposed and promulgated federal implementation plans (FIPs) that included, among other elements, BART determinations and BART emission limitations for subject-to-BART sources and reasonable progress goals. In a number of cases, EPA promulgated regional haze FIPs where a submitted SIP would have, in EPA's view, inadequately controlled visibility-impairing emissions and thus disapproved all or key parts of the SIP.[41]

Most of these EPA rulemaking actions were controversial and engendered significant litigation in the federal courts of appeals. Each rulemaking and litigation matter involved facts specific to the individual states, emission sources, Class I areas, and technical assessments and factors that were at issue. But important questions underlying virtually all of them concerned the respective roles, authority, and decision-making discretion of EPA and the states in implementing the regional haze program in a system of what EPA and several courts have termed "cooperative federalism."[42] Some courts adopted a view that called on EPA to accord broad deference to states' judgments on regional haze control decisions. For instance, the U.S. Court of Appeals for the Fifth Circuit, in a decision staying the effectiveness of a FIP imposing reasonable progress emission controls on sources in Texas for the first implementation period, stated that "[t]he structure of the Clean Air Act indicates a congressional preference that states, not EPA, drive the regulatory process."[43] In that court's view, the Act "confines EPA's role in implementing air quality standards [including regional haze program requirements] 'to the ministerial function of reviewing SIPs for consistency with the Act's requirements.'"[44] On the other hand, in a case concerning Arizona BART requirements, the U.S. Court of Appeals for the Ninth Circuit—citing regional haze SIP and FIP decisions by the Tenth and Eighth Circuits concerning Oklahoma[45] and North Dakota,[46] respectively—wrote that

> EPA may only approve SIPs, or portions of SIPs, that "meet[] all the applicable requirements" of the Act. [CAA § 110(k)(3),] 42 U.S.C. § 7410(k)(3). Thus, while the Act "gives states discretion in balancing the five BART factors, it also mandates that the state adhere to certain requirements when conducting a BART analysis." *Oklahoma,* 723 F.3d at 1208. Consequently, when reviewing regional haze SIPs, EPA may not approve "a BART determination that is based upon an

analysis that is neither reasoned nor moored to the [Act]'s provisions." *N. Dakota,* 730 F.3d at 761. In short, EPA is not limited to the "ministerial" role of verifying whether a determination was made; it must "review the substantive content of the BART determination." *Id.*[47]

E. Reliance on Other EPA Rules To Satisfy BART Obligations

EPA's regional haze rules allow states to adopt a "BART alternative" in lieu of requiring BART provided the alternative emission controls "will achieve greater reasonable progress toward natural visibility conditions" than BART.[48] EPA's authority to approve BART alternatives was specifically upheld by the D.C. Circuit.[49] EPA promulgated FIPs and approved SIPs with BART alternatives for individual emission sources and in other circumstances.[50] EPA has also approved state reliance on other broadly applicable EPA regulations as valid BART alternatives. First, in conjunction with EPA's promulgation of the Clean Air Interstate Rule (CAIR), a NOx and SO_2 emissions trading program applicable to twenty-eight eastern states and the District of Columbia, EPA promulgated a rule declaring that states subject to CAIR's emission trading programs could rely on compliance with CAIR's requirements instead of requiring source-by-source BART for emissions of NOx and SO_2 from EGUs within those states. This rule was sometimes called the "CAIR=BART" rule.[51] CAIR was challenged in the D.C. Circuit, and after EPA had promulgated the CAIR=BART rule, the court found CAIR invalid and remanded the rule to EPA.[52] The court decided, however, to leave CAIR in place until EPA could promulgate a valid replacement rule.[53]

In 2011, EPA promulgated the Cross-State Air Pollution Rule (known as CSAPR) as a replacement for CAIR. Like CAIR, CSAPR is a NOx and SO_2 emissions trading program applicable to fossil fuel-fired EGUs in most states in the eastern half of the United States, using statewide emission budgets and marketable emission allowances as compliance mechanisms. After it promulgated CSAPR, EPA promulgated a final rule[54] that: (1) deemed CSAPR a valid BART alternative for NOx and SO_2 emissions from EGUs for states covered by CSAPR and promulgated a "CSAPR=BART" rule;[55] (2) removed EPA's CAIR=BART determination from its regulations; (3) finalized "limited disapprovals" of the SIPs of fourteen states[56] that relied on the CAIR=BART rule; and (4) promulgated FIPs for twelve states[57] that replaced those states' reliance on the CAIR=BART rule with reliance on the CSAPR=BART rule. After EPA's promulgation of the CSAPR=BART rule, the D.C. Circuit ruled on challenges that had been filed against CSAPR and initially vacated CSAPR. The court ordered that

CAIR continue in effect until EPA promulgated a valid replacement rule, creating a prolonged period of uncertainty over the status of the CSAPR=BART rule and SIPs and FIPs related to that rule.[58] The Supreme Court's 2014 decision reversing the D.C. Circuit's invalidation of CSAPR as a whole[59] and the subsequent D.C. Circuit decision on remand—which kept all of CSAPR in place even while remanding to EPA certain statewide emission budgets[60]—resulted in the continued effectiveness of the CSAPR=BART rule.

Several parties challenged various aspects of the CSAPR=BART rule; industry parties and two states (Texas and Louisiana) challenged EPA's revocation of the CAIR=BART determination and disapproval of SIPs that relied on that determination, while two environmental advocacy organizations challenged the CSAPR=BART determination. After an extended period during which the court held this litigation in abeyance pending the Supreme Court appeal and D.C. Circuit remand proceedings in the litigation on CSAPR itself, the D.C. Circuit issued its decision on the challenges to the CSAPR=BART rule.[61] The court denied all of the challenges, leaving EPA's rule intact and the CSAPR=BART determination valid and effective.[62]

While the CSAPR=BART litigation challenges were still pending in the D.C. Circuit, however, EPA undertook a public notice-and-comment proceeding to affirm the continued validity of the CSAPR=BART determination notwithstanding certain changes in the geographic coverage of CSAPR—most notably, the removal of Texas from CSAPR's SO_2 emission allowance trading program—that resulted from the D.C. Circuit's 2015 remand to EPA of several statewide emission budgets in CSAPR at the final stage of the litigation on CSAPR. In its 2017 final rulemaking action, EPA reaffirmed that compliance with CSAPR would still achieve greater reasonable progress than source-by-source BART for SO_2 and NOx emissions from EGUs in states covered by CSAPR.[63] The next month, EPA published a final rule establishing a FIP with a new intrastate SO_2 emission allowance trading program for Texas—a BART-alternative program for Texas EGUs' SO_2 emissions to take the place of Texas's now-withdrawn participation in CSAPR's interstate SO_2 trading program.[64]

Environmental advocacy organizations petitioned EPA for reconsideration of the September 2017 CSAPR=BART reaffirmation rule, in part because, they argued, EPA afforded commenters no opportunity to consider the effect of the new intrastate trading FIP for Texas. They also petitioned for reconsideration of that FIP. EPA then offered new opportunities for public comment on the October 2017 Texas FIP[65] and, after considering comments, both reaffirmed the FIP (with some modifications)[66] and denied the petition for reconsideration of the September 2017 CSAPR=BART reaffirmation rule.[67]

All the above actions related to CSAPR=BART and the Texas FIP were challenged judicially. As of the end of March 2023, those actions remain in abeyance pending EPA's consideration of a second administrative petition for reconsideration of the September 2017 CSAPR=BART rule and voluntary reconsideration of the August 2020 Texas FIP. According to EPA's fall 2022 regulatory agenda, the Agency anticipates issuing a proposal in spring 2023.

F. Rulemaking, Guidance, and Litigation Regarding the Second Planning Period

In January 2017—just days before President Trump was inaugurated—EPA published revisions to its visibility program rules, including the regional haze regulations.[68] The principal focus of the rule revisions was on requirements for SIPs addressing the second implementation period. One change that was generally favored by states as well as industry was a three-year deferral of the deadline, from July 31, 2018, to July 31, 2021, for states to submit SIPs to EPA for the second implementation period. (SIPs for the third and subsequent implementation periods remain due by July 31, 2028, and each 10 years thereafter.[69]) The revisions also addressed a range of other elements of the program. Among other things, the January 2017 rule:

- Continued to require states to submit visibility-improvement "progress reports" to EPA every five years—with the next report due by January 31, 2025, and subsequent reports by July 31, 2033, and at 10-year intervals thereafter—but discontinued the requirement that the progress reports be in the form of SIP revisions that EPA would have to approve or disapprove (although states still must allow for public review of and comment on the reports before submittal to EPA);[70]
- Established requirements for interstate consultation in the development of regional haze SIPs;[71]
- "[C]odified" EPA's "clarification" of what it characterized as its "longstanding" interpretation of the regional haze rules to the effect that states, in developing their periodic comprehensive regional haze SIP revisions, must consider the statutory reasonable progress factors for emission sources as the basis for their long-term strategies and must set reasonable progress goals for Class I areas based on the collection of emission controls included in the long-term strategies;[72]
- Made clear that states may not rely on meeting the uniform rate of progress, or glidepath, in a given ten-year implementation period but instead must apply the reasonable progress factors and determine whether (and which) emission limits are warranted to achieve reasonable progress by

the end of that period, even if the relevant Class I areas already are meeting, or are projected to meet, the uniform rate of progress in the absence of any additional emission controls;[73]

- Provided that if a state's reasonable progress goal for a given Class I area "is above the [uniform rate of progress] line"—i.e., is less accelerated or less ambitious than a goal that would reflect the glidepath for that area—"then the state has an additional analytical obligation to ensure that no reasonable controls were left off the table";[74] and
- Expressly recognized that states may, in calculating glidepaths for Class I areas, account for the visibility-impairing effects of anthropogenic emissions from sources located outside the United States and emissions from certain types of "prescribed fires"—adjustments that in effect would make it less burdensome to meet some Class I areas' glidepaths—and required that states use a method specifically detailed in the regulations if they chose to make such adjustments (which are subject to EPA's review and approval or disapproval as part of the SIP-approval process).[75]

A number of provisions of the rule—as well as EPA's rejection of some revisions proposed by rulemaking commenters—were controversial, and four states (Texas, Alaska, Arkansas, and North Dakota), several industry parties, and four environmental advocacy organizations challenged various aspects of it.[76] In addition, Alaska and four industry parties petitioned for reconsideration of some aspects of the rule revisions. In response, EPA in early 2018 announced that it intended to consider potential amendments to provisions and to develop guidance documents to address some of the concerns raised by the parties seeking reconsideration. And, in 2018, EPA issued a "Regional Haze Reform Roadmap" memorandum that provided more specific information about EPA's plans in that regard.[77] In light of EPA's statements about its expected future administrative actions, EPA asked the D.C. Circuit to hold the litigation on the January 2017 rule revisions in abeyance, and the court granted that request.

Beginning in late 2018, EPA issued a series of guidance documents and technical memoranda related to states' implementation of the regional haze program for the second planning period. First, EPA issued Technical Guidance on Tracking Visibility Progress for the Second Implementation Period of the Regional Haze Program.[78] Second, in August 2019, EPA issued perhaps its most important guidance document for the second planning period, addressing the requirements of the January 2017 rule for state regional haze SIP submissions due on July 31, 2021.[79] The recommendations in the 2019 Final Guidance are generally less prescriptive with respect to states' planning obligations than was EPA's 2016 draft version of the guidance.[80] The 2019 Final Guidance addresses issues concerning ambient data analysis, a state's determination of affected Class I areas in other states, states' selection of emission sources to evaluate for potential reasonable progress emission controls, characterization of each of the four statutory reasonable progress factors and an optional visibility-benefits factor,[81] states' determinations as to what control measures are necessary to make reasonable progress, and other matters.

In 2019, EPA issued another important document for use by states, RPOs, and others in connection with preparation of SIPs for the second implementation period.[82] The Modeling TSD presented specific results of EPA's modeling projections of visibility conditions at Class I areas (or, more precisely, at IMPROVE ambient air quality monitoring sites representing the various Class I areas) in 2028, the end of the second implementation period. Among other things, EPA's modeling projected that more than half of the IMPROVE sites will have in 2028—even in the absence of additional emission controls—visibility conditions that are better than the relevant "unadjusted glidepath" (i.e., the glidepath without any adjustment to account for visibility effects of emissions from non-U.S. anthropogenic sources and prescribed fires).[83] Indeed, essentially all sites in the eastern half of the country were projected to do better than their unadjusted glidepaths.[84] The Modeling TSD also presented information on 2028 glidepaths after EPA adjusted the glidepaths to account for effects of anthropogenic non-U.S. emissions.[85] Specifically, the TSD presented, for each IMPROVE site (and, by extension, each Class I area), a 2028 "default" adjusted glidepath as well as 2028 "minimum alternative" and "maximum alternative" adjusted glidepaths. Based on the data displayed in the TSD for the Class I areas,[86] EPA noted that "[a]fter applying the 'default' glidepath adjustment to account for international anthropogenic emissions sources, there are only 8 IMPROVE sites [out of a total of 99 IMPROVE sites nationwide] projected to be above the adjusted glidepath [i.e., projected to have worse visibility than the adjusted glidepath] in 2028" without additional reasonable progress emission controls.[87]

In 2020, EPA issued additional technical information for states to use in developing SIPs for the second implementation period.[88] And, in 2021, EPA issued a memorandum providing clarifications regarding regional haze SIPs in response to questions and information received from states and stakeholders.[89]

As of August 31, 2022, EPA had received thirty-seven SIPs addressing the second planning period. In September 2022, EPA issued findings of failure to submit for fifteen states.[90] The findings establish a 2-year deadline for the EPA to promulgate FIPs to address these requirements for a given state unless, prior to the EPA promulgating a FIP, the state submits, and the EPA approves, a SIP that meets the applicable requirements.

Finally, regarding additional rulemaking to address possible amendments to the January 2017 rule, EPA's fall 2022 regulatory agenda states that, consistent with prior letters to the petitioners for reconsideration, EPA plans to issue a rulemaking to address portions of the rule, including the Reasonably Attributable Visibility Impairment provisions, the provisions regarding Federal Land Manager consultation, and any other elements of the rule EPA may identify for additional consideration. However, EPA's agenda provides no projected date for the proposal other than to identify it as an action more than 12 months in the future.

Notes

1. CAA § 169A(a)(1), 42 U.S.C. § 7491(a)(1).
2. *Id.* § 169A(a)(2), 42 U.S.C. § 7491(a)(2); 40 C.F.R. pt. 81, subpt. D.
3. Visibility Protection for Federal Class I Areas, 45 Fed. Reg. 80,084 (Dec. 2, 1980).
4. EPA's regulations define regional haze as "visibility impairment that is caused by the emission of air pollutants from numerous anthropogenic sources located over a wide geographic area. Such sources include, but are not limited to, major and minor stationary sources, mobile sources, and area sources." 40 C.F.R. § 51.301.
5. *See Cent. Ariz. Water Conservation Dist. v. EPA*, 990 F.2d 1531 (9th Cir. 1993).
6. CAA § 169B, 42 U.S.C. § 7492.
7. Regional Haze Regulations, 64 Fed. Reg. 35,714 (July 1, 1999).
8. *Am. Corn Growers Ass'n v. EPA*, 291 F.3d 1, 8 (D.C. Cir. 2002) (per curiam).
9. Regional Haze Regulations and Guidelines for Best Available Retrofit Technology (BART) Determinations, 70 Fed. Reg. 39,104 (July 6, 2005).
10. *Id.* at 39,108; CAA § 169A(b), 42 U.S.C. § 7491(b).
11. 70 Fed. Reg. at 39,158.
12. CAA § 110(a)(2)(J), 42 U.S.C. § 7410(a)(2)(J).
13. 40 C.F.R. § 51.308(b).
14. *Id.* § 51.308(d)(1), (f)(3). States have discretion to extend their target dates for achieving "natural" visibility conditions. *Id.* § 51.308(d)(1)(i), (ii), (f)(3)(i), (ii).
15. *Id.* § 51.308(d)(4), (f)(6).
16. *Id.* § 51.308(d)(1), (f)(3).
17. *Id.* § 51.308(e).
18. *Id.* § 51.308(d)(3), (f)(2).
19. For practical purposes, an organization known as the Southeastern Air Pollution Control Agencies (SESARM) became the successor to VISTAS; the Lake Michigan Air Directors Commission (LADCO) succeeded the MRPO; and the Central States Air Resource Agencies (CenSARA) succeeded CenRAP. The other RPOs—MANE-VU and WRAP—continued their activities.

20. *See, e.g.*, Air Plan Approval; MS [Mississippi]; BART SIP and Regional Haze Progress Report, 86 Fed. Reg. 55,501 (Oct. 6, 2021).

21. *See* 40 C.F.R. § 51.301 (definitions of "BART-eligible source" and "existing stationary facility," among other relevant terms).

22. *See* CAA § 169A(b)(2)(A), (g)(7), 42 U.S.C. § 7491(b)(2)(A), (g)(7); 40 C.F.R. § 51.301 (definitions of "in existence" and "in operation").

23. 40 C.F.R. § 51.308(e).

24. 70 Fed. Reg. at 39,107.

25. A deciview is defined as "the unit of measurement on the deciview index scale for quantifying in a standard manner human perceptions of visibility"; "deciview index" in turn is defined as "a value for a day that is derived from calculated or measured light extinction, such that uniform increments of the index correspond to uniform incremental changes in perception across the entire range of conditions, from pristine to very obscured." 40 C.F.R. § 51.301. The latter definition includes an equation for calculating the deciview index. EPA stated that a change in visibility of 1.0 deciview is "a humanly perceptible change in visibility in virtually all situations." 70 Fed. Reg. at 39,120 n.32.

26. 70 Fed. Reg. at 39,161.

27. 40 C.F.R. § 51.308(e)(1)(ii).

28. CAA § 169A(g)(2), 42 U.S.C. § 7491(g)(2); 40 C.F.R. § 51.308(e)(1)(ii)(A).

29. 70 Fed. Reg. at 39,131–36, 39,171–72.

30. *Id.* at 39,131.

31. *See id.* at 39,117.

32. CAA § 169A(g)(1), 42 U.S.C. § 7491(g)(1); *see* 40 C.F.R. § 51.308(d)(1)(i)(A), (f)(2)(i).

33. 40 C.F.R. § 51.308(f)(2)(i).

34. *Id.* § 51.308(f)(1).

35. *See, e.g.*, 70 Fed. Reg. at 39,143; 40 C.F.R. § 51.308(f)(1)(vi)(A).

36. *See, e.g., id.* Moreover, a reasonable progress goal for a given Class I area may be less, or more, ambitious or accelerated than the uniform rate of progress for that area.

37. 40 C.F.R. § 51.308(f)(3)(i).

38. *Id.*

39. *See, e.g.*, Approval and Promulgation of Implementation Plans; State of Montana; State Implementation Plan and Regional Haze Federal Implementation Plan, 77 Fed. Reg. 57,864 (Sept. 18, 2012).

40. *See, e.g.*, Approval of Air Quality Implementation Plans; Navajo Nation; Regional Haze Requirements for Navajo Generating Station, 79 Fed. Reg. 46,514 (Aug. 8, 2014); Source Specific Federal Implementation Plan for Implementing Best Available Retrofit Technology for Four Corners Power Plant: Navajo Nation, 77 Fed. Reg. 51,620 (Aug. 24, 2012).

41. *See, e.g.*, Approval, Disapproval and Promulgation of Air Quality Implementation Plans; Arizona; Regional Haze State and Federal Implementation Plans, 77 Fed. Reg. 72,512 (Dec. 5, 2012); Approval and Promulgation of Implementation Plans; North Dakota; Regional Haze State Implementation Plan; Federal Implementation Plan for

Interstate Transport of Pollution Affecting Visibility and Regional Haze, 77 Fed. Reg. 20,894 (Apr. 6, 2012); Approval and Promulgation of Implementation Plans; Oklahoma; Federal Implementation Plan for Interstate Transport of Pollution Affecting Visibility and Best Available Retrofit Technology Determinations, 76 Fed. Reg. 81,728 (Dec. 28, 2011); Approval and Promulgation of Implementation Plans; New Mexico; Federal Implementation Plan for Interstate Transport of Pollution Affecting Visibility and Best Available Retrofit Technology Determination, 76 Fed. Reg. 52,388 (Aug. 22, 2011); *see also* CAA §§ 110(c)(1), 302(y), 42 U.S.C. §§ 7410(c)(1), 7602(y) (providing EPA with authority to promulgate a FIP where a state fails to submit a SIP, or submits an incomplete SIP, or where EPA disapproves a submitted SIP).

42. *See, e.g.*, *Texas v. EPA*, 829 F.3d 405, 411 (5th Cir. 2016) ("The Clean Air Act is 'an experiment in cooperative federalism.'") (quoting *Michigan v. EPA*, 268 F.3d 1075, 1083 (D.C. Cir. 2001)).

43. *Id.*

44. *Id.* (quoting *Luminant Generation Co., L.L.C. v. EPA*, 675 F.3d 917, 921 (5th Cir. 2012)).

45. *Oklahoma v. EPA*, 723 F.3d 1201 (10th Cir. 2013).

46. *North Dakota v. EPA*, 730 F.3d 750 (8th Cir. 2013).

47. *Arizona ex rel. Darwin v. EPA*, 815 F.3d 519, 531 (9th Cir. 2016). Additional cases in which federal courts addressed the respective roles of EPA and states in making determinations on BART and reasonable progress issues, the degree of deference EPA should extend to state judgments, and related regional haze program implementation matters in the first planning period include, among others, *Sierra Club v. EPA*, 939 F.3d 649 (5th Cir. 2019) (requirements for Louisiana); *Arizona ex rel. Darwin v. EPA*, 852 F.3d 1148 (9th Cir. 2017); *Nat'l Parks Conservation Ass'n v. McCarthy*, 816 F.3d 989 (8th Cir. 2016), *amending on reh'g* 811 F.3d 1005 (8th Cir. 2016) (Minnesota); *Nebraska v. EPA*, 812 F.3d 662 (8th Cir. 2016); *Nat'l Parks Conservation Ass'n v. EPA*, 803 F.3d 151 (3d Cir. 2015) (Pennsylvania); *WildEarth Guardians v. EPA*, 770 F.3d 919 (10th Cir. 2014) (New Mexico, Utah, and Wyoming). A case in which a court reviewed a FIP that EPA promulgated because the state (Montana) declined to submit any regional haze SIP is *National Parks Conservation Ass'n v. EPA*, 788 F.3d 1134 (9th Cir. 2015) (granting in part and denying in part petitions for review filed by industry and environmental advocacy organizations challenging various provisions of the regional haze FIP for Montana).

48. 40 C.F.R. § 51.308(e). Criteria for determining whether an alternative measure achieves greater reasonable progress than source-specific BART are set out at 40 C.F.R. § 51.308(e)(2)(i)(E) and (e)(3).

49. *Util. Air Regulatory Grp. v. EPA*, 471 F.3d 1333 (D.C. Cir. 2006); *Ctr. for Energy & Econ. Dev. v. EPA*, 398 F.3d 653, 660 (D.C. Cir. 2005).

50. *See, e.g.*, 77 Fed. Reg. at 51,620 (Four Corners Power Plant, located within the borders of the Navajo Nation); Approval and Promulgation of Air Quality Implementation Plans; Arizona; Regional Haze State and Federal Implementation Plans, 82 Fed. Reg. 46,903 (Oct. 10, 2017) (Coronado Generating Station in Arizona); *WildEarth Guardians*, 770 F.3d at 919 (upholding interstate BART-alternative program applicable to sources of SO_2 emissions in New Mexico, Utah, and Wyoming).

51. 70 Fed. Reg. at 39,106, 39,138–43.

52. CAIR and its replacement rule are discussed in more detail in chapter 2.

53. *North Carolina v. EPA*, 531 F.3d 896 (D.C. Cir.) (per curiam), *modified in part on reh'g*, 550 F.3d 1176 (D.C. Cir. 2008) (per curiam).

54. Regional Haze: Revisions to Provisions Governing Alternatives to Source-Specific Best Available Retrofit Technology (BART) Determinations, Limited SIP Disapprovals, and Federal Implementation Plans, 77 Fed. Reg. 33,642 (June 7, 2012).

55. The CSAPR=BART rule is codified at 40 C.F.R. § 51.308(e)(4).

56. The fourteen states were Alabama, Georgia, Indiana, Iowa, Louisiana, Michigan, Mississippi, Missouri, North Carolina, Ohio, Pennsylvania, South Carolina, Texas, and Virginia. In separate rulemaking proceedings, EPA also promulgated final limited disapprovals of the regional haze SIPs of Kentucky, Tennessee, and West Virginia because of their reliance on the CAIR=BART rule.

57. The twelve states were Georgia, Indiana, Iowa, Kentucky, Michigan, Missouri, Ohio, Pennsylvania, South Carolina, Tennessee, Virginia, and West Virginia. EPA did not promulgate FIPs for Alabama, Louisiana, Mississippi, North Carolina, and Texas to allow those states time to revise their SIPs. In addition, EPA had separately proposed a limited disapproval and FIP for Florida but ended up not finalizing either proposal because EPA had changed Florida's status under CSAPR after CSAPR's promulgation and EPA determined it was appropriate to allow Florida time to revise its SIP as well.

58. *EME Homer City Generation, L.P. v. EPA*, 696 F.3d 7 (D.C. Cir. 2012), *cert. granted,* 570 U.S. 916 (2013), *rev'd*, 572 U.S. 489 (2014).

59. *EPA v. EME Homer City Generation, L.P.*, 572 U.S. 489 (2014).

60. *EME Homer City Generation, L.P. v. EPA*, 795 F.3d 118 (D.C. Cir. 2015).

61. *Util. Air Regulatory Grp. v. EPA*, 885 F.3d 714 (D.C. Cir. 2018).

62. In two separate cases, the Eighth Circuit earlier had affirmed application of the CSAPR=BART determination to EGUs in Minnesota and Nebraska. *Nat'l Parks Conservation Ass'n v. McCarthy*, 816 F.3d 989, 994–96 (8th Cir. 2016), *amending on reh'g* 811 F.3d 1005 (8th Cir. 2016) (Minnesota); *Nebraska v. EPA*, 812 F.3d 662, 669–70 (8th Cir. 2016). When presented with a challenge to EPA's application of the CSAPR=BART determination to EGUs in Pennsylvania, the U.S. Court of Appeals for the Third Circuit held that only the D.C. Circuit had jurisdiction to adjudicate that issue under CAA section 307(b)(1), 42 U.S.C. § 7607(b)(1), and thus did not address the merits of the issue. *Nat'l Parks Conservation Ass'n*, 803 F.3d at 158–60.

63. Interstate Transport of Fine Particulate Matter: Revision of Federal Implementation Plan Requirements for Texas, 82 Fed. Reg. 45,481 (Sept. 29, 2017).

64. Promulgation of Air Quality Implementation Plans; State of Texas: Regional Haze and Interstate Visibility Transport Federal Implementation Plan, 82 Fed. Reg. 48,324 (Oct. 17, 2017).

65. Promulgation of Air Quality Implementation Plans, State of Texas; Regional Haze and Interstate Visibility Transport Federal Implementation Plan: Proposal of Best Available Retrofit Technology (BART) and Interstate Transport Provisions, 83 Fed. Reg. 43,586 (proposed Aug. 27, 2018); Promulgation of Air Quality Implementation Plans;

State of Texas; Regional Haze and Interstate Visibility Transport Federal Implementation Plan: Proposal of Best Available Retrofit Technology (BART) and Interstate Visibility Transport Provisions, 84 Fed. Reg. 61,850 (proposed Nov. 14, 2019).

66. Promulgation of Air Quality Implementation Plans; State of Texas; Regional Haze and Interstate Visibility Transport Federal Implementation Plan, 85 Fed. Reg. 49,170 (Aug. 12, 2020).

67. Petition for Partial Reconsideration of Interstate Transport of Fine Particulate Matter: Revision of Federal Implementation Plan Requirements for Texas; Notice of Action Denying Petition for Reconsideration, 85 Fed. Reg. 40,286 (July 6, 2020).

68. Protection of Visibility: Amendments to Requirements for State Plans, 82 Fed. Reg. 3078 (Jan. 10, 2017) ("January 2017 rule"). EPA also gave the rule revisions an effective date of January 10, 2017, contrary to EPA's typical practice of making such regulations effective at least thirty days after *Federal Register* publication. *See id.* at 3078, 3079. That action on the timing of the rule revisions' effectiveness precluded possible revocation or amendment of the rule revisions by the incoming administration in the absence of new rulemaking proceedings.

69. 40 C.F.R. § 51.308(f).

70. *Id.* § 51.308(g); 82 Fed. Reg. at 3119–20.

71. 40 C.F.R. § 51.308(f)(2)(ii); *see also id.* § 51.308(f)(2)(iii); 82 Fed. Reg. at 3088, 3095–96.

72. 82 Fed. Reg. at 3080, 3090–96.

73. *Id.* at 3093 ("The [uniform rate of progress] is not a safe harbor . . . , and states may not subsequently reject control measures that they have already determined are reasonable.").

74. *Id.* This "additional analytical obligation" is described and codified at 40 C.F.R. § 51.308(f)(3)(ii).

75. 40 C.F.R. § 51.308(f)(1)(vi)(B).

76. *Texas v. EPA*, No. 17-1021 (and consolidated cases) (D.C. Cir. filed Jan. 23, 2017).

77. *See* Memorandum from Andrew R. Wheeler, Acting Adm'r, EPA, to Assistant Adm'r for Air & Radiation, Gen. Counsel, & Reg'l Adm'rs, Regional Haze Reform Roadmap (Sept. 11, 2018).

78. EPA-454/R-18-010 (Dec. 20, 2018) ("December 2018 Technical Guidance").

79. EPA, Guidance on Regional Haze State Implementation Plans for the Second Implementation Period, EPA-457/B-19-003 (Aug. 20, 2019) ("2019 Final Guidance").

80. EPA, EPA-457/P-16-001, Draft Guidance on Progress Tracking Metrics, Long-term Strategies, Reasonable Progress Goals and Other Requirements for Regional Haze State Implementation Plans for the Second Implementation Period (July 2016). The 2019 Final Guidance supersedes the July 2016 draft, except for Section 5 of that draft, which is superseded by the December 2018 Technical Guidance.

81. Although section 169A(g)(1) of the Act does not list visibility benefits of emission controls as one of the factors that states must consider in determining reasonable progress, the guidance recognizes that states may consider that factor, given that visibility improvement is the purpose of the program. *See, e.g.*, 2019 Final Guidance at 28, 34–36.

82. EPA, Technical Support Document for EPA's Updated 2028 Regional Haze Modeling (Sept. 2019) ("Modeling TSD").

83. Modeling TSD at 30–31.

84. *Id.* at 31 and Fig. 3–3.

85. For a number of reasons, the Modeling TSD did not present specific adjustments to glidepaths to account for effects of prescribed fires, although it did quantify those effects. *Id.* at 54–55; *see id.* at 44–53 Tbl. 5-1 (last column).

86. *Id.* at 56–65 Tbl. 5-2.

87. *Id.* at 67. EPA cautioned, however, "that number climbs to 26 sites (above the adjusted glidepath) when comparing 2028 projected visibility impairment to the 'minimum alternative' adjusted glidepath." *Id.* EPA added that "[d]ue to the uncertainty in many of the calculations and modeling and ambient data, additional scrutiny of the initial glidepath adjustments [is] warranted." *Id.*

88. *See* Memorandum from Richard A. Wayland, Div. Dir., Air Quality Assessment Div., EPA, to Reg'l Air Div. Dirs., Regions 1–10, Recommendation for the Use of Patched and Substituted Data and Clarification of Data Completeness for Tracking Visibility Progress for the Second Implementation Period of the Regional Haze Program (June 3, 2020) (with Technical Addendum).

89. *See* Memorandum from Peter Tsirigotis, Dir, Office of Air Quality Planning & Standards, EPA, to Reg'l Air Div. Dirs., Regions 1–10, Clarifications Regarding Regional Haze State Implementation Plans for the Second Implementation Period (July 8, 2021).

90. Finding of Failure To Submit Regional Haze State Implementation Plans for the Second Planning Period, 87 Fed. Reg. 52,856 (Aug. 30, 2022).

Chapter 7

CLIMATE CHANGE

Addressing climate change was not a focus of Congress when it enacted the Clean Air Act (CAA or Act) and made major amendments to it between 1970 and 1990. As climate change began to become a larger concern and as congressional efforts to address climate change stalled, however, advocacy organizations turned to the Act as a vehicle to limit greenhouse gas (GHG) emissions and address climate change, despite the fact that climate change, with its global causes and impacts, does not fit neatly into the Act's statutory construct. Every step along the road to regulating GHGs under the Act has been highly controversial, with each attempt yielding record-setting comment submissions, followed by multiple legal challenges.

With little congressional appetite to adopt mandatory restrictions on GHG emissions, regulatory action under the Act may be one of the few sources of mandatory restrictions on GHG emissions facing the U.S. economy for the foreseeable future.

I. CAA Authority to Regulate GHG Emissions

In the late 1990s and early 2000s, dueling memoranda and statements by three general counsels of the U.S. Environmental Protection Agency (EPA or Agency) considered the question of the Agency's authority to regulate GHGs under the Act. Two general counsels interpreted the Act as giving the Agency authority to regulate carbon dioxide (CO_2), while one did not.[1] Even though not legally binding, these statements expressed the changing policy views of the Agency on the question of whether it could regulate GHG emissions and served as the foundation for a petition for rulemaking filed with EPA by the International Center for Technology Assessment (ICTA) and 18 other entities in 1999.

The ICTA petition asked EPA to regulate emissions of CO_2 and three other GHGs—methane (CH_4), nitrous oxide (N_2O), and hydrofluorocarbons (HFCs)—from new motor vehicles and new motor vehicle engines under section 202(a)

(1) of the Act to address global climate change. Section 202(a)(1) authorizes the EPA Administrator to:

> [B]y regulation prescribe (and from time to time revise) in accordance with the provisions of this section, standards applicable to the emission of any air pollutant from any class or classes of new motor vehicles or new motor vehicle engines, which in his judgment cause, or contribute to, air pollution which may reasonably be anticipated to endanger public health or welfare.[2]

EPA asked for public comment on the ICTA petition in 2001[3] but failed to take final action on it.

When ICTA filed suit to enforce their right to a reasonably timely response, EPA responded by denying the petition, citing lack of statutory authority, various policy reasons, and conflict with the Energy Policy and Conservation Act's (EPCA's) directive that regulation of fuel economy standards lie solely with the Department of Transportation.[4] Numerous parties challenged EPA's denial. When the U.S. Court of Appeals for the District of Columbia Circuit (D.C. Circuit) upheld the denial in a divided three-part opinion,[5] petitioners appealed to the U.S. Supreme Court, which granted review.

The Supreme Court's landmark decision in *Massachusetts v. EPA* held that GHGs are within the scope of "air pollutants" as defined by the Act and that section 202(a)(1) authorizes EPA to regulate GHG emissions from new motor vehicles if EPA determines that such emissions meet the "endangerment" test for regulation under section 202(a)(1).[6] Specifically, the Court held that GHGs are air pollutants covered by the Act, that the definition of "air pollutant" under the Act is "sweeping," encompassing "'all airborne compounds of whatever stripe,'"[7] and that EPA must determine whether GHG emissions from new motor vehicles cause or contribute to endangerment of public health or welfare.[8]

The Court found that EPA failed to provide a legally adequate justification for its denial of the ICTA petition because it improperly considered factors outside the scope of the Act.[9] With regard to the question of whether the Department of Transportation has exclusive jurisdiction over fuel economy standards, the Court found "no reason to think the two agencies cannot both administer their obligations and yet avoid inconsistency."[10] The Court made clear that EPA could regulate under section 202(a)(1) only "[i]f EPA makes a finding of endangerment" and that "EPA no doubt has significant latitude as to the manner, timing, [and] content" of any regulations.[11] The Court added, however, that "EPA can avoid taking further action only if it determines that [GHGs] do not contribute to climate change or if it provides some reasonable explanation as to why it cannot or will not exercise its discretion to determine whether they do."[12] The Court then sent the matter back to EPA for further consideration.

A dissent authored by Chief Justice Roberts and joined by Justices Scalia, Thomas, and Alito stated that those justices would not have found standing by any petitioner.[13] A separate dissent authored by Justice Scalia and joined by the Chief Justice and Justices Thomas and Alito addressed the merits of the case and argued that the majority substituted "its own desired outcome for the reasoned judgment of the responsible agency."[14]

II. EPA'S First Efforts to Regulate GHG Emissions Under the Act

A. The GHG Reporting Rule

In 2007, following the Supreme Court's decision in *Massachusetts*, Congress included a provision in an appropriations bill requiring EPA to adopt a mandatory GHG reporting rule for large stationary and certain mobile sources.[15] EPA adopted this rule in October 2009,[16] and has periodically revised it since to add source categories and make other adjustments. With few exceptions, the rule generally requires stationary sources emitting more than 25,000 metric tons of carbon dioxide equivalent (CO_2e) per year[17] to report to EPA their annual GHG emissions for the prior year. It also requires reporting from manufacturers and suppliers of certain products, including mobile sources, that would result in GHG emissions if released, combusted, or oxidized. The first emission reports under the rule were submitted in September 2011 for the 2010 emissions year. Most reported data are available to the public electronically on EPA's website.

B. EPA's Advance Notice of Proposed Rulemaking

In 2008, EPA published an Advance Notice of Proposed Rulemaking (ANPR) regarding how it might regulate GHGs under the Act.[18] In the ANPR, EPA sought comment on a broad array of issues relevant to EPA's possible regulation of GHGs under various Clean Air Act programs and how the Agency should respond to the *Massachusetts* decision. Recognizing that GHG emissions, particularly CO_2 emissions, are ubiquitous, EPA noted that "[t]he potential regulation of greenhouse gases under any portion of the Clean Air Act could result in an unprecedented expansion of EPA authority that would have a profound effect on virtually every sector of the economy and touch every household in the land."[19]

C. The Endangerment Finding

In December 2009, EPA made two distinct findings: first, that the combination of "'well-mixed [GHGs]" of CO_2, CH_4, N_2O, HFCs, perfluorocarbons (PFCs), and sulfur hexafluoride (SF_6) "in the atmosphere may reasonably be anticipated both to endanger public health and to endanger public welfare,"[20] and that the combined emissions of four of those GHGs (CO_2, CH_4, N_2O, and HFCs) from new motor vehicles and new motor vehicle engines contribute to that endangering air pollution.[21] EPA made clear that the findings "are in response to the Supreme Court's decision in *Massachusetts v. EPA*" and that they "are for purposes of [Clean Air Act] section 202(a)."[22] It also stated, in response to public comments, that the test for endangerment does not require that any resulting regulations be able to "fruitfully attack" the endangerment: "EPA's belief one way or the other regarding whether regulation of greenhouse gases from new motor vehicles would be 'effective' is irrelevant in making the endangerment and contribution decisions before EPA."[23]

The findings were a prerequisite for EPA's regulation of GHG emission standards for light-duty vehicles. Once EPA finalized GHG emission standards for motor vehicles, it then said that it was compelled to regulate GHGs from stationary sources under the Prevention of Significant Deterioration (PSD) and Title V permitting programs of the Act.

Between December 2009 and March 2010, numerous petitions for administrative reconsideration were filed with EPA, including a petition by nine members of the U.S. House of Representatives, asking EPA to reconsider the endangerment finding. Several judicial challenges also were filed. EPA denied the petitions for administrative reconsideration, which focused on the validity of the climate science on which the Agency had relied in its determination.[24] Challenges by numerous parties to that denial were consolidated with the petitions filed challenging the endangerment finding itself. Subsequently, between 2017 and 2019, EPA received four additional petitions asking the Agency either to reconsider or to initiate rulemaking in connection with the 2009 endangerment finding. In 2022, EPA denied those petitions, and that denial also was challenged.[25] The legal challenges to the endangerment finding and the denial of reconsideration of the endangerment finding are discussed in Section V.

III. Regulation of GHG Emissions From Mobile Sources and Fuels Under Title II of the Clean Air Act

A. The California Waiver

Although EPA was initially hesitant to regulate GHG emissions under the Act and did not attempt to do so until after the Supreme Court's 2007 decision in *Massachusetts*, California's first attempt to limit GHG emissions from mobile sources dates back to 2004. The Act generally preempts state regulation of mobile source emissions, but section 209(b) permits California to implement state emissions standards that are more protective of public health and welfare than federal standards if EPA grants the state a waiver to do so.[26] In 2004, the California Air Resources Board (CARB) adopted standards to regulate GHG emissions from new passenger cars, light-duty trucks, and medium-duty vehicles, which California's Office of Administrative Law approved; and, in 2005, CARB submitted a waiver request to EPA under section 209(b).[27]

EPA denied CARB's waiver request in 2008.[28] However, shortly after taking office in 2009, President Obama directed EPA to reconsider the request,[29] and EPA subsequently granted a waiver of Clean Air Act preemption for California's GHG emissions standards.[30] EPA granted California a second waiver for GHG emission standards in 2013 as part of the state's Advanced Clean Car Program for model years 2015 through 2025.[31] The waiver permitted the state to promulgate a new suite of regulations concerning emission standards for smog-causing pollutants, emission standards for GHGs, and the state's Zero Emission Vehicle (ZEV) program.[32] Although the Trump administration revoked California's waiver in 2019, the Biden administration rescinded the withdrawal in 2022.[33] The final rules and the related litigation are discussed in chapter 8.

B. Federal-State-Automobile Manufacturers' Agreement and Standards for Light-Duty Vehicles

Since 2009, at least seventeen other states have adopted some portion of California's GHG emissions standards for light-duty motor vehicles as permitted by section 177 of the Act, potentially subjecting a significant portion of the national market for new light-duty vehicles to California's standards.[34] Faced with the prospect of having to comply with two sets of motor vehicle emissions standards, auto manufacturers joined environmental advocacy organizations in calling for federal action to develop a uniform national regulatory scheme for GHG emissions from motor vehicles.

In a May 2009 Rose Garden ceremony attended by representatives of several major auto manufacturers, President Obama announced the establishment of a "National Program" in accordance with a new National Fuel Efficiency Policy to coordinate the efforts of EPA, the Department of Transportation, and California in developing harmonized regulations governing GHG emissions from light-duty vehicles for model years 2012–2016.[35] The new policy was supported by auto manufacturers, environmental advocacy organizations, the United Auto Workers, and several states.[36] The Department of Transportation, which establishes motor vehicle fuel economy standards through the National Highway Traffic Safety Administration (NHTSA), was an important part of this coordinated approach because reducing fuel consumption through greater fuel economy is the primary method of reducing GHG emissions from motor vehicles.

C. Light-Duty Vehicle Standards

Seven months after President Obama announced the National Fuel Efficiency Policy, EPA finalized the endangerment finding. Once EPA made that finding, it was then required to regulate GHG emissions from motor vehicles.[37] Section 202(a) requires EPA to regulate the emission of air pollutants from "any class or classes of new motor vehicles or new motor vehicle engines, which . . . cause, or contribute to, air pollution which may reasonably be anticipated to endanger public health or welfare."[38]

In May 2010, EPA and NHTSA jointly published what is known as the "Tailpipe Rule," which implemented the National Fuel Efficiency Policy and fulfilled EPA's requirements under section 202(a).[39] Numerous states and industry groups challenged the Tailpipe Rule. That litigation is discussed in Section V.

The "National Program" concept was extended with the issuance of another EPA/NHTSA joint final rule in 2012. In that rule, EPA finalized a set of more stringent GHG emission standards for model years 2017 through 2025, and NHTSA issued final Corporate Average Fuel Economy (CAFE) standards for model years 2017 through 2021 and projected standards for model years 2022 to 2025, to be finalized in a future rulemaking.[40] More recently, in 2021, EPA finalized standards for model years 2023–2026,[41] revising less-stringent standards adopted by the prior administration the year before.[42] Each of those rules also was challenged judicially.

All of the above rules, related litigation, and EPA's plans for new standards, are discussed in chapter 8.

D. Heavy-Duty Vehicle Standards

Following on the example of the light-duty National Fuel Efficiency Policy, in May 2010, President Obama held another Rose Garden ceremony during which he signed a presidential memorandum directing EPA and NHTSA to cooperate again in developing fuel economy and GHG emissions standards for commercial medium- and heavy-duty vehicles beginning with model year 2014.[43] As with the light-duty vehicle regulations, this coordinated regulatory approach to heavy-duty vehicles was supported by California and by the automobile and truck manufacturing industry.[44]

In 2011, EPA (in a joint final rule with NHTSA) adopted final Phase 1 GHG emission standards for heavy-duty vehicles and engines over 8,500 pounds gross vehicle weight rating (GVWR) beginning in model year 2014.[45] In 2016, EPA (again, in a joint final rule with NHTSA) adopted final Phase 2 GHG emission standards for these vehicles through model year 2027.[46] In March 2022, EPA proposed more stringent GHG standards for certain commercial vehicle categories in the heavy-duty Phase 2 program, starting with model year 2027.[47] These standards, related litigation, and EPA's plans for future standards are discussed in detail in chapter 8.

E. Renewable Fuel Standard Program

In the Energy Policy Act of 2005,[48] Congress created the renewable fuel standard (RFS) program to expand the renewable fuels sector, thus reducing greenhouse gas emissions and reliance on imported oil. As enacted, the program required that a minimum volume of renewable fuel be used in gasoline sold in the United States each year, ramping up from 4 billion gallons in 2006 to 7.5 billion gallons in 2012.[49] In the Energy Independence and Security Act of 2007, Congress strengthened the RFS program by substantially increasing the volumes of renewable fuel required to be used each year, extending the time frame over which those volumes ramp up through at least 2022, differentiating renewable fuels into four nested categories, and expanding the program to cover nearly all transportation fuels.[50] To carry out the program's mandate, EPA must determine and publish the applicable renewable fuel obligation for fuel refineries, blenders, and importers for each calendar year by November 30 of the preceding year, expressed as a volume percentage of transportation fuel sold or introduced into commerce in the United States.[51] EPA has the discretion to waive the mandate if the Agency determines that it would "severely harm the economy or environment" or that there is an "inadequate domestic supply."[52]

The RFS program is discussed in greater detail in chapter 8. EPA's implementation of the program has been the subject of significant controversy as the Agency's annual renewable fuel obligations have routinely exceeded the production capacity of the nation's renewable fuel suppliers.

F. Aircraft Standards

Initial efforts to regulate GHG emissions from aircraft came only months after the Supreme Court's decision in *Massachusetts*. A coalition of environmental advocacy organizations submitted a petition for rulemaking requesting that EPA issue an endangerment finding for aviation emissions under section 231 of the Act, which specifically addresses aircraft.[53] Section 231(a) requires EPA to regulate the emission of air pollutants from "any class or classes of aircraft engines, which in [its] judgment, causes, or contributes to, air pollution which may reasonably be anticipated to endanger public health or welfare."[54]

In 2010, the coalition successfully sued EPA for failure to respond to the petition.[55] Relying heavily on *Massachusetts*, the U.S. District Court for the District of Columbia held that an endangerment finding under section 231 was a necessary prerequisite to regulate aircraft emissions.[56] While the court acknowledged that EPA has broad discretion to determine what standards are appropriate for aircraft emissions, it held that this discretion "does not extend to eschewing a required component of the regulatory process."[57] EPA issued its response the next year and informed the petitioners that it was "not prepared at this time to initiate the rulemaking."[58]

In 2016, EPA reversed its position and issued an endangerment finding for GHG emissions from aircraft.[59] EPA concluded that the combination of six "well-mixed" GHGs from certain classes of aircraft engines contributes to air pollution that "may reasonably be anticipated to endanger the public health and welfare of current and future generations."[60] EPA noted that the GHGs were the same six GHGs that were defined in the 2009 endangerment finding for motor vehicles.[61] Accordingly, in 2021, EPA issued GHG emission standards for certain classes of airplanes and airplane engines, including new commercial airplanes and large passenger jets.[62] GHG rules for aircraft engines and related litigation are discussed further in chapter 8.

IV. Regulating GHGs Under the Act's Prevention of Significant Deterioration (PSD) and Title V Permitting Programs

As discussed in greater detail in chapter 4, new and modified major stationary sources of regulated air pollutants must obtain preconstruction permits to prevent significant deterioration of air quality in those areas. EPA's PSD regulations require newly constructed or modified major sources that emit one or more "regulated [new source review (NSR)] pollutant[s]"[63] above certain thresholds to obtain a PSD permit and to install "best available control technology" (BACT) for those regulated NSR pollutants.[64] The definition of "regulated NSR pollutant" includes "[a]ny pollutant that otherwise is subject to regulation under the Act."[65]

A. In re: Deseret Power Electric Cooperative

Four months after the decision in *Massachusetts*, EPA's Region 8 issued a PSD permit to Deseret Power Electric Cooperative to build a new waste-coal-fired electric generating unit (EGU) in Bonanza, Utah, without addressing the plant's eventual CO_2 emissions.[66] Sierra Club petitioned EPA's Environmental Appeals Board (EAB) for review of the decision, arguing that Region 8 erred in failing to require BACT for the plant's CO_2 emissions.[67]

Sierra Club argued that CO_2 is a pollutant "subject to regulation" under the Act for PSD purposes through section 821 of the 1990 amendments. Section 821 requires EGUs subject to the Act's Acid Rain Program to monitor and report their CO_2 emissions. Sierra Club took issue with EPA's position that "subject to regulation" for PSD purposes means subject to emission controls or other emission standards.[68] Under Sierra Club's interpretation, CO_2 became subject to the PSD permitting program as early as 1993, when certain EGUs were required to monitor and report their CO_2 emissions under section 821.

In November 2008, the EAB rejected the Sierra Club's argument that the language of the Act clearly renders CO_2 "subject to regulation" under the Act for purposes of the PSD program and its requirement for an analysis of BACT based on the CO_2 monitoring and reporting requirements of the Act. At the same time, however, the EAB found a clear error in the Region's assertion that it had no authority to subject CO_2 to BACT based on EPA's asserted historical interpretation of "subject to regulation" under the Act as requiring actual control of emissions.[69] In other words, the EAB found that EPA had not been "sufficiently clear and consistent" on this issue to bind the Regions in responding to permit applications.[70] The EAB remanded the permit back to Region 8 to "reconsider whether or not to impose a CO_2 BACT limit in light of the Agency's discretion to interpret, consistent with the [Act], what constitutes a 'pollutant subject to regulation under this Act.'"[71]

B. The PSD Interpretive Memorandum and "Timing Rule"

The EAB's *Deseret* opinion left PSD permitting decisions in a state of uncertainty. In response, Administrator Johnson issued a memorandum stating with immediate effect that a pollutant becomes "subject to regulation" under the Act when "a provision in the Clean Air Act or regulation adopted by EPA under the Clean Air Act . . . requires actual control of emissions of that pollutant."[72] This statement distinguished pollutants that "are subject only to monitoring and reporting requirements," which the memorandum made clear were not subject to PSD.[73] EPA expressly left open for the future the question of whether the Agency should take action to subject CO_2 and other GHGs to emission controls under the Act.

In 2009, following a change in administration, EPA granted a petition by Sierra Club to reconsider the PSD Interpretive Memorandum, but denied a request to stay the interpretation during the reconsideration period.[74] In 2010, EPA took final action maintaining the interpretation in the memorandum. The reconsideration further stated that the PSD permitting requirements "will not apply to a newly regulated pollutant [like GHGs] until a regulatory requirement to control emissions of that pollutant 'takes effect.'"[75] The reconsideration specifically provided that GHG emissions from stationary sources were to become "subject to regulation" on the first date a model year 2012 light-duty vehicle could become available, which was January 2, 2011.[76] EPA's final rule on reconsideration of the PSD Interpretive Memorandum is sometimes referred to as the "Timing Rule." Numerous states and industry groups filed petitions for review of the Timing Rule. That litigation is discussed in Section V.

C. The Tailoring Rule

In October 2009, EPA proposed a rule to "tailor" statutory provisions of the Act so that the PSD and Title V permitting programs would initially apply only to the largest-emitting stationary sources of GHGs.[77] Under the Act, any stationary source emitting as few as 100 or 250 tons per year (tpy) of one or more GHGs would be required to obtain such permits, a threshold that many churches, hospitals, and office buildings would easily surpass. EPA stated the action was necessary because direct application of the statutory PSD and Title V thresholds (which were written with traditional pollutants in mind) to sources of GHG emissions would cause "immense" administrative burdens that "would immediately and completely overwhelm the permitting authorities" and impose "burdens on the small sources."[78] EPA estimated that, without relief, six million sources would need to obtain Title V operating permits (compared to only 15,000 with the rule).[79]

In 2010, EPA finalized a rule—commonly called the "Tailoring Rule"—to phase in the statutory applicability thresholds in two steps.[80] The first step applied, beginning January 2, 2011, to projects with existing Title V and PSD permits for non-GHG pollutants (or to new sources obtaining Title V or PSD permits) that would increase GHG emissions by at least 75,000 tpy of CO_2e, but "only if the project also significantly increases emissions of at least one non-GHG pollutant."[81] The second step took effect on July 1, 2011, and required PSD preconstruction and Title V operating permits for sources undertaking new projects that would emit at least 100,000 tpy of GHGs (measured as CO_2e).[82] Modifications at existing facilities that would result in an increase in GHG emissions of 75,000 tpy of CO_2e would also require a PSD permit. Title V permits would be required for sources emitting at least 100,000 tpy of CO_2e. GHG emissions above these thresholds would trigger PSD and Title V requirements even if the source did not exceed permitting thresholds for other non-GHG pollutants.

EPA conducted a rulemaking in 2012 as step 3 of the Tailoring Rule and determined at that time not to lower further the applicability thresholds established in steps one and two.[83] EPA also committed to completing a study on the administrative burdens associated with PSD and Title V permitting by April 30, 2015, and to complete a step 4 rulemaking to determine whether to lower the applicability thresholds further by April 30, 2016.[84]

In promulgating the Tailoring Rule and phasing in the applicability requirements, EPA relied on deference it is given in interpreting the Act,[85] as well as the judicial doctrines of "absurd results," "administrative necessity," and "one-step-at-a-time."[86] EPA described the "absurd results" doctrine as "authoriz[ing] agencies to apply statutory requirements differently than a literal reading would indicate, as necessary to effectuate congressional intent and avoid absurd results."[87] It described the "administrative necessity doctrine" as "authoriz[ing] agencies to apply statutory requirements in a way that avoids impossible administrative burdens."[88] EPA also relied on the so-called "one-step-at-a-time" doctrine, which, as the name would suggest, "authorizes agencies to implement statutory requirements a step at a time."[89] EPA also cited section 301(a) of the Act, "which authorizes the Administrator 'to prescribe such regulations as are necessary to carry out his functions under [the Clean Air Act].'"[90]

Numerous states and industry groups filed petitions for review challenging the Tailoring Rule. That litigation, in which portions of the rule were ultimately vacated by the Supreme Court, is discussed in Section V.

D. The PSD SIP Call and FIPs

After finalizing the Tailoring Rule in 2010, EPA conducted several rulemakings to address potential issues with states' implementation of their PSD programs for sources of GHGs. After notice and comment, EPA issued a "SIP Call" finding the PSD provisions in thirteen states' EPA-approved state implementation plans (SIPs) were "substantially inadequate" to meet Clean Air Act requirements because they did not authorize application of PSD requirements to sources' GHG emissions.[91] The final rule established the deadline for each state's submission of SIP revisions to incorporate GHGs into the state's PSD program. Seven of the states chose to accept the earliest SIP submittal deadline of December 22, 2010.[92] When those states failed to meet that deadline, EPA simultaneously issued a finding of failure to submit,[93] and a federal implementation plan (FIP) for those seven states.[94] On that same day, EPA also issued a proposed SIP Call and FIP rule for Texas,[95] along with an interim final rule.[96] In the interim final rule, EPA partially disapproved Texas's PSD SIP under the Act's "error correction" provisions of section 110(k)(6) asserting that it made an error when it previously approved Texas's PSD SIP because Texas did not address how its program would apply to pollutants newly subject to regulation or provide assurances that the program had adequate legal authority to apply to such pollutants.[97] The interim final rule expired on its own terms, and EPA published its final rule disapproving Texas's PSD SIP and imposing a FIP on Texas.[98]

All of the rules were challenged judicially. That litigation is discussed in Section V.

V. Litigation Challenging the Endangerment Finding, the 2010 Light-Duty Vehicle Tailpipe Rule, the Timing Rule, and the Tailoring Rule

A. *Coalition for Responsible Regulation, Inc. v. EPA*

Numerous states and industry groups petitioned for review of EPA's first suite of GHG rules. Those ended up being consolidated into four separate cases, as follows: (1) petitions for review of EPA's 2009 endangerment finding, consolidated with petitions for review of EPA's 2010 denial of petitions for administrative reconsideration of the endangerment finding; (2) petitions for review of the Tailpipe Rule; (3) petitions for review of the Timing Rule, consolidated with petitions for review of the Tailoring Rule; and (4) petitions for review of EPA's past PSD rules on the basis of "grounds arising after." In 2012, the D.C. Circuit upheld all of EPA's rules in *Coalition for Responsible Regulation, Inc. v. EPA*,[99] finding that petitioners lacked standing to challenge the Timing and Tailoring Rules, and that the endangerment finding and Tailpipe Rule were not arbitrary or capricious. The court further held that EPA's interpretation of the Act in promulgating those rules (and its prior PSD regulations) was "unambiguously correct."[100]

With regard to the endangerment finding, petitioners argued in part that EPA failed to consider the "absurd results" that would stem from its action, as the Agency was required to do under section 202(a)(1).[101] Petitioners said that the endangerment finding would likely (and in fact did) lead to regulation of GHG emissions from even very small, non-industrial stationary sources under the PSD provisions of the Act, something Congress could not have intended.[102] Petitioners also challenged the record on which EPA relied in promulgating the endangerment finding and accused the Agency of "improperly 'delegat[ing]' its judgment" to the authors of secondary studies it relied on in making the finding.[103] Petitioners further alleged that EPA's failure to "'quantify'" the risks created by climate change was incorrect, and that EPA erred in defining the term "air pollutant" in the finding as the aggregate of six GHGs.[104]

The court found that EPA properly relied on "substantial record evidence"[105] in making the finding and that the finding was consistent with both *Massachusetts* and the Clean Air Act.[106] It held that EPA did not improperly rely on scientific evidence compiled by others: "EPA is not required to re-prove the existence of the atom every time it approaches a scientific question."[107] The court further held that EPA was not required to do anything more than make a "'scientific judgment' about the potential risks greenhouse gas emissions pose to public health or welfare,"[108] and that "[t]he statute speaks in terms of endangerment, not in terms of policy, and EPA has complied with the statute."[109] The court further found that the absurdity of what might result from a finding is "irrelevant to the endangerment inquiry."[110] EPA is also not required to make a quantitative determination of risk or harm in its endangerment finding process, the court held.[111] With regard to the argument that EPA was arbitrary and capricious in determining that the aggregate of six "well-mixed" GHGs was the "air pollutant" at issue in the endangerment finding, the D.C. Circuit found that no petitioner had shown any injury-in-fact in making the argument and therefore did not have standing to do so.[112]

Petitioners also challenged EPA's interpretation that the Tailpipe Rule necessarily triggered regulation of GHGs from stationary sources, and that EPA improperly failed to consider and justify the cost impacts of this triggering.[113] The court upheld the Tailpipe Rule, stating that once the Agency made its endangerment finding for GHG emissions from motor vehicles, "EPA lacked discretion to defer promulgation of the Tailpipe Rule" on the basis of its triggering other Clean Air Act requirements or its overlapping authority with NHTSA to regulate fuel economy.[114]

The court found that EPA's interpretation of the term "any air pollutant" in the PSD provisions of the Act to include GHGs was reasonable, because that term "unambiguously" includes "'any pollutant regulated under the [Clean Air Act].'"[115] Industry petitioners listed a number of reasons why the PSD program should not be construed to require permitting for GHG emissions. On these points, the court said that it is "crystal clear that PSD permittees must install BACT for greenhouse gases," despite petitioners' contentions to the contrary.[116] The court also said that despite the traditionally local and regional focus of the PSD program, nothing in the Act limits the PSD provisions to such a focus, and, indeed, Congress, according to the court, apparently intended for the program to address broad public health and welfare impacts.[117]

Industry petitioners further argued that PSD permits are required only for facilities that emit pollutants for which the area where the facility is located has reached attainment. In other words, a facility is subject to PSD permitting requirements for fine particulate matter when the area where the facility is located has reached attainment under the NAAQS program for fine particulate matter, since the PSD program is of course aimed at "preventing significant deterioration" of attainment with NAAQS standards.[118] Because EPA has chosen not to regulate GHGs under the NAAQS program, this "situs" argument leads to the conclusion that GHGs cannot be regulated under the PSD program. The court disposed of this argument by stating that it agreed with EPA's longstanding interpretation of the PSD program to mean that as long as a source is located in an area that is either unclassified or classified as in attainment with the NAAQS program generally, it must obtain a PSD permit for *any* pollutant the source will emit (in significant amounts) that is regulated under the Act.[119]

In finding that the petitioners lacked standing to challenge the Timing and Tailoring Rules, the court said that they had failed to demonstrate injury-in-fact, "much less injury that could be redressed by the Rules' vacatur."[120] The court said that it was not EPA's action in the Tailoring and Timing Rules that imposed the administrative burdens of the PSD and Title V permitting programs on certain Petitioners' stationary sources, but rather that the statute itself "automatic[ally] operat[ed]" to impose these burdens once EPA made the endangerment finding.[121] The court also stated that the Timing and Tailoring Rules "actually mitigate" the impacts of the imposition of the PSD program on stationary sources because the Act's thresholds for application are much lower than the thresholds EPA established in the Tailoring Rule.[122]

Petitioners filed petitions for rehearing *en banc*, which the court denied. Judges Brown and Kavanaugh each filed lengthy dissents to the denial of rehearing.[123] Judge Brown started her dissent with a personal story of her experience with Los Angeles air pollution and argued that despite the *Massachusetts* opinion, Congress never intended to address climate change through the statute. She further argued that EPA had not made the requisite determination regarding the "nexus" between the air pollutant CO_2 and the object of the harm—in other words, that CO_2 had not yet been found to *directly* harm public health and welfare.[124] She concluded that *Massachusetts* does not apply to and should not apply to the PSD and Title V programs. Judge Kavanaugh's dissent focused on EPA's "strange" interpretation of the statute in rewriting the 100- and 250-ton thresholds to arrive at the Tailoring Rule, arguing that the PSD program should be limited to the NAAQS pollutants and not extended to GHG emissions.[125] Like Brown, Kavanaugh would not have found that the holding in *Massachusetts* extended to the PSD and Title V programs.[126] He concluded that "the ultimate clincher in this case is one simple point: EPA chose an admittedly absurd reading over a perfectly natural reading of the relevant statutory text. An agency cannot do that."[127]

In responding to the dissents, Chief Judge Sentelle, joined by Judges Rogers and Tatel (the original panel in the case), argued that while "the stakes here are high, . . . [t]he legal issues presented . . . are straightforward, requiring no more than the application of clear statutes and binding Supreme Court precedent."[128] Chief Judge Sentelle also argued that despite Judge Brown's contentions, EPA *did* find the requisite nexus between CO_2 and the alleged harms to public health and welfare and alleged that Judge Brown's real "quarrel is with the Supreme Court['s]" decision in *Massachusetts*.[129] As to Judge Kavanaugh's point, Chief Judge Sentelle said that Congress's use of the term "any air pollutant" was meant to encompass *any* air pollutant in the PSD program, not just the NAAQS pollutants.[130]

B. *Utility Air Regulatory Group v. EPA*

Nine petitions for a writ of certiorari were filed, seeking review of the D.C. Circuit's decision in *Coalition for Responsible Regulation, Inc. v. EPA* by the U.S. Supreme Court. The Court granted six of the petitions, limiting its review to the Timing and Tailoring Rules by directing the parties to address the following issue: "'Whether EPA permissibly determined that its regulation of greenhouse gas emissions from new motor vehicles triggered permitting requirements under the Clean Air Act for stationary sources that emit greenhouse gases.'"[131] The Court denied those petitions that sought solely to review the D.C. Circuit's decision upholding the endangerment finding and EPA's model year 2012–2016 Light-Duty Vehicle GHG emission standards.

The Court's 2014 decision in *Utility Air Regulatory Group v. EPA* held that EPA incorrectly determined that sources could become subject to PSD and Title V permit requirements based solely on their potential to emit GHGs.[132] However, the Court found that EPA could require BACT for GHGs emitted by sources that were otherwise subject to PSD review under the Act.[133] Although the Supreme Court framed the case as a single issue in its order granting *certiorari*, the Court's majority opinion, authored by Justice Scalia, separated the question into two distinct challenges.[134]

First, the Court addressed whether EPA permissibly interpreted the Clean Air Act to provide that a source may be required to obtain a PSD or Title V permit on the sole basis of its potential GHG emissions. The Court disagreed with the D.C. Circuit's position that the Act "compelled" EPA to regulate GHG under the PSD or Title V permitting programs.[135] The Court explained that while its decision in *Massachusetts* interpreted the term "air pollutant" broadly to include GHGs, EPA is permitted to give the term a "narrower, context-appropriate meaning" when the term appears in the statute's "operative provisions," such as the PSD and Title V contexts.[136] Thus, the Court concluded that *Massachusetts* "does not strip EPA of authority to exclude greenhouse gases from the class of regulable air pollutants under other parts of the Act where their inclusion would be inconsistent with the statutory scheme."[137]

The Supreme Court also rejected EPA's alternative argument that the inclusion of GHGs as an "air pollutant" for purposes of the PSD program was a reasonable interpretation of the Clean Air Act entitled to deference under *Chevron*.[138] The Court stated that the Act unambiguously requires permits for sources with the potential to emit more than 100 or 250 tpy.[139] Therefore, EPA exceeded its statutory authority when it established a threshold of 100,000 tpy for GHG emissions.[140]

Next, the Court considered whether EPA was permitted to require BACT for those sources that would otherwise be subject to PSD permits based on their emissions of other regulated air pollutants. It held that EPA's decision to require BACT for these "'anyway sources'" was permissible.[141] Under the BACT provision, sources must install BACT for "each pollutant subject to regulation" under the statute.[142] The Court explained that BACT's mandate to reduce emissions of "each pollutant subject to regulation" is more clear and "far less open-ended" than the term "any air pollutant" used in the PSD statutory triggering language.[143] Even if the text was ambiguous, the Court reasoned that EPA's interpretation would still be reasonable because applying BACT to "'anyway sources'" would not result in "a dramatic expansion of agency authority."[144]

Justice Breyer authored an opinion, which was joined by Justices Ginsburg, Sotomayor, and Kagan, concurring with the majority's opinion with regard to the application of BACT for "'anyway' sources," but dissenting as to the Court's opinion that the term "air pollutant" excluded the regulation of GHGs in the PSD context.[145] Rather than read "any air pollutant" to exempt GHGs, Justice Breyer argued that the phrase "any source" should be read to include an "implicit source-related exception" for small-scale GHG emissions.[146]

A separate opinion authored by Justice Alito and joined by Justice Thomas agreed with the majority's opinion with regard to EPA's interpretation of the PSD and Title V programs, but dissented with the Court's ruling that EPA could require sources already regulated by PSD and Title V to require BACT for GHGs.[147] In his opinion, Justice Alito reiterated his belief that *Massachusetts* had been wrongly decided and expressed that the Clean Air Act was not suited to regulate GHG emissions.[148]

Following the Supreme Court's ruling, the D.C. Circuit amended its order and vacated portions of the Tailoring Rule that required PSD and Title V permits solely based on a source's greenhouse gas emissions.[149] In 2015, EPA amended its PSD and Title V regulations in accordance with the D.C. Circuit's amended order.[150]

C. *Texas v. EPA*

All of the challenges to the PSD SIP Call rules and FIPs were consolidated. In its 2013 opinion in *Texas v. EPA*, the D.C. Circuit dismissed all of the petitions for review for lack of jurisdiction, finding that none of the petitioners had standing to challenge EPA's actions.[151] In finding that petitioners lacked standing, the court relied on its decision upholding EPA's suite of rules to regulate GHGs under the PSD and Title V permitting programs (discussed above). The court stated that "[b]ecause we now hold that under the plain text of [sections 165(a) and 167 of the Clean Air Act] the permitting requirements are self-executing without regard to previously approved SIPs, industry petitioners fail to show how they have been injured in fact by the rules enabling issuance of the necessary permits."[152] The court also held that Texas and Wyoming lacked standing because they could not show "in the face of Congress's mandate in [section] 165(a) . . . how vacating the rules would redress their purported injuries."[153]

Judge Kavanaugh filed a dissenting opinion. He would have vacated all of EPA's rules and said that "[i]n [his] view, this case is straightforward. The relevant EPA regulation [40 C.F.R. § 51.166(a)(6)] plainly gives States three years to revise their SIPs whenever new pollutants, like [GHGs], are regulated under EPA's PSD regulations."[154] He stated that "[d]uring that time, States may still issue PSD construction permits."[155] Judge Kavanaugh also rejected EPA's alternative theory for the Texas FIP—correction of an error in the Texas SIP under section 110(k)(6)—as flawed because Texas's SIP was valid when approved in 1992 and was not "'in error.'"[156] He also rejected EPA's alternative theory for the PSD SIP Call, Finding of Failure, and FIP rules, which was that those states' SIPs could be retroactively disapproved because they failed to update automatically to include GHGs. Judge Kavanaugh noted that it is not a requirement of either the Clean Air Act or EPA's regulations that SIPs update automatically to include new pollutants.[157]

Petitioners urged the D.C. Circuit to grant rehearing in the case after the Supreme Court's decision in *Utility Air Regulatory Group*. Petitioners argued that the D.C. Circuit's dismissal for lack of standing was based on the court's incorrect position that PSD permitting requirements are unambiguously self-executing. This interpretation, petitioners asserted, was specifically rejected and reversed by the Supreme Court in *Utility Air Regulatory Group.* The D.C. Circuit denied the petitions for rehearing following the D.C. Circuit's amended order rescinding the regulations.[158]

D. Ongoing Challenges to the Endangerment Finding

As discussed above in Section II, between 2017 and 2019 EPA received several additional petitions seeking administrative reconsideration of the 2009 endangerment finding based on more recent research reports and data purporting to undermine the 2009 finding. EPA denied the petitions, concluding that the petitioners had "provided inadequate, erroneous, and deficient arguments and evidence for their assertions that the underlying science supporting the 2009 Endangerment Finding is flawed, misinterpreted, or inappropriately applied by EPA."[159]

Two industry groups challenged that denial, arguing that EPA's decision was arbitrary and capricious and that the court should review EPA's scientific determinations under a less deferential standard.[160] Oral argument was held April 14, 2023.

VI. New Source Performance Standards For GHG Under Section 111

Section 111(b) of the Act requires EPA to issue standards of performance for new and modified sources, referred to as new source performance standards (NSPS).[161] Under the process set out in section 111, EPA first defines the source category that will be regulated and then sets the standard applicable to that category. It also typically sets different standards for different subcategories within that category. Once set, all sources across the country that construct or make major modifications after the date of *proposal* must meet the final standard.[162]

Section 111(d) of the Act governs the regulation of emissions from existing sources of air pollutants that are not listed as criteria air pollutants pursuant to section 108 of the Act or listed as hazardous air pollutants (HAPs) under section 112. After NSPS have been issued for a source category under section 111(b), section 111(d) requires EPA to issue regulations that establish a procedure for states to submit plans that establish performance standards for existing sources in the same source category.[163] Section 111(d) does not directly authorize EPA to establish standards of performance for existing sources. Rather, it directs EPA to issue regulations governing the procedure by which states are to submit plans to EPA regarding how the states will regulate existing sources within their borders. EPA's regulations set forth a process that is much like the one used by states to develop SIPs.[164] Historically, regulation of existing sources under this provision has rarely occurred.[165] Following the issuance of the first proposed GHG NSPS by the Obama administration in 2012, EPA has looked to section 111(d) as a means to regulate CO_2 emissions from certain source categories.

Any attempt to regulate GHG emissions under section 111 has proven to be highly controversial and has repeatedly led to extensive litigation. Regulations passed under the Obama administration (2008–2016) were consistently challenged by industry groups and a coalition of states, while rules promulgated during the Trump presidency (2016–2020) were challenged by environmental advocacy organizations and a coalition of opposing states. As the Biden administration completes its actions, additional litigation seems inevitable. The following describes activities related to regulation of GHGs for two industry sectors—electric generating units and oil and natural gas production.

A. Electric Generating Units

1. *Standards for New Sources Under Section 111(b)*

In 2006, prior to the Supreme Court's 2007 decision in *Massachusetts v. EPA*, EPA issued NSPS for new EGUs under section 111(b) of the Act without establishing GHG emission standards, concluding that the Agency did not have authority to regulate GHGs under the Act.[166] Several states and environmental advocacy organizations challenged that decision, claiming that EPA was required to set GHG emission standards as part of the NSPS. After the Supreme Court's decision, the D.C. Circuit entered an order remanding the EGU NSPS rulemaking to EPA.[167] EPA ultimately entered into a settlement agreement to propose and finalize NSPS under section 111(b) of the Act for GHG emissions from new and modified EGUs by May 26, 2012. EPA also agreed to issue emission guidelines for existing EGUs under section 111(d) of the Act.

EPA missed that deadline and first proposed an NSPS for new EGUs in April 2012.[168] The proposed rule addressed only CO_2 (not all GHGs)[169] and only new sources.[170] The proposed source category included all new oil-fired, gas-fired, and coal-fired EGUs over 73 MW in capacity and designed to meet baseload or intermediate demand.[171] The proposal also was unusual in that it set a single standard across all EGUs—1,000 pounds of CO_2 per megawatt hour (lbs CO_2/MWh) of electricity generated on a gross basis—an emissions rate achievable only by a natural gas combined cycle facility.[172] Thus, in essence, no new coal-fired EGUs could be built. EPA did propose an alternative method to meet the standard, however. If the facility used coal or petroleum coke as fuel, it could comply with the standard by emitting as much as 1,800 lbs of CO_2/MWh for the first ten years of the facility's operation and then a third of that for the following twenty years of its operation (i.e., comply with the standard on a 30-year average basis). EPA noted that the initial rate could be met with supercritical steam conditions, integrated gasification combined cycle (IGCC) facilities, and pressurized circulating fluidized bed boilers.[173] The subsequent standard was designed to be met by a carbon capture and storage (CCS) facility.[174]

Several industry parties filed suit challenging the proposed rule on the basis that it constituted final agency action with immediate effect because it prevented the construction of new coal-fired EGUs. Under section 111(a)(2) of the Act, a final NSPS must be adhered to by all new sources that commenced construction after the date of proposal—not the date of the final rule.[175] The D.C. Circuit dismissed the challenge, saying it was unripe because the proposal did not constitute final agency action.[176]

Because of concerns that had been raised regarding the 2012 proposed rule's legality, President Obama directed EPA to withdraw the rule and issue a new proposed rule setting NSPS for CO_2 emissions from new EGUs as part of his Climate Action Plan. The President's 2013 Climate Action Plan specifically directed EPA to repropose and finalize by specific deadlines both an NSPS addressing CO_2 emissions from new EGUs and carbon pollution standards, regulations, or guidelines, as appropriate, for modified, reconstructed, and existing power plants.[177]

EPA released a reproposed NSPS addressing CO_2 emissions from new EGUs before the deadline specified in the Climate Action Plan, and published it in early 2014.[178] For fossil fuel-fired steam generating boilers and IGCC units, EPA proposed a rate of 1,100 lbs CO_2/MWh (on a 12-operating-month rolling average) or a lower rate with an 84-operating-month averaging period and a determination that the best system of emission reduction (BSER) that had been adequately demonstrated for these units was "partial implementation of [CCS]."[179]

For natural gas-fired stationary combustion turbines, EPA proposed: (1) a rate of 1,000 lbs CO_2/MWh for larger units; (2) a rate of 1,100 lbs CO_2/MWh for smaller units; and (3) a determination that BSER for these units was natural gas combined cycle operation without CCS.[180] The proposal exempted or otherwise did not include: (1) modified and reconstructed sources; (2) simple-cycle "peaking" stationary combustion turbines that sell less than one-third of potential electrical output to the grid; (3) EGUs that primarily fire biomass and oil; and (4) three specific plants that might be exempted because they were under development or construction.[181] EPA also formally rescinded the 2012 proposed rule.[182] The only GHG covered by the reproposed rule was CO_2.[183]

In June 2014, EPA also issued first-time proposed standards of performance to limit CO_2 emissions from modified and reconstructed fossil fuel-fired and natural gas-fired fired EGUs.[184] For modified and reconstructed fossil fuel-fired EGUs, EPA's proposed BSER was based on a combination of best operating practices and equipment upgrades.[185] For natural gas-fired turbines, EPA proposed establishing the same emission rate and BSER for reconstructed and modified sources as the Agency had proposed for new natural gas turbines.

The final rule, published in 2015, included a number of significant changes from the Agency's proposals.[186] For newly constructed fossil fuel-fired EGUs, EPA established a standard of 1,400 lbs CO_2/MWh and a determination that BSER is efficient generation (in the form of a new supercritical pulverized coal (SCPC) utility boiler) combined with partial CCS.[187] For modified sources, the final standard was to be determined by the unit's best demonstrated historical performance (from 2002 to the time of modification), which EPA determined could be met through a combination of best operating practices and equipment upgrades.[188] For reconstructed sources, EPA established standards based on size and the most efficient generating technology for reconstructed units.[189]

For newly constructed and reconstructed natural gas-fired stationary combustion turbines, EPA established three subcategories of natural gas-fired stationary combustion turbines: (1) base load, (2) non-base load, and (3) multi-fuel-fired units, determining that the BSER for base load combustion turbines was efficient generation (i.e., the use of natural gas combined cycle or "NGCC" technology), and the BSER for non-base load and multi-fuel-fired combustion turbines was the use of clean fuels.[190] EPA did not promulgate final standards for modified stationary combustion turbines under 111(b).[191]

Multiple parties filed petitions for judicial review of both the 2015 standards and EPA's denial of petitions for administrative reconsideration of the standards,[192] and the cases were consolidated.[193] Petitioners argued that EPA failed to show that BSER technologies outlined in the final standards were "adequately demonstrated" as required by section 111(a).[194] Instead, petitioners contended that EPA's determination consisted of various component technologies, such as CCS, that exist only in highly-subsidized, pilot-scale, or experimental form and are not commercially available. By mid-January 2017, briefing of the case was almost complete.

After taking office in January 2017, President Trump moved quickly to halt or undo GHG regulations proposed and finalized under the Obama administration. In March, President Trump signed an executive order that directed EPA to review and, if appropriate, revise or withdraw the final performance standards for new, modified, and reconstructed EGUs.[195] In accordance with the executive order, EPA issued a notice announcing its review of the action.[196] The court then granted a request by EPA to hold the challenges to the rule in abeyance.[197]

In the end of 2018, EPA issued proposed revisions to the 2015 NSPS for new, modified, and reconstructed fossil fuel-fired EGUs amending its previous determination that BSER for newly constructed coal-fired EGUs is partial CCS.[198] EPA concluded that the limited geographic availability of CCS and high costs associated with implementing the technology do not make it the BSER.[199] Instead, EPA proposed to find that BSER is the most efficient demonstrated steam cycle in combination with best operating practices.[200] Specifically, EPA proposed that BSER be supercritical steam conditions for large units and subcritical steam conditions for small units.[201] EPA further proposed to revise the emission limits and BSER for reconstructed EGUs to make them consistent with the standards for newly constructed EGUs and propose separate standards of performance for newly constructed and reconstructed coal refuse-fired units. For these units, EPA proposed a determination that BSER is best available subcritical steam condition.[202] With regard to modified sources, EPA proposed to retain its BSER determination but proposed to revise the emissions rate for large modified sources so that the standard could be no lower than the new source standards.[203]

In January 2021, just before President Trump left office, EPA took final action on a portion of the 2018 proposal that determined whether GHG emissions from any particular source category "contribute significantly" to endangerment under section 111(b)(1).[204] The rule, generally referred to as the "Significant Contribution Rule," finalized (1) a new finding of significant contribution for GHG emissions from EGUs (thus affirming that they remain a listed source category for GHG) and (2) a new framework for determining whether other NSPS source categories' emissions contribute significantly to endangerment. In the 2015 NSPS, EPA interpreted the Act to require such a finding only once as to the source category and not as to the specific pollutant being regulated, thus allowing EPA to regulate any pollutant as long as it had a rational basis for doing that. The 2021 Significant Contribution Rule revised that interpretation to articulate a specific threshold (defined as a percent of total U.S. GHG emissions) that would be considered a significant contribution.[205] When the final rule was challenged in the D.C. Circuit by states and environmental advocacy organizations, the Biden EPA moved for voluntary vacatur and remand of the rule based on procedural deficiencies because EPA had not proposed the action it finalized, and the court granted the motion.[206]

As of April 2023, the cases challenging the 2015 NSPS remained in abeyance—but this time to allow the Biden EPA to complete its review of the standards in light of the 2018 proposal. EPA's fall 2022 regulatory agenda projects issuance of a new proposal in the spring of 2023 and a final rule in 2024.

2. *Existing Source Performance Standards*

a. Clean Power Plan

In 2013, EPA began stakeholder outreach regarding its plans to issue emission guidelines to address GHG emissions from existing EGUs under section 111(d) as part of President Obama's Climate Action Plan.[207] EPA also announced plans for a series of "listening sessions" throughout the country where stakeholders could raise with EPA issues that they thought the Agency should consider as part of the section 111(d) guideline development process.[208]

Following the outreach, in 2014, EPA issued its first proposed rule to regulate CO_2 emissions from existing fossil fuel-fired EGUs.[209] The proposal had two main components: (1) state-specific emission rate-based CO_2 goals; and (2) guidelines for the development, submission, and implementation of state plans.[210] State goals were set based on a state's mix of energy sources and opportunities to achieve reductions.[211] Under the proposal, states were given significant autonomy to choose the best methods to achieve an interim CO_2 goal over the 10-year period from 2020–2029, as well as a final, more stringent emission target in 2030.[212]

EPA proposed to determine that BSER for EGUs was a combination of measures that include activities taken at the source or "inside the fence," as well as measures that take place outside of the facility, or "beyond the fenceline."[213] In the proposal, EPA categorized these measures into four "building blocks."[214] The building blocks consisted of: (1) increasing the operational efficiency of existing coal-fired steam EGUs through heat rate improvements and other measures; (2) substituting increased generation at existing NGCC units for generation at existing steam EGUs; (3) substituting generation from low- and zero-carbon generating capacity for generation at existing fossil fuel-fired EGUs; and (4) increasing demand-side energy efficiency to reduce the amount of fossil fuel-fired generation.[215]

EPA finalized the rule—known as the Clean Power Plan (CPP)—on the same day it released the 2015 NSPS for EGUs.[216] The final rule significantly refined the building block approach described in the proposed rule. For building block 1, EPA quantified the emission reductions achievable through heat rate improvements on a regional basis rather than a national basis as originally proposed.[217] As a result, EPA determined that heat rate improvements achievable by coal-fired steam EGUs were only between 2.1 percent and 4.3 percent depending on region, rather than the 6 percent stated in the proposed rule.[218] EPA also modified building block 2 and determined that an annual utilization rate of 75 percent on a net summer basis was more appropriate than the proposed rule's annual utilization rate of 70 percent on a nameplate basis, for the purposes of calculating the potential utilization level of existing NGCCs.[219] With regard to building block 3, EPA placed a greater emphasis on renewable energy and concluded that nuclear power should be excluded from BSER for substituting generation from low- and zero-carbon generating capacity.[220] Lastly, EPA eliminated building block 4 from its BSER determination.[221] As was the case with the proposal, EPA crafted the building block approach to offer "states and utilities substantial flexibility and latitude" to achieve CO_2 reductions from EGUs.[222]

Due to the changes in BSER, EPA also drastically modified the state-specific emission rates and mass-based targets.[223] Based on the refined building blocks, EPA set a standard of 1,305 lbs CO_2/MWh for fossil fuel-fired steam generating units and 771 lbs CO_2/MWh for stationary combustion turbines.[224] EPA derived a "state rate-based goal" by applying the national uniform rates to each individual state's power mix.[225] Additionally, EPA calculated a "mass-based" target—the total amount of CO_2 that EGUs cumulatively are permitted to emit in each state—based on the state rate-based goal.[226] Under the CPP, states were allowed to comply with the final rule by: (1) applying the national emission rates directly to EGUs within its borders; (2) achieving overall compliance with the rate-based goals established for the state; or (3) meeting the mass-based approach.[227]

The CPP Rule maintained the 2030 deadline to achieve final CO_2 emission rates or state-based equivalents but pushed back the period for mandatory emission reductions to 2022, two years later than EPA's original proposal.[228] In addition, EPA established three separate interim step periods (2022–2024, 2025–2027, and 2028–2029)—where increasingly stringent emission performance rates or state emission goals must be met.[229] EPA estimated that the CPP would reduce emissions from the utility power sector by approximately 32 percent from 2005 levels.[230]

Opposition to the CPP was almost immediate. Members of the House and Senate attempted to block the implementation of the final rule legislatively through a resolution of disapproval under the Congressional Review Act.[231] President Obama vetoed the resolution in December 2015.[232] Numerous petitions for administrative reconsideration were filed, which EPA ultimately denied.[233] And, a number of states and industry members immediately challenged the CPP in the D.C. Circuit, later arguing in their brief that the plan exceeded EPA's statutory authority because (1) the NSPS for new sources included technology, such as CCS, that was not adequately demonstrated; (2) EPA lacked statutory authority to impose "beyond the fenceline" emission reduction measures; and (3) the CPP sought to establish a federal renewable portfolio standard not authorized by Congress.[234] Petitioners also sought an immediate stay of the rule by the D.C. Circuit, which denied the request.[235]

Rather than file a petition for *certiorari* or challenge the D.C. Circuit's decision to deny their stay request, petitioners applied directly to the Supreme Court for a stay pending initial judicial review of the rule in the D.C. Circuit. In a surprising move, the Supreme Court, by a 5–4 vote, granted the stay, halting the CPP from going into effect.[236] Chief Justice Roberts and Justices Scalia, Thomas, Alito, and Kennedy voted to grant the stay applications, and Justices Ginsburg, Breyer, Sotomayor, and Kagan were in favor of denying the stay applications.[237] Following the Supreme Court's issuance of a stay, the D.C. Circuit moved directly to hear the case en banc.[238] Oral argument in the case was held in September 2016.

Following the January 2017 change in administration, the court granted a request by EPA to hold the cases in abeyance while EPA reviewed the CPP as directed by President Trump's Executive Order 13783.[239] As with the 2015 NSPS, EPA issued a notice announcing its review of the final action to determine whether it should be suspended, revised, or rescinded.[240] EPA also withdrew the proposed implementing regulations.[241] The cases challenging the CPP remained in abeyance for over two years as EPA conducted its review and repeal. After finalizing its rule repealing the CPP, discussed below, EPA filed, and the court granted, a motion to dismiss the petitions for review as moot.[242]

b. Affordable Clean Energy Rule

EPA issued its proposal to repeal the CPP in 2017, concluding that the CPP exceeded the Agency's statutory authority because it set CO_2 emission guidelines that would require measures that extend "beyond-the-source itself."[243] The next year, EPA released its proposal to replace the CPP, known as the Affordable Clean Energy (ACE) rule.[244] In it, EPA proposed (1) establishing heat rate improvement as the BSER for coal-fired EGUs;[245] (2) providing states with a list of "'candidate technologies'" of heat rate improvement measures that can be used to establish standards of performance;[246] (3) updating EPA's NSR permitting program to incentivize efficiency improvements at existing power plants;[247] and (4) amending general implementing regulations that govern the Agency's issuance of emission guidelines under section 111(d) and states' submission of their GHG plans.[248]

In 2019, in one action, EPA finalized the repeal of the CPP, promulgation of the ACE rule, and amendments to the section 111(d) implementing regulations.[249] EPA chose not to finalize the updates to the NSR provisions it had proposed, stating that it would do that in a separate action.[250] For the final ACE rule, EPA affirmed its determination that BSER for coal-fired EGUs is heat rate improvement.[251] EPA identified six "candidate technologies" for heat rate improvements: neural network/intelligent sootblowers; boiler feed pumps; air heat and duct leakage control; variable frequency drives; blade path upgrade; and redesign/replace economizer.[252] EPA also amended the general section 111(d) implementing regulations to provide states three years, rather than nine months, to develop their plans.[253] EPA reasoned, based on its decades of experience in the SIP context, that states might need the additional time to develop plans that include "unit-specific standards, and implementation and enforcement measures" that are tailored to those standards.[254] EPA estimated that the ACE rule would decrease CO_2 emissions by 11 million short tons in 2030.[255]

On the same day EPA finalized the ACE rule, the American Lung Association and American Public Health Association filed a petition for review in the D.C. Circuit.[256] Subsequently, a coalition of twenty-two states, a group of environmental advocacy organizations, and various other petitioners also brought suits challenging the final rule.[257] The petitioners argued that EPA improperly interpreted the definition of BSER to exclude measures that go beyond a single source.[258] Petitioners asserted that EPA's selected heat rate improvements alone cannot constitute BSER because it would result in only negligible emission reductions.[259] Additionally, petitioners alleged that the ACE rule lacked any "crucial guardrails" for state plans because it did not quantify a minimum degree of emission limitation.[260] According to petitioners, the ACE rule also contravened section 116 of the Act, which preserves states' right to adopt more stringent standards, because it prohibited state plans that allow emission averaging and trading.[261]

At the same time, some industry petitioners sought review of the ACE rule to challenge EPA's authority to regulate GHGs from EGUs under section 111(d), arguing that existing EGUs could not be regulated under section 111(d) because they are already regulated under section 112 of the Act.[262] Some industry petitioners also argued that EPA had failed to make the requisite endangerment finding that is required to regulate CO_2 emissions from EGUs.[263] Lastly, some industry petitioners contended that EPA must regulate CO_2 emissions through the NAAQS process.[264]

In response, EPA argued that the promulgation of the CPP was illegal because the Act strictly limits EPA's authority when selecting a BSER to measures that can be applied to a particular, individual source.[265] According to EPA, the ACE rule remedied that deficiency by establishing BSER as heat rate improvements.[266] Despite the illegality of the CPP, EPA maintained that it had authority to regulate CO_2 emissions from existing EGUs.[267] EPA claimed its authority to regulate the source category derived from the Agency's 2015 NSPS for CO_2, and did not require a new endangerment finding.[268] EPA also asserted that regulation under section 112 does not bar regulation of coal-fired EGUs under section 111(d).[269]

In its 2021 decision in *American Lung Ass'n v. EPA*,[270] issued just one day before President Trump left office, the D.C. Circuit vacated the ACE rule and the embedded repeal of the CPP holding that both "rested critically on a mistaken reading of the Clean Air Act."[271] More specifically, following a detailed parsing of the statutory text, the court concluded that the statute "does not unambiguously bar a system of emission reduction that includes generation shifting."[272] The court also vacated the ACE rule's revision of the implementing regulations under section 111(d) that extended the compliance timeline for submission of state plans and FIPs as arbitrary and capricious.[273] The court rejected application of the "major questions doctrine" to enhance the standard of review, concluding that "EPA's consideration of already-in-use generation shifting as part of the [BSER]" was not of extraordinary significance.[274] Finally, the majority of the court held that section 111(d) allows EPA to regulate CO_2 emissions from power plants, adopting EPA's long-standing interpretation of the Act that section

111 precludes regulation of pollutants regulated under section 112, not source categories.[275]

At the time of the D.C. Circuit's decision, the Supreme Court's stay of implementation of the CPP had been in place for years and the deadlines for action in the rule had long passed. Following the D.C. Circuit's vacatur of the ACE rule and embedded CPP repeal, the court granted a motion by EPA to prevent the CPP from taking effect while EPA worked on a replacement rule.[276]

In October, 2021, the Supreme Court granted petitions by states (including a coalition led by West Virginia) and coal companies to review whether section 111(d) of the Act authorizes EPA to impose standards that apply beyond the individual source level.[277] The Court declined to review the issue of EPA's authority to impose section 111(d) standards on existing stationary sources that are regulated under the HAP program in section 112, thus leaving the D.C. Circuit's holding in place. No party sought review of the court's vacatur of the revisions to the 111(d) implementing regulations.

c. *West Virginia v. EPA*

In its 2022 opinion in *West Virginia v. EPA*,[278] the Supreme Court held that EPA does not have authority under the Act to regulate GHG emissions from existing EGUs based on the generation shifting approach it took in the CPP. The 6-3 opinion, authored by Chief Justice Roberts, relied on the "major questions doctrine," which provides that with respect to issues of major national significance, a regulatory agency cannot rely on its general authority but rather must point to clear congressional authorization for its action.[279] Examining section 111, the majority rejected the idea that Congress' direction to establish standards at a level reflecting "the application of the best system of emission reduction . . . adequately demonstrated" clearly authorized EPA to mandate generation shifting that would "substantially restructure the American energy market."[280] The Court declined to opine as to whether BSER refers exclusively to measures applied at the individual source level, finding only that it did not authorize the measures in the CPP.[281] Thus, the Court reversed the D.C. Circuit's vacatur of the ACE rule and the embedded repeal of the CPP and remanded the case for further consideration.

In October 2022, after considering motions to govern by the parties in the case, the D.C. Circuit responded to the Supreme Court's remand by issuing an amended judgment that in effect reinstated the ACE rule.[282] Because EPA had informed the court that it was working on a new rule to replace the ACE rule, the court held the case (and remaining legal issues that were not resolved in its 2021 decision) in abeyance pending completion of that rulemaking. To prevent the ACE rule (the deadlines under which had all since passed) from taking effect in the interim, EPA issued a rule extending the ACE rule deadlines for state plan submittal until April 15, 2024, thus providing a period of extension equal to the time that the ACE rule had been vacated.[283] EPA's fall 2022 regulatory agenda estimates proposal of a new replacement rule in the first half of 2023.

B. Oil and Natural Gas Sector

Under the Obama administration, EPA also first moved to regulate GHG emissions from new and modified oil and natural gas production sources under section 111(b) of the Act. In 2012, EPA finalized its NSPS for the oil and natural gas sector to regulate volatile organic compounds (VOCs).[284] However, the 2012 standards did not include regulations for methane (or CH_4)—a key constituent of natural gas.[285] Three years later, EPA proposed to amend them to include standards for CH_4, noting that CH_4 has a global warming potential more than 25 times greater than CO_2.[286] The proposal also sought to expand standards for VOCs to include additional emission sources within the source category.

In the 2016 final rule, EPA set standards for GHGs in the form of CH_4 emission limits for natural gas well sites, oil well sites, production gathering and boosting stations, natural gas processing plants, and natural gas compressor stations.[287] The 2016 NSPS also required owners and operators to find and repair leaks, known as "fugitive emissions."[288] The Agency estimated that the standards would reduce CH_4 emissions from the source category by 40 to 45 percent from 2012 levels by 2025.[289] The final rule also noted EPA's issuance of an Information Collection Request (ICR) to aid in the development of regulations to reduce CH_4 emissions from existing oil and gas sources.[290]

As in the case of the GHG NSPS for EGUs, shortly after President Trump's inauguration in 2017, EPA acted to avoid implementing the rule's requirements. First, EPA withdrew the ICR for existing sources.[291] Next, EPA delayed the compliance deadlines for core elements of the 2016 NSPS by 90 days to allow a voluntary reconsideration.[292] Two weeks after the initial 90-day delay, EPA proposed to stay the standards for two years.[293] A coalition of environmental advocacy organizations and attorneys general successfully challenged the 90-day stay in the D.C. Circuit, which held that the agency could not unilaterally delay compliance deadlines in existing rules without conducting a full notice-and-comment rulemaking proceeding.[294] While the two-year stay proposal was pending, fifteen states also filed a lawsuit in the U.S. District Court for the District of Columbia (D.C. District Court) alleging that EPA was unreasonably delaying its mandatory duty to control CH_4 emissions from existing sources in the oil and gas sector under section 111(d) of the Act.[295]

Over the next several years, EPA proposed[296] and finalized two rules revising the 2016 oil and gas NSPS. The first of those final actions, referred to as the oil and gas "Policy Rule," among other things, rescinded the CH_4 standards for new sources,[297] thus removing the predicate for the states' suit seeking CH_4 standards for existing sources. The second final action, referred to as the oil and gas "Technical Rule," included revisions to the "fugitive emissions" provisions in the rule.[298]

On the day of publication of the Policy Rule in September 2020, a coalition of states and environmental advocacy organizations, including the petitioners in the D.C. District Court litigation, petitioned for review of the final rules in the D.C. Circuit.[299] In February, 2021, after the change of administration, EPA moved to place the case in abeyance to allow review of the rule under President Biden's Executive Order 13990, which directed review of all EPA actions taken by the prior administration.[300] Then, in June 2021, President Biden signed into law a joint resolution under the Congressional Review Act (CRA) disapproving the 2020 final Policy Rule.[301] The CRA resolution had the effect of reinstating the 2012 VOC and 2016 VOC and methane standards for the oil and gas segment. Subsequently, the petitioners in the challenges moved for, and the court granted, voluntary dismissal of the cases challenging the "Policy Rule."[302] The cases challenging the "Technical Rule" remain in abeyance pending EPA's review.

In November 2021, EPA published a proposed rule to revise the existing VOC and CH_4 standards, establish existing source emission guidelines under section 111(d), and take other actions stemming from the CRA's disapproval of the Policy Rule.[303] EPA supplemented that proposal in December 2022 to strengthen the requirements after receiving comments on the 2021 proposal.[304] In the meantime, the states' suit in the D.C. District Court seeking to compel issuance of existing source standards remains in abeyance while EPA completes that rulemaking.[305] EPA's fall 2022 regulatory agenda projects a final rule in the second half of 2023.

C. Revisions to EPA's Implementing Regulations for Emission Guidelines for Existing Source Performance Standards

The regulations governing the processes and timelines for state and federal plans to implement the existing source guidelines under section 111(d) are codified in 40 C.F.R. part 60, subpart B. As noted above, in 2021, the D.C. Circuit vacated the revised timelines EPA had provided in those implementing regulations as part of the ACE rule. In December 2022, EPA proposed amendments to those rules to, among other things, address the court's vacatur, add "regulatory mechanisms to improve flexibility and efficiency" in the process, and clarify requirements for when a state can apply a less-stringent standard to a facility or class of facilities.[306] EPA's fall 2022 regulatory agenda estimates issuance of a final rule in the first half of 2023.

VII. Pending Petitions for Rulemaking Under Other Clean Air Act Provisions

EPA has been petitioned by environmental advocacy organizations a number of times to initiate additional rulemakings to regulate GHG emissions under the Clean Air Act.

In December 2009, the Center for Biological Diversity and an organization called 350.org (based on the parts per million level that they believe is the safe upper limit for CO_2 in the atmosphere) filed a petition for rulemaking with EPA seeking to have seven GHGs (CO_2, CH_4, N_2O, HFCs, PFCs, SF_6, and nitrogen trifluoride) listed as criteria air pollutants under section 108 of the Act.[307] If, as a result of this petition for rulemaking, EPA chose to (or is required to, as the petition argues) list these GHGs as criteria air pollutants, EPA would then have to establish NAAQS for those pollutants.[308]

In February 2013, the New York University School of Law's Institute for Policy Integrity petitioned EPA to make certain findings and to regulate GHG emissions under sections 111, 115, 615, and Title II of the Clean Air Act.[309] Pursuant to section 111 (NSPS), the petition requests EPA to list additional source categories that "contribute significantly to greenhouse gas pollution," including agricultural sources and coal mines.[310] The petition also asked EPA to revise performance standards for already-listed categories to cover significant GHG emissions (including landfills, natural gas and petroleum systems, iron and steel producers, cement producers, nitric acid plants, wastewater treatment facilities, and manufacturing).[311]

Pursuant to Title II of the Act (mobile sources), the petition restates the Institute for Policy Integrity's 2009 request to EPA to establish a cap-and-trade system for vehicle fuels, and newly petitions EPA, in the alternative, to promulgate emissions standards for mobile sources not yet regulated for their GHG emissions, including motorcycles, trailers of heavy-duty trucks, aircraft, marine vessels, buses, and locomotives.[312] With regard to section 115 (international air pollution) of the Act, the petition asks EPA (i) to find that all prerequisites under section 115 for controlling GHG emissions have been satisfied; (ii) to require states to revise their SIPs to control GHG emissions to meet the requirements of section 115; and (iii) to advise states on their options under section 115, "including flexible regulatory tools like market incentives"[313] such as "an integrated, nationwide cap-and-auction control system."[314]

Pursuant to section 615 of the Clean Air Act (stratospheric ozone), the petition asks EPA to "[i]nitiate a public call for information under Title VI regarding the effect of [GHGs] on the stratosphere and ozone in the stratosphere," to issue an endangerment finding under section 615 if warranted,[315] and then to control GHG emissions "through flexible regulatory tools like markets."[316] The petition notes that simultaneous regulation under all four of these sections is not necessary and that regulation under one of the more "comprehensive" sections, sections 115 and 615, might be sufficient.[317]

In April 2019, Food & Water Watch petitioned EPA to regulate GHGs as HAPs under section 112 of the Act.

In 2019, during the Trump administration, EPA issued an eighteen-page letter denying the pending petitions largely on the basis that the cited sections of the Act are not "well suited" to address the diffuse, global nature of GHG pollution.[318] After the change in administrations in 2021, EPA issued three largely identical letters withdrawing the denial, stating that "the agency did not fully and fairly assess the issues raised" and that "EPA intends to further consider the important issues raised by your petition before responding."[319] In response, the Center for Biological Diversity submitted a supplement to its 2009 petition to address "additional information regarding developments in climate research and policy since 2009, and address some of the concerns raised in the Petition Denial."[320] To date, EPA has not made any additional public response to those petitions.

VIII. The Inflation Reduction Act

In August 2022, Congress enacted the Inflation Reduction Act (IRA)[321]—a sweeping piece of legislation with almost $400 billion in federal funding related to climate and clean energy. More specifically, the IRA amended Title I, Part A, of the Clean Air Act by adding the following new sections:

- Section 132. Clean Heavy-Duty Vehicles—providing, among other things, grants and rebates for the cost of zero-emission replacement vehicles, and infrastructure, training, and planning to support those vehicles;

- Section 133. Grants to Reduce Air Pollution at Ports;
- Section 134. Greenhouse Gas Reduction Fund—appropriating funds to assist with, among other things, zero-emission technologies;
- Section 135. Low Emissions Electricity Program;
- Section 136. Methane Emissions and Waste Reduction Incentive Program for Petroleum and Natural Gas Systems—establishing, among other things, a first-ever escalating pollution fee on excessive methane emissions;
- Section 137. Greenhouse Gas Air Pollution Plans and Implementation Grants; and
- Section 138. Environmental and Climate Justice Block Grants.[322]

The IRA also appropriates funds for, among other things, diesel emissions reductions under the 2005 Energy Policy Act; grants under Clean Air Act sections 103 and 105 for air pollution monitoring and other activities related to reducing air pollution at schools; funding to implement the RFP under Clean Air Act section 211(o), including investments in advanced biofuels; funding for implementation of the AIM Act of 2020; funding for enforcement technology and public information; and funding to develop and carry out programs for Low-Embodied Carbon Labeling for Construction Materials.[323]

Notes

1. *See* Memorandum from Jonathan Z. Cannon, Gen. Counsel, EPA, to Carol M. Browner, Adm'r, EPA, EPA's Authority to Regulate Pollutants Emitted by Electric Power Generation Sources (Apr. 10, 1998) (concluding that CO_2 is a "pollutant" subject to regulation under the CAA); Letter from Gary S. Guzy, Gen. Counsel, EPA, to David M. McIntosh, Chairman, Subcomm. on Nat'l Econ. Growth, Nat. Res. & Regulatory Affairs, Comm. on Gov't Reform, U.S. House of Representatives (Dec. 1, 1999) (stating that CO_2 may be regulated under the Clean Air Act if other requirements of Act are met); Memorandum from Robert E. Fabricant, Gen. Counsel, EPA, to Marianne L. Horinko, Acting Adm'r, EPA, EPA's Authority to Impose Mandatory Controls to Address Global Climate Change Under the Clean Air Act (Aug. 28, 2003) (concluding CAA does not authorize EPA to regulate GHGs to address global climate change); *see also Joint Hearing of the Subcomm. on Nat'l Econ. Growth, Nat. Res. & Regulatory Affairs of the Comm. on Gov't Reform & the Subcomm. on Energy & Env't of the Comm. on Sci., U.S. House of Representatives*, 106th Congress (Oct. 6, 1999) (testimony of Gary S. Guzy, General Counsel, EPA).

2. CAA § 202(a)(1), 42 U.S.C. § 7521(a)(1). Regulation of mobile sources is discussed in chapter 8.

3. Control of Emissions From New and In-use Highway Vehicles and Engines; Notice, Request for Comment, 66 Fed. Reg. 7486 (Jan. 23, 2001).

4. Control of Emissions from New Highway Vehicles and Engines, Notice of Denial of Petition for Rulemaking, 68 Fed. Reg. 52,922, 52,925–52,931 (Sept. 8, 2003).

5. *Massachusetts v. EPA*, 415 F.3d 50 (D.C. Cir. 2005), *rev'd* 549 U.S. 497 (2007).

6. *Massachusetts v. EPA*, 549 U.S. 497, 528–532 (2007).

7. *Id.* at 528–29 (Stevens, J., op.), 558 n.2 (Scalia, J., dissenting).

8. *Id.* at 552 (Scalia, J., dissenting) (citing CAA § 202(a)(1), 42 U.S.C. § 7521(a)(1)); *see also id.* at 514, 528, 532–533 (Stevens, J., op.).

9. *Id.* at 532-35 (Stevens, J., op.).

10. *Id.* at 532.

11. *Id.* at 533.

12. *Id.*

13. *Id.* at 535–36, 543–44 (Roberts, C.J., dissenting).

14. *Id.* at 560 (Scalia, J., dissenting).

15. Consolidated Appropriations Act, 2008, Pub. L. No. 110-161, tit. II, 121 Stat. 1844, 2128 (2007).

16. Mandatory Reporting of Greenhouse Gases, 74 Fed. Reg. 56,260 (Oct. 30, 2009) (adopting 40 C.F.R. pt. 98 and amending 40 C.F.R. pt. 86).

17. "CO_2e" is a reference that enables the expression of the volumes of different GHGs in a single metric relative to CO_2. It is calculated based on how potent each gas is in terms of its ability to accelerate global warming (the gas's "global warming potential"). For instance, one ton of N_2O is roughly equivalent to 300 tons of CO_2 according to its global warming potential.

18. Regulating Greenhouse Gas Emissions Under the Clean Air Act; Advance Notice of Proposed Rulemaking, 73 Fed. Reg. 44,354 (July 30, 2008).

19. *Id.* at 44,355.

20. Endangerment and Cause or Contribute Findings for Greenhouse Gases Under Section 202(a) of the Clean Air Act, 74 Fed. Reg. 66,496, 66,496, 66,497 (Dec. 15, 2009).

21. *Id.* at 66,499 (finding that section 202 sources as a whole contribute "just over 23 percent of total U.S. well-mixed greenhouse gas emissions" and "about 4 percent of total global well-mixed greenhouse gas emissions").

22. *Id.*

23. *Id.* at 66,507.

24. EPA's Denial of the Petitions To Reconsider the Endangerment and Cause or Contribute Findings for Greenhouse Gases Under Section 202(a) of the Clean Air Act, 75 Fed. Reg. 49,556 (Aug. 13, 2010).

25. Endangerment and Cause or Contribute Findings for Greenhouse Gases Under Section 202(a) of the Clean Air Act; Final Action on Petitions, 87 Fed. Reg. 25,412 (Apr. 29, 2022).

26. CAA § 209(b), 42 U.S.C. § 7543(b). Other states may adopt the California emission standards if they prefer those to the federal standards. *Id.* § 177, 42 U.S.C. § 7507.

27. California State Motor Vehicle Pollution Control Standards; Notice of Decision Denying a Waiver of Clean Air Act Preemption for California's 2009 and Subsequent

Model Year Greenhouse Gas Emission Standards for New Motor Vehicles, 73 Fed. Reg. 12,156, 12,157 (Mar. 6, 2008).

28. *Id.*

29. Memorandum of January 26, 2009, State of California Request for Waiver Under 42 U.S.C. § 7543(b), the Clean Air Act, *reprinted in*, 74 Fed. Reg. 4905 (Jan. 28, 2009).

30. California State Motor Vehicle Pollution Control Standards; Notice of Decision Granting a Waiver of Clean Air Act Preemption for California's 2009 and Subsequent Model Year Greenhouse Gas Emission Standards for New Motor Vehicles, 74 Fed. Reg. 32,744, 32,746 (July 8, 2009).

31. California State Motor Vehicle Pollution Control Standards; Notice of Decision Granting a Waiver of Clean Air Act Preemption for California's Advanced Clean Car Program and Within the Scope Confirmation for California's Zero Emission Vehicle Amendments for 2017 and Earlier Model Years, 78 Fed. Reg. 2112 (Jan. 9, 2013).

32. *Id.* at 2112–14.

33. California State Motor Vehicle Pollution Control Standards; Advanced Clean Car Program; Reconsideration of a Previous Withdrawal of a Waiver of Preemption; Notice of Decision, 87 Fed. Reg. 14,332 (Mar. 14, 2022).

34. *See* CAA § 177, 42 U.S.C. § 7507 (allowing state adoption of California standards in nonattainment areas); Press Release, Office of the Attorney General of California, California and States Representing Over 40 Percent of U.S. Car Market Sue to Defend National Clean Car Rules (May 1, 2018).

35. Press Release, Office of the Press Secretary, The White House, President Obama Announces National Fuel Efficiency Policy (May 19, 2009). In 2011, President Obama announced an extension of the agreement to cover a new round of standards through model year 2025. Press Release, Office of the Press Secretary, The White House, President Obama Announces Historic 54.5 mpg Fuel Efficiency Standard (July 29, 2011).

36. *See, e.g.*, Letter from Dave McCurdy, President & CEO, Alliance of Auto. Mfrs., to Ray LaHood, Sec'y of Transp., & Lisa Jackson, Adm'r, EPA (May 18, 2009).

37. 74 Fed. Reg. at 66,497.

38. CAA § 202(a)(1), 42 U.S.C. § 7521(a)(1).

39. Light-Duty Vehicle Greenhouse Gas Emission Standards and Corporate Average Fuel Economy Standards, 75 Fed. Reg. 25,324 (May 7, 2010).

40. 2017 and Later Model Year Light-Duty Vehicle Greenhouse Gas Emissions and Corporate Average Fuel Economy Standards, 77 Fed. Reg. 62,624 (Oct. 15, 2012).

41. Revised 2023 and Later Model Year Light-Duty Vehicle Greenhouse Gas Emissions Standards, 86 Fed. Reg. 74,434 (Dec. 30, 2021).

42. The Safer Affordable Fuel-Efficient (SAFE) Vehicles Rule for Model Years 2021–2026 Passenger Cars and Light Trucks, 85 Fed. Reg. 24,174 (Apr. 30, 2020).

43. Memorandum of May 21, 2010, Improving Energy Security, American Competiveness and Job Creation, and Environmental Protection Through a Transformation of Our Nation's Fleet of Cars and Trucks, *reprinted in*, 75 Fed. Reg. 29,399 (May 26, 2010).

44. *See, e.g.*, Letter from Dave McCurdy, President & CEO, Alliance of Auto. Mfrs., to Ray LaHood, Sec'y of Transp., & Lisa Jackson, Adm'r, EPA (May 20, 2010).

45. Greenhouse Gas Emissions Standards and Fuel Efficiency Standards for Medium- and Heavy-Duty Engines and Vehicles, 76 Fed. Reg. 57,106 (Sept. 15, 2011).

46. Greenhouse Gas Emissions and Fuel Efficiency Standards for Medium- and Heavy-Duty Engines and Vehicles—Phase 2, 81 Fed. Reg. 73,478 (Oct. 25, 2016).

47. Control of Air Pollution From New Motor Vehicles: Heavy-Duty Engine and Vehicle Standards, 87 Fed. Reg. 17,414 (proposed Mar. 28, 2022).

48. Energy Policy Act of 2005, Pub. L. No. 109-58, § 1501, 119 Stat. 594, 1067, 1069 (2005) (codified as amended at CAA § 211(*o*), 42 U.S.C. § 7545(*o*)).

49. *Id.*

50. Energy Independence and Security Act of 2007, Pub. L. No. 110-140, §§ 201–210, 121 Stat. 1492, 1519–32 (codified at CAA § 211(*o*), 42 U.S.C. § 7545(*o*)).

51. CAA § 211(*o*)(3)(B), 42 U.S.C. § 7545(*o*)(3)(B).

52. *Id.* § 211(*o*)(7), 42 U.S.C. § 7545(*o*)(7).

53. Friends of the Earth et al., Petition for Rulemaking Under the Clean Air Act to Reduce the Emissions of Air Pollutants from Aircraft that Contribute to Global Climate Change (Dec. 5, 2007).

54. CAA § 231(a)(2)(A), 42 U.S.C. § 7571(a)(2)(a).

55. *See Ctr. for Biological Diversity v. EPA*, 794 F. Supp. 2d 151, 162 (D.D.C. 2011).

56. *Id.* at 159.

57. *Id.* at 162.

58. Letter from Gina McCarthy, Asst. Adm'r, EPA, to J. Martin Wagner, Earthjustice at 1, and enclosed Memorandum In Response to Petition Regarding Greenhouse Gas Emissions from Aircraft (June 14, 2012).

59. Finding That Greenhouse Gas Emissions From Aircraft Cause or Contribute to Air Pollution That May Reasonably Be Anticipated to Endanger Public Health and Welfare, 81 Fed. Reg. 54,422 (Aug. 15, 2016).

60. *Id.* at 54,423.

61. *Id.* at 54,423 n.2.

62. Control of Air Pollution from Airplanes and Airplane Engines: GHG Emission Standards and Test Procedures, 86 Fed. Reg. 2136 (Jan. 11, 2021).

63. 40 C.F.R. § 52.21(b)(50) (defining "[r]egulated NSR pollutant").

64. *Id.* § 52.21(j)(3); *see also* CAA §§ 165, 169, 42 U.S.C. §§ 7475, 7479.

65. 40 C.F.R. § 52.21(b)(50)(iv).

66. EPA, Region 8, Final Air Pollution Control Prevention of Significant Deterioration (PSD) Permit to Construct, Permit No. PSD-OU-0002-04.00, Deseret Power Electric Cooperative, at 1, 2 (Aug. 30, 2007).

67. Order Granting Review, *In re: Deseret Power Electric Coop.*, PSD Appeal No. 07-03 (EAB Nov. 21, 2007).

68. In January 2008, the EAB had denied review of a similar challenge in the *In re Christian County Generation* case, *see In re Christian Cty. Generation, LLC*, 13 E.A.D. 449 (EAB 2008), where Sierra Club had also raised the BACT CO_2 issue. In its *Christian County* ruling, the EAB determined that Sierra Club had waived that issue by failing to raise it in its initial comments on the Christian County permit. The EAB further noted

Massachusetts did not address the BACT CO_2 issue, so that issue "remains a matter of considerable dispute." *Id.* at 461.

69. *In re Deseret Power Elec. Coop.*, 14 E.A.D. 212 (EAB 2008).

70. *Id.* at 239, 243.

71. *Id.* at 258.

72. Memorandum from Stephen L. Johnson, Adm'r, EPA, to Reg'l Adm'rs, EPA, EPA's Interpretation of Regulations That Determine Pollutants Covered by Federal Prevention of Significant Deterioration (PSD) Permit Program at 1 (Dec. 18, 2008) ("PSD Interpretive Memorandum"); *see also* 73 Fed. Reg. 80,300 (Dec. 31, 2008) (public notice of memorandum). The PSD Interpretive Memorandum sometimes is also referred to as the "Johnson Memorandum."

73. PSD Interpretive Memorandum at 1.

74. Letter from Lisa P. Jackson, Adm'r, EPA, to David Bookbinder, Chief Climate Counsel, Sierra Club (Feb. 17, 2009) (responding to amended petition for reconsideration dated Jan. 6, 2009).

75. Reconsideration of Interpretation of Regulations That Determine Pollutants Covered by Clean Air Act Permitting Programs, 75 Fed. Reg. 17,004, 17,004 (Apr. 2, 2010).

76. *Id.* at 17,004, 17,007, 17,015.

77. Prevention of Significant Deterioration and Title V Greenhouse Gas Tailoring Rule, 74 Fed. Reg. 55,292 (proposed Oct. 27, 2009).

78. *Id.* at 55,295.

79. *Id.*

80. Prevention of Significant Deterioration and Title V Greenhouse Gas Tailoring Rule, 75 Fed. Reg. 31,514 (June 3, 2010).

81. *Id.* at 31,516.

82. *Id.*

83. Prevention of Significant Deterioration and Title V Greenhouse Gas Tailoring Rule Step 3 and GHG Plantwide Applicability Limits, 77 Fed. Reg. 41,051, 41,051 (July 12, 2012).

84. *Id.* at 41,054.

85. *See Chevron, U.S.A., Inc. v. Nat. Res. Def. Council*, 467 U.S. 837 (1984).

86. 75 Fed. Reg. at 31,517.

87. *Id.* at 31,516.

88. *Id.*

89. *Id.*

90. *Id.*

91. Action To Ensure Authority To Issue Permits Under the Prevention of Significant Deterioration Program to Sources of Greenhouse Gas Emissions: Finding of Substantial Inadequacy and SIP Call, 75 Fed. Reg. 77,698 (Dec. 13, 2010).

92. *Id.* at 77,705.

93. Action To Ensure Authority To Issue Permits Under the Prevention of Significant Deterioration Program to Sources of Greenhouse Gas Emissions: Finding of Failure To

Submit State Implementation Plan Revisions Required for Greenhouse Gases, 75 Fed. Reg. 81,874 (Dec. 29, 2010).

94. Action To Ensure Authority To Issue Permits Under the Prevention of Significant Deterioration Program to Sources of Greenhouse Gas Emissions: Federal Implementation Plan, 75 Fed. Reg. 82,246 (Dec. 30, 2010).

95. Determinations Concerning Need for Error Correction, Partial Approval and Partial Disapproval, and Federal Implementation Plan Regarding Texas Prevention of Significant Deterioration Program, 75 Fed. Reg. 82,365 (proposed Dec. 30, 2010).

96. Determinations Concerning Need for Error Correction, Partial Approval and Partial Disapproval, and Federal Implementation Plan Regarding Texas Prevention of Significant Deterioration Program; Interim Final Rule, 75 Fed. Reg. 82,430 (Dec. 30, 2010).

97. *Id.* at 82,431, 82,435.

98. Determinations Concerning Need for Error Correction, Partial Approval and Partial Disapproval, and Federal Implementation Plan Regarding Texas's Prevention of Significant Deterioration Program, 76 Fed. Reg. 25,178 (May 3, 2011).

99. *Coal. for Responsible Regulation, Inc. v. EPA*, 684 F.3d 102, 113–14 (D.C. Cir. 2012) (per curiam), *rev'd in part on other grounds sub nom Util. Air Regulatory Grp. v. EPA*, 573 U.S. 302 (2014).

100. *Id.* at 113.

101. *Id.* at 118–19.

102. *Id.* at 119.

103. *Id.*

104. *Id.* at 117.

105. *Id.* at 121.

106. *Id.* at 122.

107. *Id.* at 120.

108. *Id.* at 117–18.

109. *Id.* at 118.

110. *Id.* at 119.

111. *Id.* at 122–23.

112. *Id.* at 123–24.

113. *Id.* at 126.

114. *Id.* at 126–27.

115. *Id.* at 136; *see also id.* at 134–35.

116. *Id.* at 137.

117. *Id.* at 137–38.

118. *See id.* at 138–41.

119. *Id.* at 143.

120. *Id.* at 146.

121. *Id.*

122. *Id.*

123. *Coal. for Responsible Regulation, Inc. v. EPA,* No. 09–1322, 2012 WL 6621785 (D.C. Cir. Dec. 20, 2012) (denial of rehearing).

124. *Id.* at *7–8 (Brown, J., dissenting).
125. *Id.* at *15–16 (Kavanaugh, J., dissenting).
126. *Id.* at *19 (Kavanaugh, J., dissenting).
127. *Id.* at *21 (Kavanaugh, J., dissenting).
128. *Id.* at *3 (Sentelle, C.J., concurring in the denials of rehearing en banc).
129. *Id.* at *1 (Sentelle, C.J., concurring in the denials of rehearing en banc).
130. *Id.* at *2 (Sentelle, C.J., concurring in the denials of rehearing en banc).
131. *Util. Air Regulatory Grp. v. EPA*, 571 U.S. 951 (2013).
132. 573 U.S. 302, 333–34 (2014).
133. *Id.*
134. *Id.* at 313.
135. *Id.* at 315.
136. *Id.* at 315–16.
137. *Id.* at 319.
138. *Id.* at 321.
139. *Id.* at 325–26.
140. *Id.*
141. *Id.* at 329–33.
142. CAA § 165(a)(4); 42 U.S.C. § 7475(a)(4).
143. *Util. Air Regulatory Grp.*, 573 U.S. at 331.
144. *Id.* at 332.
145. *Id.* at 339–43 (Breyer, J., concurring/dissenting).
146. *Id.* at 341.
147. *Id.* at 344 (Alito, J., concurring/dissenting).
148. *Id.*
149. *Coal. for Responsible Regulation, Inc. v. EPA,* 606 F. App'x 6 (D.C. Cir. 2015) (per curiam) (amending decision).
150. Prevention of Significant Deterioration and Title V Permitting for Greenhouse Gases: Removal of Certain Vacated Elements, 80 Fed. Reg. 50,199 (Aug. 19, 2015).
151. 726 F.3d 180, 183 (D.C. Cir. 2013).
152. *Id.*
153. *Id.*
154. *Id.* at 200 (Kavanaugh, J., dissenting).
155. *Id.*
156. *Id.* at 204 (Kavanaugh, J., dissenting).
157. *Id.*
158. Order, *Texas v. EPA*, No. 10-1425 (D.C. Cir. May 4, 2015) (per curiam), ECF No. 1550576 (order denying rehearing).
159. EPA, Denial of Petitions Relating to the Endangerment and Cause or Contribute Findings for Greenhouse Gases Under Section 202(a) of the Clean Air Act at 1 (undated), Docket ID No. EPA-HQ-OAR-2022-0129-0053, cited at 87 Fed. Reg. at 25,412 n.2.
160. Corrected Petitioners' Reply Brief, *Concerned Household Electricity Consumers Council v. EPA*, No. 22-1139 (and consolidated case) (D.C. Cir. filed Feb. 8, 2023), ECF No. 1985108.

161. CAA § 111(b), 42 U.S.C. § 7411(b).
162. *Id.* § 111(a)(2), 42 U.S.C. § 7411(a)(2).
163. *Id.* § 111(d)(1); 42 U.S.C. § 7411(d)(1).
164. SIPs are discussed in more detail in chapter 2.
165. *See, e.g.*, State Plans for the Control of Certain Pollutants From Existing Facilities, 40 Fed. Reg. 53,340 (Nov. 17, 1975).
166. Standards of Performance for Electric Utility Steam Generating Units for Which Construction Is Commenced After September 18, 1978; Standards of Performance for Industrial-Commercial-Institutional Steam Generating Units; and Standards of Performance for Small Industrial-Commercial-Institutional Steam Generating Units, 71 Fed. Reg. 9866, 9869 (Feb. 27, 2006).
167. Order, *New York v. EPA*, No. 06-1322 (D.C. Cir. Sept. 24, 2007) (per curiam), ECF No. 1068502 (remanding to EPA).
168. Standards of Performance for Greenhouse Gas Emissions for New Stationary Sources: Electric Utility Generating Units, 77 Fed. Reg. 22,392 (proposed Apr. 13, 2012).
169. *Id.* at 22,406.
170. *Id.* at 22,395, 22,421.
171. *Id.* at 22,405, 22,436.
172. *Id.* at 22,394.
173. *Id.* at 22,406.
174. This is sometimes also referred to as "carbon capture and sequestration."
175. CAA § 111(a)(2), 42 U.S.C. § 7411(a)(2).
176. Order at 1, *Las Brisas Energy Ctr., LLC v. EPA*, No. 12-1248 (and consolidated cases) (D.C. Cir. Dec. 13, 2012) (per curiam), ECF No. 1409856 (granting motions to dismiss).
177. Executive Office of the President, The President's Climate Action Plan (June 2013).
178. Standards of Performance for Greenhouse Gas Emissions From New Stationary Sources: Electric Utility Generating Units, 79 Fed. Reg. 1430 (proposed Jan. 8, 2014).
179. *Id.* at 1433.
180. *Id.*
181. *Id.* at 1433, 1434, 1435 n.8, 1446 n.83, 1461–62.
182. Withdrawal of Proposed Standards of Performance for Greenhouse Gas Emissions From New Stationary Sources: Electric Utility Generating Units, 79 Fed. Reg. 1352 (Jan. 8, 2014).
183. 79 Fed. Reg. at 1432.
184. Carbon Pollution Standards for Modified and Reconstructed Stationary Sources: Electric Utility Generating Units, 79 Fed. Reg. 34,960 (proposed June 18, 2014).
185. *Id.* at 34,962.
186. Standards of Performance for Greenhouse Gas Emissions From New, Modified, and Reconstructed Stationary Sources: Electric Utility Generating Units, 80 Fed. Reg. 64,510 (Oct. 23, 2015).
187. *Id.* at 64,512, tbl. 1.

188. *Id.* at 64,514.

189. *Id.*

190. *Id.* at 64,513, tbl. 1.

191. *Id.* at 64,622.

192. Reconsideration of Standards of Performance for Greenhouse Gas Emissions from New, Modified, and Reconstructed Stationary Sources: Electric Utility Generating Units, 81 Fed. Reg. 27,442 (May 6, 2016).

193. *North Dakota v. EPA*, No. 15–1381 (and consolidated cases) (D.C. Cir. filed Oct. 23, 2015).

194. CAA § 111(a)(1); 42 U.S.C. § 7411(a)(1).

195. Exec. Order No. 13783, Promoting Energy Independence and Economic Growth (Mar. 28, 2017), *reprinted in* 82 Fed. Reg. 16,093, 16,095 (Mar. 31, 2017).

196. Review of the Standards of Performance for Greenhouse Gas Emissions From New, Modified, and Reconstructed Stationary Sources: Electric Generating Units, 82 Fed. Reg. 16,330 (Apr. 4, 2017).

197. Order, *North Dakota v. EPA*, No. 15–1381 (D.C. Cir. Apr. 28, 2017) (per curiam), ECF No. 1673072 (holding cases in abeyance).

198. Review of Standards of Performance for Greenhouse Gas Emissions From New, Modified, and Reconstructed Stationary Sources: Electric Utility Generating Units, 83 Fed. Reg. 65,424 (proposed Dec. 20, 2018).

199. *Id.* at 65,426.

200. *Id.*

201. *Id.* at 65,430.

202. *Id.* at 65,431, tbl. 3.

203. *Id.*

204. Pollutant-Specific Significant Contribution Finding for Greenhouse Gas Emissions From New, Modified, and Reconstructed Stationary Sources: Electric Utility Generating Units, and Process for Determining Significance of Other New Source Performance Standards Source Categories, 86 Fed. Reg. 2542 (Jan. 13, 2021).

205. *Id.* at 2546, 2552–53

206. Order, *California v. EPA*, No. 21–1035 (and consolidated cases) (D.C. Cir. Apr. 5, 2021) (per curiam), ECF No. 1893155 (vacating and remanding).

207. EPA, Considerations in the Design of a Program to Reduce Carbon Pollution from Existing Power Plants (Sept. 23, 2013).

208. *See* EPA, Outreach on Reducing Carbon Pollution from Existing Power Plants (undated).

209. Carbon Pollution Emission Guidelines for Existing Stationary Sources: Electric Utility Generating Units, 79 Fed. Reg. 34,830 (proposed June 18, 2014).

210. *Id.* at 34,833.

211. *Id.* at 34,892–95.

212. *Id.* at 34,892.

213. *Id.* at 34,848, 34,888.

214. *Id.* at 34,858.

215. *Id.* at 34,856–58.

216. Carbon Pollution Emission Guidelines for Existing Stationary Sources: Electric Utility Generating Units, 80 Fed. Reg. 64,662 (Oct. 23, 2015).

217. *Id.* at 64,727.

218. *Id.*

219. *Id.* at 64,799.

220. *Id.* at 64,737.

221. *Id.* at 64,738.

222. *Id.* at 64,663.

223. *See id.* at 64,824.

224. *Id.* at 64,667.

225. *See id.* at 64,823.

226. *Id.* at 64,822.

227. *Id.* at 64,833–35.

228. *Id.* at 64,828.

229. *Id.* at 64,837.

230. *Id.* at 64,924.

231. S.J. Res. 24, 114th Cong. (2015).

232. Press Release, Office of the Press Secretary, The White House, Memorandum of Disapproval on S.J. Res. 24 (Dec. 18, 2015).

233. Denial of Reconsideration and Administrative Stay of the Emission Guidelines for Greenhouse Gas Emissions and Compliance Times for Electric Utility Generating Units, 82 Fed. Reg. 4864 (Jan. 17, 2017).

234. *See, e.g.,* Opening Br. of Pet'rs' on Core Legal Issues, *West Virginia v. EPA*, No. 15-1363 (and consolidated cases) (D.C. Cir. Feb. 19, 2016), ECF No. 1610010.

235. Order, *West Virginia v. EPA*, No. 15-1363 (and consolidated cases) (D.C. Cir. Jan. 21, 2016) (per curiam), ECF No. 1594951 (denying motion to stay).

236. *West Virginia v. EPA*, 136 S. Ct. 1000 (2016).

237. *Id.*

238. Order, *West Virginia v. EPA*, No. 15-1363 (and consolidated cases) (D.C. Cir. May 16, 2016) (per curiam), ECF No. 1613489 (on *en banc* review).

239. Order, *West Virginia v. EPA*, No. 15-1363 (and consolidated cases) (D.C. Cir. Apr, 28, 2017) (per curiam), ECF No. 1673071 (holding cases in abeyance).

240. Review of the Clean Power Plan, 82 Fed. Reg. 16,329 (Apr. 4, 2017).

241. Withdrawal of Proposed Rules: Federal Plan Requirements for Greenhouse Gas Emissions from Electric Utility Generating Units Constructed on or Before January 8, 2014; Model Trading Rules; Amendments to Framework Regulations; and Clean Energy Incentive Program Design Details, 82 Fed. Reg. 16,144 (Apr. 3, 2017).

242. Order, *West Virginia v. EPA*, No. 15-1363 (and consolidated cases) (D.C. Cir. Sept. 17, 2019) (per curiam), ECF No. 1806952 (granting motion to dismiss as moot).

243. Repeal of Carbon Pollution Emission Guidelines for Existing Stationary Sources: Electric Utility Generating Units, 82 Fed. Reg. 48,035, 40,040 (proposed Oct. 16, 2017).

244. Emission Guidelines for Greenhouse Gas Emissions From Existing Electric Utility Generating Units; Revisions to Emission Guideline Implementing Regulations; Revisions to New Source Review Program, 83 Fed. Reg. 44,746 (proposed Aug. 31, 2018).

245. *Id.* at 44,749.

246. *Id.* at 44,756.

247. *Id.* at 44,776–77.

248. *Id.* at 44,769.

249. Repeal of the Clean Power Plan; Emission Guidelines for Greenhouse Gas Emissions From Existing Electric Utility Generating Units; Revisions to Emission Guidelines Implementing Regulations, 84 Fed. Reg. 32,520 (July 8, 2019).

250. *Id.* at 32,537.

251. *Id.* at 32,536.

252. *Id.* at 32,537, tbl. 1.

253. *Id.* at 32,565, tbl. 8.

254. *Id.* at 32,567–68.

255. *Id.* at 32,561, tbl. 3.

256. *Am. Lung Ass'n v. EPA*, No. 19-1140 (D.C. Cir. filed July 8, 2019).

257. *New York v. EPA*, No. 19-1165 (D.C. Cir. filed Aug. 13, 2019); *Appalachian Mountain Club v. EPA*, No. 19-1166 (D.C. Cir. filed Aug. 14, 2019).

258. Final Opening Br. of State and Municipal Pet'rs' & Pet'r Intervenor Nevada at 42, *Am. Lung Ass'n v. EPA*, No. 19-1140 (and consolidated cases) (D.C. Cir. Apr. 17, 2020), ECF No. 1856250.

259. *Id.* at 26.

260. *Id.* at 27, 61–64.

261. *Id.* at 65–69.

262. Coal Industry Pet'rs' Final Opening Br. at 20, *Am. Lung Ass'n v. EPA*, No. 19−1140 (and consolidated cases) (D.C. Cir. Apr. 17, 2020), ECF No. 1856447.

263. *Id.* at 7–15.

264. Corrected Final Br. of Pet'rs Robinson Enterprises, Inc. et al. at 16-20, *Am. Lung Ass'n v. EPA*, No. 19-1140 (and consolidated cases) (D.C. Cir. Apr. 17, 2020), ECF No. 1856307.

265. Corrected Final Br. for the U.S. EPA and EPA Adm'r Andrew Wheeler at 58, *Am. Lung Ass'n v. EPA*, No. 19-1140 (and consolidated cases) (D.C. Cir. June 16, 2020), ECF No. 1856430.

266. *Id.* at 14–15.

267. *Id.* at 50.

268. *Id.* at 162.

269. *Id.* at 172–73.

270. 985 F.3d 914 (D.C. Cir. 2021) (per curiam), *rev'd sub nom. West Virginia v. EPA*, 142 S. Ct. 2587 (2022).

271. *Id.* at 995.

272. *Id.* at 951.

273. *Id.* at 930.

274. *Id.* at 967–68.

275. *Id.* at 986–88.

276. Order, *Am. Lung Ass'n v. EPA*, No. 19–1140 (and consolidated cases) (D.C. Cir. Feb. 22, 2021) (per curiam), ECF No. 1886386 (withholding issuance of the mandate with respect to the vacatur of the Clean Power Plan Repeal Rule until the EPA responds to the court's remand in a new rulemaking action).

277. *West Virginia v. EPA*, 142 S. Ct. 420 (2021).

278. 142 S. Ct. 2587 (2022).

279. *Id.* at 2610.

280. *Id.* at 2610, 2614.

281. *Id.* at 2615–16.

282. *Am. Lung Ass'n v. EPA*, No. 19-1140, 2022 WL 15163000 (D.C. Cir. Oct. 27, 2022).

283. Delay of Submittal Date for State Plans Required Under the Affordable Clean Energy Rule, 88 Fed. Reg. 14,918 (Mar. 10, 2023).

284. Oil and Natural Gas Sector: New Source Performance Standards and National Emission Standards for Hazardous Air Pollutants Reviews, 77 Fed. Reg. 49,490 (Aug. 16, 2012) (amending 40 C.F.R. pt. 60, subpt. OOOO and adding subpt. OOOOa).

285. *Id.* at 49,513.

286. Oil and Natural Gas Sector: Emission Standards for New and Modified Sources, 80 Fed. Reg. 56,593, 56,599 (proposed Sept. 18, 2015).

287. Oil and Natural Gas Sector: Emission Standards for New, Reconstructed, and Modified Sources, 81 Fed. Reg. 35,824, 35,827 (June 3, 2016) (adopting 40 C.F.R. pt. 60, subpt. OOOOa).

288. *Id.* at 35,846.

289. *Id.* at 35,830.

290. *Id.* at 35,832.

291. Notice Regarding Withdrawal of Obligation To Submit Information, 82 Fed. Reg. 12,817 (Mar. 7, 2017).

292. Oil and Natural Gas Sector: Emission Standards for New, Reconstructed, and Modified Sources; Grant of Reconsideration and Partial Stay, 82 Fed. Reg. 25,730 (June 5, 2017).

293. Oil and Natural Gas Sector: Emission Standards for New, Reconstructed, and Modified Sources: Stay of Certain Requirements, 82 Fed. Reg. 27,645 (proposed June 16, 2017).

294. *See Clean Air Council v. Pruitt*, 862 F.3d 1, 6, 9 (D.C. Cir. 2017) (per curiam).

295. *New York v. EPA*, No. 1:18-cv-00773-RBW (D.D.C. filed Apr. 5, 2018).

296. Oil and Natural Gas Sector: Emission Standards for New, Reconstructed, and Modified Sources Reconsideration, 83 Fed. Reg. 52,056 (proposed Oct. 15, 2018); Oil and Natural Gas Sector: Emission Standards for New, Reconstructed, and Modified Sources Review, 84 Fed. Reg. 50,244 (proposed Sept. 24, 2019).

297. Oil and Natural Gas Sector: Emission Standards for New, Reconstructed, and Modified Sources Review, 85 Fed Reg. 57,018 (Sept. 14, 2020).

298. Oil and Natural Gas Sector: Emission Standards for New, Reconstructed, and Modified Sources Reconsideration, 85 Fed. Reg. 57,398 (Sept. 15, 2020).

299. *California v. Regan*, No. 20-1357 (and consolidated cases) (D.C. Cir. filed Sept. 14, 2020); *Env't Def. Fund v. EPA*, No. 20-1360 (and consolidated cases) (D.C. Cir. filed Sept. 15, 2020).

300. Exec. Order No. 13990, Protecting Public Health and the Environment and Restoring Science To Tackle the Climate Crisis (Jan. 20, 2021), *reprinted in* 86 Fed. Reg. 7037 (Jan. 25, 2021).

301. *See* EPA, Office of Air Quality Planning & Standards, Congressional Review Act Resolution to Disapprove EPA's 2020 Oil and Gas Policy Rule—Questions and Answers (June 30, 2021).

302. Order, *California v. Regan*, No. 20-1357 (and consolidated cases) (D.C. Cir. Aug. 25, 2021) (granting motion for voluntary dismissal), ECF No. 1911434.

303. Standards of Performance for New, Reconstructed, and Modified Sources and Emissions Guidelines for Existing Sources: Oil and Natural Gas Sector Climate Review, 86 Fed. Reg. 63,110 (proposed Nov. 15, 2021).

304. Standards of Performance for New, Reconstructed, and Modified Sources and Emissions Guidelines for Existing Sources: Oil and Natural Gas Sector Climate Review; Supplemental Notice, 88 Fed. Reg. 74,702 (proposed Dec. 6, 2022).

305. *New York v. EPA*, No. 1:18-cv-00773-RBW (D.D.C. filed Apr. 5, 2018).

306. Adoption and Submittal of State Plans for Designated Facilities: Implementing Regulations Under Clean Air Act Section 111(d), 87 Fed. Reg. 79,176 (proposed Dec. 23, 2022).

307. Center for Biological Diversity & 350.org, Petition to Establish National Pollution Limits for Greenhouse Gases Pursuant to the Clean Air Act (Dec. 2, 2009).

308. The NAAQS program is discussed in detail in chapter 2.

309. Institute for Policy Integrity at New York University School of Law, Petition for Rulemakings and Call for Information under Section 115, Title VI, Section 111, and Title II of the Clean Air Act to Regulate Greenhouse Gas Emissions (Feb. 19, 2013).

310. *Id.* at 18.

311. *Id.*

312. *Id.* at 30.

313. *Id.* at 1.

314. *Id.* at 15.

315. *Id.* at 2.

316. *Id.* at 31.

317. *Id.*

318. Letter from Andrew Wheeler, Adm'r, EPA, to Kassie Siegel, Dir., Climate Law Inst., Ctr. for Biological Diversity et al., Denial of Petitions to Establish National Ambient Air Quality Standards for Greenhouse Gases, to Regulate Greenhouse Gases under Clean Air Act Section 115, and to Regulate Greenhouse Gases as Hazardous Air Pollutants (Jan. 19, 2021).

319. Letter from Jane Nishida, Acting Adm'r, EPA, to Kassie Siegel, Dir., Climate Law Inst., Ctr. for Biological Diversity (Mar. 4, 2021).

320. Letter from Kassie Seiegal, Dir., Climate Law Inst., Ctr. for Biological Diversity et al., to Michael Regan, Adm'r, EPA at 1, Supplemental Information in Support of Petition to Establish National Pollution Limits for Greenhouse Gases Pursuant to the Clean Air Act (Apr. 14, 2021).

321. Pub. L. No. 117-169, 136 Stat. 1818 (2022).

322. *Id.* at §§ 60101–60103, 60107, 60113–60114, 60201, 136 Stat. at 2063–67, 2069–70, 2073–79.

323. *Id.* at §§ 60104–60106, 60108–60110, 60116, 136 Stat. at 2067–72, 2077–78.

Chapter 8

MOBILE SOURCES

The reach of the Clean Air Act (CAA or Act) is perhaps at its broadest with respect to the regulation of mobile sources of air pollution. Although the regime principally focuses on motor vehicles, it extends far beyond them. Almost any mobile source, no matter how big or small, potentially falls within the U.S. Environmental Protection Agency's (EPA or Agency) regulatory domain. The list of regulated mobile sources is both extensive and impressive, including cars, trucks, buses, motorcycles, construction and farm equipment, off-road recreational vehicles, locomotives, aircraft, marine vessels, and lawn and garden equipment.

The source of EPA's authority to regulate mobile sources is Title II of the Act,[1] which essentially establishes two different forms of regulation. The first form of regulation involves the establishment of performance standards for emissions from the subset of mobile sources considered to be significant sources of air pollution. These standards limit the amount of certain pollutants that can be emitted by the source. The pollutants typically covered by these emission standards are carbon monoxide (CO), volatile organic carbons (VOCs) or non-methane hydrocarbons (NMHC), nitrogen oxides (NOx), and particulate matter (PM). In 2010, EPA also began to regulate greenhouse gas (GHG) emissions from mobile sources, including carbon dioxide (CO_2), methane (CH_4), nitrous oxide (N_2O), and hydrofluorocarbons (HFCs).[2] The emission standards for mobile sources, usually expressed in terms of a mass of emissions per unit measurement (e.g., grams per mile), are technology-forcing. Emission control systems consist of several components, which, for cars and light trucks, generally include three-way catalytic converters, onboard diagnostic computers, and oxygen sensors. As emission standards are tightened, these and other emission-related components must be developed or improved.

The second form of regulation involves the fuels upon which mobile sources operate. The purpose of the fuel provisions is twofold. They are designed either to (1) reduce further the emission of various pollutants from mobile sources or (2) require an assessment of the public health implications of the fuel's use. If information indicates that a particular fuel can result in emission reductions, the use of the fuel in certain mobile sources can be mandated. Conversely, if information indicates that the fuel will adversely affect the operation of emission control systems or present a significant risk to public health, the use of the fuel can be limited or prohibited.

The discussion here tracks these two forms of regulation. The first section provides an overview of the mobile source emission standards either developed or proposed by EPA. The focus of this section is on the crosscutting, common elements of the various emission control programs EPA has developed for each category of mobile sources. The second section, which focuses on fuel regulation, summarizes a series of complex regulations developed by EPA to regulate the composition of gasoline and other fuels and to assess their potential impact on public health.

I. Mobile Source Emission Standards

A. State Regulatory Authority: California and the Preemption Waiver

The preemptive scope of the Act's regulatory regime for mobile sources is unique from any other program in the Act. Although section 209(a) broadly and explicitly preempts any state regulation of emissions from new motor vehicles or new motor vehicle engines, section 209(b) provides for such preemption to be waived for California's motor vehicle emission standards in certain circumstances.[3] California was leading national efforts to regulate motor vehicle emissions long before the adoption of the Clean Air Act. In recognition of the state's "pioneering efforts" in emission control,[4] Congress directed EPA to waive the Act's preemptive effect with regard to mobile source standards adopted by California if the state submits a request and determines that its standards "will be, in the aggregate, at least as protective of public health and welfare as applicable Federal standards."[5] Courts have recognized that the purpose of the Act's waiver provision is "to afford California the broadest possible discretion in selecting the best means to protect the health of its citizens and the public welfare."[6]

A waiver is not permitted where the Administrator finds that (1) the state's "at least as protective" determination is arbitrary and capricious; (2) California does not need its state-specific standards to meet "compelling and extraordinary conditions" in the state; or (3) California standards and accompanying enforcement procedures are not consistent with section 202(a) of the Act.[7] Where such a waiver is granted, EPA must treat compliance with the California standard as compliance with applicable federal standards.[8] As a result of this dual system of regulatory authority, motor vehicle manufacturers face the prospect of having to produce a "second vehicle" for each model: one for sale in California that will comply with its state standards, and one for sale in the rest of the United States that will comply with federal mobile source standards.

EPA granted its first waiver to California for its GHG emissions standards for light-duty cars and trucks starting with model year 2009.[9] In 2013, EPA granted a second waiver for California's GHG tailpipe emission standards established as part of its Advanced Clean Car Program, which included a Zero Emission Vehicle (ZEV) sales mandate for model years 2021–2025.[10] However, the controversial nature of those waivers was highlighted in 2019 when, following the change in administrations, EPA withdrew the 2013 waiver based on its determination that California does not need these standards to meet "compelling and extraordinary conditions" with respect to GHG emissions in the state.[11] In that same action, the National Highway Traffic Safety Administration (NHTSA) finalized regulatory text making explicit a determination that state programs to limit or prohibit tailpipe GHG emissions or to establish ZEV mandates are preempted by the Energy Policy and Conservation Act (EPCA).[12] However, in 2021, following the next presidential election and change in administration, EPA published notice of its intent to reconsider those actions.[13] EPA completed that reconsideration in 2022, rescinding the interpretation and restoring the waiver.[14] EPA's more recent actions and the resulting litigation are discussed in this chapter.

In addition to the waiver, Congress allows other states containing nonattainment areas to opt into California's regime under section 177.[15] Any state standards adopted must be completely identical to their California counterparts in order to avoid requiring manufacturers to produce a "third vehicle."[16] Several states have availed themselves of the section 177 authority for various California emission requirements, including Connecticut, Colorado, Delaware, Maryland, Maine, Massachusetts, New Jersey, New Mexico, Minnesota, Nevada, New York, Pennsylvania, Oregon, Rhode Island, Vermont, Virginia, and Washington.[17]

Like the section 209(a) prohibition on state regulation of emissions from new motor vehicles and motor vehicle engines, section 209(e) prohibits states from adopting or enforcing "any standard or other requirement relating to the control of emissions" from certain new nonroad engines or vehicles, including: (1) new engines used in construction and farm equipment or vehicles that are smaller than 175 horsepower; and (2) new locomotives or locomotive engines.[18] There is no process for California to obtain a preemption waiver for any state-specific emission standards applicable to these types of nonroad engines or vehicles, although California may seek a waiver for its standards applicable to other types of nonroad engines.[19] Other states may adopt and enforce standards for which California has obtained a waiver, as long as they are identical to California's approved standards and are adopted at least two years before they take effect.[20]

B. Primary Contributors: Cars and Light Trucks

The principal focus of the mobile source regulatory program has long been the control of emissions from cars and light trucks, the primary contributors to mobile source pollution.[21] The basic framework for this regulatory program was laid out in the 1970 Clean Air Act. The 1990 amendments to the Act largely retained this framework while making its requirements substantially more prescriptive and stringent.

EPA's general authority to regulate mobile sources comes from section 202(a) of the Act, which directs the Administrator to prescribe "standards applicable to the emission of any air pollutant from any class or classes of new motor vehicles or new motor vehicle engines, which in his judgment cause, or contribute to, air pollution which may reasonably be anticipated to endanger public health or welfare."[22] These standards are to apply for the entire "useful life" of the vehicle, as determined by the Administrator.[23] Mobile source standards promulgated under section 202(a) are intended to be technology-forcing, but feasible: EPA must allow sufficient lead time for the "development and application of the requisite technology" before standards take effect, "giving appropriate consideration to the cost of compliance within [that] period."[24] To support its prediction that its standards are feasible, EPA must "answer[] any theoretical objections . . . , identif[y] the major steps necessary in refinement of the [technology], and offer[] plausible reasons for believing that each of those steps can be completed in the time available."[25] For parties challenging the standards, "evidence that current technology is inadequate is not enough to show that the EPA was arbitrary in predicting future success."[26]

1. Standards for Smog, Soot, and Other Pollution

The 1990 Clean Air Act amendments specified detailed NMHC, CO, NOx, and PM emission standards for "light-duty vehicles" (i.e., cars) and "light-duty trucks" (i.e., light trucks) to be phased in beginning with model year 1994.[27] These standards are commonly known as the "Tier 1" standards. In addition, the amendments laid out a framework for EPA to adopt more stringent "Tier 2" standards for model years 2004 and later. Congress directed EPA to study whether further emission reductions would be required from light-duty vehicles and certain light-duty trucks in order to attain or maintain the national ambient air quality standards.[28] Based on this study, EPA was required to promulgate more stringent standards if: (1) further emission reductions were needed; (2) the necessary technology would be available, considering the costs, lead time, energy, and safety impacts; and (3) further reductions would be cost-effective.[29]

EPA submitted the required study to Congress in 1998 concluding that all three criteria were satisfied.[30] In 2000, the Agency promulgated Tier 2 standards for light-duty vehicles and trucks to be phased in beginning with model year 2004.[31] EPA was able to adopt substantially more stringent emission limitations due to advances in control technologies and EPA's simultaneous adoption of limits on the content of sulfur in gasoline, which interferes with the effectiveness of these technologies.[32] This "system" approach, in which the engine and its fuel are regulated together, has been a fundamental part of EPA's recent mobile source standards. The Tier 2 standards establish a system of certification "bins," each with its own set of increasingly stringent emission requirements.[33] Manufacturers have the choice to certify particular vehicles to any one of these bins, but must meet a fleetwide average NOx standard.[34] In addition, EPA expanded its emission standards to include a new class of "medium-duty passenger vehicles," such as minivans and sport utility vehicles, which had previously been subject to less-stringent limitations.[35]

In 2014, EPA took further steps to limit emissions from mobile sources by finalizing Tier 3 standards for light-duty vehicles and trucks beginning in model year 2017.[36] Unlike the Tier 2 standards, which were guided by strict directions from Congress, the new Tier 3 limits are based on EPA's general authority over mobile source emissions under section 202(a). Like the Tier 2 standards, the Tier 3 standards rely on a "system" approach, in which EPA regulates both the vehicle's emissions and the content of the fuel used to simultaneously reduce the sulfur content of fuels and thereby make the emission standards feasible. EPA estimated that the fully phased-in Tier 3 standards for light-duty vehicles and trucks and medium-duty passenger vehicles would reduce fleet average emissions of non-methane organic gases and NOx by 80 percent and reduce per-vehicle PM emissions by 70 percent as compared to the Tier 2 standards.[37]

2. Standards for Greenhouse Gas Emissions

In 2009, EPA issued findings under section 202(a) of the Act that the combined emissions of six GHGs from new motor vehicles and new motor vehicle engines contribute to pollution that endangers public health and welfare.[38] This endangerment finding, which is discussed in more detail in chapter 7, triggered authority to regulate those emissions. Since then, EPA has significantly expanded the scope of its mobile source regulatory regime by promulgating standards for the emission of GHGs to address climate change.

a. The Tailpipe Rule (Model Years 2012–2016)

In 2010, EPA adopted its first suite of GHG emission standards for light-duty vehicles and trucks for model years 2012 through 2016.[39] These standards, known as the "Tailpipe Rule," were issued in a joint final rule with NHTSA, which sets motor vehicle Corporate Average Fuel Economy (CAFE) standards under authority delegated in the EPCA and the Energy Independence and Security Act of 2007 (EISA).[40] The purpose of the jointly issued standards was to harmonize EPA's tailpipe GHG emission standards with NHTSA's fuel economy standards covering the same model years to establish a National Program under President Obama's 2019 National Fuel Efficiency Policy.[41] Under the rule, vehicles faced increasingly stringent GHG emission limits each year, including a CO_2 emissions rate and caps on emissions of other GHGs, including N_2O and CH_4.[42] Although the CO_2 standards called for greater reductions than those afforded by meeting the CAFE standards alone, EPA allowed manufacturers to achieve full compliance by earning carbon dioxide equivalent (CO_2e) credits for reducing emissions of HFCs and CO_2 from vehicle air conditioning systems.[43]

EPA expected manufacturers to achieve these standards through the use of technologies such as gasoline direct injection, downsized engines, advanced transmissions, increased use of start-stop technology, improvements in tire rolling resistance, reductions in vehicle weight, increased use of hybrid technologies, and the commercialization of electric vehicles and plug-in hybrids.[44] EPA and NHTSA predicted that these standards would result in 960 million metric tons of total CO_2e emissions reductions over the lifetime of model year 2012–2016 vehicles, and that fuel savings would offset the estimated increase in the average vehicle cost.[45]

Consistent with the National Fuel Efficiency Policy, California took steps to harmonize its light-duty vehicle standards with the Tailpipe Rule. In 2009, the California Air Resources Board (CARB) adopted provisions allowing manufacturers to pool vehicle sales across California and other states that adopt its standards and to submit federal CAFE program data for compliance determinations.[46] And, in 2010, California adopted amendments providing that compliance with EPA's GHG standards will be deemed compliance with the California standards for model years 2012–2016.[47]

b. The 2012 Light-Duty Rule (Model Years 2017–2025)

In October 2012, EPA and NHTSA built on the Tailpipe Rule by enacting GHG emissions and CAFE standards for model year 2017–2025 light-duty vehicles.[48] Like the Tailpipe Rule, the 2012 Light-Duty Rule required manufacturers to meet increasingly stringent standards for each model year. Light-duty trucks initially faced a lower rate of annual reductions in CO_2 emissions than passenger cars to preserve their utility while transitioning into these stricter standards. Because NHTSA is authorized to issue fuel economy standards for periods of only five model years at a time, the 2012 Light-Duty Rule included final CAFE standards only for model years 2017–2021, but NHTSA also published projected standards for model years 2022–2025.[49]

The 2012 Light-Duty Rule provided flexible compliance options. Manufacturers could earn credits for achieving greater improvements in GHG emissions or fuel economy than required in a given model year, which could have been carried forward or traded. EPA continued to give manufacturers credit for GHG emission reductions from air conditioning systems but capped those credits. In addition, the rule provided incentives for the production of electric vehicles, plug-in hybrid electric vehicles, and fuel cell vehicles sold in model years 2017–2021 in the form of an incentive multiplier for CO_2 emissions compliance purposes.[50] EPA estimated that its emissions standards would reduce GHG emissions by approximately 2 billion metric tons over the lifetimes of model year 2017–2025 light-duty vehicles, and that the average cost increase of $1,800 to new light-duty vehicles in model year 2025 would be offset by reduced spending on fuel.[51]

As part of the 2012 rulemaking, EPA made a regulatory commitment to conduct a Midterm Evaluation (MTE) of the standards for model years 2022–2025. EPA, NHTSA, and CARB issued a joint Draft Technical Assessment Report in 2016, assessing the appropriateness of retaining the standards.[52] EPA also released a proposed determination finding that the standards remained appropriate and that a rulemaking to change them was unwarranted.[53] During the last week of the Obama administration, EPA issued the MTE Final Determination to retain the standards.[54]

c. The 2019 Withdrawal of the California Waiver and Adoption of the 2020 SAFE Vehicles Rule (Model Years 2021–2026)

Following the inauguration of President Trump in 2017, EPA and NHTSA announced it would reconsider the model year 2022–2025 standards.[55] In 2018, EPA formally withdrew the MTE Final Determination, after concluding that the standards were based on "outdated information" and "may be too stringent."[56] A coalition of states led by California, environmental advocacy organizations, and electric industry representatives challenged the withdrawal of the determination, alleging that it was arbitrary and capricious.[57] The U.S. Court of Appeals for the District of Columbia Circuit (D.C. Circuit) held that EPA's withdrawal of the determination was not a judicially reviewable final action under the Administrative Procedure Act or Clean Air Act because it did not result in any change to emission standards.[58]

Later in 2018, EPA and NHTSA proposed a rollback of federal GHG and CAFE standards, known as the Safer Affordable Fuel-Efficient (SAFE) Vehicles Rule.[59] The proposal called for freezing CAFE and GHG standards at model year 2020 standards for model years 2021–2025 and revocation of California's 2013 Clean Air Act waiver.[60] EPA and NHTSA offered three justifications for withdrawing California's 2013 waiver. First, NHTSA claimed that California's GHG and ZEV standards are preempted by the EPCA and cannot be afforded a valid wavier of preemption under the Clean Air Act. Second, EPA asserted that "California does not need its GHG and ZEV standards to meet compelling and extraordinary conditions," as required by section 209 of the statute.[61] Finally, EPA argued that California's standards and enforcement procedures "are inconsistent with" the requirements for federal emissions standards under Clean Air Act section 202(a).[62]

The Trump administration ultimately passed the major components of the SAFE Vehicle Rules in two parts. Part one (initially referred to as the One National Program rule, but later called SAFE-1) consisted of (1) NHTSA's decision that state standards related to fuel economy are preempted by the EPCA; and (2) EPA's withdrawal of the waiver.[63] Part two set new CAFE and GHG emission standards the agencies estimated would decrease regulatory costs by $86 to $126 billion through 2029.[64] However, rather than freeze standards as originally proposed, the final rule increased the stringency of the CAFE and GHG standards by one and one half percent annually from model year 2021 through 2026 over model year 2020 levels. The agencies estimated that the lower standards would decrease regulatory costs by $86 to $126 billion through 2029.[65]

A coalition of twenty-three states led by California and multiple health and environmental advocacy organizations challenged the 2019 withdrawal of the California waiver in both the D.C. Circuit and the U.S. District Court for the District of Columbia (D.C. District Court).[66] Petitioners in the D.C. Circuit sought review of EPA's withdrawal of the California wavier, and litigants at the district court level challenged the NHTSA component of the rule that found the EPCA preempted states from setting their own vehicle emission standards. Litigation was proceeding in both courts simultaneously until the district court issued an order staying the cases before it pending resolution of the consolidated cases in the D.C. Circuit. A number of challenges to the 2020 SAFE Vehicles Rule also were filed in the D.C. Circuit.[67] All of those cases were held in abeyance after the change in administration to allow EPA to reconsider the rule.

d. The 2021 Revised GHG Emission Standards (Model Years 2023 and Later) and 2022 Reinstatement of the California Waiver

A few months after the inauguration of President Biden in 2021, EPA announced it was taking comments on reconsideration of the prior withdrawal of the waiver for California's Advanced Clean Car Program.[68] Later that year, EPA finalized more stringent GHG standards for light-duty vehicles for model years

2023–2026.[69] EPA based the standards on "earlier EPA actions and supporting analyses" and "updated analyses that consider the most recent technical and scientific data and continuing developments in the automotive industry."[70] Although EPA stated that it had coordinated with NHTSA, the rulemaking only addressed emission standards under section 202(a) of the Act, leaving NHTSA to review and revise its CAFE standards under EPCA and the EISA in a separate rulemaking.[71] With respect to the California waiver, EPA completed that reconsideration and restored the waiver in 2022.[72]

A coalition of states led by Ohio and multiple industry groups challenged the reinstatement.[73] Challenges to the 2021 revisions to the Light-Duty Vehicle GHG standards also are pending.[74] Both cases likely will be argued in the fall of 2023. The prior challenges to the 2019 withdrawal of the California waiver, and to the 2020 SAFE Vehicles Rule now are being held in abeyance pending resolution of the later cases.

3. New Multipollutant Standards for Model Years 2027 and Later

In 2021, President Biden issued an executive order establishing a goal that "50 percent of all new passenger cars and light trucks sold in 2030 be zero-emission vehicles" and directing EPA to consider establishing "new multi-pollutant emissions standards, including for greenhouse gas emissions, for light- and medium-duty vehicles beginning with model year 2027 and extending through and including at least model year 2030."[75] EPA's fall 2022 regulatory agenda estimates issuing a proposal in the first half of 2023 to implement the order.

4. Additional Requirements

In addition to limits on tailpipe emissions generally, EPA also operates several other regulatory programs addressing pollutants from mobile sources. Sections 202(a)(6) and 202(k) require the control of evaporative emissions from fuel during refueling, running, and nonoperation.[76] In response to these provisions, EPA promulgated rules requiring onboard vapor recovery systems to address evaporative emissions from refueling[77] and adopted new test procedures for other evaporative emissions.[78] The Agency has adopted special limits for emissions of CO at temperatures below 20 degrees Fahrenheit because of research showing that such emissions are significantly higher at very cold temperatures.[79] In addition, pursuant to Congress's mandate in section 202(m), EPA requires manufacturers to install onboard diagnostics systems on light-duty vehicles and trucks to assess whether a vehicle's emissions control equipment is functioning properly.[80]

C. Heavy-Duty Vehicles and Engines

Heavy-duty vehicles and engines, such as large trucks and buses, are regulated under a scheme similar to that for light-duty vehicles and trucks. Emission standards for these mobile sources must reflect "the greatest degree of emission reduction achievable through the application of technology which the Administrator determines will be available for the model year to which such standards apply," considering cost, energy, and safety.[81] In adopting these standards, EPA may differentiate heavy-duty vehicles or engines into classes based on "gross vehicle weight, horsepower, type of fuel used, or other appropriate factors."[82] EPA allows manufacturers to comply with these standards by averaging emissions across different engine families or by banking emission credits.[83]

1. Standards for Smog, Soot, and Other Pollution

As with the standards for light-duty vehicles and trucks, the 1990 amendments led EPA to significantly tighten its requirements for heavy-duty vehicles and engines. The first round of new emission standards for these mobile sources imposed new standards for NOx emissions from new heavy-duty trucks for model years 1998 and later.[84] EPA followed up with stricter emission standards for heavy-duty diesel engines starting in model year 2004[85] and for heavy-duty gasoline engines in model year 2005.[86]

In 2001, EPA adopted a set of substantially tighter emission limitations for heavy-duty vehicles known as the Phase 2 rule.[87] Like the Tier 2 standards for light-duty vehicles and trucks, the Phase 2 rule relied on the "system" approach to make its significant further cuts in tailpipe emissions achievable by simultaneously requiring reductions in the sulfur content of diesel fuel. The new standards were phased in beginning in model year 2007 for diesel engines and 2008 for gasoline engines.

EPA placed further limits on certain heavy-duty vehicle emissions in its Tier 3 regulations, which were finalized in 2014 and included the light-duty car and truck standards.[88] The Tier 3 standards apply to heavy-duty vehicles and engines between 8,501 and 14,000 pounds gross vehicle weight rating (GVWR) (i.e., Class 2b and Class 3 vehicles) beginning in model year 2018. EPA estimated in its Tier 3 final rule that these limits would reduce emissions of PM and combined NOx and non-methane organic gases from such sources by 60 percent compared to the Phase 2 standards.[89]

EPA announced in November 2018 plans to further update emission standards for NOx and other pollutants for highway heavy-duty engines, as part of its Cleaner Trucks Initiative.[90] EPA issued an advanced notice of proposed rulemaking in 2020 seeking pre-proposal comment on the regulatory approaches under consideration for various elements of the program, including emission control technologies, standards and test cycles, in-use emission standards, regulatory useful life, and durability testing.[91]

In August 2021, after a change in administration, EPA unveiled a new version of its truck initiative called the Clean Trucks Plan, under which it committed to set more stringent NOx standards in several phases.[92] In the first step of that plan, EPA, in January 2023, finalized more stringent standards for NOx and PM for model years starting in 2027 that cover a wider range of engine operating conditions and that must be met for a longer period of time.[93] The additional steps in EPA's new plan involve combined rulemakings that will also strengthen standards for light-duty vehicles and GHG standards for trucks.

2. Standards for Greenhouse Gas Emissions

To address climate change, EPA and NHTSA adopted GHG emissions and CAFE standards for heavy-duty vehicles in 2011.[94] Those standards apply to "all vehicles with a gross vehicle weight rating above 8,500 pounds, and the engines that power them," excluding medium-duty passenger vehicles.[95] To reflect the significant diversity of heavy-duty vehicles and engines, EPA and NHTSA divided these vehicles into three groups—Combination Tractors, Heavy-Duty Pickup Trucks and Vans, and Vocational Vehicles (such as buses and dump trucks)—and developed GHG emissions and CAFE standards for subcategories within each group based on gross vehicle weight and design.[96] The 2011 Heavy-Duty Rule also limited emissions of other GHGs from some types of heavy-duty vehicles, such as N_2O and CH_4 from engines and HFCs from air conditioning system leakage.[97] Although EPA's GHG emission standards for heavy-duty vehicles took effect in model year 2014, NHTSA's CAFE standards were voluntary in model years 2014 and 2015 (and model year 2016 for diesel engines) to provide the four full model years of regulatory lead time required by the EISA.[98] EPA estimated that those standards would reduce CO_2 emissions by 273 million metric tons over the lifetime of all model year 2014–2018 heavy-duty vehicles.[99]

A plant-oil diesel company and a group of businesses, associations, and individuals in California sought review of EPA and NHTSA's 2011 Heavy-Duty Rule in the D.C. Circuit.[100] The court dismissed all challenges to the Heavy-Duty Rule based on petitioners' lack of standing. The court held that the plant-oil diesel company's claim that the rule made its products economically infeasible fell outside the zone of interests protected by the Clean Air Act.[101] The D.C. Circuit also rejected California petitioners' claim that EPA unlawfully promulgated both the Heavy-Duty Rule and the Tailpipe Rule[102] without providing the standards to the Science Advisory Board (SAB)—the expert body tasked with providing scientific information to the Agency.[103] Under the controlling statute, EPA is required to provide SAB with "any proposed criteria, document, standard, limitation, or regulation under the Clean Air Act."[104] The court explained, however, that the SAB requirement only applied to EPA and would not affect the regulations promulgated by NHTSA, which would have the same effect on petitioners. Thus, the court held that petitioners' claim was not redressable.[105]

In 2016, EPA and NHTSA jointly published the second phase of CAFE and GHG standards for medium- and heavy-duty vehicles and engines.[106] The Heavy-Duty Phase 2 Rule continues to divide heavy-duty vehicles by category. In addition to the three groups featured in the original rule, the Heavy-Duty Phase 2 Rule also regulated trailers.[107] However, in 2021, the D.C. Circuit vacated all portions of the rule that apply to trailers themselves. The court held that EPA lacked authority to regulate trailers because the Act defines "motor vehicle" to exclude anything that does not propel itself, and trailers are not "self-propelled."[108] The court further held that NHTSA did not have authority to impose fuel economy standards on trailers because trailers do not "use fuel."[109] The Court affirmed, however, that both agencies still "can regulate *tractors* based on the *trailers* they pull."[110]

The standards phase in between model years 2021–2027 for engines and vehicles and model years 2018–2027 for trailers and gliders.[111] While the final rule maintains the regulatory structure developed by the Phase 1 program, the Heavy-Duty Phase 2 Rule sets "technology advancing standards"[112] based on currently available technologies, as well as the utilization of technologies under development or not yet widely deployed.[113] EPA estimated that these standards will reduce CO_2 emissions by 1.1 billion metric tons over the lifetime of all model year 2018–2029 heavy-duty vehicles and save the trucking industry up to $8.5 billion annually.[114]

In its 2021 Clean Truck Plan, EPA committed to strengthening certain Phase 2 standards, and setting Phase 3 GHG standards for heavy-duty vehicles beginning with model year 2030 and beyond.[115] Although EPA proposed targeted Phase 2 standard revisions in 2022,[116] EPA chose not to finalize those with the rest of the proposal.[117] According to EPA's fall 2022 regulatory agenda, EPA plans to issue a new proposal covering both Phase 2 and Phase 3 GHG standards for heavy-duty trucks in the first half of 2023.

3. *Additional Requirements*

Over time, EPA has also extended numerous supplemental requirements applicable to light-duty vehicles and trucks to include heavy-duty vehicles. For example, in 2000 EPA promulgated a rule requiring onboard diagnostics systems for heavy-duty vehicles and engines under 14,000 pounds GVWR,[118] and later extended that requirement to the entire heavy-duty fleet.[119] In addition, EPA has promulgated evaporative emission standards for heavy-duty vehicles and engines[120] and required onboard refueling vapor recovery systems in heavy-duty gasoline vehicles under 10,000 pounds GVWR.[121]

D. Nonroad Sources: From Chainsaws and Lawnmowers to Planes and Trains

EPA has developed emission standards for several other mobile sources of air pollution as well, in recognition of their increasing impact on the national emissions inventory. This category of "nonroad engines" includes any internal combustion engine that is not used in a motor vehicle.[122] These "other" sources employ a far more diverse array of engine sizes and specifications, fuel-metering methods, and emission control systems than cars and trucks.

Congress granted EPA the authority to regulate nonroad engines in the 1990 amendments to the Act. For nonroad engines other than locomotives (and engines used in locomotives), section 213(a) directs EPA to determine whether emissions of CO, NOx, and VOCs are significant contributors to ozone or CO concentrations in more than one nonattainment area for those pollutants.[123] If so, EPA must promulgate for the classes of nonroad engines that contribute to such pollution standards that provide "the greatest degree of emission reduction achievable," considering cost and noise, energy, and safety factors.[124] EPA published the requisite finding in 1994.[125] EPA may also regulate other pollutants from such nonroad engines if they significantly contribute to air pollution that may reasonably be anticipated to endanger public health or welfare.[126] The Act separately directs EPA to promulgate emission standards for locomotives[127] and aircraft.[128]

The regulated categories of nonroad engines include construction equipment,[129] off-road recreational vehicles,[130] marine vessels,[131] lawn and garden equipment,[132] locomotives and locomotive engines,[133] and aircraft.[134] Notwithstanding these regulations, which now encompass all nonroad engines, the relative contribution of pollutants from these mobile sources has steadily increased, owing in part to the increasing populations of nonroad engines.

E. Aircraft

Section 231 of Act directs EPA to regulate emissions of air pollutants from any class or classes of aircraft or aircraft engines which endanger public health or welfare.[135] EPA first regulated several classes of airplanes under that authority in 1973 with standards for vented fuel, smoke, and exhaust (hydrocarbons, NOx, and CO) emissions.[136] Starting in 1997, EPA began aligning its standards with those of the United Nations International Civil Aviation Organization (ICAO), of which the United States is a member.[137]

In 2016, EPA issued a finding under section 231(a) of the Act that GHG emissions from certain classes of engines used in aircraft contribute to the air pollution that causes climate change, thus endangering public health and welfare.[138] Although that finding triggered a requirement for EPA to promulgate standards addressing GHG emissions from engines on covered aircraft, in addition to the standards it already had issued, EPA initially failed to act.

In 2020, EPA proposed GHG emission standards for aircrafts[139] after environmental advocacy organizations threatened to sue the Agency for its inaction.[140] The final rule, issued in 2021, aligned the United States' emission standards with standards created by the ICAO.[141] The standards apply to civil subsonic jet airplanes (those powered by turbojet or turbofan engines with a maximum takeoff mass (MTOM) greater than 5,700 kilograms), as well as larger civil subsonic propeller-driven airplanes (those powered by turboprop engines with a MTOM greater than 8,618 kilograms).[142] In doing so, EPA acknowledged that domestic airplane manufacturers already had developed or are developing technologies that will allow affected airplanes to comply with the ICAO standards.[143] As a result, EPA did not anticipate that the rule would result in any additional emission reductions from the aviation sector.[144] A coalition of states, led by California, and an environmental advocacy organization have judicially challenged the sufficiency of the standards.[145] A decision in that suit is expected in 2023.

More recently, EPA finalized PM standards for certain classes of civil subsonic jet engines that are equivalent to the more recent ICAO standards.[146] Those standards also have been challenged judicially by a coalition of environmental advocacy organizations, but the case is being held in abeyance pending resolution of the prior similar challenge to the new standards for GHGs.[147]

Finally, in 2022, EPA further extended its potential regulation of aircraft emissions proposing to find under section 231(a) of the Act that lead emissions from aircraft that operate on leaded fuel (generally small piston-engine passenger planes) endanger public health or welfare.[148] EPA likely will finalize any determination in 2023.

F. Crosscutting Approach to Emission Reductions

Although the emission standards for each mobile source may be different, the primary elements of the regulatory programs that implement and enforce the standards are essentially the same. Each program contains three core components: (1) certification; (2) assembly line testing; and (3) in-use testing and recall authority.[149] These components are designed to ensure compliance by the source with the applicable emission standards over the life cycle of the source.

1. Certification

Certification refers to a process in which manufacturers of the regulated mobile source demonstrate to EPA's satisfaction that a prototype engine will meet applicable emission control standards. The process occurs in advance of full-scale production of the mobile source, whether it be a leaf blower or a bulldozer. Based on test procedures established by EPA, the manufacturer submits detailed information about the design, operation, and emission performance of the regulated source in an application for certification. If the manufacturer meets the specified requirements, EPA issues a "certificate of conformity" signifying that the source complies with applicable emission standards. Once the manufacturer obtains the necessary certification, full-scale production can begin. The sale by a manufacturer or dealer of sources not covered by a certificate of conformity is strictly prohibited, punishable by a fine of up to $55,808 per day of violation for fines assessed after January 6, 2023.[150]

The test procedures used in the certification process have been the subject of substantial attention and revision. Since 1999, test procedures for motor vehicles, for example, have been promulgated, challenged, vacated, revised, then challenged again. Prior to 1999, EPA had imposed a relatively proscriptive series of test procedures to be used in the motor vehicle certification process. To demonstrate the long-term durability of emission control systems, manufacturers were required to accumulate a substantial amount of mileage on a prototype vehicle over a prescribed standard road cycle, then to test that vehicle's emissions at periodic intervals.[151] As time passed, however, EPA became increasingly concerned that this fixed cycle was too expensive, too time-consuming, and too outdated.[152] The Agency therefore began to vest manufacturers with increasing discretion to determine what test procedures to use to demonstrate compliance with emission standards.[153] Eventually, this trend manifested itself in what is commonly referred to as the "CAP 2000" rule, which allowed manufacturers to customize their own test procedures, subject to EPA approval.[154]

Shortly after CAP 2000's issuance, however, a fuel additive manufacturer petitioned for its review on the basis that it did not comport with EPA's statutory obligation to establish test procedures "by regulation."[155] In 2002, the D.C. Circuit agreed and vacated the CAP 2000 program, prompting EPA to respond with yet another revision to the test procedures.[156] A subsequent challenge to that action was held in abeyance pending action on a petition for administrative reconsideration, but after sixteen years the petitioner concluded that EPA was unlikely to take action and voluntarily dismissed its case.[157]

2. Assembly Line Testing

Because the certification process focuses on the performance of a prototype engine, EPA has established a program to ensure that the sources coming off the assembly line also conform to emission standards. In the case of motor vehicles, section 206(b) authorizes EPA to test, or to require manufacturers to test, samples of new vehicles or engines covered by a certificate of conformity.[158] EPA implements this mandate through the "selective enforcement audit" or "SEA" program, which allows the Agency to sample randomly motor vehicle assembly lines using specified test procedures.[159] If a sufficient sampling fails to comply with applicable emission standards, EPA can suspend or revoke the applicable certificate of conformity, forcing the manufacturer to remedy related deficiencies before it can be reinstated. Although EPA appears to be reducing its reliance on SEAs in favor of in-use testing,[160] the program may continue to serve as a deterrent value, spurring manufacturers to perform their own self-audits to ensure compliance. EPA's regulations allow up to a specific percent of vehicles to fail emission standards before the certificate of conformity will be suspended or revoked.[161]

3. In-Use Testing and Recall Authority

The Clean Air Act typically requires manufacturers of regulated mobile sources to design and produce sources that will remain in compliance with emission standards throughout their useful lives, or else face potential recall. The "useful life" is an administratively defined period of source operation during which the source is subject to emission control standards.[162] The useful life for a car, for example, is 10 years or 120,000 miles of operation, whichever is reached first.[163] If in-use testing indicates a problem with the emissions performance of a particular make and model within this period, then it may be subject to recall by EPA. As provided in section 207(c)(1):

> If the Administrator determines that a substantial number of any class or category of vehicles or engines, although properly maintained and used, do not conform to [emission standards] . . . when in actual use throughout their useful life . . . he shall immediately notify the manufacturer thereof of such nonconformity, and he shall require the manufacturer to submit a plan for remedying the nonconformity . . . .[164]

Courts have interpreted the requirement of a "substantial number" of nonconforming vehicles to mean "any number large enough to show that a 'systematic or pervasive problem in a particular class or category of vehicles' exists."[165] A plan for remedying the nonconformity must include, among other things, a description of how the vehicle owners subject to the recall will be notified and a description of the specific remedial measures to be undertaken at the manufacturer's expense.[166]

Most emission-related motor vehicle recalls, however, are now executed voluntarily by manufacturers in connection with EPA's "in-use verification program" (IUVP). The IUVP is the primary program by which EPA implements its recall authority. The IUVP requires manufacturers to conduct their own in-use emissions performance testing[167] and to report the results of such testing to EPA.[168] Manufacturers that discover potential noncompliance issues or defects during IUVP testing often initiate voluntary recalls to circumvent, among other things, an EPA-mandated recall. Voluntary recalls play a key role in mobile source enforcement. For example, in 2017, manufacturers voluntarily recalled over 4.9 million light-duty vehicles for emission-related problems—a number that is lower than the previous year.[169]

II. The Regulation of Fuels

A comprehensive framework governing both mobile sources and the fuels upon which they operate is essential for a sound regulatory program. According to EPA, "[t]he systems approach of combining the engine and fuel standards into a single program is critical to the success of our overall efforts to reduce emissions, because the emission standards will not be feasible without the fuel change."[170] The emission products of fuels and fuel additives can not only impair the efficacy of emission control systems, but can independently cause or contribute to tailpipe emissions. EPA's fuel regulations therefore impact nearly every aspect of fuel production and use in the United States. The bulk of EPA's authority to regulate fuels arises under section 211.[171]

Prior to 2021, all of EPA's fuels regulations were in 40 C.F.R. parts 79 and 80. Part 79 contained provisions related to the registration of fuel and fuel additives, while part 80 contained the renewable fuel standard (RFS) and provisions for fuel quality, including the reformulated gasoline (RFG) program. In 2020, to consolidate and streamline rules for its gasoline and diesel fuel programs, EPA moved all of the regulations related to fuel quality into a single set of provisions under a new part 1090. The fuel registration requirements in part 79 and the RFS program in part 80, which EPA deemed different in scope, were not moved.[172]

A. Registration and Testing

Section 211(a) requires the "regist[ration]" of "designate[d]" fuels and fuel additives prior to introduction of the fuel or additive into commerce.[173] Designated fuels and fuel additives generally include commercially produced motor vehicle gasoline and diesel fuel and the additives produced or sold for use in them.[174] Registration requires, among other things, the submission of information, including the name of any additive that will or may be used in the fuel, the "range of concentration," "purpose-in-use," and "chemical composition" of any such additive, and the test data and other information required in the testing process.[175]

Section 211(b) requires that designated fuels and fuel additives be tested for registration purposes "to determine potential public health and environmental effects of the fuel or additive."[176] "The primary purpose" of this registration program, according to EPA, is "to establish registration requirements which will provide information for identifying and evaluating the potential adverse effects of designated [fuel and fuel additive] emissions and for guiding the direction of related regulatory actions in the future."[177] The regulations that implement section 211(b) set forth three tiers of testing, each of which is designed to assess whether the combustion or evaporative emissions of the fuels and fuel additives present a significant risk to public health:

- Tier 1 requires the fuel or fuel additive manufacturer to conduct tests to characterize the nature of the emissions (both combustion and evaporative) associated with use of the fuel or fuel additive, and to perform a literature search on health and welfare effects.[178]
- Tier 2 sets forth a battery of biological testing for specific health effect endpoints, including carcinogenic or mutagenic effects, teratogenic and reproductive effects, general toxicity and pulmonary effects, and neurotoxic effects.[179] EPA may, at its discretion, require Alternative Tier 2 testing[180] in lieu of the standard Tier 2 if EPA concludes that, among other things: (1) available information caused EPA to be concerned about potential health effects unrelated to an endpoint not specifically addressed in Tier 2; or (2) EPA identifies a "potentially significant public health risk related to a Tier 2 endpoint, such that EPA knows that more definitive testing will be required."[181]
- Tier 3 testing authorizes EPA to impose additional testing requirements on a case-by-case basis depending upon the results of testing from Tiers 1 and 2.[182] According to EPA, a decision to impose testing under its Tier 3 authority requires the exercise of "expert scientific judgment" and

depends upon "the availability of adequate data to enable a health risk evaluation and the need for more definitive information for developing regulatory decisions."[183] The scope of Tier 3 tests is determined at EPA's discretion as well.

To alleviate some of the burden associated with the health effects testing regulations, EPA developed a framework that allows manufacturers of similar fuel products to "group" their resources to conduct the necessary testing.[184] EPA's goal was to reduce duplicative testing and to reduce the cost burden for individual fuel product manufacturers.

B. Controls and Prohibitions

In addition to EPA's "pre-clearance" authority under section 211(a) and (b), EPA has a broad grant of authority under section 211(c) to control or prohibit the use of certain fuels or fuel additives. As interpreted by EPA, the Agency's authority to control or prohibit the use of certain fuels or fuel additives "must be read in conjunction with" its testing authority.[185] As a result, "[t]he purpose of obtaining data on fuels and fuel additives is," according to EPA, "to provide a basis for further risk characterization and possible regulation under section 211(c)."[186] Section 211(c) provides EPA with the authority to control or prohibit the use of fuels or fuel additives based on either of two criteria:

- "[I]f, in the judgment of the Administrator, any . . . emission product of [a] fuel or fuel additive causes, or contributes, to air pollution or water pollution . . . that may reasonably be anticipated to endanger the public health or welfare"; or
- "[I]f emission products of [a] fuel or fuel additive will impair to a significant degree the performance of any emission control device or system which is in general use, or which the Administrator finds has been developed to a point where in a reasonable time it would be in general use were such regulation to be promulgated."[187]

EPA has availed itself of its section 211(c) authority in the context of lead and sulfur, among other pollutants. The steps taken to control lead have been a true success story. By EPA estimates, blood-lead levels in the United States decreased 78 percent from 1978 to 1991 as a result of EPA-imposed fuel controls, five years before the statutory prohibition on leaded gasoline in section 211(n) even took effect.[188] Since 2000, EPA has been aggressively targeting sulfur in fuels as a key part of its "system" approach to limiting mobile source emissions, based on the Agency's finding that "gasoline sulfur degrades the effectiveness of catalytic converters and that high sulfur levels in commercial gasoline could affect the ability of future automobiles—especially those designed for very low emissions—to meet more stringent standards in use."[189] EPA's Tier 2 program applied both an annual average and per-gallon cap for sulfur content in gasoline.[190] In 2014, EPA finalized its Tier 3 rules, which lowered gasoline sulfur content standards to 10 parts per million (ppm) beginning in 2017 for large refiners and 2020 for small refiners, while maintaining a per-gallon cap of 80 ppm for all refiners and importers.[191]

C. Reid Vapor Pressure (RVP) Requirements

Reid vapor pressure is a measure of the volatility of gasoline (i.e., the rate at which it evaporates). Evaporative emissions from gasoline include VOCs that contribute to the formation of ground level ozone or smog. To address this issue, the 1990 amendments to the Act added a new subsection 211(h)(1) requiring that gasoline volatility not exceed 9.0 pounds per square inch (psi) during the ozone season, and that nonattainment areas meet a lower, or more stringent, RVP standard.[192] At the same time, a separate provision—section 211(m)—mandated the use of oxygenated fuels in certain nonattainment areas to address CO nonattainment in the winter months (sometimes called the "Oxyfuels" program). The blending of ethanol with gasoline is a common means of oxygenating fuel and most gasoline sold today is a blend of gasoline with 10 percent ethanol, also known as E10. Because the blending of ethanol into gasoline increases its volatility, Congress included in section 211(h)(4) a waiver of the RVP limit for ethanol fuels "containing gasoline and 10 percent denatured anhydrous ethanol."[193] The Energy Policy Act of 2005 modified section 211(h) by requiring EPA to impose the more stringent RVP upon notification by a state that applying the waiver in (h)(4) would "increase emissions that contribute to air pollution in any area in the State."[194] The amendment specifies that the removal be effective on the later of two dates, but authorizes EPA to extend the effective date if the Administrator determines that the removal "would result in an insufficient supply of gasoline in the State."[195]

In 2019, EPA issued a final rule—referred to as the "E15 Rule"—interpreting the section 211(h)(4) RVP waiver to apply to blends containing "*at least* 10 percent ethanol."[196] The interpretation would have allowed use of gasoline blends with 15 percent ethanol (i.e., E15) year-round. In a challenge by both petroleum industry groups and agricultural groups, the D.C. Circuit vacated the rule finding that EPA's interpretation was contrary to the section's plain language and legislative history.[197]

In 2022, a number of state governors petitioned EPA to remove the E10 waiver in their state starting in the summer of 2023 based on modeling results indicating removal of the waiver would result in reductions in VOCs, NOx, and CO.[198] Subsequently, EPA received numerous petitions asking EPA to delay the effectiveness of any removal until 2024 based on concerns about the sufficiency of the gas supply in those states.[199] In interpreting the Act, EPA concluded that although it lacked discretion to consider other issues, like economic impacts, in deciding whether to remove the waiver, the Administrator had discretion to consider a number of factors when making a determination of "insufficient supply," including "the possibility of supply disruptions, and the ability of the fuel to be physically produced and transported to the petitioning states."[200] After considering those factors, when EPA proposed removal of the waiver EPA also proposed to extend the effectiveness of the removal until 2024.[201] If EPA finalizes its proposal, refineries will have to produce a lower volatility conventional gasoline before oxygenate or ethanol blending to meet the RVP standard. The availability of that lower RVP gasoline for blending also would allow for expanded use of E15.

D. The Reformulated Gasoline and Anti-Dumping Programs

Faced with repeated difficulties that metropolitan areas were experiencing in meeting air quality goals, Congress established the reformulated gasoline (RFG) and anti-dumping programs in the 1990 amendments to the Act.[202] The RFG program seeks to improve air quality by requiring refiners to reformulate the gasoline used in certain areas to make it burn more completely and, thereby, reduce motor vehicle emissions. The program is based upon the understanding that changes in the composition of the gasoline (i.e., its "reformulation") will reduce emissions of certain "air toxics,"[203] VOCs, and NOx from motor vehicles.[204] To achieve the goal of cleaner burning gasoline, section 211(k) imposes both composition and performance requirements for RFG. Conversely, the companion anti-dumping program prohibits refiners, blenders, and importers from "dumping" relatively dirtier fuel components generated from the production of RFG into "conventional" gasoline sold in all other areas of the nation not using RFG.

The RFG program, which commenced January 1, 1995, imposes VOC and air toxics standards based on either a fuel formula or an emission reduction performance standard.[205] The fuel formula includes controls on benzene and aromatic hydrocarbons, a lead prohibition, and a requirement to add detergents to prevent the accumulation of deposits in engines or vehicle fuel supply systems. The emission reduction performance standard requires the aggregate emissions of ozone-forming VOCs and air toxics from baseline vehicles when using RFG to be 25 percent below (on a mass basis) the aggregate emissions of these materials from vehicles using conventional gasoline. EPA has the discretion to provide for a lesser (but not below 20 percent) or greater reduction based on "technological feasibility" and "considering the cost of achieving such reductions in VOC emissions."[206]

To achieve these targets, EPA developed two statistical "models" to be used by refiners to evaluate how changes in the composition of the gasoline they produce will affect motor vehicle emissions. The first model, applicable in the early years of the program, was known as the "simple model."[207] The second model was known as the "complex model."[208] EPA developed both models after extensive discussions with fuel and fuel additive manufacturers, the automotive industry, and several other stakeholders based on emission data derived from extensive vehicle testing using a wide range of different fuel parameters. Using these models, a refiner could mix and match different fuel parameters in keeping with refiner-specific technological and economic constraints to achieve the RFG emission reduction targets in a cost-effective manner. The models allowed the formula for RFG to vary from one refiner to the next so long as the underlying emission reduction targets are achieved.

In 2020, EPA amended the RFG standards by translating the current summer RFG volatile organic compound standard into a RVP per-gallon cap of 7.4 psi.[209] According to EPA, "[t]his change allows us to remove the use of the Complex Model as a requirement to certify batches of gasoline and remove all the provisions associated with demonstrating compliance on average."[210] Accordingly, the Complex Model no longer is required under the regulations and is maintained by EPA solely for compliance oversight.[211]

RFG "covered areas" include the nation's nine largest metropolitan areas with the most severe summertime ozone levels.[212] Congress also authorized certain other areas to "opt-in" to the RFG program, provided those areas were classified as marginal, moderate, serious, or severe ozone nonattainment areas.[213] As of March 2023, certain counties in the following states are included in the RFG program: California, Connecticut, Delaware, Illinois, Indiana, Kentucky, Maryland, Massachusetts, Missouri, New Hampshire, New Jersey, New York,

Pennsylvania, Rhode Island, Texas, Virginia, and Wisconsin.[214] The District of Columbia is also part of the program.[215]

The anti-dumping program, which applies everywhere else in the country, was essentially designed to protect conventional gasoline from the potential adverse impacts associated with the RFG refining process. Section 211(k)(8) directs that motor vehicle emissions associated with the use of conventional gasoline after January 1, 1995, must meet refiner-specific "baseline" emission standards attributable to gasoline sold in the year 1990.[216] EPA's regulations direct refiners to apply statistical models corresponding to the simple and complex models to calculate both their 1990 baseline emission limitations for conventional gasoline and subsequent compliance with those standards for all conventional gasoline produced after January 1, 1995.

E. Renewable Fuels Mandate

With the enactment of the Energy Policy Act of 2005, Congress wrought considerable changes in fuel and fuel additive regulation by introducing a national renewable fuels mandate, which was incorporated into the Act as section 211(*o*).[217] In its original form, the renewable fuel standard (RFS) program required that a minimum volume of renewable fuel be used to replace petroleum-based fuel sold in the United States each year, ramping up from 4 billion gallons in 2006 to 7.5 billion gallons in 2012.[218] To achieve these goals, EPA is required to determine and publish the applicable renewable fuel obligation for fuel refineries, blenders, and importers for each calendar year by November 30 of the preceding year, expressed as a volume percentage of transportation fuel sold or introduced into commerce in the United States.[219] In 2007, EPA enacted regulations to implement and enforce the RFS program and established the 2007 renewable fuel obligation for refiners, blenders, and importers.[220]

In the 2007 EISA, Congress amended the RFS program by substantially increasing the volumes of renewable fuel required to be used each year, extending the time frame over which those volumes ramp up through at least 2022, and expanding the program to cover nearly all transportation fuels.[221] The total minimum volume of required renewable fuels gradually increased from 4.7 billion gallons in 2007 to 36 billion gallons in 2022.[222] After 2022, EPA is responsible for determining the annual volume requirements.[223] In addition, the EISA divided renewable fuels into four categories: total renewable fuels, advanced biofuel, cellulosic biofuel, and biomass-based diesel.[224] Each category faces a separate annual statutory minimum volume, and EPA must determine the applicable renewable fuel obligation for fuel refineries, blenders, and importers to meet these requirements for each category.[225]

Based on the annual obligations, EPA determines RFS renewable volume obligations (RVOs), which establish the amount of credits or renewable identification numbers (RINs) fuel refineries, blenders, and importers must submit to EPA.[226] A RIN is attached to each gallon of qualifying renewable fuel. The RINs are credits that may be submitted for compliance, traded, or saved for future use. The Act also provides for exemption from the renewable fuel obligations for small refineries based on "disproportionate economic hardship."[227]

Furthermore, to qualify for inclusion in the RFS program, renewable fuels must meet certain GHG emission thresholds demonstrating that their lifecycle GHG emissions—the aggregate direct and indirect emissions related to the fuel, from feedstock generation through its final use—are sufficiently less than those of the gasoline or diesel fuel they would replace.[228] Advanced biofuel and biomass-based diesel must achieve lifecycle GHG emission reductions of "at least 50 percent" compared to the gasoline or diesel baseline.[229] Cellulosic biofuel must achieve "at least 60 percent" lifecycle GHG emission reductions, while the threshold for other renewable fuels from new sources is "20 percent."[230] Eligible renewable fuels must also be made from feedstocks that qualify as "renewable biomass" based on their type and source.[231]

EPA may waive or reduce these minimum volumes if the Administrator determines that there is an inadequate domestic supply of any fuel or that the requirements would cause severe economic or environmental harm.[232] In addition to this general waiver, the statute includes a cellulosic waiver[233] and biomass-based diesel waiver.[234] Under these waivers, EPA is required to reduce the applicable volume requirement for these categories in response to projected fuel unavailability (for cellulosic biofuel) or price shocks (for biomass-based diesel). Additionally, the statute contains a "reset" provision that authorizes the EPA to adjust the applicable volume of the RFS, if EPA waives "20 percent" of the applicable volume for a fuel type for two consecutive years or "50 percent" of the applicable volume for a single year.[235]

In 2010, EPA adopted a new set of RFS regulations, known as RFS2, to implement the 2007 amendments to the program.[236] The Agency identified several types of renewable fuels as meeting the applicable lifecycle GHG emissions thresholds based on EPA's modeling.[237] The rule also established mechanisms for renewable fuel producers to petition for new pathways to qualify a fuel under the program based on feedstock, production process, and fuel type.[238] Since enacting RFS2, EPA has identified a number of renewable fuels that meet the applicable lifecycle GHG emissions thresholds making them eligible to generate RINs.[239]

EPA subsequently published the renewable fuel obligations and associated percentage standards that apply to transportation fuel refiners, blenders, and importers in each category of renewable fuels for 2010, 2011, and 2012.[240] The D.C. Circuit, however, struck down the Agency's 2012 renewable fuel obligation for cellulosic biofuel.[241] The Act required the use of 500 million gallons of cellulosic biofuel in 2012, but EPA adjusted that year's renewable fuel obligation downward under the Act's waiver provision to 8.65 million gallons because the industry was still incapable of producing that fuel at a commercial scale.[242] The court held that the reduced obligation was still impermissibly high, noting that while other parts of the RFS program may be technology-forcing, EPA must base its annual cellulosic biofuel requirement on a projection that "aims at accuracy" and is not merely "aspirational."[243]

A number of parties also sought review of EPA's final rule setting renewable fuel volume requirements for 2014, 2015, 2016, and 2017 for biomass-based diesel.[244] In *Americans for Clean Energy*, the D.C. Circuit upheld all of the challenged provisions of the final rule except for EPA's decision to reduce the total renewable fuel volume requirements for 2016 based on an alleged "inadequate domestic supply."[245] When finalizing the total renewable fuel volume requirements, EPA interpreted the general waiver to allow it to consider both supply-side and demand-side constraints in the market when determining whether there is an adequate domestic supply of fuel.[246] The court held this interpretation was incorrect and explained that the term "inadequate domestic supply" refers only to the supply of renewable fuel available to refiners, blenders, and importers.[247] The court vacated the total renewable fuel volume requirements for 2016.[248]

EPA's more recent renewable fuel volume determinations also have been the subject of litigation. In late 2019, EPA set the RFS final volume requirements for 2020.[249] Consistent with its policy since 2014, EPA used the cellulosic biofuel wavier to set volume requirements at amounts less than established in the statute, but slightly greater than the previous year's volumes. Pursuant to its cellulosic wavier authority, EPA reduced the volume requirement for cellulosic biofuel by 9.91 billion gallons, and reduced the final volume requirements for total renewable fuel and advanced biofuel "by the same magnitude as the reduction in the cellulosic biofuel reduction."[250] The 2020 rule triggered the "reset" provision for total renewable fuel, while the final rule for 2014 through 2016 triggered the provision for advanced biofuel and cellulosic biofuel.[251]

Multiple refiners and renewable fuel producers challenged the 2020 rule judicially.[252] After briefing started, the litigation was paused several times to await decisions in subsequent cases and rulemakings with the potential to narrow the scope of the dispute. At one point briefing was halted to await a decision by the

U.S. Supreme Court interpreting the "small refineries" exemption in section 211(*o*)(9) of the Act. In that case, the Court held that "small refineries whose exemptions have lapsed in one year may still seek an 'extension' in a following year."[253]

In addition, in 2022, EPA finalized a package of actions that, in addition to setting new standards for 2021 and 2022, revised the volume and percentage requirements in the 2020 rule for certain renewable fuel types.[254] In that rule, EPA also established a 250 million gallon "supplemental" obligation to the volumes finalized for 2022 and stated its intent to add another 250 million gallons in 2023, to address the remand of the 2014–2016 annual rule in *Americans for Clean Energy*.[255] Multiple refiners and renewable fuel producers have challenged the 2022 rule raising a litany of issues, including EPA's action on the remand.[256] The challenges to the 2020 rule remain in abeyance pending the outcome of that case, which will be briefed in 2023, and the outcome of a set of consolidated cases challenging EPA's denials of multiple small refinery petitions for exemption from the RFS program under 211(*o*)(9).[257]

EPA proposed the RFS volumes and percentage standards for 2023, 2024, and 2025 at the end of 2022.[258] This proposal is the first time EPA is not bound by statutory volume targets, but instead must set volumes based on a review of the "implementation of the program for prior years," and an analysis of six statutory factors.[259] EPA's fall 2022 regulatory agenda projects issuance of a final rule in June 2023.

Notes

1. Titles of the CAA correspond to subchapters in the U.S. Code.
2. The regulation of GHGs generally is discussed more fully in Chapter 7.
3. CAA § 209(b), 42 U.S.C. § 7543(b).
4. S. REP. No. 90-403, at 33 (1967).
5. CAA § 209(b)(1), 42 U.S.C. § 7543(b)(1).
6. *Motor & Equip. Mfrs. Ass'n v. EPA*, 627 F.2d 1095, 1110 (D.C. Cir. 1979) (citation omitted).
7. CAA § 209(b)(1), 42 U.S.C. § 7543(b)(1).
8. *Id.* § 209(b)(3), 42 U.S.C. § 7543(b)(3).
9. California State Motor Vehicle Pollution Control Standards; Notice of Decision Granting a Waiver of Clean Air Act Preemption for California's 2009 and Subsequent Model Year Greenhouse Gas Emission Standards for New Motor Vehicles, 74 Fed. Reg. 32,744, 32,746 (July 8, 2009).
10. California State Motor Vehicle Pollution Control Standards; Notice of Decision Granting a Waiver of Clean Air Act Preemption for California's Advanced Clean Car

Program and a [*sic*] Within the Scope Confirmation for California's Zero Emission Vehicle Amendments for 2017 and Earlier Model Years, 78 Fed. Reg. 2112–14 (Jan. 9, 2013).

11. *See* The Safer Affordable Fuel-Efficient (SAFE) Vehicles Rule Part One: One National Program, 84 Fed. Reg. 51,310, 51,328 (Sept. 27, 2019).

12. *Id.* at 51,314, 51,362.

13. California State Motor Vehicle Pollution Control Standards; Advanced Clean Car Program; Reconsideration of a Previous Withdrawal of a Waiver of Preemption; Opportunity for Public Hearing and Public Comment, 86 Fed. Reg. 22,421 (Apr. 28, 2021).

14. California State Motor Vehicle Pollution Control Standards; Advanced Clean Car Program; Reconsideration of a Previous Withdrawal of a Waiver of Preemption; Notice of Decision, 87 Fed. Reg. 14,332 (Mar. 14, 2022).

15. CAA § 177, 42 U.S.C. § 7507.

16. *Id.*

17. California Air Resources Board, "States that have Adopted California's Vehicle Standards under Section 177 of the Federal Clean Air Act" (May 13, 2022).

18. CAA § 209(e)(1), 42 U.S.C. § 7543(e)(1).

19. *Id.* § 209(e)(2)(A), 42 U.S.C. § 7543(e)(2)(A).

20. *Id.* § 209(e)(2)(B), 42 U.S.C. § 7543(e)(2)(B).

21. The regulations controlling emissions from cars and light trucks are located at 40 C.F.R. part 86.

22. CAA § 202(a)(1), 42 U.S.C. § 7521(a)(1).

23. *Id.*

24. *Id.* § 202(a)(2), 42 U.S.C. § 7521(a)(2).

25. *Nat. Res. Def. Council, Inc. v. EPA*, 655 F.2d 318, 332 (D.C. Cir. 1981). *See also Am. Petroleum Inst. v. EPA*, 706 F.3d 474, 480 (D.C. Cir. 2013) (explaining that "an agency may base a standard or mandate on future technology when there exists a rational connection between the regulatory target and the presumed innovation").

26. *Nat'l Petrochemical & Refiners Ass'n v. EPA*, 287 F.3d 1130, 1136 (D.C. Cir. 2002) (per curiam).

27. CAA § 202(g), (h), 42 U.S.C. § 7521(g), (h).

28. *Id.* § 202(i)(1), (2), 42 U.S.C. § 7521(i)(1), (2).

29. *Id.* § 202(i)(3)(C), 42 U.S.C. § 7521(i)(3)(C).

30. EPA, EPA 420-R-98-008, Tier 2 Report to Congress (July 31, 1998).

31. Control of Air Pollution From New Motor Vehicles: Tier 2 Motor Vehicle Emissions Standards and Gasoline Sulfur Control Requirements, 65 Fed. Reg. 6698 (Feb. 10, 2000).

32. EPA's regulation of fuel content is addressed in Section II below.

33. 40 C.F.R. § 86.1811-04(c)(6).

34. *Id.* § 86.1811-04(d).

35. 65 Fed. Reg. at 6750.

36. Control of Air Pollution From Motor Vehicles: Tier 3 Motor Vehicle Emission and Fuel Standards; 79 Fed. Reg. 23,414 (Apr. 28, 2014).

37. *Id.* at 23,417.

38. Endangerment and Cause or Contribute Findings for Greenhouse Gases Under Section 202(a) of the Clean Air Act, 74 Fed. Reg. 66,496, 66,497 (Dec. 15, 2009).

39. Light-Duty Vehicle Greenhouse Gas Emission Standards and Corporate Average Fuel Economy Standards, 75 Fed. Reg. 25,324 (May 7, 2010) ("Tailpipe Rule").

40. *Id.*

41. *Id.* at 25,326. *See also id.* at 25,327 ("The National Program is both needed and possible because the relationship between improving fuel economy and reducing CO_2 tailpipe emissions is a very direct and close one. The amount of those CO_2 emissions is essentially constant per gallon combusted of a given type of fuel. Thus, the more fuel efficient a vehicle is, the less fuel it burns to travel a given distance.").

42. *Id.* at 25,330, 25,396.

43. *Id.* at 25,399 & n.161.

44. *Id.* at 25,332.

45. *Id.* at 25,328.

46. *See* California State Motor Vehicle Pollution Control Standards; Within-the-Scope Determination for Amendments to California's Motor Vehicle Greenhouse Gas Regulations; Notice of Decision, 76 Fed. Reg. 34,693, 34,693 (June 14, 2011) (approving amendments to California standards as consistent with 2009 preemption waiver).

47. *Id.*

48. 2017 and Later Model Year Light-Duty Vehicle Greenhouse Gas Emissions and Corporate Average Fuel Economy Standards, 77 Fed. Reg. 62,624 (Oct. 15, 2012) ("2012 Light-Duty Rule").

49. *Id.* at 62,638–39.

50. *Id.* at 62,628.

51. *Id.* at 62,631.

52. Notice of Availability of Midterm Evaluation Draft Technical Assessment Report for Model Year 2022–2025 Light-Duty Vehicle GHG Emissions and CAFE Standards, 81 Fed. Reg. 49,217 (July 27, 2016).

53. Proposed Determination on the Appropriateness of the Model Year 2022–2025 Light-Duty Vehicle Greenhouse Gas Emissions Standards Under Midterm Evaluation, 81 Fed. Reg. 87,927 (Dec. 6, 2016).

54. EPA, EPA-420-R-17-001, Final Determination on the Appropriateness of the Model Year 2022–2025 Light-Duty Vehicle Greenhouse Gas Emissions Standards under the Midterm Evaluation (Jan. 2017) ("MTE Final Determination").

55. Notice Of Intention to Reconsider the Final Determination of the Mid-Term Evaluation of Greenhouse Gas Emissions Standards for Model Year 2022–2025 Light Duty Vehicles, 82 Fed. Reg. 14,671 (Mar. 22, 2017).

56. Mid-Term Evaluation of Greenhouse Gas Emissions Standards for Model Year 2022–2025 Light-Duty Vehicles, 83 Fed. Reg. 16,077, 16,077 (Apr. 13, 2018).

57. *California v. EPA*, 940 F.3d 1342 (D.C. Cir. 2019).

58. *Id.* at 1351.

59. The Safer Affordable Fuel-Efficient (SAFE) Vehicles Rule for Model Years 2021–2026 Passenger Cars and Light Trucks, 83 Fed. Reg. 42,986 (proposed Aug. 24, 2018).

60. *Id.* at 42,988, 42,999.
61. *Id.* at 43,240.
62. *Id.*
63. 84 Fed. Reg. at 51,311, 51,328.
64. The Safer Affordable Fuel-Efficient (SAFE) Vehicles Rule for Model Years 2021–2026 Passenger Cars and Light Trucks, 85 Fed. Reg. 24,174, 24,176 (Apr. 30, 2020).
65. *Id.* at 24,175–76.
66. *Union of Concerned Scientists v. NHTSA*, No. 19-1230 (and consolidated cases) (D.C. Cir. filed Oct. 28, 2019); *California v. Chao,* No. 1:19-cv-02826-JMC (and consolidated cases) (D.D.C. filed Sept. 20, 2019, voluntarily dismissed Aug. 29, 2022).
67. *Competitive Enter. Inst. v. NHSTA* (and consolidated cases) No. 20-1145 (D.C. Cir. filed May 1, 2020).
68. California State Motor Vehicle Pollution Control Standards; Advanced Clean Car Program; Reconsideration of a Previous Withdrawal of a Waiver of Preemption; Opportunity for Public Hearing and Comment, 86 Fed. Reg. 22,421 (Apr. 28, 2021).
69. Revised 2023 and Later Model Year Light-Duty Vehicle Greenhouse Gas Emissions Standards, 86 Fed. Reg. 74,434 (Dec. 30, 2021).
70. *Id.* at 74,435.
71. *Id.* at 74,456.
72. California State Motor Vehicle Pollution Control Standards; Advanced Clean Car Program; Reconsideration of a Previous Withdrawal of a Waiver of Preemption; Notice of Decision, 87 Fed. Reg. 14,332 (Mar. 14, 2022).
73. *Ohio v. EPA*, No. 22-1081 (and consolidated cases) (D.C. Cir. filed May 12, 2022).
74. *Texas v. EPA*, No. 22-1031 (and consolidated cases) (D.C. Cir. filed Feb. 28, 2022).
75. Exec. Order 14307, Strengthening American Leadership in Clean Cars and Trucks (Aug. 5, 2021), *reprinted in* 86 Fed. Reg. 43,583 (Aug. 10, 2021).
76. CAA § 202(a)(6), (k), 42 U.S.C. § 7521(a)(6), (k).
77. *See, e.g.,* Control of Air Pollution From New Motor Vehicles and New Motor Vehicle Engines; Refueling Emission Regulations for Light-Duty Vehicles and Light-Duty Trucks, 59 Fed. Reg. 16,262 (Apr. 6, 1994).
78. *See, e.g.,* Control of Air Pollution From New Motor Vehicles and New Motor Vehicle Engines: Evaporative Emission Regulations for Gasoline- and Methanol-Fueled Light-Duty Vehicles, Light-Duty Trucks and Heavy-Duty Vehicles, 58 Fed. Reg. 16,002 (Mar. 24, 1993).
79. CAA § 202(j), 42 U.S.C. § 7521(j); *see, e.g.,* Control of Air Pollution From New Motor Vehicles and New Motor Vehicle Engines; Cold Temperature Carbon Monoxide Emissions From 1994 and Later Model Year Gasoline-Fueled Light-Duty Vehicles and Light-Duty Trucks, 57 Fed. Reg. 31,888 (July 17, 1992).
80. CAA § 202(m), 42 U.S.C. § 7521(m); *see, e.g.,* Control of Air Pollution From New Motor Vehicles and New Motor Vehicle Engines; Regulations Requiring On-Board

Diagnostic Systems on 1994 and Later Model Year Light-Duty Vehicles and Light-Duty Trucks, 58 Fed. Reg. 9468 (Feb. 19, 1993); Control of Air Pollution From Motor Vehicles and New Motor Vehicle Engines; Modification of Federal On-board Diagnostic Regulations for Light-Duty Vehicles and Light-Duty Trucks; Extension of Acceptance of California OBD II Requirements, 63 Fed. Reg. 70,681 (Dec. 22, 1998).

81. CAA § 202(a)(3), 42 U.S.C. § 7521(a)(3).

82. *Id.* § 202(a)(3)(ii), 42 U.S.C. § 7521(a)(3)(ii).

83. 40 C.F.R. §§ 86.004-15, 86.007-15.

84. Control of Air Pollution From New Motor Vehicles and New Motor Vehicle Engines; Particulate Emission Regulations for 1993 Model Year Buses, Particulate Emission Regulations for 1994 and Later Model Year Urban Buses, Test Procedures for Urban Buses, and Oxides of Nitrogen Emission Regulations for 1998 and Later Model Year Heavy-Duty Engines, 58 Fed. Reg. 15,781 (Mar. 24, 1993).

85. Control of Emissions of Air Pollution From Highway Heavy-Duty Engines, 62 Fed. Reg. 54,694 (Oct. 21, 1997).

86. Control of Emissions of Air Pollution from 2004 and Later Model Year Heavy-Duty Highway Engines and Vehicles; Revision of Light-Duty On-Board Diagnostics Requirements, 65 Fed. Reg. 59,896, 59,926 (Oct. 6, 2000).

87. Control of Air Pollution from New Motor Vehicles: Heavy-Duty Engine and Vehicle Standards and Highway Diesel Fuel Sulfur Control Requirements, 66 Fed. Reg. 5002 (Jan. 18, 2001).

88. 79 Fed. Reg. at 23,414.

89. *Id.* at 23,422.

90. *See* EPA, News Releases from Headquarters, Office of the Administrator, EPA Acting Administrator Wheeler Launches Cleaner Trucks Initiative; Agency to update nitrogen oxide emission standards for heavy-duty trucks (Nov. 13, 2018).

91. *See* Control of Air Pollution from New Motor Vehicles: Heavy-Duty Engine Standards; Advanced Notice of Proposed Rulemaking, 85 Fed. Reg. 3306 (Jan. 21, 2020).

92. EPA, EPA-420-F-21-057, Regulatory Update: EPA Announces the "Clean Trucks Plan," Office of Transportation and Air Quality (Aug. 2021).

93. Control of Air Pollution from New Motor Vehicles: Heavy-Duty Engine and Vehicle Standards, 88 Fed. Reg. 4296 (Jan. 24, 2023).

94. Greenhouse Gas Emissions Standards and Fuel Efficiency Standards for Medium- and Heavy-Duty Engines and Vehicles, 76 Fed. Reg. 57,106 (Sept. 15, 2011) ("2011 Heavy-Duty Rule").

95. *Id.* at 57,109.

96. *See id.* at 57,117 (model year 2017 standards for Combination Tractors); *id.* at 57,121–22 (model year 2017 standards for Vocational Vehicles).

97. *Id.* at 57,117.

98. *Id.* at 57,110.

99. *Id.* at 57,126.

100. *Delta Constr. Co. v. EPA*, 783 F.3d 1291 (D.C. Cir. 2015) (per curiam).

101. *Id.* at 1300.

102. The court acknowledged that it had already upheld the 2010 Tailpipe Rule in *Coalition for Responsible Regulation, Inc. v. EPA*, 684 F.3d 102 (D.C. Cir. 2012), which is discussed in more detail in Chapter 7, and described petitioners' claim in this case as a procedural "collateral attack." *Id.* at 1293–95.

103. *Id.* at 1296.

104. *Id.* (quoting 42 U.S.C. § 4365(c)(1)).

105. *Id.* at 1296–97.

106. Greenhouse Gas Emissions and Fuel Efficiency Standards for Medium- and Heavy-Duty Engines and Vehicles—Phase 2, 81 Fed. Reg. 73,478 (Oct. 25, 2016).

107. *Id.* at 73,521.

108. *Truck Trailer Mfrs. Ass'n v. EPA*, 17 F.4th 1198, 1201 (D.C. Cir. 2021).

109. *Id.* at 1206.

110. *Id.* at 1208.

111. 81 Fed. Reg. at 73,682, 73,644.

112. *Id.* at 73,495.

113. *Id.*

114. *Id.* at 73,482.

115. Press Release, EPA, Office of Air and Radiation, Final EPA Standards for Heavy-Duty Vehicles to Slash Dangerous Pollution and Take Key Step Toward Accelerating Zero-Emissions Future (Dec. 20, 2022).

116. Control of Air Pollution from New Motor Vehicles: Heavy-Duty Engine and Vehicle Standards, 87 Fed. Reg. 17,414 (proposed Mar. 28, 2022).

117. 88 Fed. Reg. at 4298.

118. 65 Fed. Reg. at 59,916, 59,929.

119. Control of Air Pollution From New Motor Vehicles and New Motor Vehicle Engines; Regulations Requiring Onboard Diagnostic Systems on 2010 and Later Heavy-Duty Engines Used in Highway Applications Over 14,000 Pounds; Revisions to Onboard Diagnostic Requirements for Diesel Highway Heavy-Duty Vehicles Under 14,000 Pounds, 74 Fed. Reg. 8310 (Feb. 24, 2009).

120. 66 Fed. Reg. at 5044.

121. 65 Fed. Reg. at 59,924.

122. CAA § 216(10), 42 U.S.C. § 7550(10).

123. *Id.* § 213(a), 42 U.S.C. § 7547(a).

124. *Id.* § 213(a)(3), 42 U.S.C. § 7547(a)(3).

125. Control of Air Pollution; Determination of Significance for Nonroad Sources and Emission Standards for New Nonroad Compression-Ignition Engines At or Above 37 Kilowatts, 59 Fed. Reg. 31,306 (June 17, 1994).

126. CAA § 213(a)(4), 42 U.S.C. § 7547(a)(4).

127. *Id.* § 213(a)(5), 42 U.S.C. § 7547(a)(5).

128. *Id.* § 231, 42 U.S.C. § 7571.

129. 40 C.F.R. pt. 1039; *see also* Control of Emissions of Air Pollution From Nonroad Diesel Engines and Fuel, 69 Fed. Reg. 38,958 (June 29, 2004).

130. 40 C.F.R. pt. 1051; *see also* Control of Emissions From Nonroad Large Spark-Ignition Engines, and Recreational Engines (Marine and Land-Based), 67 Fed. Reg. 68,242 (Nov. 8, 2002).

131. 40 C.F.R. pts. 89 and 94; *see also* Control of Emissions of Air Pollution From Locomotive Engines and Marine Compression-Ignition Engines Less Than 30 Liters per Cylinder; Republication, 73 Fed. Reg. 37,096 (June 30, 2008); Control of Emissions From Nonroad Spark-Ignition Engines and Equipment, 73 Fed. Reg. 59,034 (Oct. 8, 2008); Control of Emissions From New Marine Compression-Ignition Engines at or Above 30 Liters per Cylinder, 75 Fed. Reg. 22,896 (Apr. 30, 2010).

132. 40 C.F.R. pt. 90; *see also* Phase 2 Emission Standards for New Nonroad Spark-Ignition Handheld Engines At or Below 19 Kilowatts and Minor Amendments to Emission Requirements Applicable to Small Spark-Ignition Engines and Marine Spark-Ignition Engines, 65 Fed. Reg. 24,268 (Apr. 25, 2000).

133. 40 C.F.R. pt. 92; *see also* 73 Fed. Reg. at 37,096.

134. 40 C.F.R. pt. 87; *see also* Control of Air Pollution From Airplanes and Airplane Engines: GHG Emission Standards and Test Procedures, 86 Fed. Reg. 2136 (Jan. 11, 2021).

135. CAA § 231(a)(2)(A), 42 U.S.C. § 7571(a)(2)(A).

136. *See, e.g.*, Part 87—Control of Air Pollution from Aircraft and Aircraft Engines; Emission Standards and Test Procedures for Aircraft, 38 Fed. Reg. 19,088 (July 17, 1973).

137. *See, e.g.*, Control of Air Pollution From Aircraft and Aircraft Engines: Emission Standards and Test Procedures, 62 Fed. Reg. 25,356 (May 8, 1997).

138. *See* Finding That Greenhouse Gas Emissions From Aircraft Cause or Contribute to Air Pollution That May Reasonably Be Anticipated To Endanger Public Health and Welfare, 81 Fed. Reg. 54,422 (Aug. 15, 2016).

139. Control of Air Pollution From Airplanes and Airplane Engines: GHG Emission Standards and Test Procedures, 85 Fed. Reg. 51,556 (proposed Aug. 20, 2020).

140. *See* Letter from Sarah Burt, Earthjustice, & Clare Lakewood, Ctr. for Biological Diversity, to Andrew Wheeler, Adm'r, EPA, & Sarah Dunham, Dir., Office of Transp. & Air Quality, EPA, Notice of Intent to File Suit Under Section 304 of the Clean Air Act with Respect to Proposed Rulemaking to Reduce Greenhouse Gas Emissions from Aircraft (Jan. 30, 2020).

141. 86 Fed. Reg. at 2136, 2137.

142. *Id.*

143. *Id.* at 2138.

144. *Id.*

145. *California v. EPA*, No. 21-1018 (and consolidated case) (D.C. Cir. argued Oct. 6, 2022).

146. Control of Air Pollution From Aircraft Engines: Emission Standards and Test Procedures, 87 Fed. Reg. 72,312 (Nov. 23, 2022).

147. Order, *Ctr for Biological Diversity v. EPA*, No. 23-1019 (and consolidated case) (D.C. Cir. Feb. 7, 2023), ECF No. 1984899 (holding cases in abeyance).

148. Proposed Finding That Lead Emissions From Aircraft Engines That Operate on Leaded Fuel Cause or Contribute to Air Pollution That May Reasonably Be Anticipated To Endanger Public Health and Welfare, 87 Fed. Reg. 62,753 (proposed Oct. 17, 2022).

149. EPA establishes emission standards for aircraft, but the Federal Aviation Administration of the U.S. Department of Transportation enforces the standards. For this reason, the regulation of aircraft emission control standards is somewhat different from the other mobile source programs discussed here.

150. CAA § 205(a), 42 U.S.C. § 7524(a); 40 C.F.R. § 19.4 (adjusting statutory penalties for inflation).

151. *See, e.g.*, Emission Durability Procedures for New Light-Duty Vehicles, Light-Duty Trucks and Heavy-Duty Vehicles, 71 Fed. Reg. 2810, 2811 (Jan. 17, 2006) (providing a history of the durability demonstration process).

152. *Id.*

153. *See, e.g.*, Letter from Robert E. Maxwell, Dir., Office of Mobile Sources, EPA, to automobile manufacturers (July 29, 1994) (providing manufacturers with alternative durability guidance for model years 1994 through 1998).

154. Control of Air Pollution From New Motor Vehicles; Compliance Programs for New Light-Duty Vehicles and Light-Duty Trucks, 64 Fed. Reg. 23,906 (May 4, 1999) (adopting CAP 2000, which established emissions compliance procedures for new light-duty vehicles and trucks).

155. *Ethyl Corp. v. EPA*, 306 F.3d 1144 (D.C. Cir. 2002) (holding that EPA's CAP 2000 rulemaking did not satisfy the requirements of section 206(d) of the Act to establish methods and procedures "by regulation").

156. 71 Fed. Reg. at 2810 (revising the methods used to determine emissions deterioration for the purposes of certification in light of the *Ethyl Corp.* decision).

157. Order, *Afton Chem. Corp. v. EPA*, No. 06-1095 (and consolidated cases) (D.C. Cir. May 17, 2022), ECF No. 1946918 (granting voluntary dismissal).

158. CAA § 206(b), 42 U.S.C. § 7525(b).

159. 40 C.F.R. pt. 86, subpt. G.

160. *See, e.g.*, Control of Emissions of Air Pollution From New Motor Vehicles: In-Use Testing for Heavy-Duty Diesel Engines and Vehicles, 70 Fed. Reg. 34,594, 34,615 (June 14, 2005) (anticipating that a "robust, mature manufacturer-run in-use program would significantly reduce the role SEA plays in EPA's compliance program").

161. 40 C.F.R. § 86.610-98(a).

162. *Id.* § 86.1803-01.

163. *Id.* § 86.1805-12.

164. CAA § 207(c)(1), 42 U.S.C. § 7541(c)(1).

165. *Chrysler Corp. v. EPA*, 631 F.2d 865, 891 n.133 (D.C. Cir. 1980).

166. *See* 40 C.F.R. § 85.1803(a).

167. *See, e.g.*, *id.* § 86.1845-04.

168. *Id.* § 86.1847-01.

169. EPA, EPA-420-R-19-003, 2014–2017 Progress Report, Vehicle Engine & Compliance Activities, at 38–39 (Apr. 2019).

170. 66 Fed. Reg. at 5005.

171. Other provisions of the Act address fuel issues either directly or indirectly, including section 104 (research relating to fuels and vehicles), section 212 (loans, appropriations, and grants for renewable fuel research and development), and sections 241 to 246 (clean-fueled vehicle fleet requirements for promoting use of "clean" alternative fuels), 42 U.S.C. §§ 7404, 7546, 7581–7586.

172. Fuels Regulatory Streamlining, 85 Fed. Reg. 78,412, 78,413 (Dec. 4, 2020).

173. CAA § 211(a), 42 U.S.C. § 7545(a).

174. 40 C.F.R. §§ 79.30–79.33.

175. *Id.* §§ 79.10–79.24.

176. CAA § 211(b), 42 U.S.C. § 7545(b).

177. Fuels and Fuel Additives Registration Regulations, 59 Fed. Reg. 33,042 (June 27, 1994).

178. 40 C.F.R. § 79.52.

179. *Id.* § 79.53.

180. *Id.* § 79.58(c).

181. 59 Fed. Reg. at 33,081.

182. 40 C.F.R. § 79.54.

183. 59 Fed. Reg. at 33,082.

184. 40 C.F.R. § 79.56.

185. Fuels and Fuel Additives Registration Regulations; Notice of Proposed Rulemaking, 57 Fed. Reg. 13,168, 13,173 (Apr. 15, 1992).

186. 57 Fed. Reg. at 13,174.

187. CAA § 211(c)(1), 42 U.S.C. § 7545(c)(1).

188. EPA, EPA-420-R-05-011, Toward A Cleaner Future; Office of Transportation and Air Quality Progress Report 2005, at 31 (Nov. 2005).

189. 65 Fed. Reg. at 6703.

190. 79 Fed. Reg. at 23,540.

191. *Id.* at 23,414, 23,424.

192. CAA § 211(h)(1), 42 U.S.C. § 7545(h). In 2020, as part of its Fuels Regulatory Streamlining rule, EPA adopted revised criteria and procedures for states with areas subject to the more stringent federal 7.8 psi RVP standard to request a relaxation of that standard. 85 Fed. Reg. at 78,425–26.

193. 42 U.S.C. § 7545(h)(4).

194. CAA § 211(h)(5)(A), 42 U.S.C. § 7545(h)(5)(A).

195. *Id.* § 211(h)(5)(B) and (C), § 7545(h)(5)(B) and (C).

196. Modifications to Fuel Regulations to Provide Flexibility for E15; Modifications to RFS RIN Market Regulations, 84 Fed. Reg. 26,980, 26,983 (June 10, 2019).

197. *Am. Fuel & Petrochemical Mfrs. v. EPA* 3 F.4th 373 (D.C. Cir. 2021).

198. Request From States for Removal of Gasoline Volatility Waiver, 88 Fed. Reg. 13,758 (proposed Mar. 6, 2023).

199. *Id.* at 13,759.

200. *Id.* at 13,762.

201. *Id.* at 13,767.

202. CAA § 211(k), 42 U.S.C. § 7545(k).

203. Air toxics emissions in this context are defined as the emission of benzene, 1,3-butadiene, polycyclic organic matter, acetaldehyde, and formaldehyde. *Id.* § 211(k)(10)(C), 42 U.S.C. § 7545(k)(10)(C).

204. VOC and NOx emissions can contribute to the formation of ozone, causing certain areas—particularly urban areas—to fall into ozone nonattainment.

205. Notably, the RFG program initially contained a 2 percent oxygen content requirement, which was repealed in the Energy Policy Act of 2005. Although this requirement was a core element of the original design of the RFG program, numerous factors—including advanced fuel technologies, a renewable fuels mandate (described below), and groundwater contamination associated with the use of methyl tertiary-butyl ether ("MTBE") (one of the two most predominantly used oxygenates)—led to its eventual repeal. Congress left in place, however, the "Oxyfuels" program in section 211(m), which relies on the use of oxygenated fuels to limit CO emissions as opposed to ozone.

206. CAA § 211(k)(3)(B), 42 U.S.C. § 7545(k)(3)(B).

207. *See* 40 C.F.R. § 80.42 (2020).

208. *See id.* § 80.45 (2020).

209. 85 Fed. Reg. at 78,414, 78,420.

210. *Id.* at 78,414 (footnote omitted).

211. *Id.* at 78,421.

212. CAA § 211(k)(10)(D), 42 U.S.C. § 7545(k)(10)(D).

213. *Id.* § 211(k)(6), 42 U.S.C. § 7545(k)(6).

214. 40 C.F.R. § 1090.285.

215. *Id.*

216. CAA § 211(k)(8), 42 U.S.C. § 7545(k)(8).

217. Energy Policy Act of 2005, Pub. L. No. 109-58, § 1501, 119 Stat. 594, 1067 (2005) (codified as amended at CAA § 211(*o*), 42 U.S.C. § 7545(*o*)).

218. *Id.* § 1501(a), 119 Stat. at 1069 (codified as amended at CAA § 211(*o*)(2)(B), 42 U.S.C. § 7545(*o*)(2)(B)).

219. CAA § 211(*o*)(3)(B), 42 U.S.C. § 7545(*o*)(3)(B).

220. Regulation of Fuels and Fuel Additives: Renewable Fuel Standard Program, 72 Fed. Reg. 23,900 (May 1, 2007).

221. Energy Independence and Security Act of 2007, Pub. L. No. 110-140, §§ 201–210, 121 Stat. 1492, 1519–32 (codified at CAA § 211(*o*), 42 U.S.C. § 7545(*o*)).

222. CAA § 211(*o*)(2)(B)(i)(I), 42 U.S.C. § 7545(*o*)(2)(B)(i)(I).

223. *Id.* § 211(*o*)(2)(B)(ii), 42 U.S.C. § 7545(*o*)(2)(B)(ii).

224. *Id.* § 211(*o*)(2)(B)(i), 42 U.S.C. § 7545(*o*)(2)(B)(i).

225. *Id.* § 211(*o*)(2)(B), (3)(B), 42 U.S.C. § 7545(*o*)(2)(B), (3)(B).

226. *Id.* § 211(*o*)(5), 42 U.S.C. § 7545(*o*)(5); 40 C.F.R. § 80.1427(a)(1).

227. CAA. § 211(*o*)(9), 42 U.S.C. § 7545(*o*)(9).

228. *Id.* § 211(*o*)(1)(H), 42 U.S.C. § 7545(*o*)(1)(H) (defining lifecycle GHG emissions).

229. *Id.* § 211(*o*)(1)(B), (D), 42 U.S.C. § 7545(*o*)(1)(B), (D).

230. *Id.* § 211(*o*)(1)(E), (2)(A)(i), 42 U.S.C. § 7545(*o*)(1)(E), (2)(A)(i).

231. *Id.* § 211(*o*)(1)(I)-(J), 42 U.S.C. § 7545(*o*)(1)(I)-(J).

232. *Id.* § 211(*o*)(7)(A), 42 U.S.C. § 7545(*o*)(7)(A).

233. *Id.* § 211(*o*)(7)(D), 42 U.S.C. § 7545(*o*)(7)(D).

234. *Id.* § 211(*o*)(7)(E), 42 U.S.C. § 7545(*o*)(7)(E).

235. *Id.* § 211(*o*)(7)(F)(i)-(ii), 42 U.S.C. § 7545(*o*)(7)(F)(i)-(ii).

236. Regulation of Fuels and Fuel Additives: Changes to Renewable Fuel Standard Program, 75 Fed. Reg. 14,670 (Mar. 26, 2010).

237. *Id.* at 14,677.

238. *Id.* at 14,679–81.

239. *See, e.g.,* 40 C.F.R. § 80.1426.

240. *See* 75 Fed. Reg. at 14,670 (adopting renewable fuel standards for 2010); Regulation of Fuels and Fuel Additives: 2011 Renewable Fuel Standards, 75 Fed. Reg. 76,790 (Dec. 9, 2010) (renewable fuel standards for 2011); Regulation of Fuels and Fuel Additives: 2012 Renewable Fuel Standards, 77 Fed. Reg. 1320 (Jan. 9, 2012) (renewable fuel standards for 2012).

241. *Am. Petroleum Inst. v. EPA*, 706 F.3d 474 (D.C. Cir. 2013).

242. *Id.* at 476. Despite Energy Information Administration projections that production would reach 5 million and 3.9 million gallons in 2010 and 2011, respectively, the domestic industry was unable to produce any cellulosic biofuel in those years. *Id.* at 478.

243. *Id.* at 479, 480.

244. *Americans for Clean Energy v. EPA*, 864 F.3d 691 (D.C. Cir. 2017).

245. *Id.* at 737.

246. *Id.* at 700.

247. *Id.* at 710–13.

248. *Id.* at 737.

249. Renewable Fuel Standard Program: Standards for 2020 and Biomass-Based Diesel Volume for 2021 and Other Changes, 85 Fed. Reg. 7016, 7018, tbl. I-1 (Feb. 6, 2020).

250. *Id.* at 7017.

251. Renewable Fuel Standard Program: Standards for 2014, 2015, and 2016 and Biomass-Based Diesel Volume for 2017, 80 Fed. Reg. 77,420 (Dec. 14, 2015).

252. *RFS Power Coal. v. EPA*, No. 20-1046 (and consolidated cases) (D.C. Cir. filed Feb. 21, 2020).

253. *HollyFrontier Cheyenne Refining, LLC v. Renewable Fuels Ass'n.*, 141 S. Ct. 2172, 2177 (2021),

254. Renewable Fuel Standard (RFS) Program: RFS Annual Rules, 87 Fed. Reg. 39,600 (July 1, 2022).

255. 864 F.3d at 691.

256. *Sinclair Wyo. Ref. Co. LLC v. EPA*, No. 22-1210 (and consolidated cases) (D.C. Cir. filed Aug. 17, 2022). A separate petition by an environmental advocacy organization challenging EPA's compliance with the Endangered Species Act, *Center for Biological Diversity v. EPA*, 22-1164 (D.C. Cir. filed July 20, 2022), was severed from those cases.

See Order, *Ctr. for Biological Diversity v. EPA*, No. 22-1164 (D.C. Cir. Nov. 29, 2022), ECF No. 1975429 (severing case).

257. *Sinclair Wyo. Ref. Co. LLC v. EPA*, No. 22-1073 (and consolidated cases) (D.C. Cir. filed May 4, 2022). In the challenged denials, EPA found that "no small refineries face disproportionate costs of compliance due to the RFS program." *See, e.g.*, April 2022 Denial of Petitions for Small Refinery Exemptions Under the Renewable Fuel Standard Program, 87 Fed. Reg. 24,300, 24,300 (Apr. 25, 2022).

258. Renewable Fuel Standard (RFS) Program: Standards for 2023–2025 and Other Changes, 87 Fed. Reg. 80,582 (proposed Dec. 30, 2022).

259. *Id.* at 80,583.

Chapter 9

THE ACID DEPOSITION CONTROL PROGRAM

Title IV of the Clean Air Act (CAA or Act),[1] added by the 1990 amendments, established a new program to control electric generating units' emissions of sulfur dioxide (SO_2) and nitrogen oxides (NOx), air pollutants that are believed to be major contributors to acid deposition. Congress designed this title to reduce electric utility SO_2 emissions by 10 million tons and achieve substantial reductions in NOx emissions from 1980 levels by the year 2000.[2]

The U.S. Environmental Protection Agency (EPA or Agency) published most of the regulations required for the SO_2 emission reduction program and the acid rain permitting program in 1993 (the "Title IV Core rules").[3] EPA published the principal regulations to implement the NOx program in 1994, 1995, and 1996.[4] The acid rain rules—contained in 40 C.F.R. parts 72 through 78—have undergone several revisions, particularly on emission monitoring requirements.

This chapter first reviews the two-phase program applicable to SO_2 emissions. It then discusses the NOx control requirements of the acid deposition program, the treatment of specific types of utility and non-utility facilities under Title IV, and the permitting and compliance requirements applicable to affected facilities.

I. SO_2 Emission Limitations

The basic feature of the Title IV SO_2 program is a system of SO_2 emission allowances, which imposes a cap on total SO_2 emissions from the electric utility industry. Each allowance entitles the allowance holder to emit one ton of SO_2. These allowances can be traded among affected facilities and others. The following sections describe the allowance system and how that system is put in place through a two-phased program of SO_2 control.

A. The Allowance Allocation and Trading System

1. Allowances

Rather than mandating traditional "command and control" regulation of SO_2, which would dictate absolute emission limits for each regulated source, Title IV provides for a market-based approach to SO_2 emission control. Under this approach, each existing affected facility is allocated a certain number of allowances to emit SO_2 each year, based on a prescribed emission limit. These allowances can be used in that year, saved for future years, or sold to other sources. Thus, allowance holders can buy and sell allowances on the open market, encouraging reduction of emissions in the most cost-effective manner.

Title IV defines an "allowance" as "an authorization, allocated to an affected unit by the EPA Administrator under [Title IV], to emit, during or after a specified calendar year, one ton of sulfur dioxide."[5] (A "unit" is "a fossil fuel-fired combustion device," such as a boiler or a turbine that is connected to an electric generator.[6]) Although allowance holders may not use an allowance before the calendar year for which EPA issued it, allowances can be carried forward and banked for use in future years or sold to others for their use in the future.[7]

Under Title IV, allowance holders may trade allowances freely. Although some proposed versions of the 1990 amendments considered by Congress would have restricted trading for existing units to allowance holders within two major geographic regions, the enacted statute did not restrict trading in any way.[8] Allowance transfers are not effective, however, until EPA receives and records a written certification of the transfer signed by a responsible official representing each party to the transaction.[9] In addition, allowance holders may transfer allowances before the calendar year in which they become effective even though the allowances may not actually be used for compliance purposes before that year.

EPA issued SO_2 emission allowances to affected units in two phases.[10] For Phase I units—that is, units that first became subject to the allowance-holding requirement in 1995—EPA issued a certain number of annual allowances, as specified in section 404 of the Act.[11] For both Phase I units and Phase II units—that is, units that first became subject to the allowance-holding requirement in 2000—allowances are allocated for Phase II (2000 and later) according to twenty-eight specific allowance allocation formulas set out in section 405 of the Act.[12] With limited exceptions, only existing affected units (basically, electric utility units that began commercial operation before November 15, 1990) are entitled to allowance allocations; most "new units" (units that commenced commercial operation on or after November 15, 1990) must acquire allowances in the market.[13] Allowances are allocated to an existing affected unit even if it was removed from commercial operation after November 15, 1990.

Except for 50,000 annual allowances for Phase I units in certain states and up to 530,000 "bonus allowances" annually for 2000–2009 for certain Phase II units, the total number of allowances is limited by statute to 8.9 million each year in Phase II.[14] If the total of annual Phase II allowances that would be provided through application of the statutory allocation formulas would exceed this 8.9-million "cap," EPA must reduce the number of allowances on a pro rata basis; EPA in fact did this when it allocated allowances in 1993.

Title IV specifies that an allowance is not a property right and that "[n]othing in this [Title] or in any other provision of law shall be construed to limit the authority of the United States to terminate or limit such authorization [to emit]."[15] In addition, issuance of allowances in no way alters the compliance requirements imposed under other provisions of the Act, including the national ambient air quality standard and state implementation plan programs.

2. Allowance Trading

Under Title IV, allowance holders can trade allowances without restriction on a nationwide basis.[16] Although EPA may issue allowances only to the owners or operators of affected units, allowances can be transferred to any person, whether or not that person owns or operates an affected unit. The regulations addressing allowance tracking and trading are in 40 C.F.R. part 73.

Allowances may be traded for compliance purposes for a given calendar year as late as sixty days after the end of the year.[17] The purpose of this sixty-day "true-up period" following the end of a calendar year is to allow completion of allowance trades after a full year of emissions data has been obtained, thereby permitting determination of each unit's allowance needs for that year.

In keeping with the statutory scheme, EPA's allowance trading rules provide for minimal EPA involvement in allowance transfers, other than the recording and certification functions contemplated by the statute. For example, the price and other terms of allowance transactions need not be disclosed to EPA. In drafting the rules, EPA recognized the importance of fostering the development of an open and flexible allowance market.

B. Applicability

The Title IV SO_2 requirements apply to affected utility units. An "affected unit" is "a unit that is subject to emission reduction requirements or limitations under this [T]itle."[18] The SO_2 allowance program, in turn, applies to "existing" and "new" "utility units." An "existing unit" is "a unit . . . that commenced commercial operation before November 15, 1990."[19] A "new unit" is "a unit that commences commercial operation on or after November 15, 1990."[20] A "utility unit" is "(i) a unit that serves a generator in any State that produces electricity for sale, or (ii) a unit that, during 1985, served a generator in any State that produced electricity for sale."[21]

The statute carves out several exceptions to this general definition. For example, a unit that cogenerates steam and electricity is not a "utility unit" unless the unit supplies "more than one-third of its potential electric output capacity and more than 25 megawatts electrical output to any utility power distribution system for sale."[22] Section 72.6 of EPA's rules elaborates on these and other applicability requirements, which should be reviewed carefully in individual cases to determine whether Title IV requirements apply to a facility. Section 72.6 addresses applicability criteria for various categories of facilities, including cogeneration facilities, independent power production facilities, and solid waste incinerators. Moreover, section 72.6(c) establishes a procedure by which a binding applicability determination can be requested and obtained from EPA.

In addition, EPA's rules provide for a "de minimis" exemption for new units that serve "one or more generators with total nameplate capacity of 25 MWe or less" and that use fuels with a sulfur content of no more than 0.05 percent by weight.[23] EPA's rules also provide a means to obtain an exemption from Title IV requirements for units that are permanently retired.[24]

II. NOx Emission Limitations

Title IV also addresses emissions of NOx by directing EPA to set NOx emission limitations for coal-fired utility boilers in two phases.[25] Under EPA's rules, the first phase began in 1996 and the second in 2000.[26] Part 76 sets out specific NOx emission limitations for various categories of coal-fired utility boilers. Unlike the SO_2 part of Title IV, the Title IV NOx provisions do not include emission allowances and allowance trading. The Title IV NOx provisions offer some flexibility, however, through options for averaging of NOx emissions rates[27] and, subject to certain restrictions, alternative emission limitations.[28]

III. Permits, Penalties, and Emission Monitoring

A. Title IV Permits

Title IV contains permitting and compliance plan requirements that are in addition to the general operating permit requirements of Title V of the Act.[29] EPA must implement the Title IV permitting requirements in accordance with Title V, except in cases where the requirements of these titles conflict; in such cases, Title IV requirements govern.

Under Title IV, owners and operators of units subject to SO_2 and NOx emission requirements must prepare and submit acid rain permit applications and compliance plans. Unless certain specific compliance options are chosen, a simple statement that the unit will hold enough allowances to cover its SO_2 emissions and will meet any applicable NOx emission limit will satisfy the compliance plan requirement.[30]

A Title IV permit is applicable for five years.[31] For Phase I units, EPA issued the Phase I permit.[32] For Phase II, designated state permitting authorities[33] issue permits.[34] A new unit must submit a Phase II permit application and compliance plan to the permitting authority no later than twenty-four months before it begins operation.[35]

B. Excess Emissions Penalty

Section 411 of the Act imposes a penalty of $2,000 per ton (increased yearly for inflation) for a unit's SO_2 emissions that exceed the number of allowances held in the applicable source's compliance account[36] as of the applicable allowance transfer deadline and for NOx emissions that exceed the level of emissions permissible under section 407 of the Act.[37] Very few units have had to pay this penalty because there have been very few cases in which units have had emission exceedances under Title IV. In addition, a unit must have deducted from its allowance account (generally for the year following the exceedance) one allowance for each ton of excess SO_2 emissions.[38] Moreover, any violation of Title IV requirements is potentially subject to the Act's other enforcement provisions discussed in chapter 11.[39]

C. Emission Monitoring, Reporting, and Recordkeeping Requirements

The owner or operator of an affected unit under Title IV must install and operate continuous emission monitoring systems (CEMS), and must quality-assure the data, for SO_2, NOx, opacity, and volumetric flow.[40] The Act, however, authorizes EPA to allow use of alternative monitoring systems that have "the same precision, reliability, accessibility, and timeliness" as CEMS.[41] EPA used that authority to authorize use of fuel sampling and analysis to report SO_2 emissions and an estimation protocol to report NOx emissions from certain oil- and gas-fired units, rather than installing CEMS.[42] The Act also requires sources to provide data for each hour of operation, or other information "satisfactory to the Administrator," when data from a required monitoring system is not available.[43] To fulfill that requirement, EPA's part 75 rules require reporting for "missing data" periods using estimation protocols that are increasingly more conservative depending on the length of the missing data period and total number of hours of missing data during the year.[44]

Facilities are required to submit all hourly data from their monitoring systems, and other supporting information, in electronic format to EPA in a format specified by the Administrator,[45] which currently is a system called the Emissions Collection and Monitoring Plan System or ECMPS. All information submitted must be certified by a representative chosen by the unit's owners and operators as "true, accurate, and complete" based on a standard of reasonable inquiry set out in the rules.[46]

EPA has periodically updated the highly technical and complex rules implementing the CEMS provisions, and the associated reporting and recordkeeping requirements, to reflect advancements in technology and address issues that arise in implementation. However, the last significant update was in 2011.

Notes

1. Titles of the CAA correspond to subchapters in the U.S. Code.
2. CAA § 401(b), 42 U.S.C. § 7651(b).
3. Acid Rain Program: General Provisions and Permits, Allowance System, Continuous Emissions Monitoring, Excess Emissions and Administrative Appeals, 58 Fed. Reg. 3590 (Jan. 11, 1993) (promulgating 40 C.F.R. pts. 72, 73, 75, 77, 78).
4. Acid Rain Program: Nitrogen Oxides Emission Reduction Program, 59 Fed. Reg. 13,538 (Mar. 22, 1994); Acid Rain Program: Nitrogen Oxides Emission Reduction Program; Response to Court Remand, 60 Fed. Reg. 18,751 (Apr. 13, 1995); Acid Rain Program: Nitrogen Oxides Emission Reduction Program, 61 Fed. Reg. 67,112 (Dec. 19, 1996).
5. CAA § 402(3), 42 U.S.C. § 7651a(3).
6. 40 C.F.R. § 72.2.
7. CAA § 403(g), 42 U.S.C. § 7651b(g).

8. A 2000 New York law that purported to restrict interstate allowance transfers on a geographic basis was struck down as unconstitutional. *Clean Air Mkts. Grp. v. Pataki*, 194 F. Supp. 2d 147 (N.D.N.Y. 2002), *aff'd*, 338 F.3d 82 (2d Cir. 2003).

9. CAA § 403(b), 42 U.S.C. § 7651b(b).

10. Allowance allocations are listed in tables in 40 C.F.R. § 73.10.

11. 42 U.S.C. § 7651c.

12. *Id.* § 7651d.

13. CAA § 402(10), 42 U.S.C. § 7651a(10); *but see id.* § 405(g), 42 U.S.C. § 7651d(g) (authorizing allowance allocations for certain new units that commenced operation between 1986 and December 31, 1995).

14. *Id.* §§ 403(a)(1), 405(a)(2), (3), 42 U.S.C. §§ 7651b(a)(1), 7651d(a)(2), (3).

15. *Id.* § 403(f), 42 U.S.C. § 7651b(f).

16. *Id* § 403(b), 42 U.S.C. § 7651b(b).

17. *See* 40 C.F.R. § 72.2 (definition of "allowance transfer deadline").

18. CAA § 402(2), 42 U.S.C. § 7651a(2).

19. *Id.* § 402(8), 42 U.S.C. § 7651a(8). The definition does *not* include existing simple combustion turbines or existing units that serve a generator with a nameplate capacity of 25 megawatts (MW) or less.

20. *Id.* § 402(10), 42 U.S.C. § 7651a(10).

21. *Id.* § 402(17)(A)(i)-(ii), 42 U.S.C. § 7651a(17)(A)(i)-(ii).

22. *Id.* § 402(17)(C), 42 U.S.C. § 7651a(17)(C).

23. 40 C.F.R. § 72.7(a).

24. *Id.* § 72.8.

25. CAA § 407, 42 U.S.C. § 7651f.

26. 40 C.F.R. pt. 76 ("Part 76").

27. 40 C.F.R. § 76.11.

28. *Id.* § 76.10.

29. CAA § 408, 42 U.S.C. § 7651g. The Title IV permitting rules are in 40 C.F.R. part 72. Title V permitting is discussed in Chapter 4.

30. CAA § 408(b), 42 U.S.C. § 7651g(b).

31. *Id.* § 408(a), 42 U.S.C. § 7651g(a).

32. *Id.* § 408(c), 42 U.S.C. § 7651g(c).

33. *Id.* § 402(11), 42 U.S.C. § 7651a(11), defines "permitting authority" as "the Administrator, or the State or local air pollution control agency, with an approved permitting program . . . ."

34. *Id.* § 408(d), 42 U.S.C. § 7651g(d).

35. *Id.* § 408(e), 42 U.S.C. § 7651g(e).

36. As initially promulgated by EPA, the SO_2 allowance rules were implemented on a unit-by-unit basis using individual unit allowance accounts. In 2005, EPA revised the program to implement the SO_2 allowance-holding requirement on a source-by-source basis, effective July 1, 2006. Rule To Reduce Interstate Transport of Fine Particulate Matter and Ozone (Clean Air Interstate Rule); Revisions to Acid Rain Program; Revisions to the NOx SIP Call, 70 Fed. Reg. 25,162, 25,335 (May 12, 2005). Under this revised approach, a

unit at a given source may use allowances from any other unit at the same source without transferring allowances between individual unit accounts. *Id.* at 25,296.

37. CAA § 411(a), (c), 42 U.S.C. § 7651j(a), (c). As a result of cumulative annual inflation adjustments, the per-ton penalty amount for 2022 excess emissions is $4,392. Acid Rain Program: Excess Emissions Penalty Inflation Adjustments, 86 Fed. Reg. 53,959 (Sept. 29, 2021).

38. CAA § 411(b), 42 U.S.C. § 7651j(b). EPA's rules governing excess emissions penalties and offsets are in 40 C.F.R. part 77.

39. *Id.* §§ 411(e), 414, 42 U.S.C. §§ 7651j(e), 7651m.

40. *Id.* § 412, 42 U.S.C. § 7651k. EPA's implementing rules are in 40 C.F.R. part 75 ("Part 75").

41. *Id.* § 412(a), 42 U.S.C. § 7651k(a).

42. *See* 40 C.F.R. pt. 75, Apps. D and E.

43. CAA § 412(d), 42 U.S.C. § 7651k(d).

44. 40 C.F.R. §§ 75.30 to 75.39.

45. *Id.* at §§ 75.62(c), 75.63(c), 75.64(d), 75.64(f).

46. *Id.* at §§ 72.21(b), 72.24

Chapter 10

STRATOSPHERIC OZONE PROTECTION

Congress added Title VI to the Clean Air Act (CAA or Act) as part of the 1990 amendments in order to address the issue of stratospheric ozone depletion, and to implement the United States' international obligations as a signatory to the Montreal Protocol on Substances that Deplete the Ozone Layer (Protocol).[1] The Protocol, which has been amended several times since its adoption in 1987, requires its signatories (including the United States) to restrict the production and consumption (defined not as "use," but as production plus imports minus exports of bulk chemicals) of chlorofluorocarbons (CFCs), halons, methyl chloroform, carbon tetrachloride, and hydrochlorofluorocarbons (HCFCs). As amended in November 1992, the Protocol required the complete phaseout of all listed CFCs, methyl chloroform, and carbon tetrachloride by 1996, and of halons by 1994. The phaseout of HCFCs is to be accomplished over a longer period stretching out from 2020 to 2040. Finally, the 1992 amendments to the Protocol required that production and consumption of hydrobromofluorocarbons (HBFCs) be phased out beginning in 1996 and added methyl bromide to the list of controlled substances.

In 1988, the U.S. Environmental Protection Agency (EPA or Agency) issued final rules implementing the Protocol in the United States.[2] These rules established a system for allocating production and consumption allowances for ozone-depleting substances based on 1986 levels of production and imports, and established a system for trading these allowances. In 1989, this regulatory system was supplemented with an excise tax on most sales of CFCs and other ozone-depleting chemicals.

Although Title VI largely mirrors the requirements of the Montreal Protocol as they existed in 1990, it contains more stringent interim targets and an earlier phaseout of methyl chloroform. In 1993, EPA took final action to accelerate these targets in response to new scientific information, the 1992 amendments to the Montreal Protocol, and petitions to the Agency.[3] Title VI also requires EPA to promulgate regulations to (1) ensure the "lowest achievable levels" of emissions in all user sectors; (2) ban nonessential products; (3) limit the use of harmful substitutes; (4) establish standards and requirements regarding the use, recycling, and disposal of CFCs and certain other substances in appliances and industrial process refrigeration; (5) establish standards and requirements for servicing motor vehicle air conditioners; (6) mandate warning labels; and (7) establish a safe alternatives program.

This chapter describes the provisions of Title VI of the Act[4] and discusses key implementing regulations.

I. The Listing and Phaseout of Ozone-Depleting Substances

The provisions of the Montreal Protocol and of Title VI are directed at reducing and discontinuing the production and consumption of ozone-depleting substances. The statute lists the substances that are to be controlled and mandates that their production and consumption be phased out over a specified time period depending on the ozone-depletion potential of the substances. In addition, Title VI immediately bans specific uses of controlled substances that Congress deemed to be nonessential and authorizes the EPA Administrator to promulgate rules banning additional nonessential uses.

A. Listing

Under the terms of Title VI, the Administrator was required to publish an initial list of "class I" and "class II" ozone-depleting substances within sixty days of the enactment of the 1990 Clean Air Act amendments. Congress enumerated the substances that were to be included in the initial lists, all of which were contained in the London Amendments to the Montreal Protocol. Title VI requires EPA to update the lists by rulemaking "[p]eriodically, but not less frequently than every 3 years after November 15, 1990."[5]

The list of class I substances is to include "any . . . substance that the Administrator finds causes or contributes significantly to harmful effects on the stratospheric ozone layer . . . [including] all substances that the Administrator determines have an ozone depletion potential of 0.2 or greater."[6] The statutory class I substances are divided into five groups that include two groups of CFCs, a group consisting of three halons, and two single-substance groups, including carbon tetrachloride and methyl chloroform, respectively.

The list of class II substances is to include "any . . . substance that the Administrator finds is known or may reasonably be anticipated to cause or contribute to harmful effects on the stratospheric ozone layer."[7] EPA promulgated regulations in 1991 incorporating the lists exactly as set out in the statute.[8]

The Administrator is empowered to add, by rulemaking, any substance to the class I or class II lists that meets the criteria for inclusion. In addition, anyone may petition to have a substance added to the lists. Finally, the Administrator may remove a substance from the class II list by adding it to the class I list; no substance listed in the statute in class I may be removed from that list, however.[9] In response to changes in the Montreal Protocol, and to petitions submitted to the Administrator after passage of the 1990 amendments, EPA added methyl bromide and HBFCs to the class I list in 1993,[10] and added chlorobromomethane to that list in 2003.[11] Each of these new substances is listed in its own group.

B. Phaseout

Title VI provides for the total elimination of production of class I substances by January 1, 2000 (January 1, 2002, for methyl chloroform).[12] In each year from 1991 to 2000, production of class I substances was restricted to a declining percentage of the amount of each substance that was produced in the baseline year, which is defined in the statute.[13] Title VI provides for the total elimination of production of class II substances by January 1, 2030.[14] The statute also provides that, effective January 1, 2015, it was unlawful for any person (i) to produce any class II substance in an annual quantity greater than the quantity of the same substance produced by the same producer in the baseline year,[15] and (ii) to introduce into interstate commerce or use any class II substance unless such substance (1) had been used, recovered, and recycled, (2) is used and entirely consumed (except for trace quantities) in the production of other chemicals, (3) is used as a refrigerant in appliances manufactured prior to January 1, 2020, or (4) is listed as acceptable for use as a fire suppression agent for nonresidential applications in accordance with section 612(c) of the Act.[16]

The statute provides exceptions allowing for production of limited quantities of methyl chloroform for use in essential applications, for the production of limited quantities of class I substances for use in medical devices, and for the production of limited quantities of class I halons for purposes of aviation safety. Production under these exceptions is capped at annual quantities equal to 10 percent of each producer's baseline allowance for the specified substance.[17] The Administrator may grant limited exceptions for production solely for export to developing countries that are parties to the Montreal Protocol, for national security, and for fire suppression and explosion prevention.[18] The statute also authorizes the Administrator to grant limited exceptions for production of class II substances for use in medical devices and for export to developing countries that are parties to the Montreal Protocol, subject to specified caps.[19] Additional detail regarding phaseout of class I and class II substances, and applicable exceptions, is provided by regulation.[20]

C. Accelerated Schedule

Section 606 of the Act permits the Administrator to promulgate a more stringent phaseout schedule for both class I and class II substances if (1) based on an assessment of credible scientific information, the Administrator determines an accelerated phaseout is necessary to protect human health and the environment from harmful effects on the stratospheric ozone layer; (2) based on the availability of substitutes for listed substances, a more stringent schedule is practicable, taking into account technological achievability, safety, and other relevant factors; or (3) the Montreal Protocol is modified to include an accelerated phaseout schedule.[21] In addition, anyone can petition the Administrator to promulgate regulations under this section.[22]

In 1992, President Bush announced that the United States would phase out production of listed ozone-depleting substances by December 31, 1995. To effectuate this change in policy, as well as to respond to petitions to EPA from both environmental advocacy organizations and industry groups, the Administrator proposed an accelerated schedule under which production and consumption of all class I substances listed in Title VI, except halons, was to occur by January 1, 1996, and listed halons were to be phased out by January 1, 1994.[23]

EPA proposed to accelerate the phaseout schedule for certain class II HCFCs on a compound-specific basis depending on the ozone-depletion potential of each substance. The earliest phaseout date was to be January 1, 2003, for HCFC-141b. Production and consumption of other HCFCs were to be frozen as of January 1, 2010, or January 1, 2015, and complete phaseout would be required by either January 1, 2020, or January 1, 2030, depending on which HCFC is involved.[24]

In the same notice, the Agency proposed adding methyl bromide to the list of class I substances. This addition to the class I list was prompted by the 1992 amendments to the Montreal Protocol and by a petition to EPA under section 602(c)(3) of the Act.[25] In 1998, Congress amended the Act and directed EPA to conform the phaseout schedule for methyl bromide to what other industrialized nations were doing under the Protocol.[26] In response, EPA issued regulations requiring: (1) a 50 percent reduction from baseline levels beginning January 1, 2001; (2) a 70 percent reduction from baseline levels beginning January 1, 2003; and (3) complete phaseout beginning January 1, 2005.[27]

Finally, to codify the other 1992 amendment to the Montreal Protocol, EPA proposed adding HBFCs to the list of class I substances. The Agency proposed a production and consumption freeze at 1991 baseline levels beginning January 1, 1994, and a January 1, 1996 phaseout date.[28]

In 1993, EPA promulgated a final rule that implemented the accelerated phaseouts along the lines initially proposed.[29] In addition, in the final rule, EPA made certain minor revisions to its regulatory definition of "production" and implemented a ban on bulk exports of certain specified ozone-depleting substances to countries that are not signatories to the Montreal Protocol.

II. Nonessential Product Ban

In addition to mandating the gradual elimination of ozone-depleting substances, Title VI also required the Administrator to promulgate regulations within one year of the enactment of Title VI that identify nonessential products that release class I substances into the environment.[30] In determining that a product is nonessential, the Administrator must "consider the purpose or intended use of the product, the technological availability of substitutes for such product and for such class I substance, safety, health, and other relevant factors."[31] At the least, nonessential products are to include CFC-propelled plastic party streamers and noise horns, and CFC-containing cleaning fluids for noncommercial electronic and photographic equipment.[32] The Administrator was directed to include any other nonessential consumer products that release class I substances during manufacture, use, storage, or disposal.[33] Regulations banning the sale or distribution in interstate commerce of such products were to be effective twenty-four months from the enactment of Title VI.[34]

Title VI also includes a ban on the sale or distribution of nonessential products that release class II substances, including aerosol products or pressurized dispensers containing class II substances and foam products that contain or are manufactured with class II substances.[35] The Administrator may exempt any aerosol product or pressurized dispenser that is essential given flammability or worker safety concerns, where the only available alternative would be a class I substance.[36]

EPA published final regulations implementing the nonessential product ban on class I substances in January 1993, elucidating the specific product bans listed in the statute.[37] The ban on products containing class II products was promulgated later that year.[38] Since then, EPA has revised the regulations several times to add or exempt products from the banned list.[39]

III. Production and Consumption Allowance Program

The gradual elimination of ozone-depleting substances under the Montreal Protocol and Title VI has been implemented by establishing allowances based on past production and consumption of these substances.[40] These allowances are to decrease each year by a fixed percentage of the original allowance, according to the phaseout schedule for each substance. These allowances may be transferred among producers and consumers and may be increased under certain carefully defined circumstances with the approval of EPA. EPA promulgated rules governing this allowance trading system for class I substances in 1992[41] and revised them extensively in 1995.[42] EPA promulgated rules establishing an allowance system to control HCFCs in 2003.[43]

A. Allocation of Allowances

Title VI provides for the establishment of both production and consumption allowances, which are to be based on baseline production, import, and export level reports filed with EPA as directed by section 603 of the Act.[44] Regulations promulgated under Title VI in 1992 prohibit persons from producing or importing controlled substances in excess of production and consumption allowances established in those regulations.[45] Production and consumption allowances are specific to individual producers and importers and are allocated by substance.[46] Under this system, to produce any quantity of a controlled substance, a producer must have both production and consumption allowances sufficient to cover the amount of controlled substances produced. An importer need hold only consumption allowances equal to the amount imported.[47]

B. Allowance Transfer Program

In authorizing the issuance of production and consumption allowances, Title VI specifies that allowances may be transferred so long as such transactions "result in greater total reductions in the production in each year of class I and class II substances than would occur in that year in the absence of such transactions."[48] Transfers may involve either an exchange between two or more persons of production or consumption allowances, or the exchange of allowances for one substance for those of another substance. Any person holding consumption or production allowances, potential production allowances, or authorization to convert potential production allowances to actual production allowances may "transfer" such an allowance to another person, subject to EPA's determination that the transferor has sufficient allowances remaining in that year to effect the transfer. To effectuate the statutory directive that such transfers must result in greater total reductions than would occur otherwise, EPA requires a 1 percent offset from the transferor's unexpended balance of allowances.[49]

IV. Recycling Programs

Beyond introducing measures directed toward the eventual phaseout of the production and consumption of class I and class II substances, Title VI also imposes requirements intended to promote the recapture and safe disposal of such substances that have already been introduced into the product stream. To this end, Title VI requires the establishment of programs addressing industrial refrigeration, appliances, and automobile air conditioning.

A. National Recycling and Emission Reduction Program

Title VI provides for a three-part recycling and emission reduction program.[50] First, by January 1, 1992, EPA was required to have in place regulations establishing standards and requirements regarding the use and disposal of class I substances during the service, repair, or disposal of appliances and industrial process refrigeration.[51] Similar regulations were required for class II substances.[52] As defined broadly by the Act, "appliance" includes "any device which contains and uses a class I or class II substance as a refrigerant and which is used for household or commercial purposes, including any air conditioner, refrigerator, chiller, or freezer."[53] These regulations, commonly referred to as the "refrigerant recycling rules," are to be designed to reduce the use and emission of class I and class II substances to their "lowest achievable level" and to "maximize the recapture and recycling of such substances."[54]

Second, these regulations are to contain standards for safe disposal of class I and class II substances. In particular, regulatory provisions must require that (1) class I and class II substances contained in bulk in appliances, machines, or other goods be removed prior to the disposal of such items or their delivery for recycling; (2) any appliance, machine, or other good containing a class I or class II substance in bulk be equipped with a servicing aperture or an equally effective design feature that will facilitate the recapture of such substances; and (3) products in which a class I or class II substance is an "inherent element" are "disposed of in a manner that reduces, to the maximum extent practicable, the release of such substance into the environment."[55]

Third, section 608 contains a self-effectuating prohibition on the venting of class I or class II substances (and, eventually, their substitutes) during servicing of air conditioning and refrigeration equipment. Specifically, effective July 1, 1992, it became unlawful for any person

> in the course of maintaining, servicing, repairing, or disposing of an appliance or industrial process refrigeration, to knowingly vent or otherwise knowingly release or dispose of any class I or class II substances used as a refrigerant in such appliance (or industrial process refrigeration) in a manner which permits such substance to enter the environment.[56]

"De minimis releases associated with good faith attempts to recapture and recycle or safely dispose of" any class I or class II substance are not subject to this prohibition.[57] In addition, releases of substitute refrigerants that EPA has determined do not pose a threat to the environment are permitted.[58]

EPA promulgated regulations to implement the refrigerant recycling program in 1993.[59] Key elements of the regulations include service requirements for the evacuation of air conditioning and refrigeration equipment to established vacuum levels; recovery and recycling equipment certification standards; a voluntary technician certification program; mandatory certification requirements for owners of recycling or recovery equipment, including outside contractors; and standards for safe disposal.

In 2016, the Obama EPA issued a rule that revised and updated many aspects of the refrigerant management rules, and extended requirements previously applicable only to refrigerants containing an ozone-depleting substance (ODS) to non-ODS substitute refrigerants, including hydrofluorocarbons (HFCs) and hydrofluoroolefins (HFOs), with the intent of reducing emissions of substitutes that do not deplete the ozone layer but that can have high global warming potentials.[60] However, in 2020, the Trump EPA issued a rule that reversed the extension of the regulations to non-ODS substitute refrigerants.[61] Subsequently, Congress enacted the American Innovation and Manufacturing (AIM) Act of 2020,[62] which among other things, instructs EPA to issue regulations to control the servicing, repair, disposal, or installation of equipment that involves certain HFCs, and their substitutes.[63] Judicial challenges to both the 2016 rule and the 2020 rule[64] are being held in abeyance while EPA re-evaluates the rules considering the Agency's authorities under both the Clean Air Act and the AIM Act.

B. Servicing Motor Vehicle Air Conditioners

In addition to mandating recycling for class I substances used in appliances and industrial process refrigeration, Title VI requires that, as of January 1, 1992:

> [N]o person repairing or servicing motor vehicles for consideration may perform any service on a motor vehicle air conditioner involving the refrigerant for such air conditioner without properly using approved refrigerant recycling equipment and no such person may perform such service unless such person has been properly trained and certified.[65]

Title VI defines "refrigerant" to mean "any class I or class II substance used in a motor vehicle air conditioner" and, as of 1995, "any substitute substance."[66]

Regulations promulgated in 1992 define "service for consideration" to include any form of payment and any service not performed for free.[67] The regulations apply to the person performing the service, not to the owner of the vehicle; therefore, a company that owns its own fleet of vehicles is covered by the regulations because any employee who services the air conditioner is compensated for that service. The regulations define "motor vehicle" as the term is defined in Title II of the Act. This definition excludes "off-road vehicles," but covers other vehicles even if they are used off-road, such as at construction sites and on farms.[68]

These regulations have two major components. The first governs the equipment that may be used to service motor vehicle air conditioners. The second governs the training and certification of service technicians. All technicians who service motor vehicle air conditioners must attend a training and certification program approved, in advance, by EPA. Companies whose business it is to service motor vehicle air conditioners or companies that service their own fleets of motor vehicles may establish their own training and certification programs, but these programs must be approved in advance by EPA.[69] As of January 1, 1993, all persons repairing or servicing motor vehicle air conditioners for consideration must certify to the Administrator that they have purchased approved equipment and that any person authorized to use the equipment is properly trained and certified.[70]

Section 609 of the Act also makes it unlawful to sell, distribute, or offer for sale or distribution any class I or class II substance that may be used as a refrigerant for a motor vehicle air conditioner in a container holding less than 20 pounds of refrigerant. This section became effective by law on November 15, 1992.[71] EPA's regulations require proof that any sales of such small containers were made only to properly certified technicians and to those who intend to resell such containers.[72]

Since its initial regulatory actions, EPA has issued several additional rules adopting new or revised standards and authorizing the use of alternative refrigerants.[73]

V. Labeling

To promote consumer awareness, section 611 of the Act requires that, effective May 15, 1993, all containers containing class I and class II substances, products containing class I substances, and products manufactured with class I substances that are introduced into interstate commerce bear a warning statement indicating that the product contains or is manufactured with an ozone-depleting substance.[74] Section 611 further provides that after May 15, 1993, products containing or manufactured with class II substances must be labeled if the Administrator determines that safe alternatives are available. By January 1, 2015, all products manufactured with, or containing, class I or class II substances must be labeled.[75]

EPA issued a final rule implementing the labeling provisions of Title VI in 1993.[76] The rule's important features include (1) an exemption from the labeling requirement for manufacturers that have reached a total use reduction of 95 percent or greater from 1990 use levels for products manufactured using CFC-113 and methyl chloroform as solvents;[77] (2) an exclusion from the labeling requirements for products manufactured for export outside the U.S.;[78] and (3) limitations on the need for labeling information to be "pass[ed] through" by manufacturers to ultimate consumers.[79] EPA has revised the rule several times, including a revision and republication of the rule in 1995 to add several exemptions.[80]

VI. Safe Alternatives Policy

Title VI provides that, to the greatest extent possible, substitutes that are developed for controlled ozone-depleting substances must "reduce overall risks to human health and the environment."[81] To implement this policy, EPA must promulgate rules that make it illegal to replace any class I or II substance with a substitute that the Administrator determines may present adverse effects to human health or the environment, where the Administrator has identified an alternative to such replacement that (1) reduces the overall risk to human health and the environment; and (2) is currently or potentially available.[82]

The Administrator is to publish a list of prohibited alternatives and a list of safe alternatives.[83] Anyone may petition the Administrator to add a substance to or remove a substance from either the safe alternatives list or the prohibited list.[84] Finally, anyone who produces a substitute for a class I substance must provide the Administrator with any unpublished health and safety studies and must notify the Administrator not less than 90 days before the substance is placed on the market.[85]

In 1994, EPA published a rule to implement section 612, called the Significant New Alternatives Policy (SNAP) program.[86] The rule included a list of alternative substances being considered for review under the SNAP program. To evaluate the overall risk of substitutes for controlled substances, EPA considers toxicity and exposure, chlorine loading, ozone-depletion potential, global warming potential, and flammability. EPA also considers economic feasibility, the context of the risk, and the risk as measured by the intended use.

Substitutes listed as unacceptable or as acceptable subject to use restrictions are generally identified in the rule by the date of promulgation and effective date.[87] In two rules, issued in 2015 and 2016, EPA changed the status for certain HFCs in various end-uses in the aerosols, refrigeration and air conditioning, and foam blowing sections from acceptable to unacceptable.[88] As discussed above, HFCs are not ozone-depleting substances, but they can contribute to climate change. Those rules were later vacated by the D.C. Circuit and remanded to EPA.[89] Specifically, the court determined that although EPA could validly forbid current users of ozone-depleting substances from switching to HFCs, EPA lacked authority to force users who had already switched to HFCs to make a second switch to a different substitute.[90] The D.C. Circuit also vacated EPA's first attempt to revise the rule on remand without notice-and-comment rulemaking, finding it procedurally invalid.[91] EPA's fall 2022 regulatory agenda estimates issuing a new proposal to address the remand in 2023.

Notes

1. Montreal Protocol on Substances that Deplete the Ozone Layer, Sept. 16, 1987, S. TREATY DOC. NO. 100-10,1522 U.N.T.S. 3.
2. *See* Protection of Stratospheric Ozone, 53 Fed. Reg. 30,566, 30,598 (Aug. 12, 1988) (codified at 40 C.F.R. pt. 82).
3. Protection of Stratospheric Ozone, 58 Fed. Reg. 65,018 (Dec. 10, 1993).
4. Titles of the CAA correspond to subchapters in the U.S. Code.
5. CAA § 602(c), 42 U.S.C. § 7671a(c).
6. *Id.* § 602(a), 42 U.S.C. § 7671a(a). "Ozone-depletion potential" is defined in section 601(10) of the Act as "a factor established by the Administrator to reflect the ozone-depletion potential of a substance, on a mass per kilogram basis, as compared to

chlorofluorocarbon-11 (CFC–11)." *Id.* § 601(a)(10), 42 U.S.C. § 7671(10). The definition specifies that "[s]uch factor shall be based upon the substance's atmospheric lifetime, the molecular weight of bromine and chlorine, and the substance's ability to be photolytically disassociated, and upon other factors determined to be an accurate measure of relative ozone-depletion potential." *Id.*

7. *Id.* § 602(b), 42 U.S.C. § 7671a(b).

8. *See* Protection of Stratospheric Ozone: Notice Listing Ozone-Depleting Substances, 56 Fed. Reg. 2420 (Jan. 22, 1991) (codified at 40 C.F.R. pt. 82, App. A).

9. CAA § 602(c)(4), 42 U.S.C. § 7671a(c)(4).

10. *See* 58 Fed. Reg. at 65,018.

11. *See* Protection of Stratospheric Ozone: Phaseout of Chlorobromomethane Production and Consumption, 68 Fed. Reg. 42,884 (July 18, 2003).

12. CAA § 604(a), 42 U.S.C. § 7671c(a).

13. *Id.* § 601(2), 42 U.S.C. § 7671(2).

14. *Id.* § 605(b)(2), 42 U.S.C. § 7671d(b)(2).

15. *Id.* § 605(b)(1), 42 U.S.C. § 7671d(b)(1).

16. *Id.* § 605(a), 42 U.S.C. § 7671d(a).

17. *Id.* § 604(d), 42 U.S.C. § 7671c(d).

18. *Id.* § 604(e), (f), (g), 42 U.S.C. § 7671c(e), (f), (g).

19. *Id.* § 605(d), 42 U.S.C. § 7671d(d).

20. *See* 40 C.F.R. pt. 82.

21. *Id.* § 606(a), 42 U.S.C. § 7671e(a).

22. *Id.* § 606(b), 42 U.S.C. § 7671e(b).

23. *See* Protection of Stratospheric Ozone, 58 Fed. Reg. 15,014, 15,022 (proposed Mar. 18, 1993).

24. *Id.* at 15,027.

25. *Id.* at 15,030.

26. CAA § 604(h), 42 U.S.C. § 7671c(h).

27. Protection of Stratospheric Ozone: Incorporation of Clean Air Act Amendments for Reductions in Class I, Group VI Controlled Substances, 65 Fed. Reg. 70,795 (Nov. 28, 2000). In 2011, EPA promulgated rules identifying the specific parameters of the "critical use exemption" for methyl bromide and the amount of methyl bromide that may be produced, imported, or supplied from pre-phaseout inventory for those uses in 2011. Protection of Stratospheric Ozone: The 2011 Critical Use Exemption From the Phaseout of Methyl Bromide, 76 Fed. Reg. 60,736 (Sept. 30, 2011).

28. *See* 58 Fed. Reg. at 15,038.

29. 58 Fed. Reg. at 65,018.

30. CAA § 610(b), 42 U.S.C. § 7671i(b).

31. *Id.*

32. *Id.* § 610(b)(1) and (2), 42 U.S.C. § 7671i(b)(1) and (2).

33. *Id.* § 610(b)(3), 42 U.S.C. § 7671i(b)(3).

34. *Id.* § 610(c), 42 U.S.C. § 7671i(c).

35. *Id.* § 610(d)(1), 42 U.S.C. § 7671i(d)(1).

36. The ban on plastic foam products does not include foam insulation products or "an integral skin, rigid or semi-rigid foam utilized to provide for motor vehicle safety," if there is no adequate substitute. *Id.* § 610(d)(3), 42 U.S.C. § 7671i(d)(3).

37. Protection of Stratospheric Ozone, 58 Fed. Reg. 4768 (Jan. 15, 1993).

38. Protection of Stratospheric Ozone, 58 Fed. Reg. 69,638 (Dec. 30, 1993).

39. *See, e.g.,* Protection of Stratospheric Ozone: Reconsideration of the Ban on Fire Extinguishers Containing HCFCs, 61 Fed. Reg. 64,424 (Dec. 4, 1996); Protection of Stratospheric Ozone: Reconsideration of the 610 Nonessential Products Ban, 66 Fed. Reg. 57,512 (Nov. 15, 2001).

40. *See* CAA § 607, 42 U.S.C. § 7671f (providing for issuance of allowances for production and consumption of class I and class II substances and establishing basic parameters for trading).

41. Protection of Stratospheric Ozone, 57 Fed. Reg. 33,754 (July 30, 1992).

42. Protection of Stratospheric Ozone: Administrative Changes to Final Rule to Phase Out Ozone-Depleting Chemicals, 60 Fed. Reg. 24,970 (May 10, 1995).

43. Protection of Stratospheric Ozone: Allowance System for Controlling HCFC Production, Import and Export, 68 Fed. Reg. 2820 (Jan. 21, 2003). EPA subsequently promulgated additional rules adjusting the allowance system for HCFCs in 2009 and 2011. *See* Protection of Stratospheric Ozone: Adjustments to the Allowance System for Controlling HCFC Production, Import, and Export, 74 Fed. Reg. 66,412 (Dec. 15, 2009); Protection of Stratospheric Ozone: Adjustments to the Allowance System for Controlling HCFC Production, Import, and Export, 76 Fed. Reg. 47,451 (Aug. 5, 2011).

44. CAA § 603(b), 42 U.S.C. § 7671b(b).

45. As initially promulgated, the rules provided exceptions for: (1) the production of carbon tetrachloride for feedstock; (2) coincidental, unintentional by-product carbon tetrachloride that is immediately contained and destroyed using maximum available control technology; and (3) coincidentally produced, incinerated methyl chloroform. *See* 57 Fed. Reg. at 33,759, 33,766.

46. 40 C.F.R. §§ 82.5, 82.6.

47. *Id.* § 82.4.

48. CAA § 607(a), 42 U.S.C. § 7671f(a).

49. 40 C.F.R. § 82.12(a).

50. CAA § 608, 42 U.S.C. § 7671g.

51. *Id.* § 608(a)(1), 42 U.S.C. § 7671g(a)(1).

52. *Id.* § 608(a)(2), 42 U.S.C. § 7671g(a)(2).

53. *Id.* § 601(1), 42 U.S.C. § 7671(1).

54. *Id.* § 608(a)(3), 42 U.S.C. § 7671g(a)(3).

55. *Id.* § 608(b), 42 U.S.C. § 7671g(b).

56. *Id.* § 608(c)(1), 42 U.S.C. § 7671g(c)(1).

57. *Id.*

58. *See, e.g.,* Protection of Stratospheric Ozone: Revision of the Venting Prohibition for Specific Refrigerant Substitutes, 79 Fed. Reg. 29,682 (May 23, 2014).

59. Protection of Stratospheric Ozone; Refrigerant Recycling, 58 Fed. Reg. 28,660 (May 14, 1993). EPA adopted revisions to the regulations in the form of a supplemental rule effective September 7, 1995. Protection of Stratospheric Ozone: Supplemental Rule to Amend Leak Repair Provisions Under Section 608 of the Clean Air Act, 60 Fed. Reg. 40,420 (Aug. 8, 1995).

60. Protection of Stratospheric Ozone: Update to the Refrigerant Management Requirements Under the Clean Air Act, 81 Fed. Reg. 82,272 (Nov. 18, 2016) (codified at 40 C.F.R. pt. 82, subpt. F).

61. Protection of Stratospheric Ozone: Revisions to the Refrigerant Management Program's Extension to Substitutes, 85 Fed. Reg. 14,150 (Mar. 11, 2020).

62. Pub. L. No. 116-260 § 103(h)(3), 134 Stat. 1182, 2267 (2020) (codified at 42 U.S.C. § 7675).

63. 42 U.S.C. § 7675(b)(11), (c)(1), (c)(3). The AIM Act generally extended EPA's authority for regulation of ozone-depleting substances to HFCs.

64. *Nat'l Env't Dev. Ass'n's Clean Air Project v. EPA,* No. 20-1309 (and consolidated case) (D.C. Cir. severed issues docketed Aug. 17, 2020); *Nat. Res. Def. Council v. EPA*, No. 20-1150 (and consolidated case) (D.C. Cir. filed May 11, 2020).

65. CAA § 609(c), 42 U.S.C. § 7671h(c).

66. *Id.* § 609(b)(1), 42 U.S.C. § 7671h(b)(1).

67. Protection of Stratospheric Ozone, 57 Fed. Reg. 31,242, 31,261 (July 14, 1992) (codified at 40 C.F.R. § 82.32(g)).

68. *Id.* at 31,261 (codified at 40 C.F.R. § 82.32(c)).

69. *Id.* at 31,263 (codified at 40 C.F.R. § 82.42).

70. *Id.* (codified at 40 C.F.R. § 82.42(a)).

71. CAA § 609(e), 42 U.S.C. § 7671h(e).

72. *See* 57 Fed. Reg. at 31,263 (codified at 40 C.F.R. § 82.42(b)(3)).

73. *See, e.g.,* Motor Vehicle Air Conditioners and Protection of Stratospheric Ozone, 60 Fed. Reg. 21,682 (May 2, 1995); Protection of the Stratospheric Ozone, 62 Fed. Reg. 68,026 (Dec. 30, 1997); Protection of the Stratospheric Ozone: Motor Vehicle Air Conditioning System Servicing, 86 Fed. Reg. 15,587 (Mar. 24, 2021).

74. CAA § 611(b), 42 U.S.C. § 7671j(b).

75. *Id.* § 611(d), 42 U.S.C. § 7671j(d).

76. Protection of Stratospheric Ozone; Labeling, 58 Fed. Reg. 8136 (Feb. 11, 1993).

77. 40 C.F.R. § 82.106(b)(4).

78. *Id.* § 82.106(b)(5).

79. *Id.* § 82.116.

80. Protection of Stratospheric Ozone; Labeling Supplemental Rulemaking, 60 Fed. Reg. 4010 (Jan. 19, 1995).

81. CAA § 612(a), 42 U.S.C. § 7671k(a).

82. *Id.* § 612(c), 42 U.S.C. § 7671k(c).

83. *Id.*

84. *Id.* § 612(d), 42 U.S.C. § 7671k(d).

85. *Id.* § 612(e), 42 U.S.C. § 7671k(e).

86. Protection of Stratospheric Ozone, 59 Fed. Reg. 13,044 (Mar. 18, 1994).

87. *See* 40 C.F.R. pt. 82, subpt. G, Apps. A–V.

88. Protection of Stratospheric Ozone: Change of Listing Status for Certain Substitutes Under the Significant New Alternatives Policy Program, 80 Fed. Reg. 42,870 (July 20, 2015); Protection of Stratospheric Ozone: New Listings of Substitutes; Changes of Listing Status; and Reinterpretation of Unacceptability for Closed Cell Foam Products Under the Significant New Alternatives Policy Program; and Revision of Clean Air Act Section 608 Venting Prohibition for Propane, 81 Fed. Reg. 86,778 (Dec. 1, 2016).

89. *Mexichem Fluor, Inc. v. EPA*, 866 F.3d 451 (D.C. Cir. 2017); *Mexichem Fluor, Inc. v. EPA*, 760 F. App'x 6. (D.C. Cir. 2019) (per curiam).

90. *Mexichem Fluor*, 866 F.3d at 462–64.

91. *Nat. Res. Def. Council v. Wheeler*, 955 F.3d 68 (D.C. Cir. 2020).

Chapter 11

ENFORCEMENT AND JUDICIAL REVIEW

Environmental enforcement has undergone rapid and significant changes since the 1990s, and the federal government continues to bring significant environmental enforcement cases each year. The U.S. Environmental Protection Agency (EPA or Agency) has reported that the combined total of all criminal, civil, and administrative fines and penalties assessed for violations of environmental laws in fiscal year (FY) 2022 exceeded $300 million.[1]

Factors that have contributed to the Agency's enforcement activities include the Pollution Prosecution Act of 1990, which increased the number of Agency criminal investigators with a commensurate increase in support staff. According to EPA, although only 117 new environmental crime cases were opened in FY 2022, individual and corporate criminal defendants paid almost $150 million in fines and restitution along with over $7 million in court-ordered environmental projects. EPA also reported that in FY 2022, it obtained administrative and civil injunctive relief with a value of over $4.3 billion. And, in FY 2022, 942 facilities voluntarily disclosed violations pursuant to EPA's self-disclosure policies.[2]

A second factor contributing to significant enforcement activity since 1990 is the reorganization of the Agency's Office of Enforcement, to create in 1994 the Office of Enforcement and Compliance Assurance (OECA). According to the Agency, the reorganization to integrate technical and legal enforcement personnel was undertaken "to further strengthen enforcement capability and place increased emphasis on compliance assurance."[3] More importantly, locating the enforcement function outside of the program offices responsible for implementing the environmental statutes gave the EPA enforcers more ability to shape environmental policy through enforcement.

A third reason for significant enforcement activity is the enforcement tools provided by the 1990 amendments to the Clean Air Act (CAA or Act). Chief among these is the Title V operating permit program, which requires increased compliance monitoring and periodic certification of source compliance status.

Finally, the current Clean Air Act has been in place in one form or another for fifty years, and many of its basic programs are mature. With the maturation of these programs, the Agency's focus has shifted to enforcement.

I. Background

Historically, the statutory provision primarily used by EPA for enforcing the Act was section 113, which authorizes the EPA Administrator to go to court to seek civil or criminal penalties and to issue administrative enforcement orders requiring noncomplying sources to meet requirements of the Act.[4] Section 113 of the pre-1990 Act was narrowly drawn. The pre-1990 Act limited the Administrator's authority to assess penalties in cases where violations were not continuous, or where it was unclear exactly how long a source had operated in violation of a statutory provision. The Agency also was required to obtain permission of the Department of Justice to go to court before it could collect penalties.

The 1990 amendments gave the Administrator and the courts broader powers to enforce the substantive provisions of the Act. The amended Act provided for wider applicability of civil sanctions, increased criminal penalties, broadened emergency powers, broadened inspection powers, and increased citizen involvement in enforcement and administrative proceedings. The amended Act also contained an administrative penalty regime that allows EPA to use streamlined procedures to assess administrative penalties of up to $200,000 (or more, in some cases) and to issue on-the-spot citations to violators of the Act.[5]

Furthermore, the Federal Civil Penalties Inflation Adjustment Act Improvements Act of 2015 now requires EPA to adjust the statutory maximum (and minimum) amount of civil monetary penalties that can be imposed to reflect inflation annually according to a prescribed formula.[6] EPA adjusted the penalty amounts most recently in January 2023, raising the cap on penalties assessed under section 113(d)(1) to $55,808 per day of violation, and the cap on fines assessed under the administrative penalty scheme was increased to $446,456.[7]

This chapter summarizes the enforcement provisions of the Act, addressing the administrative penalty regime, the civil and criminal enforcement provisions, the impact of voluntary environmental compliance audit programs on enforcement under the Act, provisions regarding public involvement in enforcement proceedings, and judicial review provisions.

II. The Administrative Penalty Regime

The pre-1990 Act did not authorize EPA to use administrative procedures to assess monetary penalties. Section 113(d) of the 1990 amendments changed that by allowing the Administrator to assess administrative penalties for past or present violations of most Clean Air Act requirements. In addition, the administrative penalty regime was made more powerful by the standard of review for penalty assessments prescribed by the Act.

A. Administrative Penalties and Procedures

Administrative penalties may be sought by the Agency in "matters where the total penalty sought does not exceed $200,000."[8] Moreover, the action must be brought within one year of the "first alleged date of violation."[9] These limits may be extended and increased in cases where the Administrator and Attorney General agree that extending the covered period of violation or increasing the penalty is appropriate.[10] A decision to extend is not subject to judicial review.

Administrative penalties may be assessed by an administrative order for (1) violation of a state implementation plan (SIP) during federally assumed enforcement[11] or thirty days after the Administrator has issued a section 113(a)(1) notice to a state and the alleged violator that a permit or SIP provision has been violated;[12] (2) violations of any requirement relating to attainment and maintenance of national ambient air quality standards, hazardous air pollutants, acid deposition, permits, or stratospheric ozone protection; and (3) actions taken to construct or modify a major stationary source where the Administrator has made a finding that "a State is not acting in compliance with any requirement or prohibition of the [Act] relating to the construction of new sources or the modification of existing sources."[13]

The amount of the penalty that EPA seeks in any individual case will be based on the factors listed in section 113(e) of the Act, described later in this chapter with respect to civil penalties.

When commencing an administrative penalty action, the Administrator must give written notice to the alleged violator, who then has thirty days to request a hearing.[14] The fine is then assessed by an order issued after an opportunity for an adjudicatory hearing in accordance with the Administrative Procedure Act.[15] The discovery rules and hearing procedures applicable to such hearings are set out in EPA rules of practice.[16]

B. Field Citation Program

Under section 113(d)(3) of the Act, the Administrator may implement by regulation a field citation program for minor violations. This program allows Agency officials to issue on-the-spot environmental citations with fines not to exceed $5,000 per day of violation.[17] The recipient of a citation may request a hearing or may simply pay the fine.[18] The time within which a hearing must be requested is established by regulation, and such hearing "shall provide a reasonable opportunity to be heard and to present evidence."[19] Payment of a field citation penalty is not a defense to other enforcement actions if the violation continues.[20]

EPA issued proposed regulations to implement the field citation program in 1994.[21] In 2002, however, EPA announced that the field citation rulemaking had been withdrawn and that EPA planned no further action on the program.[22]

C. Appeals of Administrative Penalties

Under section 113(d)(4) of the Act, administrative penalties can be appealed to the district court in one of the following locations: the District of Columbia; the location where the violation allegedly occurred; the alleged violator's residence; or the alleged violator's principal place of business.[23]

Section 113(d)(4) is the exclusive means of review for administrative penalties. Appeals must be filed within thirty days after an administrative penalty becomes final or a final decision is rendered following a field citation hearing.[24] On appeal, the penalty shall be set aside only if there "is not substantial evidence in the record, taken as a whole, to support the finding," or if the Administrator's "assessment [of the penalty] constitutes an abuse of discretion."[25]

D. Failure to Pay a Fine

In the event of failure to pay an administrative penalty after it has become final, or after a court has entered final judgment in favor of the Administrator under section 113(d)(4) of the Act, the Administrator may request the attorney general to bring an action to recover unpaid fines.[26] The "validity, amount, and appropriateness" of the underlying fine may not be questioned in this action.[27] Furthermore, if the fine is upheld, the defendant is potentially liable for interest, the government's costs, attorneys' fees, and a nonpayment penalty of "10 percent of the aggregate amount of such person's outstanding penalties and nonpayment penalties accrued as of the beginning of such quarter."[28]

III. Civil Enforcement

Despite the existence of the new administrative penalty program, EPA has continued to use its civil judicial enforcement authority, particularly in cases where the Agency seeks penalties that are higher than $200,000. EPA reported that in FY 2022, the enforcement staff concluded approximately 1,650 civil judicial and administrative cases; of which, over 44 percent addressed facilities in areas with potential environmental justice concerns, the highest percentage since FY 2014, when EPA began tracking that metric.[29]

Besides expanding the Administrator's general civil enforcement authority, the 1990 amendments to the Act provided the Administrator with additional civil enforcement tools, discussed here.

A. Civil Penalty Actions

Section 113(b)(2) allows the Administrator to commence a civil action whenever an owner or operator[30] of a covered source has violated or is in violation of *any requirement or prohibition of* a SIP, Title I, section 303 of Title III, Title IV, Title V (including a Title V permit), or Title VI.[31] The 1990 amendments made it easier for EPA to assess penalties for past, non-continuing violations, and where the length of the period of violation is not clear. While the pre-1990 Act required a SIP violation to persist for thirty days after a notice of violation was given to the violator, amended section 113(a)(1) allows the Administrator to take action even if the violation does not persist past that thirty-day period.[32] In the case of a SIP or permit violation, however, unless EPA has assumed federal enforcement in a state, EPA may not bring a civil action until thirty days following notification by EPA of the alleged violation.[33] The Act provides that a civil penalty of up to $25,000 per day, adjusted for inflation, may be imposed for each violation.[34]

B. Inspections, Monitoring, and Entry

Under the pre-1990 Act, the Administrator had the authority to order any owner or operator of an emission source (or those subject to other requirements of the Act) to establish and maintain records; to make reports; to install, use, and maintain monitoring equipment or methods; to sample emissions; and to provide other information. Under section 114 of the Act as amended, the Administrator may also order (1) environmental audit procedures; (2) source owners and operators to keep records on control equipment parameters when direct monitoring is impractical; and (3) the submission of "compliance certifications."[35] These section 114 orders may be issued not only against owners and operators of sources but also against any manufacturer of emissions control equipment or process equipment or against any person that the Administrator believes has information "necessary for the purposes set forth in this subsection."[36]

Section 114(a)(3) authorizes (and, in the case of major stationary sources, requires) the Administrator to require compliance certifications by individual sources.[37] Such certifications are to identify the method used for determining compliance and provide information on the source's compliance status.[38] This provision is also the basis for EPA's Compliance Assurance Monitoring rule, described in chapter 4.

C. Penalty Assessment Criteria

Section 113(e) of the Act lists various factors for EPA and the courts to consider when penalties are assessed. This list of factors is nonexclusive and includes (1) "the size of the business"; (2) "the economic impact of the penalty on the business"; (3) "the violator's full compliance history and good faith efforts to comply"; (4) "the duration of the violation as established by any credible evidence"; (5) "payment by the violator of penalties previously assessed for the same violation"; (6) "the economic benefit of noncompliance"; and (7) "the seriousness of the violation."[39]

The Agency takes the position that the statutory ceilings and penalty assessment criteria set forth in the Act leave it with substantial discretion in setting civil penalties. EPA has published internal guidance documents—called civil penalty policies—that it uses to calculate the penalties it will seek in administrative enforcement actions and that it would deem acceptable in settlements of administrative and judicial actions.[40] In 1997, the Environmental Appeals Board (EAB) ruled that the Agency's penalty policies may be used to guide penalty decisions even though the policies were established informally and not through notice-and-comment rulemakings.[41] At the same time, however, the EAB reaffirmed that administrative law judges are not bound by agency penalty policies when calculating the amount of a penalty.[42]

EPA has said that its "policy is that any civil penalty should at least recapture the economic benefit the violator has obtained through its unlawful actions."[43] EPA uses computer software called the BEN (short for "benefit") model to estimate how much money a violator saved through noncompliance with environmental regulations. In August 2005, EPA issued a "[n]otice of final action" on how it will calculate the appropriate penalty based upon the BEN model.[44] The notice made changes to the existing model that EPA claimed will improve its "precision and function."[45] Two of the more significant changes involved "tailoring the discount/compound rate to the case and using a more precise inflation adjustment."[46] Although the BEN model may be used to estimate delayed or avoided compliance costs, it does not calculate the benefit gained from any illegal competitive advantage that a violator may have accrued.[47] The Agency has announced that it is committed to seeking to recover these costs and will do so on a case-by-case basis.[48]

D. Other Enforcement Authorities

1. Federally Assumed Enforcement

The Act allows the Administrator to take over the enforcement of a state plan or permit program if the state is not enforcing the plan or program effectively.[49] In addition, the Administrator has the power to assess administrative penalties while EPA is enforcing the SIP or the permit program.[50]

2. Compliance Orders

Under the pre-1990 Act, compliance orders issued by EPA had to specify a reasonable time for compliance. The amended Act requires compliance as expeditiously as possible, but in no case does it allow more than one year to attain compliance.[51] The amended Act also makes compliance orders nonrenewable, and it provides that the issuance of a compliance order does *not* affect either the right of the enforcement authority to assess penalties or the obligation of the violator to comply with the Act.[52]

In 2003, the compliance order regime was declared unconstitutional by the U.S. Court of Appeals for the Eleventh Circuit.[53] This case arose out of an administrative compliance order issued to the Tennessee Valley Authority (TVA), claiming that TVA had undertaken construction activities that triggered the new source review program without obtaining permits, and ordering TVA to obtain such permits subject to the threat of civil or criminal penalty. The court found that because the Act's regime allowed EPA to determine liability and impose penalties without a meaningful opportunity for the company to be heard, it violated the due process protections of the U.S. Constitution.[54]

3. Preventing New Source Construction

Section 113(a)(5) of the pre-1990 Act authorized the Administrator, in certain circumstances, to issue an administrative order or file a civil suit to prevent construction of new sources in *nonattainment* areas. In areas that have *attained* the ambient standards, sources are subject to review under the prevention of significant deterioration (PSD) program under section 167, rather than section 113(a)(5).[55] Section 113(a)(5) now provides that the Administrator may issue an enforcement order or file a civil suit whenever he finds that "a State is not acting in compliance with any requirement or prohibition of the [Act] relating to the construction of new sources or the modification of existing sources."[56] This provision applies in both nonattainment and attainment areas.

4. Emergency Powers

The pre-1990 Act allowed emergency orders to be issued only when there was imminent and substantial endangerment to the health of persons, and the orders were effective for twenty-four hours. The amended Act allows emergency orders when there is "imminent and substantial endangerment to public health *or welfare, or the environment.*"[57] The amended Act also removes the prohibition on EPA action where state or local authorities are already taking action.[58] The requirement that EPA consult with those authorities remains, however. Emergency orders are effective for sixty days and may be extended by the courts.[59]

5. Administrative Enforcement Subpoenas

The Administrator has authority to issue administrative enforcement subpoenas for obtaining information with respect to "any investigation, monitoring, reporting requirement, entry, compliance inspection, or administrative enforcement proceeding."[60] Penalties shall not be assessed for noncompliance with administrative subpoenas where the violator had "sufficient cause" to violate or to refuse to comply with the subpoena.[61]

E. Supplemental Environmental Projects Policy

In a 1995 policy statement, EPA indicated that supplemental environmental projects (SEPs), which are environmentally beneficial projects that a violator voluntarily agrees to perform, may be considered in settlement negotiations over civil penalties.[62] The "[p]olicy sets forth the types of projects that are permissible as SEPs, the penalty mitigation appropriate for a particular SEP, and the terms and conditions under which they may become part of a settlement."[63] In 2002, EPA updated and reaffirmed the policy stating that its continued use "provides the Agency with a useful tool for achieving environmental benefits beyond those gained by compliance with Federal and state laws."[64]

In 2020, Assistant Attorney General Clark issued a memorandum to the U.S. Department of Justice, Environment and Natural Resources Division (ENRD), deputy assistant attorney generals and section chiefs addressing SEPs in civil settlements with private defendants.[65] The memorandum prohibited ENRD from "using SEPs in consent decrees and judicial compromise settlements . . . no matter whether the party agreeing to implement the SEPs is a state or local government or whether it is a private party."[66] According to Assistant Attorney General Clark, such "SEPs violate the spirit, if not the letter, of the Miscellaneous Receipts Act, which is intended to protect Congress' constitutional power of the purse."[67] The memorandum did not apply retroactively, and did "not require the reopening of settlements that already [had] been signed or approved by Department or agency officials."[68] According to the Agency, in FY 2019 prior to issuance of the new policy, eighty-one EPA enforcement cases included SEPs, with a total estimated cost of over $26 million.[69]

After the change in administration in 2021, Deputy Assistant Attorney General Williams issued a memorandum to ENRD[70] withdrawing the 2020 memorandum on SEPs pursuant to President Biden's Executive Order 13990, which directed review of previously issued policies for consistency with the administration's objectives.[71] The 2021 memorandum also withdrew eight other enforcement-related memoranda issued during the Trump administration. EPA reports that in FY 2022, with the restoration of the power to use SEPs, EPA concluded two enforcement cases that included agreements by the violator to perform SEPs with a total estimated value of over $800,000.[72]

IV. Criminal Enforcement

A. Overview

In addition to being able to use an administrative penalty program and civil judicial mechanisms to enforce the Act, EPA has authority under section 113(c) of the Act to seek criminal sanctions against "any person" who knowingly violates almost any of the statute's prohibitions or requirements.[73] The term "person" includes both individuals and corporations, partnerships, and other business organizations.[74]

Although organizations are generally subject to larger fines for any given offense than are individuals, individuals are also subject to imprisonment.[75] Moreover, criminal sanctions may apply to individuals that are non-senior corporate officials.[76] That is, other enforcement provisions of the Act apply only to "senior management personnel or a corporate officer," and not to a person who is "carrying out his normal activities and who is acting under orders from the employer" or who is "a stationary engineer or technician responsible for the operation, maintenance, repair, or monitoring of equipment and facilities and who often has supervisory and training duties but who is not senior management personnel or a corporate officer."[77] These exemptions for non-senior personnel, however, do *not* apply in the case of knowing and willful violations covered by section 113(c) of the Act.[78]

The 1990 amendments to the Act increased most of the penalties associated with violations of the Act from misdemeanors to felonies, with corresponding increases in the maximum fines and jail terms. Criminal penalties under the 1990 amendments are doubled for second and subsequent convictions.[79] The length of prison sentences for individuals and the amount of fines for individuals and organizations are determined with reference to the Federal Sentencing Guidelines.[80] These aspects of the criminal enforcement provisions are discussed further here.[81]

B. Prohibited Conduct and Statutory Penalties

1. Violation of Emission Restrictions

Section 113(c)(1) of the 1990 Act provides that any person who knowingly violates any requirement or prohibition of a SIP, or of virtually any substantive provision of the Act,[82] or of any rule, order, waiver, or permit promulgated or approved under such provisions, is subject to a fine of up to $250,000 or a prison term of up to five years, or both, in the case of an individual defendant.[83] An organizational defendant is subject to a fine of up to $500,000.[84]

2. Falsification and Tampering

Section 113(c)(2)(C) provides that any person who knowingly "falsifies, tampers with, renders inaccurate, or fails to install any monitoring device or method required," is subject to a fine of up to $250,000 or a prison term of up to two years, or both, in the case of an individual defendant. An organizational defendant is subject to a fine of up to $500,000.[85]

3. False Statements

Section 113(c)(2)(A) provides that any person who knowingly makes any false material statement in or omission from any document or fails to file or maintain any document required under the Act, or any person who knowingly tampers with monitoring equipment, is subject to a fine of up to $250,000 or a prison term of up to two years, or both, in the case of an individual defendant. An organizational defendant is subject to a fine of up to $500,000.[86]

4. Failure to Pay Fees

A knowing failure to pay any fee owed to the United States under Titles I, III, IV-A, V, or VI is punishable by a fine of up to $100,000 or a prison term of up to one year, or both, in the case of an individual defendant. An organizational defendant is subject to a fine of up to $500,000.[87]

5. Knowing Endangerment

Section 113(c)(5)(A), a criminal provision added to the Act in 1990, imposes a fine of up to $250,000 or a prison term of up to fifteen years, or both, on any person who knowingly releases any hazardous air pollutant, or any "extremely hazardous substance" listed in EPA rules, knowing that doing so "places another person in imminent danger of death or serious bodily injury."[88] An organization convicted under this provision is subject to a fine of up to $1 million per violation.[89]

While punishment under this provision can apply only to persons with *actual* knowledge, circumstantial evidence can be used in proving a defendant's possession of actual knowledge.[90] In determining whether a defendant had actual knowledge that his action "placed another person in imminent danger of death or serious bodily injury . . . the defendant is responsible only for actual awareness or actual belief possessed; and . . . knowledge possessed by a person other than the defendant, but not by the defendant, may not be attributed to the defendant."[91]

The Act recognizes "assumption of the risk" defenses where the defendant proves by a preponderance of the evidence that the conduct charged was freely consented to and a reasonably foreseeable hazard of an occupation, business, profession, or medical treatment or medical or scientific experimentation.[92] Responsible corporate officers are specifically included as potentially liable parties under this subsection.[93] Finally, a release allowed under a permit is not subject to an action brought under this subsection.[94]

6. Negligent Endangerment

Section 113(c)(4), the only misdemeanor provision added by the 1990 amendments, imposes a fine of up to $100,000 or a prison term of up to one year, or both, on any person who *negligently* releases any hazardous air pollutant, or any "extremely hazardous substance" listed in EPA rules, and thereby negligently places another person in "imminent danger of death or serious bodily injury." For an organizational defendant, the maximum fine is $200,000.[95]

V. Enforcement and the "Credible Evidence" Rule

In February 1997, EPA promulgated regulations implementing three major Clean Air Act regulatory programs that significantly expand the kind of information the government and citizen suit plaintiffs can use to bring enforcement actions. Collectively known as the "credible evidence" (CE) rule, these regulations govern the methods and procedures for determining compliance with numerical emission limits under SIPs, new source performance standards, and the air toxics program of section 112.[96] Prior to the CE rule, if a regulation or permit issued under one of these programs specified a compliance determination procedure for a numerical emission standard, only that procedure could be used to determine compliance with that standard.[97] Under the CE rule, a violation of a numerical standard or emission limit could be established by any "credible evidence" that a violation would have been found had the applicable compliance test or procedure been performed.[98]

EPA promulgated the CE rule in response to the 1990 amendments to section 113 allowing the use of "credible evidence (including evidence other than the applicable test method)" to show the duration of a violation for purposes of determining the amount of civil penalties.[99] The CE rule, however, does not limit the use of "credible evidence" to establishing the duration of a violation.[100] Rather, the rule applies to compliance certifications as well as to establishing whether a person has violated or is in violation of any emission standard or limit.[101] As the rule provides, "nothing . . . shall preclude the use, including the exclusive use, of any credible evidence or information" relevant to whether a source would have been in compliance with the applicable standard if the prescribed performance test or procedure had been performed.[102] EPA takes the position that because the CE rule merely clarifies preexisting evidentiary rules, it applies to any alleged violation whether occurring before or after the effective date of the revisions.[103] In 2005, however, the U.S. Court of Appeals for the Eleventh Circuit held that data from a plant's continuous opacity monitoring system could not be used to prove violations before the date that the jurisdictional state adopted its own CE rule.[104]

Although the CE rule does not define the term "credible evidence," EPA states in the preamble to the rule that it expects that

> most if not all of the data that EPA would consider as potentially credible evidence of an emission violation at a unit subject to monitoring under the agency's proposed [Compliance Assurance Monitoring] rule would be generated through means of appropriate, well-designed parametric or emission monitoring submitted by the source itself and approved by the permitting authority, or through other requirements in the source's permit.[105]

"Credible evidence" would likely include any continuous monitoring, even if such monitoring was intended for purposes other than compliance with numerical emission limits.

Since its promulgation, there has been considerable debate over the practical effect of the CE rule on existing emission standards. The stringency of an emission standard depends not only on the numerical limit but also on the protocol by which compliance with the numerical standard is determined. A change in the compliance protocol can affect the stringency of a standard as much as a change in the level of the numerical standard itself. The compliance protocols for an emission standard are typically developed in rulemaking proceedings (generally the same proceedings in which the standard was developed) that explore complex technical issues regarding sampling procedures, accuracy of measurement, and other matters that ensure that the data generated by the compliance method is consistent with the data used to establish the emission standard. On this basis, many emission standards contain a specific method such as a periodic "stack test" as the compliance protocol, although the standards may also be accompanied by rules that require collection of continuous data for purposes other than determining compliance with the numerical emissions standard, for example, to determine compliance with any applicable "general duty" requirement,[106] or to determine whether to require performance of the applicable compliance test. As a result, there may be substantial questions whether an existing numerical standard would have been adopted if the compliance protocol involved continuous monitoring.

As a result of these concerns, the 1997 CE rule was challenged in the U.S. Court of Appeals for the District of Columbia Circuit (D.C. Circuit) on the grounds that the rule could result in tightening numerical emission standards without compliance with required statutory criteria or administrative procedures.[107] The D.C. Circuit dismissed the petitions as unripe, holding that pre-enforcement review was not available due to the factual questions raised and lack of hardship pending review.[108] The court indicated, however, that the CE rule could become ripe for review if EPA took an enforcement action based on CE.[109] Although EPA and states have largely ignored the CE rule as an enforcement tool, environmental advocacy organizations have used it to file citizen suits in federal district courts alleging violation of opacity standards based on data recorded by continuous opacity monitoring data.[110]

VI. Compliance Audits

In 1991, the Department of Justice released guidelines on the factors that prosecutors should consider in making criminal enforcement decisions under federal environmental statutes.[111] The guidelines encourage self-auditing and voluntary disclosure of environmental violations by the regulated community and list several factors that will weigh against criminal enforcement action, including (1) regular, comprehensive environmental audits; (2) timely voluntary disclosure of violations; (3) good faith efforts to remedy noncompliance; (4) an effective internal disciplinary system; and (5) prompt, good faith efforts to reach compliance agreements with federal and state authorities.[112]

After a formal review of its own environmental auditing guidelines, EPA in 1995 issued its own audit policy.[113] The policy sets forth the conditions under which EPA will reduce penalties assessed against regulated entities when they manage their own compliance responsibilities and disclose their own violations of environmental laws.[114]

Pursuant to the audit policy, entities that meet certain conditions are generally eligible for lower civil penalties (by eliminating the gravity-based penalties that would otherwise be assessed).[115] EPA issued minor revisions to the 1995 audit policy in 2000.[116] The 2000 revisions maintain the policy's basic structure and terms but broaden its availability. In the 1995 and 2000 renditions of the audit policy, EPA would generally not pursue criminal enforcement where a company discovered, voluntarily reported, and promptly corrected violations pursuant to a properly designed and implemented environmental audit program.[117] EPA reported that in FY 2022, 942 facilities used the audit policy to voluntarily disclose violations under EPA's self-disclosure policies.[118]

The audit policy specifically does not establish a legal privilege for environmental audits. Numerous states have adopted their own audit privilege or immunity legislation. Such action can create conflict between state law voluntary disclosure, immunity, and environmental audit objectives, and EPA's desire for enforcement goals based on state Title V operating permit programs. In this regard, interest groups in the past have threatened to sue the Agency if it approves Title V permit programs in states that have statutes creating environmental audit privileges or voluntary disclosure immunities and have filed petitions to revoke delegated or approved programs in some states. These groups have argued that such delegation or approval would interfere with a primary purpose of the Title V permit program to ease citizen enforcement by "clarify[ing] and mak[ing] more readily enforceable a source's pollution control requirements."[119]

EPA has generally opposed state privilege and immunity legislation and has issued guidance describing circumstances in which such legislation will render a state's Title V program inadequate (based on the concern that such legislation could interfere with state enforcement of Title V permits).[120] Generally, the guidance provides that a state must demonstrate that it has "adequate" enforcement authority to secure delegation.[121] In addition, a state must preserve its ability to obtain immediate and complete injunctive relief, to obtain significant penalties, and to obtain criminal fines and sanctions.[122] The guidance encourages states to use audit "policies," not statutes.[123]

In 2012, EPA concluded that, since implementation of the audit policy began in 1995, "internal reviews of compliance have become more widely adopted by the regulated community, as part of good management."[124] In addition, EPA found that "most violations disclosed under the Policy are not in the highest priority enforcement areas for protecting human health and the environment" and that the Agency "can reduce investment in the program to a limited national presence without undermining the incentives for regulated entities to do internal compliance reviews to find and correct violations."[125]

While EPA continues to stress the importance and value of its self-disclosure policies, the Agency's priorities related to compliance and enforcement have historically changed from one administration to the next. For example, in 2018 EPA shifted its focus to encouraging voluntary disclosure and compliance support. OECA's Assistant Administrator Bodine issued a memorandum describing a transition in enforcement focus from "National Enforcement Initiatives" to "National Compliance Initiatives."[126] According to Bodine, EPA's FY 2018–22 strategic plan for enforcement-related measures would focus on increasing the environmental law compliance rate and reducing the average time from violation identification to correction by promoting sound environmental governance and accountability measures.[127] Pursuant to this policy, EPA committed to work closely with states to promote compliance using a broad range of compliance assurance tools, which could range from general compliance assistance to inspections to informal and formal enforcement actions.[128] More recently, in December 2022, Acting Assistant Administrator for OECA, Lawrence Starfield, announced an updated policy, reemphasizing "the role of federal enforcement in ensuring that those who violate [federal] environmental laws or contribute to serious environmental problems are held accountable, even [while] continu[ing] to strive to promote greater compliance with [federal] environmental laws."[129] The change in nomenclature is, according to Starfield, an effort to reflect the comprehensive approach—criminal and civil enforcement, informal enforcement, and compliance assurance—the agency takes to advance national initiatives that address serious noncompliance, hold polluters accountable, and create general deterrence.[130]

VII. Citizen Enforcement Authority

A. Citizen Suits

Congress included citizen suit provisions in the 1970 amendments to the Act and broadened the ability of citizens to function as "private attorneys general" under the 1990 amendments. The following paragraphs discuss the citizen suit provisions.

1. Civil Penalty Awards

Section 304 of the Act gives citizens authority to file suit against EPA for its failure to perform a nondiscretionary duty, or against individual sources or states alleged to be in violation of statutory requirements.[131] Before 1990, the Act gave federal district courts the authority to issue injunctive relief (that is, to order EPA to take certain actions or to order an individual source to cease violating the Act). The 1990 amendments added another remedy in such cases: the district courts now have the power to award civil penalties against defendants other than EPA.[132]

The penalties collected in citizen suits are held in a penalty fund to be used by the Administrator "to finance air compliance and enforcement activities."[133] The 1990 amendments also provided that instead of ordering payment to the fund, district courts may order that civil penalties up to $100,000 be used in "beneficial mitigation projects which are consistent with this [Act] and enhance the public health or the environment."[134]

2. Past Violations

The 1990 amendments allowed citizens to sue for past violations "if there is evidence that the alleged violation has been *repeated*."[135]

3. Effect of Citizen Suits on the United States

Suits in which the United States is not a party have no binding effect on the United States. No consent judgment can be entered prior to forty-five days following receipt of the proposed consent judgment by the Administrator and the attorney general. The United States can intervene in a citizen suit as of right at any time.[136]

4. Which District Courts Have Jurisdiction

The pre-1990 Act gave any federal district court the power to order the Administrator to perform any nondiscretionary duty. Under the amended Act, citizens may still sue in federal district court to compel performance of a nondiscretionary duty, including a failure to act that constitutes unreasonable delay. In some cases, though, the choice of district court is not open. Specifically, in unreasonable delay suits involving final agency action referred to in section 307(b) (e.g., many of the national rulemakings required by the Act), citizen suit plaintiffs may file only in a district court within the circuit in which such action would be reviewable under section 307(b).[137] Because many actions reviewable under section 307(b) must be brought in the D.C. Circuit,[138] such unreasonable delay cases will often have to be brought in the U.S. District Court for the District of Columbia.

At least 180 days before a citizen suit can be commenced for "unreasonable delay," the filing party must give notice to the Administrator, the state, and any alleged violator.[139]

B. Public Involvement in Settlements

The amended Act requires that thirty days before the filing of a consent order or settlement to which the United States is a party, such orders or settlements must be open to public comment by notice in the *Federal Register*.[140] This requirement applies to all consent orders or settlement agreements to which the United States is a party, except enforcement actions under sections 113 or 120 (a little-used section that authorizes noncompliance penalties) or Title II. Because of this provision, the United States must seek comment on the agreements that the government reaches with environmental advocacy organizations and others suing EPA for not meeting statutory deadlines.

C. Scope of Injunctive Relief Available in Citizen Suits

Historically, citizen suit plaintiffs have sought broad injunctive relief in citizen suits, even as an intervenor in an enforcement action brought by the government. Typically, a citizen suit plaintiff will seek relief to benefit its member, for example, by securing funding for projects promoted by the group. In 2020, the Department of Justice began to resist relief by citizen groups that is broader than what the government seeks.

According to a brief filed by the Government in *United States & Sierra Club v. DTE Energy Co.*, the Clean Air Act "does *not* permit citizen suits to seek types of relief that the [government] chose to forgo."[141] Nor, according to the government, may citizen intervenors "compel a consent decree on their own terms, since doing so would enable citizens to commandeer the federal enforcement machinery."[142] On this ground, the government refused to include in the consent agreement resolving the case additional relief (e.g., local environmental projects) sought by Sierra Club, and also opposed entry by the Court of a separate agreement with Sierra Club containing that relief.

D. Bounty System

The Act allows the Administrator to award up to $10,000 to private citizens for information leading to penalties or convictions.[143] The payment is subject to "available appropriations for such purposes as provided in annual appropriation Acts."[144] The Administrator may by regulation prescribe eligibility requirements.

In 1994, the Agency proposed rules setting forth the criteria and procedures for granting citizen awards.[145] The proposed rule described the criteria that the

Agency would use in assessing the value of information and services and what is needed to adequately petition the Administrator for consideration of payment. The proposal also addressed confidentiality matters (because some citizens provide information or services on a confidential basis), and directions for providing information to the Agency.[146] EPA never finalized the proposal.

The Agency has taken the position, however, that section 113(f) is self-implementing and that awards may be granted pending final promulgation of the rules. In 1997, the Agency approved $37,000 in monetary awards under section 113(f) to twenty citizens who helped the Agency take successful enforcement actions under the Act.[147] Those were the first monetary awards given under that section of the Act.

VIII. Judicial Review of Final Agency Action

Under section 307(b) of the Act, a judicial challenge to final Agency action must be brought in the appropriate U.S. Court of Appeals within sixty days after notice of that action is published in the *Federal Register*.[148] If the action is nationally applicable, or is of nationwide scope or effect and the Administrator publishes a determination to this effect, the petition for review must be filed in the D.C. Circuit.[149] If the action is of local or regional effect, the petition must be filed in the appropriate regional U.S. Court of Appeals.[150]

Once an Agency action becomes final and the period for judicial review has expired issues resolved in that action cannot be raised in subsequent enforcement or review proceedings.[151] To the extent that new grounds arise affecting the validity of the Agency's action after the period for judicial review has expired (e.g., the Agency issues an interpretation of the rule at odds with the basis for the rule described when it was promulgated), however, one may challenge the action within sixty days after the new grounds arise, based solely on those new grounds.[152]

The Act authorizes administrative petitions to reconsider rules based on grounds that arise after the close of the formal comment period but before the close of the period for judicial review.[153] A petition for reconsideration must show that the matter at issue could not have been raised during the public comment period and that it is of "central relevance" to the final rule.[154] The filing of an administrative petition for reconsideration is not a prerequisite to judicial review and does not extend the time for filing a petition for judicial review.[155]

Under the pre-1990 Act, an Agency decision to defer statutorily required action could give rise to confusion over whether jurisdiction over a challenge to the decision to defer would lie in the federal district court or the U.S. Court of Appeals. Under section 307(b)(2) of the 1990 amendments, it is clear that the Court of Appeals has exclusive jurisdiction where EPA has made a final decision to defer performance of a nondiscretionary statutory action.[156]

IX. The Future of Agency Guidance?

Created in 1970, EPA is now over fifty years old. Over the past half century, EPA has issued literally tens of thousands of documents explaining its extensive regulatory programs. These guidance documents come in a wide variety of forms. Some may be signed by the EPA Administrator, others by officials in program offices, and still others by Regional officials or even by technical staff. Some of these documents may provide broad national guidance, while others interpret rules in source-specific factual settings. Guidance may appear in preambles to rules, in response to "frequently asked questions" (FAQs), in applicability determinations, in EAB decisions, in General Counsel opinions, and in many other ways. And of course, as administrations change, guidance may change to reflect new policies.

Anyone who has had to manage environmental compliance is familiar with the challenges of identifying operative agency guidance. And once identified, there is no guarantee that guidance may not change periodically and in unexpected ways.

In 2019, during the Trump administration, the White House issued an executive order to promote regulatory transparency and fairness by requiring each federal agency to make its regulatory guidance available to the public on an electronic, searchable database.[157] The order required agencies to establish regulations with procedures for issuing, amending, or rescinding guidance.

Executive Order 13891 defined "guidance document" as "an agency statement of *general applicability*, intended to have future effect on the behavior of regulated parties, that sets forth a policy on a statutory, regulatory, or technical issue, or an interpretation of a statute or regulation."[158] Guidance of course cannot itself impose binding requirements on regulated entities but may only "clarify existing obligations."[159] The order went a step further, however, providing that guidance documents as defined in the order that were not on the agency's searchable database were "rescinded," meaning that the Agency could not "cite, use, or rely on" them for purposes other than "to establish historical facts." [160]

In 2020, EPA made public a web "portal" with its initial, searchable list of active Agency guidance, organized by program office and Region. EPA had about six months to complete a list of active guidance, after which significant guidance could be added to the portal only after public notice and comment. In September 2020, the Administrator signed a final rule establishing procedures for the issuance, modification, and withdrawal of guidance documents.[161]

A key question raised by commenters in the rulemaking concerned the status of guidance ***not*** on the web portal. As noted earlier, as a historical matter, EPA's regulatory guidance has taken a variety of forms and has often varied over time. EPA made clear that "the[] omission from the EPA Guidance Portal" of documents that do not meet the Executive Order's definition—e.g., legal or advisory opinions directed to particular parties—"does not imply that they are 'rescinded guidance documents'" under the Executive Order.[162]

Moreover, as the order made clear, a document presenting the agency's views on the meaning of a rule—whether in the context of a particular source or more generally—is a "historical fact[]" regardless of its inclusion on the agency's database.[163] By its plain terms, the focus of Executive Order 13891 was on preventing ***agencies*** from misusing guidance: "*No agency* [could] cite, use, or rely on guidance documents that [were] rescinded, except to establish historical facts."[164] The order did not purport to preclude non-agency parties from continuing to use and to rely on what the Agency had told them historically are reasonable ways of reading its rules regardless of whether the document is found on the guidance portal. In the words of the Supreme Court,[165] where an agency has offered alternative readings of its rules over time, this may mean that there is no "genuine ambiguity" that the regulation affords multiple ways of compliance.

However, EPA's web portal and guidance rule were short-lived. The rule was rescinded in May 2021 after the Biden EPA determined that it deprived EPA of "necessary flexibility in determining when and how best to issue public guidance based on particular facts and circumstances." The web portal established under the rule was revised to redirect users to general topical listings and webpages. EPA asserts that it will continue to make Agency guidance available and to solicit stakeholder input as appropriate.[166]

Notes

1. Press Release, EPA, Office of Enforcement and Compliance Assurance, EPA Announces FY 2022 Enforcement and Compliance Accomplishments (Dec. 16, 2022).

2. EPA, Enforcement and Compliance Annual Results for FY 2022: Data and Trends ("FY 2022 Data and Trends").

3. EPA, EPA 300-R-95-004, Enforcement and Compliance Assurance Accomplishments Report: FY 1994 at 1-1 (May 1995).

4. CAA § 113, 42 U.S.C. § 7413.

5. *Id.* § 113(d)(1), 42 U.S.C. § 7413(d)(1).

6. Civil Monetary Penalty Inflation Adjustment, 88 Fed. Reg. 986 (Jan. 6, 2023).

7. *Id.* at 989, tbl.1.

8. CAA § 113(d)(1), 42 U.S.C. § 7413(d)(1). As noted above, every year EPA raises the ceilings on penalties under its Civil Penalty Inflation Adjustment rule. For ease of discussion, however, we refer in this chapter to the unadjusted penalty figures.

9. *Id.*

10. *Id.*

11. Federally assumed enforcement occurs when the Administrator finds that "violations of an applicable implementation plan or an approved permit program under [Title] V . . . are so widespread that such violations appear to result from a failure of the State . . . to enforce the plan or permit program." *Id.* § 113(a)(2), 42 U.S.C. § 7413(a)(2).

12. *Id.*

13. *Id.* § 113(d)(1), (a)(5), 42 U.S.C. § 7413(d)(1), (a)(5).

14. *Id.* § 113(d)(2), 42 U.S.C. § 7413(d)(2).

15. *See id.*; *see also* 5 U.S.C. §§ 554, 556.

16. *See* 40 C.F.R. pt. 22.

17. CAA § 113(d)(3), 42 U.S.C. § 7413(d)(3).

18. *Id.*

19. *Id.*

20. *Id.*

21. Field Citation Program, 59 Fed. Reg. 22,776 (proposed May 3, 1994).

22. Spring 2002 Regulatory Agenda, 67 Fed. Reg. 33,724, 33,734 (May 13, 2002).

23. CAA § 113(d)(4), 42 U.S.C. § 7413(d)(4).

24. *Id.*

25. *Id.*

26. *Id.* § 113(d)(5), 42 U.S.C. § 7413(d)(5).

27. *Id.*

28. *Id.*

29. *See* FY 2022 Data and Trends, Federal Compliance Monitoring Activities Conducted by EPA FY 2012–FY 2022.

30. The term "operator" is defined to "include any person who is senior management personnel or a corporate officer. Except in the case of knowing and willful violations, such term shall not include any person who is a stationary engineer or technician responsible for the operation, maintenance, repair, or monitoring of equipment and facilities and who often has supervisory and training duties but who is not senior management personnel or a corporate officer." CAA § 113(h), 42 U.S.C. § 7413(h).

31. *Id.* § 113(b)(2), 42 U.S.C. § 7413(b)(2).

32. *Id.* § 113(a)(1), 42 U.S.C. § 7413(a)(1).

33. *Id.* § 113(a)(1)–(2), (b), 42 U.S.C. § 7413(a)(1)–(2), (b).

34. *Id.* § 113(b), 42 U.S.C. § 7413(b).

35. *Id.* § 114(a)(1)(C), (E), (F), 42 U.S.C. § 7414(a)(1)(C), (E), (F).

36. *Id.* § 114(a)(1), 42 U.S.C. § 7414(a)(1). Extensive information requests under section 114 of the Act are often EPA's first step in the enforcement process.

37. *Id.* § 114(a)(3), 42 U.S.C. § 7414(a)(3).

38. *Id.* § 114(a)(3)(B), (C), 42 U.S.C. § 7414(a)(3)(B), (C).

39. *Id.* § 113(e), 42 U.S.C. § 7413(e).

40. *See, e.g.*, Memorandum from William G. Rosenberg, Assistant Adm'r for Air & Radiation, EPA, & Edward E. Reich, Acting Assistant Adm'r for Enforcement, EPA, to EPA Reg'l Adm'rs, Regions I-X, et al., Clean Air Act Stationary Source Civil Penalty Policy (Oct. 25, 1991). In 1995, the Agency issued guidance on how penalty amounts should be pled and argued in administrative litigation. Memorandum from Robert Van Heuvelen, Dir., Office of Regulatory Enforcement, EPA, to EPA Reg'l Counsel, Regions I-X, et al., Guidance on Use of Penalty Policies in Administrative Litigation (Dec. 15, 1995).

41. *In re Employers Ins. of Wausau*, 6 E.A.D. 735, 758 (EAB 1997). The EAB explained in its ruling that administrative law judges are free to ask EPA attorneys to explain how penalties are calculated and how they are consistent with the underlying statutes, but they must give the attorneys an opportunity to respond to any concerns they may have. *Id.* at 754 & n.20, 755–59.

42. *See also In re Allegheny Power Serv. Corp.*, 9 E.A.D. 636, 655 (EAB 2001), *aff'd*, No. 6:01-cv-00241 (S.D.W.Va. Apr. 5, 2002), ECF No. 22 (EPA's civil penalty policies "provide a framework that allows a presiding officer to apply his or her discretion to statutory penalty factors, thereby facilitating a uniform application of the factors.").

43. Calculation of the Economic Benefit of Noncompliance in EPA's Civil Penalty Enforcement Cases, 70 Fed. Reg. 50,326, 50,326 (Aug. 26, 2005).

44. *Id.*

45. *Id.* at 50,327.

46. *Id.*

47. *Id.* at 50,328.

48. *Id.* at 50,331.

49. CAA § 113(a)(2), 42 U.S.C. § 7413(a)(2).

50. *Id.* § 113(d)(1), 42 U.S.C. § 7413(d)(1).

51. *Id.* § 113(a)(4), 42 U.S.C. § 7413(a)(4).

52. *Id.*

53. *Tenn. Valley Auth. v. Whitman*, 336 F.3d 1236, 1239–40, 1248–49, 1256–60 (11th Cir. 2003).

54. *Id.* at 1258–59.

55. CAA § 113(a)(5), 42 U.S.C. § 7413(a)(5) (1988); *see also id.* § 167, 42 U.S.C. § 7477 (2011). In the pre-1990 Act, section 167 authorized the Administrator and states to "take such measures, including issuance of an order, or seeking injunctive relief, as necessary to prevent the construction" of major emitting facilities that failed first to get PSD permits. *Id.* § 167, 42 U.S.C. § 7477 (1988). The 1990 amendments extended the Administrator's power under section 167 to stop both the construction and *modification*

of major emitting facilities that do not conform to PSD requirements. *Id.* § 167, 42 U.S.C. § 7477 (2011).

56. *Id.* § 113(a)(5), 42 U.S.C. § 7413(a)(5) (2011).

57. *Id.* § 303, 42 U.S.C. § 7603 (emphasis added).

58. *Id.*

59. *Id.*

60. *Id.* § 307(a), 42 U.S.C. § 7607(a).

61. *Id.* § 113(e)(1), 42 U.S.C. § 7413(e)(1).

62. Interim Revised EPA Supplemental Environmental Projects Policy Issued, 60 Fed. Reg. 24,856 (May 10, 1995), *superseded by* Final EPA Supplemental Environmental Projects Policy Issued, 63 Fed. Reg. 24,796 (May 5, 1998).

63. 63 Fed. Reg. at 24,796.

64. Memorandum from Sylvia K. Lowrance, Acting Assistant Adm'r, Office of Enforcement & Compliance Assurance, EPA, to Reg'l Adm'rs, EPA Regions I-X, & Reg'l Counsel, EPA Regions I-X, Supplemental Environmental Projects (SEP) Policy at 1 (Mar. 22, 2002).

65. Memorandum from Jeffrey Bossert Clark, Assistant Attorney Gen., U.S. Dep't of Justice, Env't & Nat. Res. Div., to ENRD Deputy Assistant Attorney Gens. & Sec. Chiefs, Supplemental Environmental Projects ("SEPs") in Civil Settlements with Private Defendants (Mar. 12, 2020).

66. *Id.* at 11.

67. *Id.*

68. *Id.* at 2 n.5.

69. EPA, Office of Enforcement & Compliance Assurance, Fiscal Year 2019, EPA Enforcement and Compliance Annual Results at 14 (Feb. 13, 2020).

70. Memorandum from Jean E. Williams, Deputy Assistant Attorney Gen., U.S. Dep't of Justice, Env't & Nat. Res. Div., to ENRD Sec. Chiefs & Deputy Sec. Chiefs, Withdrawal of Memoranda and Policy Documents (Feb. 4, 2021).

71. Exec. Order No. 13990, Protecting Public Health and the Environment and Restoring Science To Tackle the Climate Crisis (Jan. 20, 2021), *reprinted in* 86 Fed. Reg. 7037 (Jan. 25, 2021).

72. FY 2022 Data and Trends, Supplemental Environmental Projects (SEPs) FY 2012–FY 2022.

73. CAA § 113(c), 42 U.S.C. § 7413(c).

74. *Id.* § 302(e), 42 U.S.C. § 7602(e).

75. *Id.* § 113(c), (d)(1), 42 U.S.C. § 7413(c), (d)(1).

76. *See id.* § 113(h), 42 U.S.C. § 7413(h).

77. *Id.*

78. *Id.*

79. *Id.* § 113(c), 42 U.S.C. § 7413(c).

80. *See* U.S. Sentencing Comm'n, Guidelines Manual (Nov. 2021).

81. The Department of Justice also may utilize Title 18 criminal provisions in environmental enforcement, such as Sections 371 (conspiracy) and 1001 (false statements). In

some cases, these statutes are charged together with substantive Clean Air Act violations, while some cases may only charge Title 18 offenses even when the underlying conduct may also violate the Clean Air Act.

82. The specific provisions for which criminal penalties may be sought are knowing violations of SIPs, section 113(a) orders, section 111(e) (new source performance standards), section 112 (hazardous air pollutants), section 129 (solid waste combustion), section 114 (inspections), sections 165(a) and 167 (PSD), section 303 (emergency orders), sections 502(a) and 503(c) (permits), or any provision relating to acid deposition control (Title IV) or stratospheric ozone control (Title VI).

83. CAA § 113(c)(1), 42 U.S.C. § 7413(c)(1).

84. *Id.*

85. *Id.* § 113(c)(2)(C), 42 U.S.C. § 7413(c)(2)(C).

86. *Id.* § 113(c)(2)(A), 42 U.S.C. § 7413(c)(2)(A).

87. *Id.* § 113(c)(3), 42 U.S.C. § 7413(c)(3).

88. *Id.* § 113(c)(5)(A), 42 U.S.C. § 7413(c)(5)(A).

89. *Id.*

90. *Id.* § 113(c)(5)(B), 42 U.S.C. § 7413(c)(5)(B).

91. *Id.*

92. *Id.* § 113(c)(5)(C), 42 U.S.C. § 7413(c)(5)(C).

93. *Id.* § 113(c)(6), 42 U.S.C. § 7413(c)(6).

94. *Id.* § 113(c)(5)(A), 42 U.S.C. § 7413(c)(5)(A).

95. *Id.* § 113(c)(4), 42 U.S.C. § 7413(c)(4).

96. Credible Evidence Revisions, 62 Fed. Reg. 8314, 8323, 8328 (Feb. 24, 1997).

97. The only exceptions to this constraint were (i) the approval of an alternative method by the Administrator under carefully defined criteria, and (ii) the consent of the source owner or operator in the case of certain alternative methods specified in the regulations. *Id.* at 8326.

98. *Id.* at 8316.

99. *Id.* at 8321 (quoting CAA § 113(e)(1), 42 U.S.C. § 7413(e)(1)).

100. *Id.*

101. *Id.* at 8328.

102. *Id.*

103. *See* Memorandum from Steven A. Herman, Assistant Adm'r, EPA, to Reg'l Adm'rs, EPA Regions I-X, et al., Interim Policy and Guidance on the Use of "Credible Evidence" in Air Enforcement Activities at 2 (Apr. 29, 1997).

104. *Sierra Club v. Tenn. Valley Auth.*, 430 F.3d 1337, 1339–40 (11th Cir. 2005).

105. 62 Fed. Reg. at 8318. Compliance Assurance Monitoring is discussed in Chapter 4.

106. For instance, source owners and operators have a general duty under 40 C.F.R. § 60.11(d) to operate facilities subject to new source performance standards in a manner "consistent with good air pollution control practice for minimizing emissions."

107. *Clean Air Implementation Project v. EPA*, 150 F.3d 1200, 1201, 1203–04 (D.C. Cir. 1998).

108. *Id.* at 1205.

109. *Id.* at 1204.

110. *See, e.g.*, *Sierra Club v. Pub. Serv. Co. of Colorado, Inc.*, 894 F. Supp. 1455, 1456, 1458–60 (D. Colo. 1995).

111. *See, e.g.*, U.S. Dep't of Justice, Factors in Decisions on Criminal Prosecutions for Environmental Violations in the Context of Significant Voluntary Compliance or Disclosure Efforts by the Violator (July 1, 1991).

112. *Id.*

113. Incentives for Self-Policing: Discovery, Disclosure, Correction and Prevention of Violations, 60 Fed. Reg. 66,706 (Dec. 22, 1995).

114. *Id.* at 66,711–12.

115. *Id.* at 66,707–08. Specifically, the policy sets out nine conditions that a regulated entity must meet in order for EPA to decline to seek, or to reduce, gravity-based penalties: (1) systematic discovery; (2) voluntary disclosure; (3) prompt disclosure; (4) discovery and disclosure independent of government or third-party plaintiff; (5) correction and remediation; (6) prevent recurrence; (7) no repeat violations; (8) certain violations excluded; and (9) cooperation. *See id.* at 66,711–12.

116. *See* Incentives for Self-Policing: Discovery, Disclosure, Correction, and Prevention of Violations, 65 Fed. Reg. 19,618 (Apr. 11, 2000). In 2008, EPA published its interim approach for application of the audit policy to new owners, which became effective upon publication, stating that the Agency's intent to tailor Audit Policy incentives was that new owners that want to make a "'clean start'" at their recently acquired facilities can do so by addressing environmental noncompliance that began prior to acquisition of such facilities. Interim Approach to Applying the Audit Policy to New Owners, 73 Fed. Reg. 44,991, 44,991 (Aug. 1, 2008).

117. 60 Fed. Reg. at 66,707; 65 Fed. Reg. at 19,620. EPA has stated that "systematic discovery" is not a requirement for eligibility for this incentive, although the entity must be acting in good faith and adopt a systematic approach to preventing recurring violations. 60 Fed. Reg. at 66,708–09; 65 Fed. Reg. at 19,618–19, 19,620–21.

118. FY 2022 Data and Trends, EPA Voluntary Disclosure Programs—Number of Disclosures/New Owner Audit Agreements and Facilities FY 2018–FY 2022.

119. S. Rep. No. 101-228 at 347 (1989), *reprinted in* 1990 U.S.C.C.A.N. 3385, 3730.

120. Memorandum from Steven A. Herman, Assistant Adm'r, EPA, et al., to Reg'l Adm'rs, EPA, Statement of Principles, Effect of State Audit Immunity/Privilege Laws on Enforcement Authority for Federal Programs (Feb. 14, 1997).

121. *Id.* at 1–2.

122. *Id.* at 2.

123. *Id.*

124. EPA, FY 2013 Office of Enforcement and Compliance Assurance (OECA) National Program Manager (NPM) Guidance at 15 (Apr. 30, 2012).

125. *Id.*

126. Memorandum from Susan Parker Bodine, Asst. Adm'r, Office of Enforcement & Compliance Assurance, EPA, to Reg'l Adm'rs, Transition from National Enforcement Initiatives to National Compliance Initiatives (Aug. 21, 2018).

127. *Id.* at 1.

128. *Id.* at 1–4.

129. Memorandum from Lawrence E. Starfield, Acting Assistant Adm'r, Office of Enforcement & Compliance Assurance, EPA, to Reg'l Adm'rs et al., Updated Policy for EPA's Enforcement and Compliance Initiatives at 1 (Dec. 20, 2022).

130. *Id.* at 1–2.

131. CAA § 304, 42 U.S.C. § 7604.

132. *Id.* § 304(a), 42 U.S.C. § 7604(a).

133. *Id.* § 304(g)(1), 42 U.S.C. § 7604(g)(1).

134. *Id.* § 304(g)(2), 42 U.S.C. § 7604(g)(2).

135. *Id.* § 304(a)(3), 42 U.S.C. § 7604(a)(3) (emphasis added).

136. *Id.* § 304(c)(3), 42 U.S.C. § 7604(c)(3).

137. *Id.* § 304(a), 42 U.S.C. § 7604(a).

138. *Id.* § 307(b), 42 U.S.C. § 7607(b).

139. *Id.* § 304(a), 42 U.S.C. § 7604(a).

140. *Id.* § 113(g), 42 U.S.C. § 7413(g).

141. United States' Resp. to Sierra Club's Mot. to Enter Agreement Between Sierra Club & DTE or, in the alternative, Notice of that Agreement at 1, *United States & Sierra Club v. DTE Energy Co.*, No. 2:10-cv-13101-BAF-RSW (E.D. Mich. July 8, 2020), ECF No. 279 (internal quotation marks and citation omitted).

142. *Id.* (internal quotation marks and citation omitted).

143. CAA § 113(f), 42 U.S.C. § 7413(f).

144. *Id.*

145. Regulations Governing Awards Under Section 113(f) of the Clean Air Act, 59 Fed. Reg. 22,795 (proposed May 3, 1994).

146. *Id.* at 22,795–96.

147. According to the Agency, one of the awards was for the maximum amount while the others were for less. The Agency indicated that it assessed a total of more than $1.5 million in civil and administrative penalties in the cases involved. Press Release, EPA, First Monetary Awards Approved for Citizens Assistance in Enforcement Cases Under the Clean Air Act (Feb. 18, 1997).

148. CAA § 307(b), 42 U.S.C. § 7607(b).

149. *Id.*

150. *Id.*

151. *Id.* § 307(b)(2), 42 U.S.C. § 7607(b)(2).

152. *Id.* § 307(b)(1), 42 U.S.C. § 7607(b)(1).

153. *Id.* § 307(d)(7)(B), 42 U.S.C. § 7607(d)(7)(B).

154. *Id.*

155. *Id.* § 307(b)(1), 42 U.S.C. § 7607(b)(1).

156. *Id.* § 307(b)(2), 42 U.S.C. § 7607(b)(2).

157. Exec. Order No. 13891, Promoting the Rule of Law Through Improved Agency Guidance Documents (Oct. 9, 2019), *reprinted in* 84 Fed. Reg. 55,235 (Oct. 15, 2019).

158. 84 Fed. Reg. at 55,235.

159. *Id.*

160. *Id.* at 55,236.

161. EPA Guidance; Administrative Procedures for Issuance and Public Petitions, 85 Fed. Reg. 66,230 (Oct. 19, 2020).

162. *Id.* at 66,234.

163. 84 Fed. Reg. at 55,236.

164. *Id.* (emphasis added).

165. *Kisor v. Wilkie*, 139 S. Ct. 2400, 2415–16 (2019).

166. EPA Guidance; Administrative Procedures for Issuance and Public Petitions; Rescission 86 Fed. Reg. 26,842, 26,842 (May 18, 2021).

Chapter 12

TRENDS IN CLEAN AIR ACT REGULATION AND LEGISLATION

The Clean Air Act (CAA or Act) is not self-implementing; the U.S. Environmental Protection Agency (EPA or Agency) and states must implement the statute through administrative action. To ensure timely execution, Congress set numerous deadlines for EPA and states to act. Since the Act was amended in 1990, many regulatory proceedings have been completed. Many others, however, are still underway, and the Act requires periodic review and updating of state implementation plans, Title V permits, and many of the basic regulatory programs. In planning for compliance, it is important to review periodically the status of permits, of EPA and state implementation activity, and of anticipated agendas for regulatory action.

I. EPA'S Regulatory Agenda

Since 2000, there has been a flood of new Clean Air Act rules, including air toxics technology-based standards, new source performance standards, revised national ambient air quality standards, rules regarding mobile source emissions standards and fuel composition, and stratospheric ozone protection rules. In particular, the new millennium brought forth an entirely new set of regulatory initiatives focused on climate change. While many of these programs were revised during the Trump administration, many of that administration's de-regulatory activities were only partial or not completed at all. And those that were completed already have been, or are being, revisited by the Biden administration.

On his first day in office in 2021, President Biden issued a series of executive orders revoking President Trump's executive orders and instructing the heads of agencies to rescind any rules, policies, committees, or task forces implementing and enforcing those orders.[1] A separate executive order instructed all executive departments and federal agencies to immediately review all federal regulations and actions taken during the prior four years for potential suspension, revision, or rescission.[2] For some items, the order identified a specific timeframe for potential publication of notice-and-comment proceedings by EPA.

EPA publishes its regulatory agenda twice a year. The agenda can be accessed from EPA's website at https://www.reginfo.gov/public/do/eAgendaMain. The most striking aspect of the fall 2022 regulatory agenda is the number of regulatory activities still focused on reversing or revising actions taken by the prior administration. Although EPA acted quickly to reverse a number of procedural rules put in place by the prior administration,[3] most of the more substantive rules are taking more time.

In many cases, regulatory proceedings—including requirements to periodically review and revise standards—are subject to statutory deadlines. When missed, the history of Clean Air Act regulation has been the establishment of new, judicially enforceable deadlines to guide agency action. Rulemaking schedules imposed by district courts as a result of citizen suits have been a driving force behind implementation of the Act since 1990, including the revised national ambient air quality standards for ozone and particulate matter, new source performance standards, and air toxics standards. These judicial schedules for regulatory action have influenced the scope of public input and interagency review, as well as the substance of the final rules themselves. The practical problems created by statutory deadlines merit careful consideration by Congress in any new Clean Air Act legislation.

EPA's heavy regulatory agenda has also led the Agency to explore new ways to implement the Act. Soon after enactment of the 1990 amendments, EPA announced a "consensus building" approach to regulation. This approach involved increased reliance on advisory committees and regulatory negotiations in an attempt to speed the regulatory process by giving interested parties an opportunity for early input. This approach did not always result in quicker implementation, however, but often in time-consuming "negotiation" that ultimately gave way to traditional rulemaking. In the coming years, one can anticipate continued efforts to streamline regulatory proceedings, particularly if there is a heavy re-regulatory effort.

A product of the Agency's full regulatory agenda has been an increased reliance on guidance and policy statements to give substantive content to regulations. While the U.S. Court of Appeals for the District of Columbia Circuit (D.C. Circuit) has cautioned EPA on substituting guidance for rulemaking,[4] this practice has accelerated in recent decades. Subjects for Agency guidance have included Title V permit implementation,[5] new source permitting,[6] and emissions monitoring and compliance requirements.[7]

Agency guidance cannot create new regulatory obligations but only clarify existing obligations. The line between permissible and impermissible guidance is blurry, though, and will continue to receive close attention from the courts as well as the executive branch. The U.S. Supreme Court addressed the framework for consideration of deference to agency regulatory interpretations in *Kisor v. Wilkie*.[8] As the Court explained, deference is appropriate only where a regulation is "genuinely ambiguous" after application of traditional rules of regulatory construction.[9] And even if there is genuine ambiguity, deference is not appropriate where it would create unfair surprise. Over the last several years, over a hundred federal courts have cited *Kisor* in support of their decisions. Clearly, *Kisor* is being applied by courts across the country and will influence the future course of agency enforcement through guidance.

In 2019, President Trump signed an executive order requiring agencies, including EPA, to establish searchable "website" containing all active guidance of general applicability. Guidance of general applicability not on the portal were "rescinded."[10] A year later, EPA promulgated a rule implementing the order and establishing procedures for its "Guidance Portal."[11] However, that rule was rescinded in May 2021 after the Biden EPA determined that it deprived EPA of "necessary flexibility in determining when and how best to issue public guidance based on particular facts and circumstances."[12] The guidance portal established under the rule was revised to redirect users to general topical listings and webpages. EPA asserts that it will continue to make Agency guidance available and to solicit stakeholder input as appropriate.

Finally, the Agency has in the past engaged in policy development through enforcement proceedings. Perhaps the most striking example of this is the Agency's new source review enforcement initiative (discussed in chapter 11), which the Agency itself has characterized as a new approach to regulating existing facilities.[13] While this trend abated during the Trump administration, a new administration is likely to increase enforcement of existing environmental regulatory programs, bringing a renewed focus on the use of enforcement proceedings as an environmental policy tool.

Formulating compliance strategies in response to constantly evolving regulatory obligations and enforcement priorities will remain a challenge.

II. Clean Air Act Legislation

Several years after the Clean Air Act Amendments of 1990 were signed into law, Congress started to debate issues raised by EPA's implementation of that legislation. That debate has been going on almost continuously since that time, with the most prominent areas of discussion being interstate and international air pollution and climate change.

In February 2002, in response to legislative initiatives calling for new requirements to reduce power plant air emissions, the Bush administration proposed comprehensive legislation—known as "the Clear Skies Initiative"—to establish additional mandatory reductions in emissions of sulfur dioxide (SO_2), nitrogen oxides (NOx), and mercury from the electric utility sector.[14] The legislation would have established phased reductions of the three pollutants, achieving a cumulative 70 percent reduction from 2002 levels by 2018. The legislation also would have addressed other power plant Clean Air Act obligations, such as new source review and regional haze regulations, in order to conform those rules to a new timetable and provide increased regulatory certainty.

In January 2004, in the absence of action on the president's Clear Skies Initiative, EPA proposed a similar (but geographically more limited) regulatory alternative—the "Clean Air Interstate Rule" (CAIR). EPA finalized the rule in 2005.[15] According to EPA, when fully implemented, CAIR (discussed in chapter 2) would have reduced SO_2 emissions from power plants in twenty-eight eastern states and the District of Columbia by more than 70 percent and NOx emissions by more than 60 percent from 2003 levels. As discussed in chapter 2, CAIR was ultimately remanded to the D.C. Circuit and replaced by the Cross-State Air Pollution Rule.[16] Starting with this experience in the Bush administration, the inability of Congress periodically to update the Clean Air Act to address new pollution issues has led to creative efforts to use existing authorities to craft regulatory solutions.

Perhaps the most striking use of the Clean Air Act to address legislative paralysis has occurred in the area of climate change. In the early days of the Obama administration, Congress tried but failed to adopt comprehensive cap-and-trade legislation for greenhouse gases.[17] The result was a lengthy and controversial administrative effort to fashion a regulatory response, known as the Clean Power Plan (discussed at length in chapter 7). This program ultimately never went into effect as a result of a Supreme Court-issued stay and was repealed and replaced by a more traditional Clean Air Act rule in the Trump administration.

One can expect renewed efforts on climate legislation in Biden administration. In the absence of legislation, however, a new effort to find creative regulatory responses to climate change under the Clean Air Act is likely. In a memorandum outlining recommended climate-related actions for the Biden administration, a group of experts including many former Obama administration officials has recommended a return to a Clean Power Plan-type program, evaluation of Clean Air Act section 115[18] on international pollution as a potential basis for a cap-and-trade system, more stringent vehicles and fuels regulation, and use of other authorities that "have the potential to indirectly reduce GHG emissions while fulfilling other environmental protection obligations."[19] Without legislation, one can anticipate an aggressive regulatory agenda in a Biden administration.

In sum, implementation of the Clean Air Act will continue to present significant challenges for both EPA and industry—challenges that will expand in scope and complexity as interstate and international air pollution issues, including regulation of greenhouse gas emissions, increasingly become the focus of the legislative debate.

Notes

1. *See, e.g.*, Exec. Order No. 13992, Revocation of Certain Executive Orders Concerning Federal Regulation (Jan. 20, 2021), *reprinted in* 86 Fed. Reg. 7049 (Jan. 25, 2021).

2. Exec. Order No. 13990, Protecting Public Health and the Environment and Restoring Science To Tackle the Climate Crisis (Jan. 20, 2021), *reprinted in* 86 Fed. Reg. 7037 (Jan. 25, 2021).

3. *See, e.g.*, Rescinding the Rule on Increasing Consistency and Transparency in Considering Benefits and Costs in the Clean Air Act Rulemaking Process, 86 Fed. Reg. 26,406 (May, 14, 2021); Order, *California v. EPA*, No. 21-1035 (and consolidated cases) (D.C. Cir. Apr. 5. 2021), ECF No. 1893155 (vacating and remanding January 13, 2021 Pollutant-Specific Significant Contribution Rule); Strengthening Transparency in Pivotal Science Underlying Significant Regulatory Actions and Influential Scientific Information; Implementation of Vacatur, 86 Fed. Reg. 29,515 (June 2, 2021); Revisions to the Permit Appeals Process To Restore the Organization and Function of the Environmental Appeals Board, 86 Fed. Reg. 31,172 (June 11, 2021).

4. *See Appalachian Power Co. v. EPA*, 208 F.3d 1015, 1028 (D.C. Cir. 2000).

5. *See* Chapter 4 (discussing EPA White Papers on Title V permitting).

6. *See* Chapter 3 (discussing recent EPA NSR guidance).

7. For example, several states have included limits in Title V permits that transform monitoring parameters into "never-to-be-exceeded" limits. Ohio facilities have successfully appealed their Title V permits to the state's Environmental Review Appeals Commission (ERAC) on the ground that such operational restrictions are not authorized. *Gen. Elec. Lighting v. Jones*, Case No. ERAC 185017, 2005 WL 3778691 (Ohio ERAC Mar. 1, 2005); *see also Gen. Elec. Lighting v. Jones*, Case No. ERAC 185017 (ERAC Aug. 21, 2003). The ERAC found that "the inclusion of any operational restriction which can[not] be *demonstrated to directly relate to the enforceability of an existing applicable requirement* and . . . not [to] alter that underlying requirement" is not lawful. *Gen. Elec. Lighting*, 2005 WL 3778691, at *9 (emphasis in original, citation omitted).

8. 139 S. Ct. 2400 (2019).

9. *Id.* at 2414.

10. Exec. Order No. 13891, Promoting the Rule of Law Through Improved Agency Guidance Documents (Oct. 9, 2019), *reprinted in* 84 Fed. Reg. 55,235, 55,236 (Oct. 15, 2019).

11. *See* EPA Guidance; Administrative Procedures for Issuance and Public Petitions, 85 Fed. Reg. 66,230 (Oct. 19, 2020).

12. EPA Guidance; Administrative Procedures for Issuance and Public Petitions; Rescission 86 Fed. Reg. 26,842, 26,842 (May 18, 2021). The importance of guidance documents in enforcement is discussed in Chapter 11.

13. Jim Jackson & Chris Oh, EPA, Office of Enforcement & Compliance Assurance, Internal Enforcement Memorandum, *Coal-Fired Power Plants* (undated, *ca.* 1997).

14. The official title of the legislation as introduced was "To amend the Clean Air Act to reduce air pollution through expansion of cap and trade programs, to provide an alternative regulatory classification for units subject to the cap and trade program, and for other purposes." *See* Clear Skies Act of 2003, S. 485, 108th Cong. (2003); Clear Skies Act of 2003, H.R. 999, 108th Cong. (2003). Both the Senate and House of Representatives versions of this legislation were introduced on February 27, 2003.

15. *See* Rule To Reduce Interstate Transport of Fine Particulate Matter and Ozone (Clean Air Interstate Rule); Revisions to Acid Rain Program; Revisions to the NOx SIP Call, 70 Fed. Reg. 25,162 (May 12, 2005).

16. *See North Carolina v. EPA*, 531 F.3d 896 (D.C. Cir.) (per curiam), *modified in part on reh'g*, 550 F.3d 1176 (D.C. Cir. 2008) (per curiam); *EME Homer City Generation, L.P. v. EPA*, 696 F.3d 7 (D.C. Cir. 2012), *cert. granted,* 570 U.S. 916 (2013), *rev'd*, 572 U.S. 489 (2014); Federal Implementation Plans: Interstate Transport of Fine Particulate Matter and Ozone and Correction of SIP Approvals, 76 Fed. Reg. 48,208 (Aug. 8, 2011).

17. American Clean Energy and Security Act of 2009, H.R. 2454, 111th Cong. (2009).

18. 42 U.S.C. § 7415.

19. Climate Project 21, Environmental Protection Agency Transition Memo at 10 (undated).

APPENDIX 1

GLOSSARY OF ABBREVIATIONS AND ACRONYMS

$\mu g/m^3$	Micrograms per cubic meter
ACE	Affordable Clean Energy
Administrator	Administrator of the U.S. Environmental Protection Agency
AIM Act	American Innovation and Manufacturing Act of 2020
ANPR	Advance Notice of Proposed Rulemaking
AOS	Alternative operating scenario(s)
AQA	Air Quality Act
AQRV(s)	Air quality-related value(s)
BACM	Best available control measures
BACT	Best available control technology
BART	Best available retrofit technology
BSER	Best system of emission reduction
CAA	Clean Air Act
CAAAC	Clean Air Act Advisory Committee
CAFE	Corporate average fuel economy
CAIR	Clean Air Interstate Rule
CAM	Compliance assurance monitoring
CAMR	Clean Air Mercury Rule
CARB	California Air Resources Board
CASAC	Clean Air Scientific Advisory Committee
CCS	Carbon capture and storage (or carbon capture and sequestration)
CCT	Clean coal technology
CE	Credible evidence
CEMS	Continuous emission monitoring system
CENRAP	Central Regional Air Planning Association
CERCLA	Comprehensive Environmental Response, Compensation, and Liability Act
CF	Clean fuels
CFC(s)	Chlorofluorocarbon(s)

CFEA	Criminal Fine Enforcement Act
CH_4	Methane
CISWI	Commercial and industrial solid waste incineration units
CO	Carbon monoxide
CO_2	Carbon dioxide
CO_2e	Carbon dioxide equivalent
CPP	Clean Power Plan
CRA	Congressional Review Act
CSAPR	Cross-State Air Pollution Rule
CSB	Chemical Safety and Hazard Investigation Board
CTG(s)	Control technique guideline(s)
D.C. Circuit	U.S. Court of Appeals for the District of Columbia Circuit
EAB	Environmental Appeals Board
ECMPS	Emissions Collection and Monitoring Plan System
EGU(s)	Electric generating unit(s)
EHS	Extremely hazardous substance(s)
EISA	Energy Independence and Security Act
ENRD	U.S. Department of Justice, Environment and Natural Resources Division
EPA	U. S. Environmental Protection Agency
EPCA	Energy Policy and Conservation Act of 1975
EPCRA	Emergency Planning and Community Right-To-Know Act
FCPP	Four Corners Power Plant
FIP(s)	Federal implementation plan(s)
FLAG	Federal Land Managers' Air Quality Related Values Work Group
FLM	Federal land manager
FY	Fiscal year
g/mi	Grams per mile
GACT	Generally available control technology
GHG(s)	Greenhouse gas(es)
GVWR	Gross vehicle weight rating
HAP(s)	Hazardous air pollutant(s)
HBFC(s)	Hydrobromofluorocarbon(s)
HCFC(s)	Hydrochlorofluorocarbon(s)
HFC(s)	Hydrofluorocarbon(s)
HFO(s)	Hydrofluoroolefin(s)
HEW	Department of Health, Education, and Welfare

I/M	Inspection and maintenance
ICAO	International Civil Aviation Organization
ICR	Information Collection Request
ICTA	International Center for Technology Assessment
IGCC	Integrated gasification combined cycle
IRA	Inflation Reduction Act of 2022
ISA	Integrated science assessment
IUVP	In-use verification program
kg/hr	Kilograms per hour
LAER	Lowest achievable emission rate
lbs CO_2/MWh	Pounds of carbon dioxide per megawatt hour
lb/mmBtu	Pounds per million British thermal units
LEV(s)	Low emission vehicle(s)
MACT	Maximum available control technology
MANE-VU	Mid-Atlantic/Northeast Visibility Union
mmBtu/hour	Million British thermal units per hour
mpg	Miles per gallon
MRPO	Midwest Regional Planning Organization
MTBE	Methyl tertiary butyl ether
MTE	Midterm evaluation
MTOM	Maximum takeoff mass
MW	Megawatts
N_2O	Nitrous oxide
NAAQS	National ambient air quality standards
NESHAPs	National emission standards for hazardous air pollutants
NGCC	Natural gas combined cycle
NGS	Navajo Generating Station
NHTSA	National Highway Traffic Safety Administration
NMHC	Nonmethane hydrocarbons
NNSR	Nonattainment new source review
NO_2	Nitrogen dioxide
NOx	Nitrogen oxides
NSPS	New source performance standard(s)
NSR	New source review
OAQPS	Office of Air Quality Planning and Standards
ODS	Ozone-depleting substance
OSHA	Office of Health and Safety Administration
PAL(s)	Plantwide applicability limit(s)

PFC(s)	Perfluorocarbon(s)
PM	Particulate matter
$PM_{2.5}$	Fine particulate matter
PM_{10}	Coarse particulate matter
POTW(s)	Publicly owned treatment work(s)
ppb	Parts per billion
ppm	Parts per million
PSD	Prevention of significant deterioration
psi	Pounds per square inch
PSM	Process safety management
PTE	Potential to emit
RACM	Reasonably available control measures
RACT	Reasonably available control technology
RCRA	Resource Conservation and Recovery Act
RFG	Reformulated gasoline
RFP	Reasonable further progress
RFS	Renewable fuel standard
RIN	Renewable identification number
RVO	Renewable volume obligations
RVP	Reid vapor pressure
RMP	Risk management plan
RMRR	Routine maintenance, repair, and replacement
RPO(s)	Regional planning organization(s)
RTA	Regional transport area
RTR	Risk and technology review
SAB	Science Advisory Board
SCR	Selective catalytic reduction
SCRAM	EPA Support Center for Regulatory Atmospheric Modeling
SEA	Selective Enforcement Audit
SEP(s)	Supplemental environmental project(s)
SESARM	Southeastern Air Pollution Control Agencies
SF_6	Sulfur hexafluoride
SIC	Standard industrial classification
SIL(s)	Significant impact level(s)
SIP(s)	State implementation plan(s)
SNAP	Significant new alternatives policy
SO_2	Sulfur dioxide
SOx	Sulfur oxides

SSM	Startup, shutdown, and malfunction
TCM(s)	Transportation control measure(s)
tpy	Tons per year
TVA	Tennessee Valley Authority
USCC	United States Sentencing Commission
VISTAS	Visibility Improvement State and Tribal Association of the Southeast
VMT	Vehicle miles traveled
VOC(s)	Volatile organic compound(s)
WRAP	Western Regional Air Partnership
ZEV(s)	Zero-emission vehicle(s)

APPENDIX 2

SOURCE CATEGORIES SUBJECT TO CLEAN AIR ACT PROGRAMS

A. NSPS SOURCE CATEGORIES LISTED UNDER SECTION 111

(40 C.F.R. Part 60)

Source Category	Subpart
Ammonium Sulfate Manufacturing	PP
Asphalt Processing and Asphalt Roofing Manufacture	UU
Auto and Light Duty Truck Surface Coating	MM
Basic Oxygen Process Furnace (BOPF) Primary Emissions	N
Basic Oxygen Process Furnace (BOPF) Steelmaking Facilities Secondary Emissions	Na
Beverage Can Surface Coating	WW
Bulk Gasoline Terminals	XX
Calciners and Dryers in Mineral Industries	UUU
Coal Preparation and Processing Plants	Y
Electric Utility Steam Generating Units (Boilers)	D, Da
Ferroalloy Production Facilities	Z
Flexible Vinyl and Urethane Coating and Printing	FFF
Glass Manufacturing Plants	CC
Grain Elevators	DD
Graphic Arts Industry - Publication Rotogravure Printing	QQ
Hot Mix Asphalt Facilities	I
Industrial/Commercial/Institutional Steam Generating Units (Boilers)	Db - Dc
Kraft Pulp Mills	BB - BBa
Large Appliance Surface Coating	SS
Lead Acid Battery Manufacturing	KK-KKa

Source Category	Subpart
Lime Manufacturing	HH
Magnetic Tape Manufacturing	SSS
Metal Coil Surface Coating	TT
Metal Furniture Surface Coating	EE
Metallic Mineral Processing Plants	LL
Municipal Solid Waste Landfills	WWW
Nitric Acid Plants	G - Ga
Nonmetallic Mineral Processing Plants	OOO
Oil and Gas Production, Transmission, and Distribution	OOOO
Onshore Natural Gas Plants - SO_2 Emissions	LLL
Onshore Natural Gas Plants - VOC Equipment Leaks	KKK
Petroleum Dry Cleaners	JJJ
Petroleum Refineries	J - Ja
Petroleum Refineries - Wastewater Systems	QQQ
Petroleum Refineries Equipment Leaks	GGG - GGGa
Phosphate Fertilizers: Granular Triple Superphosphate Storage Facilities	X
Phosphate Fertilizers: Diammonium Phosphate Plants	V
Phosphate Fertilizers: Superphosphoric Acid Plants	U
Phosphate Fertilizers: Triple Superphosphate Plants	W
Phosphate Fertilizers: Wet-Process Phosphoric Acid Plants	T
Phosphate Rock Plants	NN
Plastic Parts for Business Machines (surface coating)	TTT - TTTa
Polymeric Coating of Substrates	VVV
Polymers Manufacturing Industry	DDD
Portland Cement Manufacturing	F
Pressure Sensitive Tape and Label Surface Coating	RR
Primary Aluminum Production	S
Primary Copper Smelting	P
Primary Lead Smelting	R
Primary Zinc Smelters	Q
Residential Wood Heaters	AAA

Source Category	Subpart
Rubber Tire Manufacturing	BBB
Secondary Brass and Bronze Production Plants	M
Secondary Lead Smelters	L
Sewage Treatment Plant Incineration	O
SOCMI Air Oxidation Unit Processes	III
SOCMI Distillation	NNN
SOCMI Equipment Leaks: Alternative Means of Emission Limitation for Leak Detection and Repair	VV-VVa
SOCMI Reactor Processes	RRR
Standards for GHG Emissions from New, Modified and Reconstructed Electric Utility Generating Units	TTTT
Stationary Combustion Turbines	KKKK
Stationary Compression Ignition Internal Combustion Engines	IIII
Stationary Gas Turbines	GG
Stationary Spark Ignition Internal Combustion Engines	JJJJ
Steel Plants: Electric Arc Furnaces (EAFs) and Argon-Oxygen Decarburization Vessels (AQD)	AA - AAa
Sulfuric Acid Plants	H
Synthetic Fiber Production	HHH
Volatile Organic Liquid Storage Vessels Including Petroleum Storage Vessels	Kb
Volatile Organic Liquid Storage Vessels Including Petroleum Storage Vessels - 1978–1984	Ka
Volatile Organic Liquid Storage Vessels Including Petroleum Storage Vessels -1973–1978	K
Wool Fiberglass Insulation Manufacturing	PPP

EPA removed the following previously listed source categories in "Revisions to the Priority List of Categories of Stationary Sources," 47 Fed. Reg. 950 (Jan. 8, 1982):

Source Category
Mineral Wool
Incineration: Non-Municipal
Secondary Copper
Potash
Secondary Zinc
Ammonia
Ceramic Clay Manufacturing
Castable Refractories
Borax and Boric Acid
Phosphoric Acid: Thermal Process
Animal Feed Defluorination
Detergent

B. Existing Sources Categories Subject to Emissions Guidelines Under Section 111(d)

(40 C.F.R. Part 60)

Source Category	**Subpart**
Large Municipal Waste Combustors	Cb
Municipal Solid Waste Landfills	Cc
Sulfuric Acid Production Units	Cd
Hospital/Medical/Infectious Waste Incinerators	Ce
Emission Guidelines and Compliance Times for Municipal Solid Waste Landfills	Cf
Small Municipal Waste Combustion Units	BBBB
Commercial and Industrial Solid Waste Incineration Units	DDDD
Other Solid Waste Incineration Units	FFFF
Existing Sewage Sludge Incineration Units	MMMM
Emission Guidelines for Greenhouse Gas Emissions and Compliance Times for Electric Utility Generating Units	UUUU

C. PSD Source Categories

(40 C.F.R. § 52.21(b)(1)(a))

The following 28 source categories are subject to the 100 tons per year (tpy) definition of "major stationary source" under the PSD rules, that is, if they emit or have the potential to emit at least 100 tpy of any pollutant subject to Clean Air Act regulation, other than hazardous air pollutants listed under Section 112. Other stationary sources are subject to PSD rules if they emit or have the potential to emit at least 250 tpy of such a pollutant. A stationary source is subject to PSD regulations for greenhouse gases if it is a major stationary source for another pollutant and emits or has the potential to emit 75,000 tpy of carbon dioxide equivalent emissions (tpy CO_2e). 40 C.F.R. § 52.21(b)(49) (2021).

Fossil Fuel-Fired Steam Electric Plants of more than 250 million Btu/hr heat input

Coal Cleaning Plants (with thermal dryers)

Kraft Pulp Mills

Portland Cement Plants

Primary Zinc Smelters

Iron and Steel Mill Plants

Primary Aluminum Ore Reduction Plants (with thermal dryers)

Primary Copper Smelters

Municipal Incinerators capable of charging more than 250 tons of refuse per day

Hydrofluoric Acid Plants

Sulfuric Acid Plants

Nitric Acid Plants

Petroleum Refineries

Lime Plants

Phosphate Rock Processing Plants

Coke Oven Batteries

Sulfur Recovery Plants

Carbon Black Plants (furnace process)

Primary Lead Smelters

Fuel Conversion Plants

Sintering Plants

Secondary Metal Production Plants

Chemical Process Plants (not including ethanol production facilities producing ethanol by natural fermentation included in NAICS codes 325193 or 312140)

Fossil-Fuel Boilers (or combinations thereof) totaling more than 250 million Btu/Hr heat input

Petroleum Storage and Transfer Units with a total storage capacity exceeding 300,000 barrels

Taconite Ore Processing Plants

Glass Fiber Processing Plants

Charcoal Production Plants

D. Source Categories Listed Under Section 112

(Major and Area Sources)

(40 C.F.R. Parts 61 and 63)

Source Category	Subpart*
Acrylic/Modacrylic Fiber (area sources)	LLLLLL
Aerospace	GG
Asbestos	M (Part 61)
Asphalt Processing and Asphalt Roofing Manufacturing (area sources)	AAAAAAA
Asphalt Processing and Asphalt Roofing Manufacturing	LLLLL
Auto and Light Duty Truck Surface Coating	IIII
Benzene Transfer Operations	BB (Part 61)
Benzene Waste Operations	FF (Part 61)
Beryllium	C (Part 61)
Beryllium Rocket Motor Firing	D
Boat Manufacturing	VVVV (Part 61)
Brick and Structural Clay Products Manufacturing (*see also* Clay Ceramics)	JJJJJ
Carbon Black Production (area sources)	MMMMMM
Cellulose Products Manufacturing Miscellaneous Viscose Processes • Cellulose Food Casing • Rayon • Cellulosic Sponge • Cellophane • Cellulose Ethers Production • Caroxymethyl Cellulose • Methyl Cellulose • Cellulose Ethers	UUUU
Chemical Manufacturing Industry (area sources): CMAS	VVVVVV
Chemical Preparations Industry (area sources)	BBBBBBB
Chromium Compounds (area sources)	NNNNNN

Source Category	**Subpart***
Chromium Electroplating • Chromic Acid Anodizing • Decorative Chromium Electroplating • Hard Chromium Electroplating	N
Clay Ceramics Manufacturing (area sources)	RRRRRR
Clay Ceramics Manufacturing (see also Brick and Clay Products)	KKKKK
Coal- and Oil-Fired Electric Utility Steam Generating Units (Mercury and Air Toxics Standards)	UUUUU
Coke Oven By-product Recovery Plants	L (Part 61)
Coke Ovens: Charging, Top Side, and Door Leaks	L
Coke Ovens: Pushing, Quenching, and Battery Stacks	CCCCC
Combustion Sources at Kraft, Soda, and Sulfite Pulp & Paper Mills (Pulp and Paper MACT II) (*see also* Pulp and Paper noncombust MACT)	MM
Dry Cleaning • Commercial drycleaning dry-to-dry • Commercial drycleaning transfer machines • Industrial drycleaning dry-to-dry • Industrial drycleaning transfer machines	M
Electric Arc Furnace Steelmaking Facilities (area sources)	YYYYY
Engine Test Cells/Stands (*see also* Beryllium Rocket Motor Firing)	PPPPP
Ethylene Oxide Emission Standards for Sterilization Facilities (*see also* Hospital Ethylene Oxide Sterilizers)	O
Fabric Printing, Coating and Dyeing	OOOO
Ferroalloys Production (area sources)	YYYYYY
Ferroalloys Production (major sources)	XXX
Flexible Polyurethane Foam Fabrication Operation	MMMMM
Flexible Polyurethane Foam Production	III
Flexible Polyurethane Foam Production and Fabrication (area sources)	OOOOOO
Friction Products Manufacturing	QQQQQ
Gasoline Dispensing Facilities (area sources)	CCCCCC
Gasoline Distribution (Stage 1)	R

Source Category	Subpart*
Gasoline Distribution Bulk Terminals, Bulk Plants, and Pipeline Facilities (area sources)	BBBBBB
Generic MACT I - Acetal Resins	YY
Generic MACT I - Acrylic/Modacrylic Fibers	YY
Generic MACT I - Hydrogen Floride	YY
Generic MACT I - Polycarbonates Production	YY
Generic MACT II - Carbon Black Production	YY
Generic MACT II - Ethylene Processes	YY
Generic MACT II - Spandex Production	YY
Glass Manufacturing - Inorganic Arsenic	N (Part 61)
Glass Manufacturing (area sources)	SSSSSS
Gold Mine Ore Processing and Production (area sources)	EEEEEEE
Halogenated Solvent Cleaning	T
Hazardous Organic NESHAP (Synthetic Organic Chemical Manufacturing Industry)	F, G, H, I
Hazardous Waste Combustors	EEE
Hospital Ethylene Oxide Sterilizers (area sources) (*see also* Ethylene Oxide Sterilizers)	WWWWW
Hydrochloric Acid Production	NNNNN
Industrial Process Cooling Towers	Q
Industrial, Commercial and Institutional Boilers (area sources)	JJJJJJ
Industrial, Commercial and Institutional Boilers and Process Heaters (major sources)	DDDDD
Inorganic Arsenic Emissions from Primary Copper Smelters	O (Part 61)
Inorganic Arsenic from Arsenic Trioxide and Metallic Arsenic Production	P (Part 61)
Integrated Iron and Steel	FFFFF
Iron and Steel Foundries (major sources)	EEEEE
Iron and Steel Foundries (area sources)	ZZZZZ
Large Appliances Surface Coating	NNNN
Lead Acid Battery Manufacturing (area sources)	PPPPPP
Leather Finishing Operations	TTTT
Lime Manufacturing	AAAAA

Source Category	**Subpart***
Magnetic Tape Surface Coating	EE
Manufacturing Nutritional Yeast (formerly Bakers Yeast)	CCCC
Marine Vessel Loading Operations	Y
Mercury Cell Chlor-Alkali Plants	IIIII
Mercury Production	E (Part 61)
Metal Can Surface Coating	KKKK
Metal Coil Surface Coating	SSSS
Metal Fabrication and Finishing Source Nine Categories (area sources)	XXXXXX
Metal Furniture Surface Coating	RRRR
Mineral Wool Production	DDD
Misc. Organic Chemical Production and Processes (MON) • Alkyd Resins Production • Ammonium Sulfate Production • Benzyltrimethylammonium Chloride Production • Carbonyl Sulfide Production • Chelating Agents Production • Chlorinated Paraffins Production • Ethyllidene Norbomene Production • Explosives Production • Hydrazine Production • Maleic Anhydride Copolymers Production • Manufacture of Paints, Coatings, &Adhesives • OBPA/1, 3-diisocyanate Production • Photographic Chemicals Production • Phthalate Plasticizers Production • Polyester Resins Production • Polymerized Vinylidene Chloride Production • Polymethyl Methacrylate Resins Production • Polyvinyl Acetate Emulsions Production • Polyvinyl Alcohol Production • Polyvinyl Butyral Production • Quaternary Ammonium Comp. Production • Rubber Chemicals Production • Symmetrical Tetrachloropyridine Production	FFFF

Source Category	Subpart*
Miscellaneous Coating Manufacturing	HHHHH
Miscellaneous Metal Parts and Products Surface Coating	MMMM
Municipal Solid Waste Landfills	AAAA
Natural Gas Transmission and Storage	HHH
Nonferrous Foundries: Aluminum, Copper, and Other (area sources)	ZZZZZZ
Off-Site Waste Recovery Operations	DD
Oil and Natural Gas Production includes Area Sources	HH
Oil-Water Separators and Organic-Water Separators	VV
Organic Liquids Distribution (non-gasoline)	EEEE
Paint Stripping and Miscellaneous Surface Coating Operations (area sources)	HHHHHH
Paints and Allied Products Manufacturing (area sources)	CCCCCCC
Paper and Other Web Surface Coating	JJJJ
Pesticide Active Ingredient Production • 4-Chloro-2-Methyl Acid Production • 2,4 Salts & Esters Production • 4,6-dinitro-o-cresol Production • Butadiene Furfural Cotrimer • Captafol Production • Captan Production • Chloroneb Production • Chlorothalonil Production • Dacthal (tm) production • Sodium Pentachlorophenate Production • Tordon (tm) Acid Production	MMM
Petroleum Refineries	CC
Petroleum Refineries • Catalytic Cracking • Catalytic Reforming • Sulfur Plant Units • Associated Bypass Lines	UUU
Pharmaceuticals Production	GGG
Phosphate Fertilizers	BB
Phosphoric Acid	AA
Plastic Parts Surface Coating	PPPP

Source Category	**Subpart***
Plating and Polishing Operations (area sources)	WWWWWW
Plywood and Composite Wood Products (formerly Plywood and Particle Board Manufacturing)	DDDD
Polyether Polyols Production	PPP
Polymers & Resins I • Butyl Rubber • Epichlorohydrin Elastomers • Ethylene Propylene Rubber • Hypalon (TM) Production • Neoprene Production • Nitrile Butadiene Rubber • Polybutadiene Rubber • Polysulfide Rubber • Styrene-Butadiene Rubber & Latex	U
Polymers & Resins II • Epoxy Resins Production • Non-Nylon Polyamides Production	W
• Polymers & Resins III • Amino Resins • Phenolic Resins	OOO
Polymers & Resins IV • Acrylonitrile-Butadiene-Styrene • Methyl Methacrylate-Acrylonitrile+ • Methyl Methacrylate-Butadiene++ • Polystyrene • Styrene Acrylonitrile • Polyethylene Terephthalate • Nitrile Resins	JJJ
Polyvinyl Chloride and Copolymers Production	HHHHHHH
Polyvinyl Chloride and Copolymers Production (area sources)	DDDDDD
Portland Cement Manufacturing	LLL
Prepared Feeds Manufacturing (area sources)	DDDDDDD
Primary Aluminum	LL
Primary Copper Smelting	QQQ
Primary Copper Smelting (area sources)	EEEEEE

Source Category	**Subpart***
Primary Lead Processing	TTT
Primary Magnesium Refining	TTTTT
Primary Nonferrous Metals-Zinc, Cadmium, and Beryllium (area sources)	GGGGGG
Printing and Publishing Surface Coating	KK
Publicly Owned Treatment Works (POTW)	VVV
Pulp and Paper (non-combust) MACT	S
Reciprocating Internal Combustion Engines (RICE) includes area sources	ZZZZ
Refractory Products Manufacturing	SSSSS
Reinforced Plastic Composites Production	WWWW
Rubber Tire Manufacturing	XXXX
Secondary Aluminum	RRR
Secondary Copper Smelting (area sources)	FFFFFF
Secondary Lead Smelters	X
Secondary Nonferrous Metals Processing (Brass, Bronze, Magnesium and Zinc) (area sources)	TTTTTT
Semiconductor Manufacturing	BBBBB
Shipbuilding and Ship Repair Surface Coating	II
Site Remediation	GGGGG
Solvent Extraction for Vegetable Oil Production	GGGG
Stationary Combustion Turbines	YYYY
Steel Pickling - HCL Process	CCC
Taconite Iron Ore Processing	RRRRR
Utility NESHAP	UUUUU
Vinyl Chloride	F
Wet Formed Fiberglass Mat Production	HHHH
Wood Building Products Surface Coating (formerly Flat Wood Paneling Products)	QQQQ
Wood Furniture Surface Coating	JJ
Wood Preserving (area sources)	QQQQQQ
Wool Fiberglass Manufacturing	NNN
Wool Fiberglass Manufacturing (area sources)	NN

* Subpart of 40 C.F.R. Part 63, unless otherwise specified.

APPENDIX 3

POLLUTANTS SUBJECT TO CLEAN AIR ACT PROGRAMS

A. NAAQS CRITERIA POLLUTANTS

(40 C.F.R. Part 50)

Sulfur Dioxide (SO_2)
Particulate Matter (PM_{10} and $PM_{2.5}$)
Carbon Monoxide (CO)
Ozone (O_3)
Nitrogen Dioxide (NO_2)
Lead (Pb)

B. PSD Pollutants and Significance Levels

(40 C.F.R. § 52.21(b)(23) and (49))

For pollutants not listed below, "any emissions rate" is deemed significant. In addition, any emissions rate or any net emissions increase associated with a major stationary source or major modification that would construct within 10 kilometers of a Class I area and have an impact on that area equal to or greater than 1 $\mu g/m^3$ (24-hour average) is considered significant.

Carbon Monoxide (100 tpy)
Nitrogen Oxides (NOx) (40 tpy)
Sulfur Dioxide(SO_2) (40 tpy)
Particulate Matter:
Total PM (25 tpy)
 PM_{10} (15 tpy)
 $PM_{2.5}$ (10 tpy of direct $PM_{2.5}$; 40 tpy of SO_2; 40 tpy of NOx unless demonstrated not to be a $PM_{2.5}$ precursor)
Ozone (40 tpy of VOCs or NOx)
Lead (0.6 tpy)
Fluorides (3 tpy)
Sulfuric Acid Mist (7 tpy)
Hydrogen Sulfide (H_2S) (10 tpy)
Total Reduced Sulfur, including H_2S (10 tpy)
Reduced Sulfur Compounds, including H_2S (10 tpy)

Municipal Waste Combustor Organics (3.2×10^{-6} megagrams per year)
Municipal Waste Combustor Metals (14 megagrams per year)
Municipal Waste Combustor Acid Gases (36 megagrams per year)
Municipal Solid Waste Landfills Emissions, measured as non-methane organic compounds (45 megagrams per year)
Greenhouse Gases: Carbon dioxide, nitrous oxide, methane, hydrofluorocarbons perfluorocarbons, and sulfur hexafluoride (75,000 tpy CO_2e)

C. Nonattainment Pollutants and Significance Levels

(40 C.F.R. § 51.165(a)(1)(x))

Carbon Monoxide (100 tpy; 50 tpy in serious CO nonattainment area if stationary sources contribute significantly)
Nitrogen Oxides (40 tpy)
Particulate Matter:
Total PM (25 tpy)
PM_{10} (15 tpy)
$PM_{2.5}$ (10 tpy direct $PM_{2.5}$; 40 tpy SO_2)
Ozone (40 tpy of VOCs or NOx; 25 tpy of VOCs or NOx in serious or severe ozone nonattainment area; any increase of VOCs or NOx in extreme ozone nonattainment area)
Lead (0.6 tpy)
Sulfur Dioxide (40 tpy)

D. Section 112 Hazardous Air Pollutants

(CAA § 112(b)(1), 42 U.S.C. § 7412(b)(1); 40 C.F.R. Part 63, Subpart C)

CAS No.	Chemical Name	CAS No.	Chemical Name
75070	Acetaldehyde	110543	Hexane
60355	Acetamide	302012	Hydrazine
75058	Acetonitrile	7647010	Hydrochloric acid
98862	Acetophenone	7664393	Hydrogen fluoride (Hydrofluoric acid)
53963	2-Acetylaminofluorene	123319	Hydroquinone

CAS No.	Chemical Name	CAS No.	Chemical Name
107028	Acrolein	78591	Isophorone
79061	Acrylamide	58899	Lindane (all isomers)
79107	Acrylic acid	108316	Maleic anhydride
107131	Acrylonitrile	67561	Methanol
107051	Allyl chloride	72435	Methoxychlor
92671	4-Aminobiphenyl	74839	Methyl bromide (Bromomethane)
62533	Aniline	74873	Methyl chloride (Chloromethane)
90040	o-Anisidine	71556	Methyl chloroform (1,1,1-Trichloroethane)
1332214	Asbestos	60344	Methyl hydrazine
71432	Benzene (including benzene from gasoline)	74884	Methyl iodide (Iodomethane)
92875	Benzidine	108101	Methyl isobutyl ketone (Hexone)
98077	Benzotrichloride	624839	Methyl isocyanate
100447	Benzyl chloride	80626	Methyl methacrylate
92524	Biphenyl	1634044	Methyl tert butyl ether
117817	Bis(2-ethylhexyl)phthalate (DEHP)	101144	4,4-Methylene bis(2-chloroaniline)
542881	Bis(chloromethyl)ether	75092	Methylene chloride (Dichloromethane)
75252	Bromoform	101688	Methylene diphenyl diisocyanate (MDI)
106945	1-Bromopropane	101779	4,4′-Methylenedianiline
106990	1,3-Butadiene	91203	Naphthalene
156627	Calcium cyanamide	98953	Nitrobenzene
133062	Captan	92933	4-Nitrobiphenyl
63252	Carbaryl	100027	4-Nitrophenol
75150	Carbon disulfide	79469	2-Nitropropane
56235	Carbon tetrachloride	684935	N-Nitroso-N-methylurea
463581	Carbonyl sulfide	62759	N-Nitrosodimethylamine
120809	Catechol	59892	N-Nitrosomorpholine
133904	Chloramben	56382	Parathion
57749	Chlordane	82688	Pentachloronitrobenzene (Quintobenzene)

CAS No.	Chemical Name	CAS No.	Chemical Name
7782505	Chlorine	87865	Pentachlorophenol
79118	Chloroacetic acid	108952	Phenol
532274	2-Chloroacetophenone	106503	p-Phenylenediamine
108907	Chlorobenzene	75445	Phosgene
510156	Chlorobenzilate	7803512	Phosphine
67663	Chloroform	7723140	Phosphorus
107302	Chloromethyl methyl ether	85449	Phthalic anhydride
126998	Chloroprene	1336363	Polychlorinated biphenyls (Aroclors)
1319773	Cresols/Cresylic acid (isomers and mixture)	1120714	1,3-Propane sultone
95487	o-Cresol	57578	beta-Propiolactone
108394	m-Cresol	123386	Propionaldehyde
106445	p-Cresol	114261	Propoxur (Baygon)
98828	Cumene	78875	Propylene dichloride (1,2-Dichloropropane)
94757	2,4-D, salts and esters	75569	Propylene oxide
3547044	DDE	75558	1,2-Propylenimine (2-Methyl aziridine)
334883	Diazomethane	91225	Quinoline
132649	Dibenzofurans	106514	Quinone
96128	1,2-Dibromo-3-chloropropane	100425	Styrene
84742	Dibutylphthalate	96093	Styrene oxide
106467	1,4-Dichlorobenzene(p)	1746016	2,3,7,8-Tetrachlorodibenzo-p-dioxin
91941	3,3-Dichlorobenzidene	79345	1,1,2,2-Tetrachloroethane
111444	Dichloroethyl ether (Bis(2-chloroethyl)ether)	127184	Tetrachloroethylene (Perchloroethylene)
542756	1,3-Dichloropropene	7550450	Titanium tetrachloride
62737	Dichlorvos	108883	Toluene
111422	Diethanolamine	95807	2,4-Toluene diamine
121697	N,N-Diethyl aniline (N,N-Dimethylaniline)	584849	2,4-Toluene diisocyanate
64675	Diethyl sulfate	95534	o-Toluidine

CAS No.	Chemical Name	CAS No.	Chemical Name
119904	3,3-Dimethoxybenzidine	8001352	Toxaphene (chlorinated camphene)
60117	Dimethyl aminoazobenzene	120821	1,2,4-Trichlorobenzene
119937	3,3′-Dimethyl benzidine	79005	1,1,2-Trichloroethane
79447	Dimethyl carbamoyl chloride	79016	Trichloroethylene
68122	Dimethyl formamide	95954	2,4,5-Trichlorophenol
57147	1,1-Dimethyl hydrazine	88062	2,4,6-Trichlorophenol
131113	Dimethyl phthalate	121448	Triethylamine
77781	Dimethyl sulfate	1582098	Trifluralin
534521	4,6-Dinitro-o-cresol, and salts	540841	2,2,4-Trimethylpentane
51285	2,4-Dinitrophenol	108054	Vinyl acetate
121142	2,4-Dinitrotoluene	593602	Vinyl bromide
123911	1,4-Dioxane (1,4-Diethyleneoxide)	75014	Vinyl chloride
122667	1,2-Diphenylhydrazine	75354	Vinylidene chloride (1,1-Dichloroethylene)
106898	Epichlorohydrin (1-Chloro-2,3-epoxypropane)	1330207	Xylenes (isomers and mixture)
106887	1,2-Epoxybutane	95476	o-Xylenes
140885	Ethyl acrylate	108383	m-Xylenes
100414	Ethyl benzene	106423	p-Xylenes
51796	Ethyl carbamate (Urethane)	()	Antimony Compounds
75003	Ethyl chloride (Chloroethane)	()	Arsenic Compounds (inorganic including arsine)
106934	Ethylene dibromide (Dibromoethane)	()	Beryllium Compounds
107062	Ethylene dichloride (1,2-Dichloroethane)	()	Cadmium Compounds
107211	Ethylene glycol	()	Chromium Compounds
151564	Ethylene imine (Aziridine)	()	Cobalt Compounds
75218	Ethylene oxide	()	Coke Oven Emissions
96457	Ethylene thiourea	()	Cyanide Compounds[1]

CAS No.	Chemical Name	CAS No.	Chemical Name
75343	Ethylidene dichloride (1,1-Dichloroethane)	()	Glycol ethers[2]
50000	Formaldehyde	()	Lead Compounds
76448	Heptachlor	()	Manganese Compounds
118741	Hexachlorobenzene	()	Mercury Compounds
87683	Hexachlorobutadiene	()	Fine mineral fibers[3]
77474	Hexachlorocyclopentadiene	()	Nickel Compounds
67721	Hexachloroethane	()	Polycylic Organic Matter[4]
822060	Hexamethylene-1,6-diisocyanate	()	Radionuclides (including radon)[5]
680319	Hexamethylphosphoramide	()	Selenium Compounds

NOTE: For all listings mentioned that contain the word "compounds" and for glycol ethers, the following applies: Unless otherwise specified, these listings are defined as including any unique chemical substance that contains the named chemical (i.e., antimony, arsenic, etc.) as part of that chemical's infrastructure.

[1] X′CN where X = H′ or any other group where a formal dissociation may occur. For example KCN or $CA(CN)_2$.

[2] Glycol ethers include mono- and di-ethers of ethylene glycol, diethylene glycol, and triethylene glycol $R\text{-}(OCH_2CH_2)_n\text{-}OR'$ where

n = 1, 2, or 3;

R = alkyl C7 or less; or

R = phenyl or alkyl substituted phenyl;

R′ = H or alkyl C7 or less; or

OR′ consisting of carboxylic acid ester, sulfate, phosphate, nitrate, or sulfonate.

[In addition, the substance ethylene glycol monobutyl ether (EGBE,2-Butoxyethanol) (CAS Number 111-76-2) is deleted from the list of hazardous air pollutants. 40 C.F.R. § 63.62.]

[3] Includes mineral fiber emissions from facilities manufacturing or processing glass, rock, or slag fibers (or other mineral derived fibers) of average diameter 1 micrometer or less.

[4] Includes organic compounds with more than one benzene ring, and which have a boiling point greater than or equal to 100°C.

[5] A type of atom that spontaneously undergoes radioactive decay.

E. Accidental Release Prevention

(40 C.F.R. § 68.130)

1. Regulated Toxic Substances and Threshold Quantities

(Alphabetical Order – 77 Substances)

Chemical Name	CAS No.	Threshold Quantity (lbs)	Basis for Listing
Acrolein [2-Propenal]	107-02-8	5,000	b
Acrylonitrile [2-Propenenitrile]	107-13-1	20,000	b
Acrylyl chloride [2-Propenoyl chloride]	814-68-6	5,000	b
Allyl alcohol [2-Propen-l-ol]	107-18-6	15,000	b
Allylamine [2-Propen-l-amine]	107-11-9	10,000	b
Ammonia (anhydrous)	7664-41-7	10,000	a, b
Ammonia (conc 20% or greater)	7664-41-7	20,000	a, b
Arsenous trichloride	7784-34-1	15,000	b
Arsine	7784-42-1	1,000	b
Boron trichloride [Borane, trichloro-]	10294-34-5	5,000	b
Boron trifluoride [Borane, trifluoro-]	7637-07-2	5,000	b
Boron trifluoride compound with methyl ether (1:1) [Boron, trifluoro[oxybis[metane]]-, T-4-	353-42-4	15,000	b
Bromine	7726-95-6	10,000	a, b
Carbon disulfide	75-15-0	20,000	b
Chlorine	7782-50-5	2,500	a, b
Chlorine dioxide [Chlorine oxide (ClO_2)]	10049-04-4	1,000	c
Chloroform [Methane, trichloro-]	67-66-3	20,000	b
Chloromethyl ether [Methane, oxybis[chloro-]	542-88-1	1,000	b

Chemical Name	CAS No.	Threshold Quantity (lbs)	Basis for Listing
Chloromethyl methyl ether [Methane, chloromethoxy-]	107-30-2	5,000	b
Crotonaldehyde [2-Butenal]	4170-30-3	20,000	b
Crotonaldehyde, (E)- [2-Butenal, (E)-]	123-73-9	20,000	b
Cyanogen chloride	506-77-4	10,000	c
Cyclohexylamine [Cyclohexanamine]	108-91-8	15,000	b
Diborane	19287-45-7	2,500	b
Dimethyldichlorosilane [Silane, dichloromethyl-]	75-78-5	5,000	b
1,1-Dimethylhydrazine [Hydrazine, 1,1- dimethyl-]	57-14-7	15,000	b
Epichlorohydrin [Oxirane, (chloromethyl)-]	106-89-8	20,000	b
Ethylenediamine [1,2-Ethanediamine]	107-15-3	20,000	b
Ethyleneimine [Aziridine]	151-56-4	10,000	b
Ethylene oxide [Oxirane]	75-21-8	10,000	a, b
Fluorine	7782-41-4	1,000	b
Formaldehyde (solution)	50-00-0	15,000	b
Furan	110-00-9	5,000	b
Hydrazine	302-01-2	15,000	b
Hydrochloric acid (conc 37% or greater)	7647-01-0	15,000	d
Hydrocyanic acid	74-90-8	2,500	a, b
Hydrogen chloride (anhydrous) [Hydrochloric acid]	7647-01-0	5,000	a
Hydrogen fluoride/Hydrofluoric acid (conc 50% or greater) [Hydrofluoric acid]	7664-39-3	1,000	a, b
Hydrogen selenide	7783-07-5	500	b
Hydrogen sulfide	7783-06-4	10,000	a, b
Iron, pentacarbonyl- [Iron carbonyl ($FE(CO)_5$), (TB-5-11)-]	13463-40-6	2,500	b

Chemical Name	CAS No.	Threshold Quantity (lbs)	Basis for Listing
Isobutyronitrile [Propanenitrile, 2-methyl-]	78-82-0	20,000	b
Isopropyl chloroformate [Carbonochloridic acid, 1-methylethyl ester]	108-23-6	15,000	b
Methacrylonitrile [2-Propenenitrile, 2- methyl-]	126-98-7	10,000	b
Methyl chloride [Methane, chloro-]	74-87-3	10,000	a
Methyl chloroformate [Carbonochloridic acid, methylester]	79-22-1	5,000	b
Methyl hydrazine [Hydrazine, methyl-]	60-34-4	15,000	b
Methyl isocyanate [Methane, isocyanato-]	624-83-9	10,000	a, b
Methyl mercaptan [Methanethiol]	74-92-1	10,000	b
Methyl thiocyanate [Thiocyanic acid, methyl ester]	556-64-9	20,000	b
Methyltrichlorosilane [Silane, trichloromethyl-]	75-79-6	5,000	b
Nickel carbonyl	13463-39-3	1,000	b
Nitric acid (conc. 80% or greater)	7697-37-2	15,000	b
Nitric oxide [Nitrogen oxide (NO)]	10102-43-9	10,000	b
Oleum (Fuming Sulfuric acid) [Sulfuric acid, mixture with sulfur trioxide] [1]	8014-95-7	10,000	e
Peracetic acid [Ethaneperoxoic acid]	79-21-0	10,000	b
Perchloromethylmercaptan [Methanesulfenyl chloride, trichloro-]	594-42-3	10,000	b
Phosgene [Carbonic dichloride]	75-44-5	500	a, b
Phosphine	7803-51-2	5,000	b

Chemical Name	CAS No.	Threshold Quantity (lbs)	Basis for Listing
Phosphorus oxychloride [Phosphoryl chloride]	10025-87-3	5,000	b
Phosphorus trichloride [Phosphorous trichloride]	7719-12-2	15,000	b
Piperidine	110-89-4	15,000	b
Propionitrile [Propanenitrile]	107-12-0	10,000	b
Propyl chloroformate [Carbonochloridic acid, propylester]	109-61-5	15,000	b
Propyleneimine [Aziridine, 2-methyl-]	75-55-8	10,000	b
Propylene oxide [Oxirane, methyl-]	75-56-9	10,000	b
Sulfur dioxide (anhydrous)	7446-09-5	5,000	a, b
Sulfur tetrafluoride [Sulfur fluoride (SF_4), (T-4)-]	7783-60-0	2,500	b
Sulfur trioxide	7446-11-9	10,000	a, b
Tetramethyllead [Plumbane, tetramethyl-]	75-74-1	10,000	b
Tetranitromethane [Methane, tetranitro-]	509-14-8	10,000	b
Titanium tetrachloride [Titanium chloride ($TiCl_4$) (T-4)-]	7550-45-0	2,500	b
Toluene 2,4-diisocyanate [Benzene, 2,4-diisocyanato-1-methyl-][1]	584-84-9	10,000	a
Toluene 2,6-diisocyanate [Benzene, 1,3-diisocyanato-2-methyl-][1]	91-08-7	10,000	a
Toluene diisocyanate (unspecified isomer) [Benzene, 1,3-diisocyanatomethyl-][1]	26471-62-5	10,000	a

Chemical Name	CAS No.	Threshold Quantity (lbs)	Basis for Listing
Trimethylchlorosilane [Silane, chlorotrimethyl-]	75-77-4	10,000	b
Vinyl acetate monomer [Acetic acid ethenyl ester]	108-05-4	15,000	b

[1] The mixture exemption in 40 C.F.R. § 68.115(b)(1) does not apply to the substance.

Note: Basis for Listing:

a Mandated for listing by Congress.
b On EHS list, vapor pressure 10 mmHg or greater.
c Toxic gas.
d Toxicity of hydrogen chloride, potential to release hydrogen chloride, and history of accidents.
e Toxicity of sulfur trioxide and sulfuric acid, potential to release sulfur trioxide, and history of accidents.

E. Accidental Release Prevention (Cont'd)

2. Regulated Flammable Substances[1] and Threshold Quantities

(Alphabetical Order – 63 Substances)

Chemical Name	CAS No.	Threshold Quantity (lbs)	Basis for Listing
Acetaldehyde	75-07-0	10,000	g
Acetylene [Ethyne]	74-86-2	10,000	f
Bromotrifluorethylene [Ethene, bromotrifuloro-]	598-73-2	10,000	f
1,3-Butadiene	106-99-0	10,000	f
Butane	106-97-8	10,000	f
1-Butene	106-98-9	10,000	f
2-Butene	107-01-7	10,000	f
Butene	25167-67-3	10,000	f
2-Butene-cis	590-18-1	10,000	f
2-Butene-trans [2-Butene, (E)]	624-64-6	10,000	f
Carbon oxysulfide [Carbon oxide sulfide (COS)]	463-58-1	10,000	f
Chlorine monoxide [Chlorine oxide]	7791-21-1	10,000	f
2-Chloropropylene [1-Propene, 2-chloro-]	557-98-2	10,000	g
1-Chloropropylene [1-Propene, 1-chloro-]	590-21-6	10,000	g
Cyanogen [Ethanedinitrile]	460-19-5	10,000	f
Cyclopropane	75-19-4	10,000	f
Dichlorosilane [Silane, dichloro-]	4109-96-0	10,000	f
Difluoroethane [Ethane, 1,1-difluoro-]	75-37-6	10,000	f

Chemical Name	CAS No.	Threshold Quantity (lbs)	Basis for Listing
Dimethylamine [Methanamine, N-methyl-]	124-40-3	10,000	f
2,2-Dimethylpropane [Propane, 2,2-dimethyl]	463-82-1	10,000	f
Ethane	74-84-0	10,000	f
Ethyl acetylene [1-Butyne]	107-00-6	10,000	f
Ethylamine [Ethanamine]	75-04-7	10,000	f
Ethyl chloride [Ethane, chloro-]	75-00-3	10,000	f
Ethylene [Ethene]	74-85-1	10,000	f
Ethyl ether [Ethane, 1,1′-oxybis-]	60-29-7	10,000	g
Ethyl mercaptan [Ethanethiol]	75-08-1	10,000	g
Ethyl nitrite [Nitrous acid, ethyl ester]	109-95-5	10,000	f
Hydrogen	1333-74-0	10,000	f
Isobutane [Propane, 2-methyl]	75-28-5	10,000	f
Isopentane [Butane, 2-methyl-]	78-78-4	10,000	g
Isoprene [1,3-Butadinene, 2-methyl-]	78-79-5	10,000	g
Isopropylamine [2-Propanamine]	75-31-0	10,000	g
Isopropyl chloride [Propane, 2-chloro-]	75-29-6	10,000	g
Methane	74-82-8	10,000	f
Methylamine [Methanamine]	74-89-5	10,000	f
3-Methyl-1-butene	563-45-1	10,000	f
2-Methyl-1-butene	563-46-2	10,000	g
Methyl ether [Methane, oxybis-]	115-10-6	10,000	f

Chemical Name	CAS No.	Threshold Quantity (lbs)	Basis for Listing
Methyl formate [Formic acid, methyl ester]	107-31-3	10,000	g
2-Methylpropene [1-Propene, 2-methyl-]	115-11-7	10,000	f
1,3-Pentadiene	504-60-9	10,000	f
Pentane	109-66-0	10,000	g
1-Pentene	109-67-1	10,000	g
2-Pentene, (E)-	646-04-8	10,000	g
2-Pentene, (Z)-	627-20-3	10,000	g
Propadiene [1,2-Propadiene]	463-49-0	10,000	f
Propane	74-98-6	10,000	f
Propylene [1-Propene]	115-07-1	10,000	f
Propyne [1-Propyne]	74-99-7	10,000	f
Silane	7803-62-5	10,000	f
Tetrafluoroethylene [Ethene, tetrafluoro-]	116-14-3	10,000	f
Tetramethylsilane [Silane, tetramethyl-]	75-76-3	10,000	g
Trichlorosilane [Silane, trichloro-]	10025-78-2	10,000	g
Trifluorochloroethylene [Ethene, chlorotrifluoro-]	79-38-9	10,000	f
Trimethylamine [Methanamine, N,N-dimethyl-]	75-50-3	10,000	f
Vinyl acetylene [1-Buten-3-yne]	689-97-4	10,000	f
Vinyl chloride [Ethene, chloro-]	75-01-4	10,000	a, f
Vinyl ethyl ether [Ethene, ethoxy-]	109-92-2	10,000	g
Vinyl fluoride [Ethene, fluoro-]	75-02-5	10,000	f

Chemical Name	CAS No.	Threshold Quantity (lbs)	Basis for Listing
Vinylidene chloride [Ethene, 1,1-dichloro-]	75-35-4	10,000	g
Vinylidene fluoride [Ethene, 1,1-difluoro-]	75-38-7	10,000	f
Vinyl methyl ether [Ethene, methoxy-]	107-25-5	10,000	f

[1] A flammable substance when used as a fuel or held for sale as a fuel at a retail facility is excluded from all provisions of this part (*see* 40 C.F.R. § 68.126).

Note: Basis for Listing:

a Mandated for listing by Congress.
f Flammable gas.
g Volatile flammable liquid.

INDEX

ABOUT THE AUTHORS

The principal author of the fifth edition of the *Clean Air Handbook* is **F. William Brownell**. He is a graduate of the Georgetown University Law Center and is former chair of the Executive Committee for Hunton & Williams LLP (now Hunton Andrews Kurth LLP or Hunton). Before ascending to overall leadership of the firm, he was the head of Hunton's environmental team for many years. His practice covers a broad range of environmental issues in proceedings before federal and state agencies, federal and state courts, and Congress. He has represented clients in most of the major rulemakings and judicial review proceedings under the Clean Air Act since the Act was amended in 1977, as well as in citizen suits and enforcement actions. Besides Clean Air Act issues, Brownell's practice extends to issues arising under many other U.S. environmental statutes. He is a member of the Bars of the District of Columbia, the Supreme Court of the United States, and most of the U.S. Circuit Courts of Appeals. He speaks and writes frequently on environmental and administrative law issues, and he has been recognized by many ranking services, including being named as a Local Litigation Star by *Benchmark Litigation* (2022), listed in *Legal 500 US'* Hall of Fame (2022), is ranked by *Chambers USA* and *Chambers Global* (2023), and named one of the five most admired environmental lawyers by *Law360* (2010).

This edition of the *Clean Air Handbook* reflects the contributions of many members of the Hunton Andrews Kurth environmental team, including the following: **F. William Brownell** with respect to all chapters, and in particular with respect to control technology, the new source permitting program, climate change, and trends; **Shannon S. Broome** with respect to the new source and operating permit programs, the hazardous air pollutants program, the mobile sources program, and climate change; **E. Carter Chandler (Carter) Clements** with respect to interstate transport, visibility protection, and the stratospheric ozone protection program; **Clare Ellis** with respect to the mobile sources and fuels programs, and the stratospheric ozone protection program; **Norman W. Fichthorn (now retired)** with respect to visibility protection, and the acid deposition program; **Lauren E. Freeman (now retired)** with respect to the operating permit program, the acid deposition program, the hazardous air pollutants program, and climate change; **Todd S. Mikolop** with respect to enforcement and the mobile sources program; **Angela Morrison** with respect to the new source and operating permit programs, and the hazardous air pollutants program; **Lucinda Minton Langworthy** with respect to the national air quality standards and nonattainment program; **Matthew Z. Leopold** with respect to enforcement; **Brent A. Rosser** with respect to visibility protection and the regional haze program; and **Penny A. Shamblin** with respect to the new source permitting program. Finally, **Lauren E. Freeman (now retired)** also was responsible for final editing and formatting of the handbook, along with **Sherry L. Fisher**, environmental policy advisor.

Hunton Andrews Kurth was named the 2023 Benchmark Litigation's National Environmental Practice of the Year. Hunton was named the *Chambers US* Environmental Law Firm of the Year in 2017 and again in 2021. Hunton's environmental practice and many of Hunton's lawyers are ranked Band 1 nationally by *Chambers USA* and *Chambers Global*. Hunton maintains the top national ranking for environmental law and water law in *US News-Best Lawyers* and is ranked regionally by *US News Best Lawyers* and *Chambers* in each state where its environmental team lawyers are based. Hunton is top-ranked by *Legal 500* and ten times has been designated an Environmental Group of the Year by *Law360* since 2012, most recently in 2021. Hunton has provided domestic and international clients with a full range of environmental services for more than fifty years. The firm has more than fifty experienced environmental lawyers covering seven of the firm's offices. They are supported by numerous other experienced environmental litigators, government relations professionals, and others. These services include developing the sophisticated legal and technical arguments needed to participate meaningfully in administrative proceedings before federal and state agencies; counseling clients on environmental permitting and enforcement issues that arise when they plan, build, and operate their facilities; providing clients with prompt and informed assessments of the environmental risks that arise in business and real estate transactions; representing clients in the development of national and state legislation; and providing clients with experienced representation in trial and appellate court proceedings on environmental issues.

Hunton's environmental experience extends to all of the major U.S. environmental statutes, including the Clean Air Act; the Clean Water Act; the Safe Drinking Water Act; the Resource Conservation and Recovery Act (RCRA); the Comprehensive Environmental Response, Compensation, and Liability Act (CERCLA or Superfund); the Emergency Planning and Community Right-to-Know Act (EPCRA); the Oil Pollution Act (OPA); the Toxic Substances Control Act (TSCA); the National Environmental Policy Act (NEPA); and to all of the major environmental initiatives undertaken by the European Community. Since the firm's team represents companies throughout the United States and abroad, its members are also familiar with many state and non-U.S. environmental statutes and regulations. The clients that Hunton represents on these environmental issues include a range of industrial and governmental organizations, including chemical and petrochemical companies, automobile manufacturers, pulp and paper companies, petroleum companies, coal companies, electric utilities, waste incinerators, water disposal facilities, breweries, telecommunications companies, urban transportation systems, flexible packagers, fiber and textile manufacturers, waste disposal companies, metal finishers, and many others.

Because environmental issues frequently affect other disciplines, Hunton has developed interdisciplinary practice groups as needed to respond to clients' needs. These groups include lawyers focusing on corporate and financial transactions, real estate law, and lobbying. Hunton has also developed working relationships with numerous technical and economic consultants and public relations firms. These interdisciplinary practice groups allow Hunton to comprehensively address the full range of complex issues related to the environment.

www.ingramcontent.com/pod-product-compliance
Ingram Content Group UK Ltd.
Pitfield, Milton Keynes, MK11 3LW, UK
UKHW020128290926
15471UKWH00003B/345

9 781641 43425